Building JavaScript Games

For Phones, Tablets, and Desktop

Arjan Egges

ISBN-13 (pbk): 978-1-4302-6538-2

ISBN-13 (electronic): 978-1-4302-6539-9

Publisher: Heinz Weinheimer
Lead Editor: Jonathan Gennick
Technical Reviewer: Jon Westfall
Editorial Board: Steve Anglin, Mark Beckner, Ewan Buckingham, Gary Cornell, Louise Corrigan, Jim DeWolf, Jonathan Gennick, Robert Hutchinson, Michelle Lowman, James Markham, Matthew Moodie, Jeff Olson, Jeffrey Pepper, Douglas Pundick, Ben Renow-Clarke, Dominic Shakeshaft, Gwenan Spearing, Matt Wade, Steve Weiss
Coordinating Editor: Jill Balzano
Copy Editor: Tiffany Taylor
Compositor: SPi Global
Indexer: SPi Global
Artist: SPi Global
Cover Designer: Anna Ishchenko

Distributed to the book trade worldwide by Springer Science+Business Media New York, 233 Spring Street, 6th Floor, New York, NY 10013. Phone 1-800-SPRINGER, fax (201) 348-4505, e-mail orders-ny@springer-sbm.com, or visit www.springeronline.com. Apress Media, LLC is a California LLC and the sole member (owner) is Springer Science + Business Media Finance Inc (SSBM Finance Inc). SSBM Finance Inc is a Delaware corporation.

For information on translations, please e-mail rights@apress.com, or visit www.apress.com.

Apress and friends of ED books may be purchased in bulk for academic, corporate, or promotional use. eBook versions and licenses are also available for most titles. For more information, reference our Special Bulk Sales–eBook Licensing web page at www.apress.com/bulk-sales.

Any source code or other supplementary material referenced by the author in this text is available to readers at www.apress.com. For detailed information about how to locate your book's source code, go to www.apress.com/source-code/.

I dedicate this book to my parents, Ap and Frida, and to my wife, Sterre.

Contents at a Glance

Contents at a Glance

Contents

About the Author

Arjan Egges, PhD, is an associate professor in Computer Science at Utrecht University in the Netherlands. He is responsible there for research in the area of computer animation, and he heads the university's motion capture lab. Arjan has written over 30 research papers on animation. He is the founder of the highly successful, annual ACM SIGGRAPH conference on Motion in Games, the proceedings of which have been published by Springer-Verlag. Arjan is responsible for having designed Utrecht University's computer animation course offerings in the Game and Media Technology master's program, and he is currently the leader of that master's program. In 2011 he designed the introductory programming course for the university's bachelor's degree offering in Game Technology. He is coauthor of the book *Learning C# by Programming Games*, published in 2013 by Springer.

About the Technical Reviewer

Jon Westfall, PhD, is an assistant professor of psychology, researcher, programmer, and speaker. He has worked as a consultant since 1997, founding his own firm, Bug Jr. Systems. As a consultant, he has developed custom software solutions (including native Windows 32 applications, Windows .NET applications, Windows Phone 7 and Android mobile applications, as well as ASP, ASP.NET, and PHP web applications). He has also served as a senior network and systems architect and administrator (on both Windows and Unix networks, and hybrids) and has been recognized as a Microsoft Most Valuable Professional (MVP) 2008–2012. He has authored several books and presented at academic as well as technology conferences and gatherings. He can be found writing on his blog at JonWestfall.com and on Twitter @jonwestfall.

Acknowledgments

Writing a book, just like creating a game, is the work of a team. I want to thank Mark Overmars of Tingly Games for the many discussions we had over the past year about HTML5 and JavaScript that ultimately led to this book. I want to thank Peter Vesterbacka of Rovio Entertainment for the interesting interview and the useful thoughts he provided. Thanks also to Jeroen Fokker, who—as a seasoned programming teacher—provided me with many insights into creating a well-structured learning method for JavaScript/HTML5. I would like to thank Jon Westfall, the technical reviewer, for his attention to detail when reviewing the book and for providing lots of useful feedback during the writing process. I also want to thank my colleagues at the university for their ideas, notably Sybren A. Stüvel and Marries van de Hoef. Thanks also to the Apress team for helping this book become a reality. In particular, I want to thank Jonathan Gennick and Jill Balzano for their involvement in the book. Finally, my thanks go to Heiny Reimes, who designed the sprites that are used in the example games.

Foreword

When I first learned programming in the 1970s you would typically write rather boring programs; for example to print the first 100 prime numbers. A lot has changed since then, and learning to program has become much more exciting. And what is more exciting than creating your own computer games? Playing games is fun, but creating them is a lot more fun. Now it is you who decide on the complexity of the puzzles, the behavior of the enemies, and the power of the weapons.

I have developed many games during the past 30 years in many different languages. I created games that ran on programmable calculators, on text terminals, on mainframe computers, and more recently on mobile devices and in web browsers. Each time, it has been hugely satisfying to make the computer do what I wanted it to do and to engage players in demanding challenges. It is a pleasure that this book will bestow on you.

The book will teach you how to program in JavaScript, the most important language for the Web. It provides a thorough treatment of the language and the programming paradigms. There are of course many other books that try to do the same. But what makes this book unique is that it does so in the most exciting way possible: while creating games. And not just prototype games, but full games that look beautiful and are actually fun to play.

The book is structured around important game-development concepts, which you immediately apply to the games you create. You learn about game loops, sprites and animations, player interaction, levels, high scores, and even some basic game physics. And while doing so, you are gradually introduced to all the major language concepts of JavaScript.

The book uses HTML5 (the canvas, to be precise) to run the games. HTML5 is the new web standard that is supported by all modern browsers on PCs, tablets, and smartphones. As a result, you can put the games you create on any web site so all your friends (and the rest of the world) can play and enjoy them. Once you've created the examples in the book, you can start varying them and then move on to designing and programming your own original games.

And once your games are of sufficient quality, you can distribute them throughout the world and even sell them. The book contains some chapters on producing and publishing your own games, to get you started. Don't forget, though, that game development is a multidisciplinary activity. In addition to a programmer (you), you might need an artist to create the visuals and somebody to do the audio for the game. But such people can easily be found on the Web. And when you have a strong team, you can form your own game company. Many successful companies have started this way.

So, reading this book could be your first step on a career path in game development. Surprise yourself and the game community with the games you produce. Enjoy the ride.

—Mark Overmars

Introduction

With the emergence of the HTML5 standard, web-based application development is becoming very popular. More and more game companies are switching to developing games in JavaScript, because currently it's the only truly platform-independent approach that works on the variety of devices we have nowadays, ranging from desktop computers to smartphones and tablets. In this book, you learn how to make your own games. At the same time, you learn in depth one of the most popular programming languages of the last decade: JavaScript. After you've finished reading this book, you'll be able to make games that are ready to be exploited commercially and that run on PCs or Macs in any browser, as well as on tablets or smartphones. The skills you acquire will help you create professional-looking games and also help you build other kinds of web-based applications. As you'll see, building games can be as much fun as playing them (or even more!).

Who This Book Is For

This book is for anyone who has an interest in learning how to create your own games. If you have no prior (JavaScript) programming experience, don't worry. This book teaches you all you need to know. If you already know how to program, then this book will still be interesting for you. I show you how to design a complete software architecture for game development that caters to all the needs of a 2D game programmer. The book illustrates the usage of this software architecture in four different games. The code for these games is carefully developed, taking into account the proper way of organizing code and making it clean, robust, and easily extensible.

Structure of This Book

Each chapter in this book has its own collection of example programs. You can find all the examples on the web site belonging to this book. I explain all the programming concepts based on these examples.

The book is globally divided into six parts. Following is an overview of what each part is about.

Part I

This part provides an overview of the JavaScript programming language, along with an introduction to its main features. I introduce the most important game programming structure—the game loop—and I show you how to implement it in JavaScript. I illustrate the game loop with a very simple JavaScript application using an HTML5 canvas object. You learn about variables and data structures that are useful for representing a game world, and you see how to include game assets such as sprites and sounds in your programs.

Part II

This part focuses on the first game you create: the *Painter* game. The goal of the game is to collect paint of three different colors: red, green, and blue. The paint is falling from the sky in cans that are kept floating by balloons, and you must make sure each can has the right color before it falls through the bottom of the screen. I show you how to react to what the player is doing by reading mouse, keyboard, or touch input. I introduce the *class* as a blueprint for an object (also called an *instance* of that class). You learn about constructor methods as the methods responsible for creating an instance of the class they belong to.

You learn how to write your own methods, properties, and classes, and how you can use these programming concepts to design different game-object classes. You see how game objects should interact with each other. As an example of this interaction, you see how to handle basic collisions between game objects. You learn how inheritance is implemented in JavaScript so that game-object classes can be hierarchically built up. You're introduced to the concept of polymorphism, which lets you call the right version of a method automatically. You finish the Painter game by adding a few extra features, such as motion effects, sounds, music, and maintaining and displaying a score.

Part III

The second game you develop in this book is *Jewel Jam*: a puzzle game in which the player needs to find combinations of jewels. Every time the player makes a valid combination of jewels, they gain points. You start by dealing with viewing games on different mobile devices. You see how to automatically adjust the canvas size to different screen sizes or because the player rotates the phone or tablet screen. A method is introduced to automatically scale sprites and scale the mouse and touch positions to compensate for this so that switching between different canvas sizes is seamless.

You learn about creating structures of game objects. The scene graph is introduced as a representation of this structure. You're also introduced to local and global (world) positions of game objects. Interaction between game objects is achieved by adding identifiers to game objects so you can search for them in a list or hierarchy. To finish the game, you add nice visual effects such as glitters.

Part IV

This part introduces the game *Penguin Pairs*, a puzzle game in which the goal is to make pairs of penguins of the same color. The player can move a penguin by clicking it and selecting the direction in which the penguin should move. A penguin moves until it's stopped by another character in the game (a penguin, a seal, a shark, or an iceberg) or drops from the playing field, in which case the penguin falls into the water and is eaten by hungry sharks. Throughout the different levels of the game, you introduce new gameplay elements to keep the game exciting. For example, there is a special penguin that can match any other penguin, penguins can get stuck in a hole (meaning they can't move anymore), and you can place penguin-eating sharks on the board.

I introduce the concepts of sprite strips and sprite sheets, allowing you to store several sprites in the same image. You create a variety of useful GUI elements for menus, such as an on/off button and a slider button. You learn about a class design for dealing with different game states such as menus, a title screen, and so on. And you see how different states can be part of the game loop and how you can switch between them.

Many games consist of different levels. Especially in casual games such as puzzles and maze games, the game may have several hundreds of levels. You see how to use the power of object literals to represent the game world based on tiles. You also see how to use the HTML5 local storage to store the player's progress through the game and recall that information when the game is started again. You learn about JSON as a useful tool for serializing object literals.

Part V

The final game you develop in this book is a platform game called *Tick Tick*. You first lay out the framework that is used for the game, which is largely based on code that was written for the previous games. You see how to add animations: in the games you developed up to this point, game objects could move around on the screen, but adding something like a running character to your game is slightly more challenging.

In the Tick Tick game, characters need to interact with the game world, which requires a basic physics system. There are two aspects of physics: giving characters the ability to jump or fall, and handling and responding to collisions between characters and other game objects. You also add some basic intelligence to enemies in the game. As a result, the player has different gameplay options and must develop different strategies to complete each level. You use inheritance to create variety in the behavior of enemies. To finish the game, you add mountains and clouds to the background to make the game visually more appealing.

Part VI

The final part of the book discusses game production and publication. The contents of this part are largely based on interviews with two people from the game industry. The first is Mark Overmars, creator of the Gamemaker tool and currently CTO of Tingly Games. The second is Peter Vesterbacka, the Mighty Eagle of Rovio Entertainment, the creators of the *Angry Birds* game. This part contains many thoughts and tips from Peter and Mark about game production and game publication.

A variety of topics are covered, including writing coherent JavaScript code, using third-party libraries, creating/buying game assets such as sprites and sounds for your game, working on a game production team, the various testing phases of a game, dealing with localization, and strategies for selling and marketing games.

> **Note** This book has an accompanying web site where you can download all the example programs, the accompanying game assets (sprites and sounds), as well as other extras. The URL is www.apress.com/9781430265382. Go there and follow the instructions to get the extra materials.

Getting and Installing the Tools

In order to develop computer games in HTML5 and JavaScript, a few tools can be useful to install on your computer. Obviously, you need some kind of browser so that you can run and test the games you're developing. You may even want to install several different browsers on your machine, to make sure your game runs on all major browsers. When JavaScript was just invented, a lot of differences existed between how browsers dealt with JavaScript code. Some scripts worked fine on one browser but gave errors on others. Fortunately, this is much less of a problem today. Almost all the code provided with this book will run fine on any browser. But in some cases, you have to deal with browser differences. So, I suggest that you install at least two browsers for testing your games. On a Windows machine, you already have Internet Explorer, and on a Mac you already have Safari. For testing games, I find that the Firefox browser (www.mozilla.org/en-US/firefox/new) and the Chrome browser (https://www.google.com/chrome) work quite well. Chrome has something called *Developer Tools*, which can be accessed in the menu by going to *Tools* ➤ *Developer tools*. There you can see a console (useful for debugging), set breakpoints in scripts, and do more. When you want to test your games with Firefox, you have to install a plug-in called Firebug (http://getfirebug.com/), which has a feature set similar to Chrome's Developer Tools.

In addition to a browser that allows you to test your game, it's useful to install an editor for editing JavaScript and HTML files. Obviously, you could do this with any text editor. However, there are several editors available that are focused on web development. This means they provide features such as code completion, syntax highlighting, code refactoring, and more. These are very useful things to have as a part of your editing environment. There are paid and free editors. A good paid editor is *WebStorm* (www.jetbrains.com/webstorm). An example of a good free editor is *Komodo Edit* (www.activestate.com/komodo-edit). Another excellent free editor is *Notepad++* (http://notepad-plus-plus.org). Although Notepad++ isn't specifically targeted toward JavaScript development, it has many useful features for editing HTML and JavaScript files, including syntax highlighting.

The Example Programs

Together with this book, I supply a large number of example programs that show the various aspects of programming HTML5 games. You can find a link to the source code on the book's information page, under the Source Code/Downloads tab. This tab is located beneath the Related Titles section of the page.

The collection of examples is contained in a single zip file. After you've downloaded this file, unpack it somewhere. When you look in the folder where you've unpacked the file, you'll see a number of different folders. Each chapter in the book has its own folder. For example, if you want to run the final version of the *Penguin Pairs* game, go to the folder belonging to Chapter 23 and double-click the file PenguinPairs.html which is located in the subfolder PenguinPairsFinal. Your browser will open and run the example game *Penguin Pairs*.

As you can see, there are quite a few different files pertaining to this particular example. A simpler example can be seen if you go the folder belonging to the Chapter 1, where you find a few very basic examples of HTML5 applications with JavaScript. You can run each of the examples by double-clicking its HTML file.

Contacting the Author

If you have any questions regarding the book, please feel free to contact me directly at the following e-mail address: `j.egges@uu.nl`.

Getting Started

The first part of this book covers the basics of developing game applications in JavaScript. You see a number of simple examples that combine HTML with JavaScript. I give you an introduction to the HTML5 standard and the new HTML elements that come with it, notably the canvas. This part covers core JavaScript programming constructs such as instructions, expressions, objects, and functions. In addition, I introduce the game loop and how to load and draw sprites (images).

Programming

This chapter talks about how programming languages have evolved over time. Since the rise of the Internet in the 1990s, a lot of languages and tools have been developed to support it. One of the best-known languages is HTML, which Is used to create web sites. Together with JavaScript and CSS style sheets, it allows the creation of dynamic web sites that can be displayed by a browser. I discuss HTML and JavaScript in detail in this chapter, and you see how to create a simple web application that uses the HTML5 canvas in combination with JavaScript.

Computers and Programs

Before you start dealing with HTML and JavaScript, this section briefly covers computers and programming in general. After that, you move on to how to create a simple HTML page in combination with JavaScript.

Processor and Memory

Generally speaking, a computer consists of a *processor* and *memory*. This is true for all modern computers, including game consoles, smartphones, and tablets. I define memory as something that you can *read things from, and/or write things to*. Memory comes in different varieties, mainly differing in the speed of data transfer and data access. Some memory can be read and written as many times as you want, some memory can only be read, and other memory can only be written to. The main processor in the computer is called the *central processing unit (CPU)*. The most common other processor on a computer is a *graphics processing unit (GPU)*. Even the CPU itself nowadays is no longer a single processor but often consists of a number of ooroo.

Input and output equipment, such as a mouse, gamepad, keyboard, monitor, printer, touch screen, and so on, seems to fall outside the *processor* and *memory* categories at first glance. However, abstractly speaking, they're actually memory. A touch screen is *read-only* memory, and a printer is *write-only* memory.

The main task of the processor is to execute *instructions*. The effect of executing these instructions is that the memory is changed. Especially with my very broad definition of memory, every instruction a processor executes changes the memory in some way. You probably don't want the computer to execute only one instruction. Generally, you have a very long list of instructions to be executed—"Move this part of the memory over there, clear this part of the memory, draw this sprite on the screen, check if the player is pressing a key on the gamepad, and make some coffee while you're at it"—and (as you probably expect) such a list of instructions that is executed by the computer is called a *program*.

Programs

In summary, a program is a long list of instructions to change the computer's memory. However, the program itself is also stored in memory. Before the instructions in the program are executed, they're stored on a hard disk, a DVD, or a USB flash disk; or in the cloud; or on any other storage medium. When they need to be executed, the program is moved to the internal memory of the machine.

The instructions that, combined together, form the program need to be expressed in some way. The computer can't grasp instructions typed in plain English, which is why you need programming languages such as JavaScript. In practice, the instructions are coded as text, but you need to follow a very strict way of writing them down, according to a set of rules that defines a programming language. Many programming languages exist, because when somebody thinks of a slightly better way of expressing a certain type of instruction, their approach often becomes a new programming language. It's difficult to say how many programming languages there are, because that depends on whether you count all the versions and dialects of a language; but suffice to say that there are thousands.

Fortunately, it's not necessary to learn all these different languages, because they have many similarities. In the early days, the main goal of programming languages was to use the new possibilities of computers. However, more recent languages focus on bringing some order to the chaos that writing programs can cause. Programming languages that share similar properties are said to belong to the same *programming paradigm*. A paradigm refers to a set of practices that is commonly used.

The Early Days: Imperative Programming

A large group of programming languages belongs to the *imperative paradigm*. Therefore, these languages are called *imperative languages*. Imperative languages are based on instructions to change the computer's memory. As such, they're well suited to the processor-memory model described in the previous section. JavaScript is an example of an imperative language.

In the early days, programming computer games was a very difficult task that required great skill. A game console like the popular Atari VCS had only 128 bytes of RAM (Random Access Memory) and could use cartridges with at most 4,096 bytes of ROM (Read-Only Memory) that had to contain both the program and the game data. This limited the possibilities considerably. For example, most games had a symmetric level design because that halved the memory requirements. The machines were also extremely slow.

Programming such games was done in an *Assembler* language. Assembler languages were the first imperative programming languages. Each type of processor had its own set of Assembler instructions, so these Assembler languages were different for each processor. Because such a limited amount of memory was available, game programmers were experts at squeezing out the last bits of memory and performing extremely clever hacks to increase efficiency. The final programs, though, were unreadable and couldn't be understood by anyone but the original programmer. Fortunately that wasn't a problem, because back then, games were typically developed by a single person.

A bigger issue was that because each processor had its own version of the Assembler language, every time a new processor came around, all the existing programs had to be completely rewritten for that processor. Therefore, a need arose for processor-independent programming languages. This resulted in languages such as *Fortran* (FORmula TRANslator) and *BASIC* (Beginners' All-purpose Symbolic Instruction Code). BASIC was very popular in the 1970s because it came with early personal computers such as the Apple II in 1978, the IBM-PC in 1979, and their descendants. Unfortunately this language was never standardized, so every computer brand used its own dialect of BASIC.

> **Note**   The fact that I made the effort to identify the paradigm of imperative programming languages implies that there are other programming paradigms that aren't based on instructions. Is this possible? What does the processor do if it doesn't execute instructions? Well, the processor always executes instructions, but that doesn't mean the programming language contains them. For example, suppose you build a very complicated spreadsheet with many links between different cells in the sheet. You could call this activity *programming* and call the empty spreadsheet the *program*, ready to process data. In this case, the program is based not on instructions but on functional links between the cells. In addition to these *functional programming languages*, there are languages based on propositional logic—the *logical programming languages*—such as Prolog. These two types of programming languages together form the *declarative paradigm*.

Procedural Programming: Imperative + Procedures

As programs became more complex, it was clear that a better way of organizing all these instructions was necessary. In the *procedural programming paradigm*, related instructions are grouped together in *procedures* (or *functions*, or *methods*, the latter of which is the more common modern name). Because a procedural programming language still contains instructions, all procedural languages are also imperative.

One well-known procedural language is C. This language was defined by Bell Labs, which was working on the development on the Unix operating system at the end of the 1970s. Because an operating system is a very complicated kind of program, Bell Labs wanted to write it in a procedural language. The company defined a new language called C (because it was a successor of earlier prototypes called A and B). The philosophy of Unix was that everybody could write their own extensions to the operating system, and it made sense to write these extensions in C as well. As a result, C became the most important procedural language of the 1980s, also outside the Unix world.

C is still used quite a lot, although it's slowly but surely making way for more modern languages, especially in the game industry. Over the years, games became much larger programs, and they were created by teams rather than individuals. It was important that the game code be readable, reusable, and easy to debug. Also, from a financial perspective, reducing the time programmers had to work on a game became more and more essential. Although C was a lot better in that respect than the Assembler languages, it remained difficult to write very large programs in a structured way.

Object-Oriented Programming: Procedural + Objects

Procedural languages like C allow you to group instructions in procedures (also called *methods*). Just as they realized that instructions belonged together in groups, programmers saw that some methods belonged together as well. The *object-oriented paradigm* lets programmers group methods into something called a *class*. The memory that these groups of methods can change is called an *object*. A class can describe something like the ghosts in a game of Pac-Man. Then each individual ghost corresponds to an object of the class. This way of thinking about programming is powerful when applied to games.

Everybody was already programming in C, so a new language was conceived that was much like C, except that it let programmers use classes and objects. This language was called *C++* (the two plus signs indicated that it was a successor to C). The first version of C++ dates from 1978, and the official standard appeared in 1981.

Although the language C++ is standard, C++ doesn't contain a standard way to write Windows-based programs on different types of operating systems. Writing such a program on an Apple computer, a Windows computer, or a Unix computer is a completely different task, which makes running C++ programs on different operating systems a complicated issue. Initially, this wasn't considered a problem; but as the Internet became more popular, the ability to run the same program on different operating systems was increasingly convenient.

The time was ripe for a new programming language: one that would be standardized for usage on different operating systems. The language needed to be similar to C++, but it was also a nice opportunity to remove some of the old C stuff from the language to simplify things. The language *Java* fulfilled this role (Java is an Indonesian island famous for its coffee). Java was launched in 1995 by the hardware manufacturer Sun, which used a revolutionary business model for that time: the software was free, and the company planned to make money via support. Also important for Sun was the need to compete with the growing popularity of Microsoft software, which didn't run on the Unix computers produced by Sun.

One of the novelties of Java was that the language was designed so programs couldn't accidentally interfere with other programs running on the same computer. In C++, this was becoming a significant problem: if such an error occurred, it could crash the entire computer, or worse—evil programmers could introduce viruses and spyware.

Web Applications

One of the interesting aspects of Java was that it could be run in a browser as a so-called *applet*. This yielded the possibility of sharing programs over the Internet. However, running a Java applet requires the installation of a plug-in; and, furthermore, there is no straightforward possibility for the Java applet to interact with the elements of a browser. Of course, the other main task of a browser is to display

HTML pages. HTML is a document formatting language, and it's an abbreviation of *HyperText Markup Language*. Its goal is to provide a way to structure documents according to a set of tags that indicate different parts of a document, such as a title or a paragraph. HTML was invented in the late 1980s by physicist Tim Berners-Lee, who was working at CERN in Switzerland at the time. He wanted to provide a way for the CERN researchers to easily use and share documents. So, in a memo to his fellow researchers, he proposed an Internet-based hypertext system. Berners-Lee specified a small set of tags that an HTML viewer could recognize. The first version of HTML contained 18 of these tags, and 11 of them are still in modern HTML.

With the Internet becoming publicly accessible, HTML became the common language for building web sites worldwide. A very popular browser at that time, Mosaic, introduced a new tag, img, which could be used to incorporate an image in an HTML document. In addition, a number of new versions of the HTML language were drafted by different groups that proposed to standardize certain elements that were already implemented by a number of browsers, such as tables or fill-out forms. In 1995, the HTML 2.0 standard was devised by the HTML Working Group, which incorporated all these elements into a single standard. After that, the World Wide Web Consortium (W3C) was created to maintain and update the HTML standard over time. A new version of HTML, HTML 3.2, was defined in January 1997. In December of the same year, the W3C recommended HTML4; and, finally, HTML4.01 became the newly accepted standard in May 2000. Currently, W3C is finalizing the fifth version of HTML, HTML5, and chances are it will be the new official HTML standard by the time you're reading this book.

Just in case you've never built a web site, this is what a simple HTML page looks like:

```
<!DOCTYPE html>
<html>
<head>
<title>Useful website</title>
</head>
<body>
This is a very useful website.
</body>
</html>
```

Companies that developed browsers soon realized they needed a way to make the pages more dynamic. The first HTML standard (2.0) was very much directed at marking up text (which was why HTML was invented in the first place). However, web site users needed buttons and fields, and a specification was necessary that would indicate what should happen if a user interacted with a page. In other words, web sites needed to become more dynamic. Of course, there was Java with its applets, but those applets ran completely independently. There was no way for an applet to modify elements of an HTML page.

Netscape, the company that developed the Netscape Navigator browser, was in fierce competition with Microsoft over which browser would become the main one that everybody used. Netscape used the programming language Java in some of its existing tools, and the company wanted to design a lightweight, interpreted language that would appeal to nonprofessional programmers (such as web site designers). This language would be able to interface with a web page and read or modify its content dynamically. Netscape invented a language called *LiveScript* to fulfill that role. Not much later, the company changed the name of the script language to *JavaScript*, given its roots in the Java language and probably because people already recognized the Java name. JavaScript was included with Netscape Navigator 2.0.

JavaScript soon gained widespread success as a script language that allowed web sites to become more dynamic. Microsoft also included it in Internet Explorer 3.0 but named it *JScript* because it was a slightly different version from the one Netscape originally defined. In 1996, Netscape submitted JavaScript to the ECMA standardization organization, which renamed the language ECMAScript (although everyone still calls it JavaScript). The version that was finally accepted in 1999 as a standard is the version that all current browsers support. The latest version of the ECMAScript standard is version 5.1, which was released in 2011. ECMAScript 6, which is under development, introduces many useful new features such as classes and default values for function parameters.

Due to its support by all major web browsers, JavaScript has become the main programming language for web sites. Because it was originally conceived as a lightweight, interpreted script language, only now are programmers starting to use JavaScript to develop more complex web-based applications. Even though JavaScript may not have all the features of modern programming languages such as Python and C#, it's still a very capable language, as you'll discover while reading this book. Currently, JavaScript is the only language integrated with HTML that works across different browsers on different platforms. Together with HTML5, it has become a powerful framework for web development.

Programming Games

The goal of this book is to teach you how to program games. Games are very interesting (and sometimes challenging!) programs. They deal with a lot of different input and output devices, and the imaginary worlds that games create can be extremely complex.

Until the beginning of the 1990s, games were developed for specific platforms. For example, a game written for a particular console couldn't be used on any other device without major effort from the programmers to adapt the game program to the differing hardware. For PC games, this effect was even worse. Nowadays, operating systems provide a *hardware abstraction layer* so programs don't have to deal with all the different types of hardware that can be inside a computer. Before that existed, each game needed to provide its own drivers for each graphics card and sound card; as a result, not much code written for a particular game could be reused for another game. In the 1980s, arcade games were extremely popular, but almost none of the code written for them could be reused for newer games because of the constant changes and improvements in computer hardware.

As games grew more complex, and as operating systems became more hardware independent, it made sense for the game companies to start reusing code from earlier games. Why write an entirely new rendering program or collision-checking program for each game, if you can simply use the one from your previously released game? The term *game engine* was coined in the 1990s, when first-person shooters such as Doom and Quake became a very popular genre. These games were so popular that their manufacturer, id Software, decided to license part of the game code to other game companies as a separate piece of software. Reselling the core game code as a game engine was a lucrative endeavor because other companies were willing to pay a lot of money for a license to use the engine for their own games. These companies no longer had to write their own game code from scratch—they could reuse the programs contained in the game engine and focus more on graphical models, characters, levels, and so on.

Many different game engines are available today. Some game engines are built specifically for a platform such as a game console or an operating system. Other game engines can be used on different platforms without having to change the programs that use the game engine code. This is especially useful for game companies that want to publish their games on different platforms.

Modern game engines provide a lot of functionality to game developers, such as a 2D and 3D rendering engine, special effects such as particles and lighting, sound, animation, artificial intelligence, scripting, and much more. Game engines are used frequently, because developing all these different tools is a lot of work and game companies prefer to put that time and effort into creating beautiful environments and challenging levels.

Because of this strict separation between the core game functionalities and the game itself (levels, characters, and so on), many game companies hire more artists than programmers. However, programmers are still necessary for improving the game engine code, as well as for writing programs that deal with things that aren't included in the game engine or that are specific to the game. Furthermore, game companies often develop software to support the development of games, such as level-editing programs, extensions of 3D modeling software to export models and animations in the right format, prototyping tools, and so on.

For JavaScript, there isn't yet an engine that everyone is using. Most people program relatively simple games in JavaScript to make sure the games run on different devices, especially devices with limited capabilities. So instead of using an engine, programmers write the game directly using HTML5 elements such as the canvas. However, this is rapidly changing. If you type *javascript game engine* in Google, you'll find many engines that you can use as a basis for developing your own games. The goal of this book is to teach you how to program games; but you won't use an engine, because I want to teach you the core of the language and its possibilities. This isn't a manual for a game engine. In fact, after reading this book, you'll be able to build your own game engine. I'm not saying you should do that, but you'll be better able to program a game from scratch and more quickly understand how a game engine library works.

Developing Games

Two approaches are commonly used in developing games. Figure 1-1 illustrates these approaches: the outer one encompasses the inner one. When people are first learning to program, they typically begin writing code immediately, and that leads to a tight loop of writing, then testing, and then making modifications. Professional programmers, by contrast, spend significant upfront time doing design work before ever writing their first line of code.

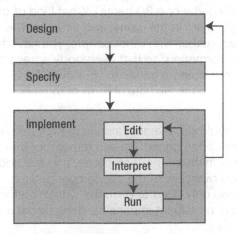

Figure 1-1. Programming on a small scale and on a large scale

Small Scale: Edit-Interpret-Run

When you want to build a game in JavaScript, you need to write a program that contains many lines of instructions. With a text editor, you can edit the script(s) you're working on. Once you're done writing down these instructions, you start the browser (preferably a recent version of a commonly used browser program) and try to run the program. When all is well, the browser interprets the script and executes it.

However, most of the time, things aren't that easy. For one thing, the source code you give to the browser/interpreter should contain valid JavaScript code, because you can't expect the browser to execute a script containing random blabbering. The browser checks whether the source code adheres to the language specifications of the JavaScript language. If not, it produces an error, and the script stops. Of course, programmers make an effort to write correct JavaScript programs, but it's easy to make a typo, and the rules for writing correct programs are very strict. So, you'll most certainly encounter errors during the interpretation phase.

After a few iterations during which you resolve minor errors, the browser interprets the entire script without encountering any problems. As the next step, the browser *executes* or *runs* the script. In many cases, you then discover that the script doesn't exactly do what you want it to do. Of course, you made an effort to correctly express what you wanted the script to do, but conceptual mistakes are easy to make.

So you go back to the editor, and you change the script. Then you open the browser again and try to interpret/run the script and hope you didn't make new typing mistakes. You may find that the earlier problem is solved, only to realize that although the script is doing something different, it still doesn't do exactly what you want. And it's back to the editor again. Welcome to life as a programmer!

Large Scale: Design-Specify-Implement

As soon as your game becomes more complicated, it's no longer a good idea to just start typing away until you're done. Before you start *implementing* (writing and testing the game), there are two other phases.

First, you have to *design* the game. What type of game are you building? Who is the intended audience of your game? Is it a 2D game or a 3D game? What kind of gameplay would you like to model? What kinds of characters are in the game, and what are their capabilities? Especially when you're developing a game together with other people, you have to write some kind of design document that contains all this information, so that everybody agrees on what game they're developing! Even when you're developing a game on your own, it's a good idea to write down the design of the game. The *design* phase is actually one of the most difficult tasks of game development.

Once it's clear what the game should do, the next step is to provide a global structure for the program. This is called the *specification* phase. Do you remember that the object-oriented programming paradigm organizes instructions in methods, and methods in classes? In the specification phase, you make an overview of the classes needed for the game and the methods in those classes. At this stage, you only need to describe what a method will do, not how it's done. However, keep in mind that you can't expect impossible things from methods: they have to be implemented later.

When the game specification is finished, you can start the *implementation* phase, which generally means going through the edit-interpret-run cycle a couple of times. After that, you can let other people play your game. In many cases, you'll realize that some ideas in the game design don't work that well. So, you begin again by changing the design, followed by changing the specification and finally doing a new implementation. You let other people play your game again, and then … well, you get the idea. The edit-interpret-run cycle is contained in a larger-scale cycle: the design-specify-implement cycle (see Figure 1-1). Although this book focuses mainly on the implementation phase, you can read a little bit more about designing games in Chapter 30.

Building Your First Web Application

In this section, you build a few very simple example applications using JavaScript. Earlier in the chapter, you saw a basic HTML page:

```
<!DOCTYPE html>
<html>
<head>
<title>Useful website</title>
</head>
<body>
This is a very useful website.
</body>
</html>
```

Open a text-editing program such as Notepad, and copy-paste this text into it. Save the file as something with a .html extension. Then double-click that file to open it in a browser. You see an almost empty HTML page, as shown in Figure 1-2. In HTML, tags are used to structure the information in the document. You can recognize these tags because they're placed between angle brackets. Each different type of content is placed between such tags. You can distinguish an opening tag from a closing tag by checking whether there is a slash in front of the tag name. For example, the title of the document is placed between the opening tag <title> and the closing tag </title>. The title itself is, in turn, part of a *header*, which is delimited by the <head> and </head> tags. The header is contained in the *html* part, which is delimited by the <html> and </html> tags. As you can see, the HTML tagging system allows you to organize the content of a document logically. The total HTML document has a kind of tree structure, where the html element is the root of the tree; the root consists of elements such as head and body, which in turn consist of more branches.

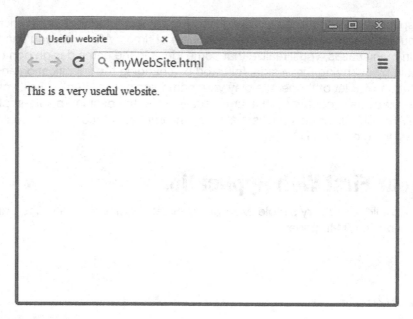

Figure 1-2. A very simple HTML page

Once you've created an HTML document, you can apply a *style* to it. For example, you might want to change the layout of the various parts of an HTML document, or you might want to use a different font or apply a background color. The style can be defined as a part of the HTML document, or you can define a style using a CSS (Cascading Style Sheet) file.

Although we do not cover style sheets (CSS files) in this book in detail, I make limited use of them for correctly positioning game content in the browser window. For example, this simple style sheet sets the margins of an html page and its body to 0:

```
html, body {
    margin: 0;
}
```

If you want your HTML page to use a CSS file (style sheet), you simply add the following line to the <head> part:

```
<link rel="stylesheet" type="text/css" href="game-layout.css"/>
```

I will use the preceding style sheet in most of the game examples in this book. In Chapter 13, I will expand the style sheet to allow for automatic scaling and positioning of the content to different devices.

You can also change the style in the HTML document itself rather than using CSS files to define the style. This is done by setting *attributes* of a tag. For example, the body of the following HTML page has an attribute tag `style` that is set to change the background color to blue (see Figure 1-3 for the page that is displayed):

```
<!DOCTYPE html>
<html>
<head>
<title>BasicExample</title></head>
<body style="background:blue">
That's a very nice background.
</body>
</html>
```

Figure 1-3. A simple web page with a blue background

You can change different aspects of the style by using a `style` attribute as in the example. For example, look at the following HTML document:

```
<!DOCTYPE html>
<html>
<head>
<title>BasicExample</title></head>
<body>
<div style="background:blue;font-size:40px;">Hello, how are you?</div>
<div style="background:yellow;font-size:20px;">I'm doing great, thank you!</div>
</body>
</html>
```

If you look at the contents of the body, you see that it contains two parts. Each part is enclosed in div tags, which are div used to divide an HTML document into *divisions.* You can apply a different style to each division. In this example, the first division has a blue background and a font size of 40 pixels, and the second division has a yellow background and a font size of 20 pixels (see also Figure 1-4).

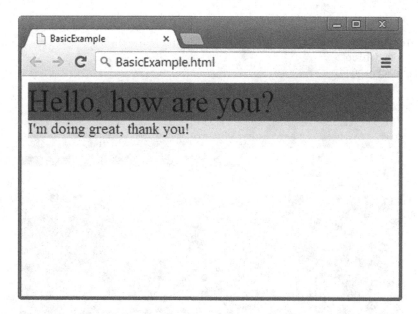

Figure 1-4. A web page consisting of two divisions, each with a different background color and font size

Instead of adding a style attribute to an HTML element, you can also use JavaScript to modify the style of that element. For example, you can change the background color of the body using JavaScript, as follows:

```
<!DOCTYPE html>
<html>
<head>
<title>BasicExample</title><script>
    changeBackgroundColor = function () {
        document.body.style.background = "blue";
    }
    document.addEventListener('DOMContentLoaded', changeBackgroundColor);
</script>
</head>
<body>
That's a very nice background.
</body>
</html>
```

The page shown by the browser looks exactly the same as the first example (shown in Figure 1-2), but there is a crucial difference between using JavaScript to do this as opposed to adding an attribute to the body tag: the JavaScript script changes the color *dynamically*. This happens because the script contains the following line:

```
document.addEventListener('DOMContentLoaded', changeBackgroundColor);
```

Inside a JavaScript application, you have access to all the elements in the HTML page. And when things happen, you can instruct the browser to execute instructions. Here, you indicate that changeBackgroundColor function should be executed when the page has finished loading.

There are many different types of these events in HTML and JavaScript. For example, you can add a button to the HTML document and execute JavaScript instructions when the user clicks the button. Here is an HTML document that illustrates this (see also Figure 1-5):

```
<!DOCTYPE html>
<html>
<head>
<title>BasicExample</title>
<script>
    sayHello = function () {
        alert("Hello World!");
    }
    document.addEventListener('click', sayHello);
</script>
</head>
<body>
<button>Click me</button>
</body>
</html>
```

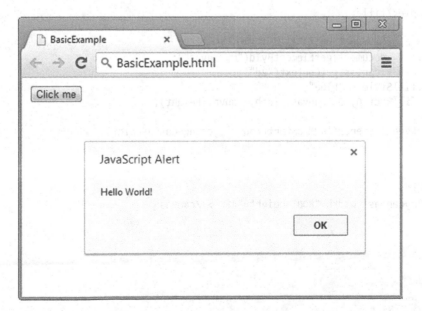

Figure 1-5. An HTML page containing a button. When the user clicks the button, an alert is displayed

This kind of dynamic interaction is possible because the browser can execute JavaScript code. If you want to program games, being able to define how the player should interact with the game is crucial.

The HTML5 Canvas

A nice thing about the new HTML standard is that it provides a couple of tags that make HTML documents a lot more flexible. A very important tag that was added to the standard is the canvas tag, which allows you to draw 2D and 3D graphics in an HTML document. Here is a simple example:

```
<!DOCTYPE html>
<html>
<head>
<title>BasicExample</title>
</head>
<body>
<div id="gameArea">
    <canvas id="mycanvas" width="800" height="480"></canvas>
</div>
</body>
</html>
```

Here you can see that the body contains a division called gameArea. Inside this division is a canvas element that has a number of attributes. It has an identifier (mycanvas), and it has a width and height. You can again modify things in this canvas element by using JavaScript. For example, the following code changes the background color of the canvas element by using a few JavaScript instructions:

```
<!DOCTYPE html>
<html>
<head>
<title>BasicExample</title>
<script>
    changeCanvasColor = function () {
        var canvas = document.getElementById("mycanvas");
        var context = canvas.getContext("2d");
        context.fillStyle = "blue";
        context.fillRect(0, 0, canvas.width, canvas.height);
    }
    document.addEventListener('DOMContentLoaded', changeCanvasColor);
</script>
</head>
<body>
<div id="gameArea">
    <canvas id="mycanvas" width="800" height="480"></canvas>
</div>
</body>
</html>
```

In the changeCanvasColor function, you first find the canvas element. This the HTML document element on which you can draw 2D and 3D graphics. Having this element ready in your code is useful, because then you can easily retrieve information about the canvas, such as its width or height. In order to perform operations on the canvas (such as drawing on it), you need a canvas *context*. The canvas context provides functions for drawing on the canvas. When you retrieve the canvas context, you need to indicate whether you want to draw in 2 or in 3 dimensions. In this example, you get a two-dimensional canvas context. You use it to choose a background fill color and fill the canvas with that color. Figure 1-6 shows the resulting HTML page displayed by the browser. The following chapters go into more detail about the canvas element and how is it used to create games.

Figure 1-6. Displaying the HTML5 canvas on a web page and filling it with a color

JavaScript in a Separate File

Instead of writing all the JavaScript code in the HTML document, you can also write JavaScript code in a separate file and include that file in the HTML document:

```
<!DOCTYPE html>
<html>
<head>
<title>BasicExample</title>
<script src="BasicExample.js"></script>
</head>
<body>
<div id="gameArea">
    <canvas id="mycanvas" width="800" height="480"></canvas>
</div>
</body>
</html>
```

The JavaScript file `BasicExample.js` then contains the following code:

```javascript
changeCanvasColor = function () {
    var canvas = document.getElementById("mycanvas");
    var context = canvas.getContext("2d");
    context.fillStyle = "blue";
    context.fillRect(0, 0, canvas.width, canvas.height)
}
document.addEventListener('DOMContentLoaded', changeCanvasColor);
```

In many cases, it's desirable to do this. By separating the script code from the HTML document, it's much easier to locate the code or use it on different web sites. All the examples used in this book have the JavaScript code separated from the HTML document, nicely organized in one or more JavaScript files.

What You Have Learned

In this chapter, you have learned:

- How computers work, and that they consist of processors to compute things and memory to store things

- How programming languages have evolved from Assembler languages to modern programming languages such as JavaScript

- How to create a simple web application using HTML5 and JavaScript

Chapter **2**

Game Programming Basics

This chapter covers the basic elements of programming games and provides a starting point for
the chapters that follow. First, you learn about the basic skeleton of any game, consisting of a
game world and a *game loop*. You see how to create this skeleton in JavaScript, by looking at
various examples such as a simple application that changes the background color. Finally, I talk
about clarifying your code by using comments, layout, and whitespace in the right places.

Building Blocks of a Game

This section talks about the building blocks of a game. I discuss the game world in general and then
show you the process of changing it using an update-draw loop, which continuously updates the
game world and then draws it on the screen.

The Game World

What makes games such a nice form of entertainment is that you can explore an imaginary world
and do things there that you would never do in real life. You can ride on the back of a dragon,
destroy entire solar systems, or create a complex civilization of characters who speak in an
imaginary language. This imaginary realm in which you play the game is called the *game world*.
Game worlds can range from very simple domains such as the Tetris world to complicated virtual
worlds in games such as Grand Theft Auto and World of Warcraft.

When a game is running on a computer or a smartphone, the device maintains an internal representation
of the game world. This representation doesn't look anything like what you see on the screen when you
play the game. It consists mostly of numbers describing the location of objects, how many hit points an
enemy can take from the player, how many items the player has in inventory, and so on. Fortunately, the
program also knows how to create a visually pleasing representation of this world that it displays on the
screen. Otherwise, playing computer games would probably be incredibly boring, with players having to
sift through pages of numbers to find out whether they saved the princess or died a horrible death.

Players never see the internal representation of the game world, but game developers do. When you want to develop a game, you also need to design how to represent your game world internally. And part of the fun of programming your own games is that you have complete control over this.

Another important thing to realize is that just like the real world, the game world is changing all the time. Monsters move to different locations, the weather changes, a car runs out of gas, enemies get killed, and so on. Furthermore, the player actually influences how the game world is changing! So simply storing a representation of the game world in the memory of a computer isn't enough. A game also needs to constantly register what the player is doing and, as a result, *update* this representation. In addition, the game needs to *show* the game world to the player by displaying it on the monitor of a computer, on a TV, or on the screen of a smart phone. The process that deals with all this is called the *game loop*.

The Game Loop

The game loop deals with the dynamic aspects of a game. Lots of things happen while a game is running. The players press buttons on the gamepad or touch the screen of their device, and a constantly changing game world consisting of levels, monsters, and other characters needs to be kept up to date. There are also special effects such as explosions, sounds, and much more. All these different tasks that need to be handled by the game loop can be organized in two categories:

- Tasks related to updating and maintaining the game world
- Tasks related to displaying the game world to the player

The game loop continuously performs these tasks, one after the other (see Figure 2-1). As an example, let's look at how you could handle user navigation in a simple game like Pac-Man. The game world mainly consists of a labyrinth with a few nasty ghosts moving around. Pac-Man is located somewhere in this labyrinth and is moving in a certain direction. In the first task (updating and maintaining the game world), you check whether the player is pressing an arrow key. If so, you need to update the position of Pac-Man according to the direction the player wants Pac-Man to go. Also, because of that move, Pac-Man may have eaten a white dot, which increases the score. You need to check whether it was the last dot in the level, because that would mean the player has finished the level. Finally, if it was a larger white dot, the ghosts need to be rendered inactive. Then you need to update the rest of the game world. The position of the ghosts needs to be updated, you have to decide whether fruit should be displayed somewhere for bonus points, you need to check whether Pac-Man collides with one of the ghosts (if the ghost isn't inactive), and so on. You can see that even in a simple game like Pac-Man, a lot of work needs to be done in this first task. From now on, I'll call this collection of different tasks related to updating and maintaining the game world the Update action.

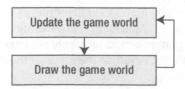

Figure 2-1. The game loop, which continuously updates and then draws the game world

The second collection of tasks is related to displaying the game world to the player. In the case of the Pac-Man game, this means drawing the labyrinth, the ghosts, Pac-Man, and information about the game that is important for the player to know, such as how many points they've scored, how many lives they have left, and so on. This information can be displayed in different areas of the game screen, such as at the top or the bottom. This part of the display is also called the *heads-up display* (HUD). Modern 3D games have a much more complicated set of drawing tasks. These games need to deal with lighting and shadows, reflections, culling, visual effects like explosions, and much more. I'll call the part of the game loop that deals with all the tasks related to displaying the game world to the player the Draw action.

Building a Game Application in JavaScript

The previous chapter showed how to create a simple JavaScript application. In that JavaScript application, you saw that instructions are grouped into a function, as follows:

```
function changeBackgroundColor () {
    document.body.style.background = "blue";
}
```

This idea of grouping is coherent with the idea that JavaScript is a procedural language: instructions are grouped in procedures/functions. The first step is setting up a simple game loop in JavaScript. Have a look at the following example:

```
var canvas = undefined;
var canvasContext = undefined;

function start () {
    canvas = document.getElementById("myCanvas");
    canvasContext = canvas.getContext("2d");
    mainLoop();
}

document.addEventListener('DOMContentLoaded', start);

function update () {
}

function draw () {
}

function mainLoop () {
    canvasContext.fillStyle = "blue";
    canvasContext.fillRect(0, 0, canvas.width, canvas.height);
    update();
    draw();
    window.setTimeout(mainLoop, 1000 / 60);
}
```

As you can see, there are a couple of different functions in this script. The `start` function is called when the body of the HTML document has loaded, because of this instruction:

```
document.addEventListener('DOMContentLoaded', start);
```

In the `start` function, you retrieve the canvas and the canvas context; you store them in *variables* so you can use them in other parts of the program (more about that later). Then, you *execute* another function called `mainLoop`. This function, in turn, contains other instructions. Two instructions take care of setting a background color. Then you call the `update` function, followed by the `draw` function. Each of these functions may again contain other instructions. The final instruction that is called is the following:

```
window.setTimeout(mainLoop, 1000 / 60);
```

What this does is simply call the `mainLoop` function again, after waiting for a certain period of time (1,000/60 = 16.6 milliseconds in this case). When the `mainLoop` function is called again, the canvas background color is set and the `update` and `draw` functions are called. At the moment, `update` and `draw` are empty, but you can start filling them with instructions to update and draw a game world. Note that using `setTimeout` to wait between loop iterations isn't always the best solution. Sometimes this approach may be adversely affected by events beyond your control, such as slow computers, other tabs that are open in your browser, concurrently running apps that need processing power, and so on. When you have to deal with sensitive time operations (such as the player needing to survive for five minutes), you may not want to rely on `setTimeout` but rather on some sort of system that schedules events at certain points in time and checks in the `update` function whether these events have occurred.

When you run the example program, the `update` and `draw` functions are continuously executed: update, draw, update, draw, update, draw, update, draw, update, draw, and so on. Furthermore, this happens at a very high speed. This particular example creates a simple game loop that runs at about 60 frames per second. This kind of loop is called a *fixed timestep* loop, and it's a very popular kind of loop for casual games. You could also design the program differently so that the game would try to execute the loop as many times as possible instead of 60 times per second.

> **Note**   When you create programs that rely on a (game) loop, you might want to avoid using fully automated loops in the early stages of implementation and testing. You might create an infinite loop that could bog down the development machine accidentally. Instead, you can set the loop to run a limited number of times, or you can let the loop run once every time you press a button. Most browsers also support debugging of JavaScript. For example, in Firebug (in the Firefox browser), you can place a breakpoint at some point in the loop. That way, you can keep track of what is happening when the program is running.

This book shows you a lot of different ways to fill the `update` and `draw` functions with the tasks you need to perform in your game. During this process, I also introduce many programming techniques that are useful for games (and other applications). The following section looks into the basic game application in more detail. Then, you fill this basic skeleton of a game with additional instructions.

The Structure of a Program

This section talks about the structure of a program in more detail. In the early days, many computer programs only wrote text to the screen and didn't use graphics. Such a text-based application is called a *console* application. In addition to printing text to the screen, these applications could also read text that a user entered on the keyboard. So, any communication with the user was done in the form of question/answer sequences (Do you want to format the hard drive (Y/N)? Are you sure (Y/N)? and so on). Before Windows-based OSs became popular, this text-based interface was very common for text-editing programs, spreadsheets, math applications, and even games. These games were called *text-based adventures*, and they described the game world in text form. The player could then enter commands to interact with the game world, such as go west, pick up matches, or Xyzzy. Examples of such early games are Zork and Adventure. Although they might seem dated now, they're still fun to play!

It's still possible to write console applications, also in a language such as JavaScript. Although it's interesting to see how to write such applications, I prefer to focus on programming modern games with graphics.

Types of Applications

The console application is only one example of a type of application. Another very common type is the *Windows* application. Such an application shows a screen containing windows, buttons, and other parts of a *graphical user interface* (GUI). This type of application is often *event-driven*: it reacts to events such as clicking a button or selecting a menu item.

Another type of application is the *app*, run on a mobile phone or a tablet PC. Screen space is generally limited in these type of applications, but new interaction possibilities are available such as GPS to find out the location of the device, sensors that detect the orientation of the device, and a touch screen.

When developing applications, it's quite a challenge to write a program that works on all the different platforms. Creating a Windows application is very different from creating an app. And reusing the code between different types of applications is difficult. For that reason, *web-based applications* are becoming more popular. In this case, the application is stored on a server, and the user runs the program in a web browser. There are many examples of such applications: think of web-based e-mail programs or social network sites. And in this book, you learn how to develop *web-based games*.

Note   Not all programs fall squarely in one application type. Some Windows applications might have a console component, such as the JavaScript console in a browser. Games often also have a window component, such as an inventory screen, a configuration menu, and so on. And nowadays the limit of what a program actually *is* has become less clear. Think about a multiplayer game that has tens of thousands of players, each running an app on a tablet or an application on a desktop computer, while these programs communicate with a complex program running simultaneously on many servers. What constitutes the *program* in this case? And what type of program is it?

Functions

Remember that in an imperative program, the *instructions* are doing the actual job of the program: they're executed one after the other. This changes the memory and/or the screen so the user notices that the program is doing something. In the BasicGame program, not all lines in the program are instructions. One example of an instruction is the line `context.fillRect(0, 0, canvas.width,` `canvas.height);` which instructs the canvas to draw a rectangle on the screen with a color specified in the previous instruction. Because this rectangle happens to be the size of the canvas, the entire canvas's color is changed.

Because JavaScript is a procedural language, the instructions can be grouped in *functions*. In JavaScript it isn't obligatory that an instruction be part of a function. For example, the following instruction in the BasicGame program doesn't belong to a function:

```
var canvas = undefined;
```

However, functions are very useful. They prevent duplication of code because the instructions are only in one place, and they allow the programmer to execute those instructions easily by calling one name. Grouping instructions in a function is done with braces ({and }). Such a block of instructions grouped together is called the *body* of a function. Above the body, you write the *header* of the function. An example of a function header is as follows:

```
function mainLoop ()
```

The header contains, among other things, the *name* of the function (in this case `mainLoop`). As a programmer, you may choose any name for a function. You have seen that the game loop consists of two parts: `update` and `draw`. In programming terms, these parts are modeled as functions, as you can see in the example program. In these functions, you then place the instructions you want to execute in order to update or draw the game world. The name of the function is preceded by the word `function`, and after the name is a pair of parentheses. These serve to provide information to the instructions that are executed inside the function. For example, take a look at the following header:

```
function playAudio (audioFileId)
```

In this header, the name of the function is `playAudio`; and between the parentheses you see the word `audioFileId`. Apparently the `playAudio` function requires an audio file identifier so it knows which audio file should be played.

Syntax Diagrams

Programming in a language such as JavaScript can be difficult if you don't know the language's rules. This book uses so-called *syntax diagrams* to explain how the language is structured. The *syntax* of a programming language refers to the formal rules that define what is a valid program (in other words: a program that a compiler or interpreter can read). By contrast, the *semantics* of a program refer to the actual *meaning* of it. To illustrate the difference between syntax and semantics, look at the phrase "all your base are belong to us". Syntactically, this phrase isn't valid (an interpreter of the English language would definitely complain about it). However, the *meaning* of this phrase is quite clear: you apparently lost all your bases to an alien race speaking bad English.

> **Note**   The phrase "all your base are belong to us" comes from the opening cut-scene of the video game Zero Wing (1991, Sega Mega Drive) as a poor translation of the original Japanese version. Since then, the phrase has appeared in my articles, television series, movies, websites, and books (such as this one!).

An interpreter can check the syntax of a program: any program that violates the rules is rejected. Unfortunately, an interpreter can't check whether the semantics of the program correspond to what the programmer had in mind. So if a program is syntactically correct, this is no guarantee that it's semantically correct. But if it isn't even syntactically correct, it can't run at all. Syntax diagrams help you to visualize the rules of a programming language such as JavaScript. For example, Figure 2-2 is a simplified syntax diagram that shows how to define a function in JavaScript.

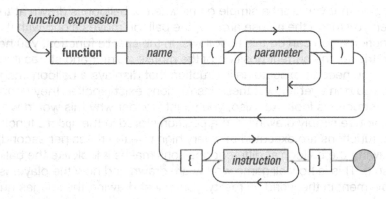

Figure 2-2. *The syntax diagram for a function expression*

You can use syntax diagrams to construct JavaScript code by starting at the top left of the diagram, in this case at the word *function*, and following the arrows. When you reach the gray dot, your piece of code is complete. Here you can clearly see that a function definition starts with the `function` keyword; then you write the name of the function. After that, you write parentheses. Between these parentheses, you can (optionally) write any number of *parameters*, separated by commas. Next you write a number of instructions, all between braces. After that, you're done because you've reached the gray dot. Throughout this book, I use syntax diagrams to show how to structure your code according to the syntactical rules of the JavaScript language.

Calling a Function

When the instruction `canvasContext.fillRect(0, 0, canvas.width, canvas.height);` is executed, you *call* the `fillRect` function. In other words, you want the program to execute the instructions grouped in the function `fillRect`. This group of instructions does exactly what you need for this example: namely, filling a rectangle with a color. However, you need to give some extra information to this function, because it needs to know the size of the rectangle that should be filled. The parameters provide this extra information. A function can have more than one parameter, as you saw in the syntax diagram. When a function is called, you always write parentheses behind it, and within the parentheses are the parameters (if required).

Do you need to know which instructions are grouped together in the `fillRect` function in order to use it? No, you don't! This is one of the nice things about grouping instructions in functions. You (or other programmers) can use the function without knowing how it works. By smartly grouping instructions in functions, it's possible to write reusable program pieces that can be used in many different contexts. The `fillRect` function is a good example of this. It can be used for various applications, and you don't need to know how the function works in order to use it. The only thing you need to know is that it takes the dimensions of a rectangle as parameters.

Update and Draw

The game loop in the BasicGame example contains `update` and `draw` functions. Because a function is basically a group of instructions, every time the `update` function is called, the instructions in that functions are executed. The same goes for `draw`.

As an example, imagine that you want a simple game where a balloon is drawn at the position of the mouse pointer. When you move the mouse around, the balloon moves along with it. In terms of the `update` and `draw` functions, you can do this as follows. In the `update` function, you need to execute an instruction that retrieves the current position of the mouse pointer and stores it in memory. In the `draw` function, you need to execute an instruction that displays a balloon image at the stored position. Of course, you don't yet know if these instructions exist (spoiler: they do!), and you don't yet know what the instructions look like. Also, you might wonder why this would work. You're not moving the balloon, you're simply drawing it at a position stored in the `update` function. Recall that the `update` and `draw` functions are executed at a very high rate (60 times per second). Because of this high rate, drawing the balloon at different positions makes it look like the balloon moves (but it actually doesn't). This is how all game worlds are drawn and how the player is lured into thinking there is movement in the world. In reality, you're just drawing the images quickly at different positions. Stay tuned—you return to this example and make it work later on!

Program Layout

This section deals with the layout of a program's source code. You first see how to add clarifying comments to your code. Then you learn how to write instructions as clearly as possible by using single or multiple lines, whitespace, and indentation.

Comments

For the human reader of a program (another programmer, or yourself in a couple of months, when you've forgotten the details of how your program worked), it can be very useful to add some clarifying comments to a program. These comments are completely ignored by the compiler, but they make for a more understandable program. There are two ways in JavaScript to mark comments in your code:

- Everything between the symbol combinations /* and */ is ignored (there can be multiple lines of comments).
- Everything between the symbol combination // and the end of the line is ignored.

It's useful to place comments in your code to explain groups of instructions belonging together, the meaning of parameters, or complete classes. If you use comments, do it to *clarify* the code, not to write the code again in words: you can assume the reader of your code knows JavaScript. To illustrate this, the following comment line adds to the clarity of the instruction:

```
// Set the background color to green.
canvasContext.fillStyle = "green";
canvasContext.fillRect(0, 0, canvas.width, canvas.height);
```

This is also a comment, but it doesn't clarify what the instruction does:

```
/* Pass the value "green" to the fillStyle variable of canvasContext and call the fillRect method of
canvasContext with the parameters 0, 0, canvas.width and canvas. */
canvasContext.fillStyle = "green";
canvasContext.fillRect(0, 0, canvas.width, canvas.height);
```

While testing your program, you can also use comment symbols to temporarily remove instructions from the program. Don't forget to remove the parts of your code that are *commented out* once you finish the program, because they can lead to confusion when other developers look at your source code.

Instructions vs. Lines

There are no strict rules about how to distribute the text of a JavaScript program over the lines in a text file. Usually you write every instruction on a separate line, even though this isn't necessary for the compiler to understand the program. Sometimes, if it makes a program clearer, the programmer writes multiple instructions on a single line. Also, sometimes a single instruction that is very long (containing function/method calls and many different parameters) can be distributed over multiple lines (you see this later in this book as well).

Whitespace and Indentation

As you can see, the BasicGame example uses whitespace liberally. There is an empty line between each function, as well as spaces between each equals sign and the expressions on either side of it. Spacing can help to clarify the code for the programmer. For the browser/interpreter, spaces have no meaning. The only place where a space is really important is between separate words: you aren't allowed to write function update() as functionupdate(). And similarly, you aren't allowed to write an extra space in the middle of a word. In text that is interpreted literally, spaces are also taken literally. There is a difference between

```
canvasContext.fillStyle = "blue";
```

and

```
canvasContext.fillStyle = "b l u e";
```

But apart from this, extra spaces are allowed everywhere. The following are good places to put extra whitespace:

- Behind every comma and semicolon (but not before).

- Left and right of the equals sign (=). You can see an example of this in the instruction `canvasContext.fillStyle = "blue";`.

- At the beginning of lines, so the bodies of methods and classes are indented (usually four positions) with respect to the braces enclosing the body.

Most editing programs help you a little by automatically performing the indentation. Also, the editor automatically places whitespace at certain spots in your code to increase readability.

What You Have Learned

In this chapter, you have learned:

- What the skeleton of a game is, consisting of the game loop and the game world the loop acts on

- How to structure a game program consisting of a few different functions that retrieve the canvas, as well as the `update` and `draw` functions that constitute the game loop

- The basic layout rules of a JavaScript program, including how to place comments in your code and where to put extra whitespace to improve readability of the code

Chapter 3

Creating a Game World

This chapter shows you how to create a game world by storing information in memory. It introduces basic types and variables and how they can be used to store or change information. Next, you see how to store more complicated information in objects that consist of member variables and methods.

Basic Types and Variables

The previous chapters discussed memory a couple of times. You have seen how to execute a simple instruction like canvasContext.fillStyle = "blue"; to set the color a shape should be filled with when drawn on the canvas. In this chapter's example, you use *memory* to store information temporarily, in order to remember the results of a few simple calculations. In this *DiscoWorld* example, you change the background color depending on the time that has passed.

Types

Types, or *data types*, represent different kinds of structured information. The previous examples used different kinds of information that were passed as parameters to functions. For example, the function fillRect wants as information four integer numbers, the start function in the BasicGame example wants a text identifier that refers to the canvas, and the update and draw functions from the same example don't need any information at all. The browser/interpreter can distinguish between all these different kinds of information and, in many cases, even convert information of one type to another. For example, in JavaScript, you can use either single or double quotes to represent text. For example, the following two instructions do the same:

```
canvas = document.getElementById("myCanvas");
```

```
canvas = document.getElementById('myCanvas');
```

Browsers are able to automatically convert between different kinds of information. For example, the following would not result in a syntax error:

```
canvas = document.getElementById(12);
```

The number passed as a parameter would simply be converted to text. In this case, of course, there is no canvas with ID 12, so the program would no longer correctly. But if you were to replace the canvas ID as follows, then the program would work just fine:

```
<canvas id="12" width="800" height="480"></canvas>
```

The browser automatically converts between text and numbers.

Most programming languages are a lot stricter than JavaScript. In languages such as Java and C#, conversion between types is done on a very limited basis. Most of the time, you have to explicitly tell the compiler that a conversion between types needs to be done. Such a type conversion is also called a *cast*.

What is the reason for having a stricter policy with regard to type conversions? For one thing, clearly defining which type a function or method expects as a parameter makes it easier for other programmers to understand how to use the function. Look at the following header for example:

```
function playAudio (audioFileId)
```

By only looking at this header, you can't be sure if `audioFileId` is a number or text. In C#, the header of a similar method looks like this:

```
void playAudio(string audioFileId)
```

You can see that in this header, not only a name is provided, but also a *type* that belongs to this name. The type in this case is `string`, which in C# means text (a string of characters). Furthermore, in front of the method name is the word `void`, which means the method doesn't have a result that can be stored (I talk more about methods/functions with results in Chapter 7).

Declaration and Assignment of Variables

It's easy to store information in JavaScript and use it later. What you need to do is provide a name that you use when you refer to this information. This name is called a *variable*. When you want to use a variable in your program, it's a good idea to *declare* it before you actually use it. This is how you declare a variable:

```
var red;
```

In this example, `red` is the name of the variable. You can use the variable in your program to store information that you need later.

When you declare a variable, you don't need to provide the type of information that you store. A variable is simply a place in memory that has a name. Quite a few programming languages require the type of a variable to be fixed when the variable is declared. For example, this is the case in languages such as C++ or Java. However, many script languages (including JavaScript) allow you to declare a variable without defining its type. When a language doesn't require a type definition for declaring a variable, then the language has *loose typing*. In JavaScript, you can declare more than a single variable at once. For example:

```
var red, green, fridge, grandMa, applePie;
```

Here you declare five different variables that you can now use in your program. When you declare these variables, they don't yet contain a value. In this case, these variables are considered *undefined*. You can assign a value to a variable by using an *assignment instruction*. For example, let's assign a value to the variable red, as follows:

```
red = 3;
```

The assignment instruction consists of the following parts:

- The name of the variable that should be assigned a value
- The = sign
- The new value of the variable
- A semicolon

You can recognize the assignment instruction by the equals sign in the middle. However, it's better to think of this sign as "becomes" rather than "equals" in JavaScript. After all, the variable isn't yet equal to the value to the right of the equals sign—it *becomes* that value after the instruction is executed. The syntax diagram describing the assignment instruction is given in Figure 3-1.

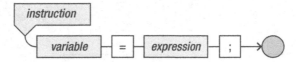

Figure 3-1. Syntax diagram of an assignment instruction

So now you have seen one instruction for declaring a variable, and another instruction to store a value in it. But if you already know which value you want to store in a variable when you declare it, you can combine the declaration of a variable and the first assignment to it:

```
var red = 3;
```

When this instruction is executed, the memory will contain the value 3, as shown in Figure 3-2.

Figure 3-2. Memory after a declaration and assignment of a variable

Here are a few examples of more declarations and assignments of numeric variables:

```
var age = 16;
var numberOfBananas;
numberOfBananas = 2;
var a, b;
a = 4;
var c = 4, d = 15, e = -3;
c = d;
numberOfBananas = age + 12;
```

In the fourth line of this example, you see that it's possible to declare multiple variables in one declaration. You can even perform multiple declarations with assignments in a single declaration, as can be seen in the sixth line of the example code. On the right side of the assignment, you can put other variables or mathematical expressions, as you can see in the last two lines. The instruction c = d; results in the value stored in variable d being stored in variable c as well. Because the variable d contains the value 15, after this instruction is executed, the variable c also contains the value 15. The last instruction takes the value stored in the variable age (16), adds 12 to it, and stores the result in the variable numberOfBananas (which now has the value 28—a lot of bananas!). In summary, the memory looks something like what is depicted in Figure 3-3 after these instructions have been executed.

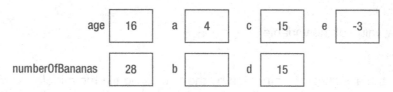

Figure 3-3. Overview of the memory after declaration and assignment of multiple variables

The syntax of declaring variables (with an optional initialization) is expressed in the diagram shown in Figure 3-4.

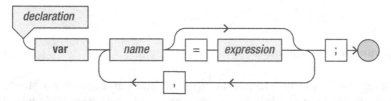

Figure 3-4. Syntax diagram of variable declaration with an optional initialization

Global Variables and Strict Mode

Instead of declaring a variable before using it, it's also possible in JavaScript to simply start using the variable without declaring it. For example, consider the following instructions:

```
var a = 3;
var b;
b = 4;
x = a + b;
```

As you can see, the variables a and b are declared in the first two instructions by using the var keyword. The variable x is never declared, but it's used to store the sum of the two variables. JavaScript allows this. However, this is very bad practice, and here is why. The problem with simply using a variable without declaring it is that the JavaScript interpreter automatically declares that variable for you without you realizing it. If you happen to use a variable with the same name somewhere else, your program may display behavior you don't expect because that variable already exists. In addition, if you use a lot of different variables, you have to keep track of these global variables as well. But an even bigger problem is shown in the following example:

```
var myDaughtersAge = 12;
var myAge = 36;
var ourAgeDifference = myAge - mydaughtersAge;
```

When programming these instructions, you would expect that the variable ourAgeDifference will contain the value 24 (36 minus 12). However, in reality it will be *undefined*. The reason is that there is a typo in the third instruction. The variable name shouldn't be mydaughtersAge, but myDaughtersAge. Instead of stopping the script and reporting an error, the browser/interpreter *silently* declares a new global variable called mydaughtersAge. Because this variable is undefined (it doesn't refer to a value yet), any calculations done with this variable will also be undefined. So, the variable ourAgeDifference is then undefined as well.

These kinds of problems are really hard to solve. Fortunately, the new EMCAScript 5 standard has something called *strict mode*. When a script is interpreted in strict mode, it isn't allowed to use variables without declaring them first. If you want a script to be interpreted in strict mode, the only thing you have to do is add a single line at the beginning of the script, as follows:

```
"use strict";
var myDaughtersAge = 12;
var myAge = 36;
var ourAgeDifference = myAge - mydaughtersAge;
```

The string/instruction "use strict"; tells the interpreter that the script should be interpreted in strict mode. If you now try to run this script, the browser will stop the script and report the error that a variable is being used without having been declared.

In addition to checking whether a variable is declared before use, strict mode includes a couple of other things that make writing correct JavaScript code easier. Furthermore, it's likely that newer versions of the JavaScript standard will be close to the JavaScript syntax restrictions imposed by strict mode.

I highly recommend that you write all your JavaScript code in strict mode. To set the model, all the remaining examples in this book are programmed in strict mode. It saves programmers a lot of headaches, and the code is readier for future versions of JavaScript.

Instructions and Expressions

If you look at the elements in the syntax diagrams, you probably notice that the value or program fragment on the right side of an assignment is called an *expression*. So what is the difference between an expression and an *instruction*? The difference between the two is that an *instruction* changes the memory in some way, whereas an *expression* has a value. Examples of instructions are method calls and assignments, as you saw in the previous section. Instructions often use expressions. Here are some examples of expressions:

```
16
numberOfBananas
2
a + 4
numberOfBananas + 12 - a
-3
"myCanvas"
```

All these expressions represent a value of a certain type. Except for the last line, all the expressions are numbers. The last expression is a string (of characters). In addition to numbers and strings, there are other kinds of expressions. I discuss the most important ones in this book. For example, in the following section I will discuss expressions with operators, and Chapter 7 describes using a function or a method as an expression.

Operators and More Complex Expressions

This section talks about the different operators that JavaScript knows. You learn the priority of each operator so you know in which order calculations are performed. You also see that sometimes, expressions can be quite complex in JavaScript. For example, a variable can consist of multiple values, or it can even refer to a function.

Arithmetic Operators

In expressions that are numbers, you can use the following arithmetic operators:

- + add
- - subtract
- * multiply
- / divide
- % division remainder (pronounced "modulus")

Multiplication uses an asterisk because the signs normally used in mathematics (·and ×) aren't found on a computer keyboard. Completely omitting this operator, as is also done in mathematics (for example, in the formula $f(x) = 3x$), isn't allowed in JavaScript because it introduces confusion with variables consisting of more than one character.

When the division operator / is used, in some cases the result is a real number (instead of an integer number). For example, after executing the following instruction, the variable y contains the value 0.75:

```
var y = 3/4;
```

The special operator % gives the division remainder. For instance, the result of 14%3 is 2, and the result of 456%10 is 6. The result always lies between 0 and the value to the right of the operator. The result is 0 if the result of the division is an integer.

Priority of Operators

When multiple operators are used in an expression, the regular arithmetic rules of precedence apply: multiplication before addition. The result of the expression 1+2*3 therefore is 7, not 9. Addition and subtraction have the same priority, and multiplication and division as well.

If an expression contains multiple operators of the same priority, then the expression is computed from left to right. So, the result of 10-5-2 is 3, not 7. When you want to deviate from these standard precedence rules, you can use parentheses: for example, (1+2)*3 and 3+(6-5). In practice, such expressions generally also contain variables; otherwise you could calculate the results (9 and 4) yourself.

Using more parentheses than needed isn't forbidden: for example, 1+(2*3). You can go completely crazy with this if you want: ((1)+(((2)*3))). However, your program will be much harder to read if you do.

In summary, an expression can be a constant value (such as 12), it can be a variable, it can be another expression in parentheses, or it can be an expression followed by an operator followed by another expression. Figure 3-5 shows the (partial) syntax diagram representing an expression.

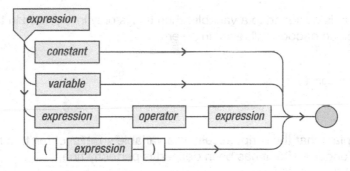

Figure 3-5. Partial syntax diagram of an expression

Assigning a Function to a Variable

In JavaScript, functions (groups of instructions) are stored in memory. And as such, functions themselves are also expressions. So, it's possible to assign a function to a variable. For example:

```
var someFunction = function () {
    // do something
}
```

This example declares a variable someFunction and assigns it a value. The value this variable refers to is an *anonymous function*. If you want to execute the instructions contained in this function, you can call it by using the variable name, as follows:

```
someFunction();
```

So what is the difference between this way of defining a function and the way you have already seen?

```
function someFunction () {
    // do something
}
```

Actually, there isn't much of a difference. The main thing is that by defining a function in the traditional way (not using a variable), the function doesn't have to be defined before it can be used. When the browser interprets a JavaScript file, it does so in two stages. In the first stage, the browser constructs a list of functions that are available. In the second stage, the browser interprets the rest of the script. This is necessary because in order to correctly interpret a script, the browser needs to know which functions are available. For example, this piece of JavaScript code will run just fine, even though the function is defined after it's called:

```
someFunction();
function someFunction () {
    // do something
}
```

However, if the function is assigned to a variable, then this is only interpreted in the second stage. And that means this piece of code will result in an error:

```
someFunction();
var someFunction = function () {
    // do something
}
```

The browser will complain that the script accesses a variable someFunction that has not yet been declared. Calling the function after it has been defined is perfectly fine:

```
var someFunction = function () {
    // do something
}
someFunction();
```

Variables Composed of Multiple Values

Instead of containing a single value, a variable can also be composed of *multiple values*. This is similar to what you do in a function, which groups instructions together. For example:

```
function mainLoop () {
    canvasContext.fillStyle = "blue";
    canvasContext.fillRect(0, 0, canvas.width, canvas.height);
    update();
    draw();
    window.setTimeout(mainLoop, 1000 / 60);
}
```

You can execute all those instructions by calling the mainLoop function. The instructions that belong to the function are grouped by using braces. Similar to grouping instructions, you can also group variables into a bigger variable. That bigger variable then contains multiple values. Have a look at the following example:

```
var gameCharacter = {
    name : "Merlin",
    skill : "Magician",
    health : 100,
    power : 230
};
```

This is an example of a *composite variable*. The variable gameCharacter consists of several values, each of which has a name and a value that the name refers to. So, in a sense, the gameCharacter variable is *composed of other variables*. You can see that, as in the body of a function, variables are grouped between braces. Each subvariable has a name, and after the colon you specify the value that this variable refers to. The expression consisting of the names and values enclosed by the braces is called an *object literal*. Figure 3-6 shows the (partial) syntax diagram of an object literal expression.

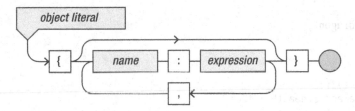

Figure 3-6. (Partial) syntax diagram of an object literal expression

After the declaration and initialization of the gameCharacter variable, the memory will look as depicted in Figure 3-7.

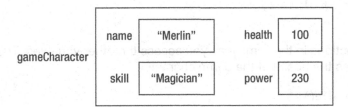

Figure 3-7. Memory structure after creating a composite variable

You can access the data in a composite variable as follows:

```
gameCharacter.name = "Arjan";
var damage = gameCharacter.power * 10;
```

As you can see, you can access the variables that are a part of gameCharacter by writing their name after a dot. JavaScript even allows you to modify the structure of a composite variable after you have declared and initialized it. For instance, look at the following code:

```
var anotherGameCharacter = {
    name : "Arthur",
    skill : "King",
    health : 25,
    power : 35000
};

anotherGameCharacter.familyName = "Pendragon";
```

The variable anotherGameCharacter now consists of five parts: name, skill, health, power, and familyName.

Because variables can also point to functions, you can even include a subvariable that points to a function. For example, you could define anotherGameCharacter as follows:

```
var anotherGameCharacter = {
    name : "Arthur",
    familyName : "Pendragon",
    skill : "King",
    health : 25,
    power : 35000,
    healMe : function () {
        anotherGameCharacter.health = 100;
    }
};
```

And just as before, you can add a function part to the variable after it has been assigned a value:

```
anotherGameCharacter.killMe = function () {
    anotherGameCharacter.health = 0;
};
```

You can call these functions in the same way you access the other variables. The following instruction fully restores the health of the game character:

```
anotherGameCharacter.healMe();
```

And if you wanted to kill the character, the anotherGameCharacter.killMe(); instruction would do the job. The nice thing about structuring variables and functions this way is that you can group related data and functions together. This example groups variables that all belong to the same game character. It also adds a few functions that are useful for this game character to have. From now on, if a function belongs to a variable, I'll call this function a *method*. I'll call a variable composed of other variables an *object*. And if a variable is a part of an object, I'll call this variable a *member variable*.

You can probably imagine how powerful objects and methods are. They provide a way to bring structure into a complicated game world. If JavaScript did not have this capability, you would be obligated to declare a very long list of variables at the beginning of the program, without knowing how the variables were related to each other or what you could do with them. By grouping variables in objects and providing methods that belong with these objects, you can write programs that are much easier to understand. In the next section, you use this power in a simple example that moves a square around the canvas.

The MovingSquare Game

This section examines a simple program that moves a square over the canvas. Its purpose is to illustrate two things:

- How the update and draw parts of a game loop work in more detail
- How to use objects to structure a program

Before you start writing this program, let's look at the code of the BasicGame example one more time:

```
var canvas = undefined;
var canvasContext = undefined;

function start () {
    canvas = document.getElementById("myCanvas");
    canvasContext = canvas.getContext("2d");
    mainLoop();
}

document.addEventListener('DOMContentLoaded', start);

function update () {
}

function draw () {
    canvasContext.fillStyle = "blue";
    canvasContext.fillRect(0, 0, canvas.width, canvas.height);
}

function mainLoop () {
    update();
    draw();
    window.setTimeout(mainLoop, 1000 / 60);
}
```

What you have here are a couple of variable declarations and a few functions that do something with those variables. With your new knowledge about grouping variables together in objects, let's make it clear that all these variables and functions belong to a *game* application, as follows:

```
"use strict";

var Game = {
    canvas : undefined,
    canvasContext : undefined
};
```

```
Game.start = function () {
    Game.canvas = document.getElementById("myCanvas");
    Game.canvasContext = Game.canvas.getContext("2d");
    Game.mainLoop();
};

document.addEventListener('DOMContentLoaded', Game.start);

Game.update = function () {
};

Game.draw = function () {
    Game.canvasContext.fillStyle = "blue";
    Game.canvasContext.fillRect(0, 0, Game.canvas.width, Game.canvas.height);
};

Game.mainLoop = function () {
    Game.update();
    Game.draw();
    window.setTimeout(mainLoop, 1000 / 60);
};
```

The main thing you do here is create a single composite variable (object) called Game. This object has two *member variables*: canvas and canvasContext. In addition, you add a number of *methods* to this object, including the methods that together form the game loop. You define the methods belonging to this object separately (in other words, they aren't a part of the variable declaration and initial assignment). The reason is that you can now easily distinguish the *data* the object consists of from the *methods that do something with the data*. Note also that you add the instruction "use strict"; to the program, as I promised!

Now let's extend this example so it shows a smaller rectangle moving on the screen. You want to change the x-position of the rectangle over time. In order to do that, you have to store the current x-position of the rectangle in a variable. That way, you can assign a value to that variable in the update method (where you change the game world) and use the variable to draw the rectangle on the screen in the draw method (where you draw the game world on the screen). The logical place to add this variable is as a part of the Game object, so you declare and initialize this object as follows:

```
var Game = {
    canvas : undefined,
    canvasContext : undefined,
    rectanglePosition : 0
};
```

You use the variable rectanglePosition to store the desired x-position of the rectangle. In the draw method, you can then use that value to draw a rectangle somewhere on the screen. In this example, you draw a smaller rectangle that doesn't cover the entire canvas so you can see it move around. This is the new draw method:

```
Game.draw = function () {
    Game.canvasContext.fillStyle = "blue";
    Game.canvasContext.fillRect(Game.rectanglePosition, 100, 50, 50);
}
```

Now the only thing you need to do is calculate what the x-position of the rectangle should be. You do this in the update method, because changing the x-position of the rectangle means you're *updating the game world*. In this simple example, let's change the position of the rectangle based on the time that has passed. In JavaScript, you can use the following two instructions to get the current system time:

```
var d = new Date();
var currentSystemTime = d.getTime();
```

You have not seen the kind of notation used in the first line before. For now, let's assume that new Date() creates a composite variable (object) that is filled with date and time information as well as a couple of useful methods. One of these methods is getTime. You call that method on the object d and store its result in the variable currentSystemTime. This variable now contains the number of milliseconds that have passed since January 1, 1970 (!). You can imagine that this number is quite large. If you wanted to set the x-position to that value, you would require a computer monitor with a huge resolution. This monitor would certainly never fit in your room (or any room, for that matter). Instead, you divide the system time by the width of the canvas, take the remainder of that division, and use that as the x-position of the rectangle. That way, you always get an x-position between zero and the width of the canvas. Here is the complete update method that does this:

```
Game.update = function () {
    var d = new Date();
    Game.rectanglePosition = d.getTime() % Game.canvas.width;
};
```

As you know, the update and draw methods are called in sequence, about 60 times per second. Every time this happens, the system time has changed (because time has passed), meaning the position of the rectangle will be changed, and it will be drawn in a different position than before.

You need to do one more thing before this example will work as it should. If you were to run the program like this, a blue bar would appear on the screen. The reason is that you're currently drawing the new rectangle on top of the old one. In order to solve this, you need to *clear the canvas* every time before you draw on it again. Clearing the canvas is done by the clearRect method. This method clears a rectangle of a given size of anything that was drawn in it. For instance, this instruction clears the entire canvas:

```
Game.canvasContext.clearRect(0, 0, Game.canvas.width, Game.canvas.height);
```

For convenience, you put this instruction in a method called clearCanvas, as follows:

```
Game.clearCanvas = function () {
    Game.canvasContext.clearRect(0, 0, Game.canvas.width, Game.canvas.height);
};
```

The only thing you have to do is make sure to call this method before update and draw are called. You do this in the mainLoop method:

```
Game.mainLoop = function() {
    Game.clearCanvas();
    Game.update();
    Game.draw();
    window.setTimeout(Game.mainLoop, 1000 / 60);
};
```

Now the example is complete! You can run this program by double-clicking the MovingSquare.html file in the folder belonging to this chapter. Figure 3-8 shows what it looks like.

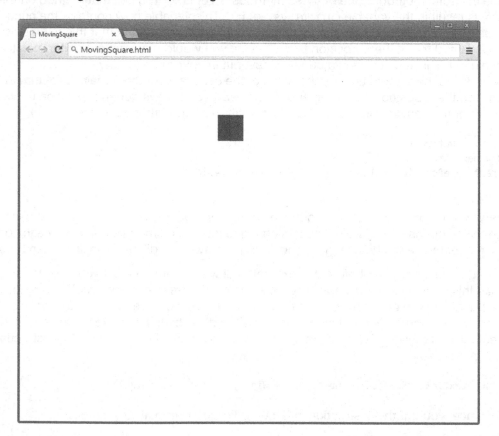

Figure 3-8. Output of the MovingSquare example

Play around with how the rectangle position is changed depending on the time. Try to get some of the following things to work correctly (if you have other ideas, don't hesitate to try them as well):

- Make the rectangle move from right to left.
- Make the rectangle move from top to bottom.
- Make the rectangle move diagonally across the screen.
- Make the rectangle move twice as slowly.

Scope of Variables

The place where you declare a variable has consequences for where you're allowed to use the variable. Look at the variable d in the MovingSquare program. This variable is declared (and assigned a value) in the update method. Because it's declared in the update method, you're only allowed to use it in this method. For example, you aren't allowed to use this variable again in the draw method. Of course, you could declare another variable called d in the draw method, but it's important to realize that the d variable declared in update would in that case not be the same d variable declared in the draw method.

Alternatively, if you declare a variable at the *object* level, you can use it anywhere, as long as you put the name of the object in front of it. You need to use the x-position of the rectangle in both the update and draw methods, because in the update method, you update this position, and in the draw method, you use it to draw a rectangle at that x-position. Therefore, it's logical that this variable needs to be declared at the object level, so that all methods belonging to the object can use the variable.

The places where a variable can be used are together called the variable's *scope*. In this example, the scope of the variable d is the update method, and the scope of the variable Game.rectanglePosition is the global scope.

What You Have Learned

In this chapter, you have learned:

- How to store basic information in memory using variables
- How to create objects that consist of member variables and methods
- How to use the update method to change the game world through variables and the draw method to display the game world on the screen

Chapter 4

Game Assets

The previous chapters have shown you how to make a very basic game application by writing your own game loop methods as a part of an object called Game. You have seen which instructions in JavaScript retrieve the canvas as well as the canvas context, which is used to perform operations on the canvas. You have seen a few simple examples where you changed the background color. You also made a rectangle move over the screen by using the current system time in combination with the game loop methods. This chapter shows how to draw images on the screen, which is the first step toward making nice-looking games. In computer graphics, these images are also called *sprites*. Sprites are generally loaded from a file. This means any program that draws sprites is no longer simply an isolated set of instructions, but relies on *game assets* that are stored somewhere. This immediately introduces a number of things that you need to think about:

- From which locations can you load sprites?
- How do you retrieve the information from an image file?
- How do you draw a sprite on the screen?

This chapter answers these questions.

Sound is another type of game asset. It is handled very similarly to sprites. So, at the end of this chapter, you also see you how to play back music and sound effects in your game.

> **Note**   The name *sprite* comes from *spriting*, which is the process of creating two-dimensional, partially transparent raster graphics that are used for video games. In the early days, creating these two-dimensional images was a lot of manual work; but it resulted in a particular style of imagery that inspired people to create similar images of their own, resulting in an artistic technique called *pixel art* or *sprite art*.

Locating Sprites

Before a program can use any kind of assets, it needs to know where to look for those assets. By default, the browser acting as interpreter looks for sprites in the same folder as the JavaScript file. Look at the SpriteDrawing example belonging to this chapter. You see a file called `spr_balloon.png` in the same folder as the HTML file and the JavaScript file. You can load this sprite and draw it on the screen.

Loading Sprites

Let's now look at how you can load a sprite from a file. Once you have done this, you store it somewhere in memory by using a variable. You need this variable in several different game-loop methods. In the `start` method, you load the sprite and store it in the variable. In the `draw` method, you can access the variable in order to draw the sprite on the screen. Therefore, you add a variable called `balloonSprite` to the `Game` object. Here you can see the declaration of the `Game` variable and its initialization:

```
var Game = {
    canvas : undefined,
    canvasContext : undefined,
    balloonSprite : undefined
};
```

In the `start` method of `Game`, you assign values to these variables. You have already seen how to retrieve the canvas and the canvas context. Just like `Game`, the canvas and canvas context are *objects* that each consist of other variables (or objects). If you load a sprite, you have *an object that represents the sprite*. You could define an object variable that contains all the information in the image:

```
Game.balloonSprite = {
    src : "spr_balloon.png",
    width : 35,
    height : 63,
    ...
}
```

This becomes problematic when you want to load hundreds of sprites for your game. Every time, you would have to define such an object by using an object literal. Furthermore, you would have to make sure you don't accidentally use other variable names in the object, because then you would have an inconsistent representation of images. Fortunately, you can avoid this trouble by using *types*.

A type is basically a definition of what an object of that type should look like; it's a *blueprint* for an object. For example, JavaScript knows a type called `Image`. This type specifies that an image object should have a width, a height, a source file, and more. There is a very simple way to create an object that has the `Image` type, using the `new` keyword:

```
Game.balloonSprite = new Image();
```

This is much easier than having to type in all the content a variable should have. The expression new Image() basically does that work for you. By using types, you now have an easy way to create objects, and you can be sure these objects always have the same structure. When an object is constructed that has the structure as dictated by the Image type, you say that this object *is of type* Image.

You didn't yet indicate what *data* should be contained in this variable. You can set the source file of this image by assigning the file name to the src variable that is always part of an Image object:

```
Game.balloonSprite.src = "spr_balloon.png";
```

Once the src variable is set, the browser begins loading the file. The browser automatically fills in the data for the width and height variables because it can extract this information from the source file.

Sometimes, loading the source file takes a while. For example, the file could be stored on a web site on the other side of the world. This means if you try to draw the image immediately after setting its source file, you may run into trouble. As a result, you need to make sure each image is loaded before you can start the game. There is a very neat way to do this, by using an *event handler* function. In Chapter 7, you see how that works. For now, just assume that loading the image will not take longer than half a second. By using the setTimeOut method, you call the mainLoop method after a delay of 500 milliseconds:

```
window.setTimeout(Game.mainLoop, 500);
```

This completes the start method, which now looks like this:

```
Game.start = function () {
    Game.canvas = document.getElementById("myCanvas");
    Game.canvasContext = Game.canvas.getContext("2d");
    Game.balloonSprite = new Image();
    Game.balloonSprite.src = "spr_balloon.png";
    window.setTimeout(Game.mainLoop, 500);
};
```

Sprites can be loaded from any location. If you're developing a game in JavaScript, then it's a good idea to think about the organization of your sprites. For example, you could put all the sprites belonging to your game in a subfolder called *sprites*. You would then have to set the source file as follows:

```
Game.balloonSprite.src = "sprites/spr_balloon.png";
```

Or perhaps you aren't even using your own images, but you refer to images that you found on another web site:

```
Game.balloonSprite.src = "http://www.somewebsite.com/images/spr_balloon.png";
```

JavaScript allows you to load image files from any location you desire. Just make sure that when you load images from another web site, the location of the image files is fixed. Otherwise, if the administrator of that web site decides to move everything without telling you, your game won't run anymore.

Drawing Sprites

Loading a sprite and storing it in memory doesn't mean the sprite is drawn on the screen. For that to happen, you need to do something in the draw method. To draw a sprite on the canvas somewhere, you use the drawImage method that is a part of the canvas context object. In JavaScript, when an image is drawn at a certain position, that position always refers to the *top-left corner* of the image. Here is the instruction that draws a sprite in the top-left corner on the screen:

```
Game.canvasContext.drawImage(sprite, 0, 0, sprite.width, sprite.height,
    0, 0, sprite.width, sprite.height);
```

The drawImage method has a number of different parameters. For example, you can indicate at which position you want to draw the sprite, or whether only a part of the sprite should be drawn. You could simply call this method and be done with it. However, if you're thinking about future games you want to build, you can use a *drawing state* to draw the sprite.

A drawing state basically is a set of parameters and transformations that will be applied to all things drawn within that state. The advantage of using a drawing state instead of separately calling the drawImage method is that you can do more complicated transformations with sprites. For example, with drawing states, you can rotate or scale sprites, which is a very useful feature in games. Creating a new drawing state is done by calling the save method:

```
Game.canvasContext.save();
```

You can then apply a variety of transformations within this drawing state. For example, you can move (or *translate*) the sprite to a certain position:

```
Game.canvasContext.translate(100, 100);
```

If you call the drawImage method now, the sprite is drawn at position (100, 100). And once you're done drawing, you can remove the drawing state as follows:

```
Game.canvasContext.restore();
```

For convenience, let's define a method that does all this work for you:

```
Game.drawImage = function (sprite, position) {
    Game.canvasContext.save();
    Game.canvasContext.translate(position.x, position.y);
    Game.canvasContext.drawImage(sprite, 0, 0, sprite.width, sprite.height,
        0, 0, sprite.width, sprite.height);
    Game.canvasContext.restore();
};
```

As you can see by looking at the *parameters*, this method requires two pieces of information: the sprite that should be drawn and the position at which it should be drawn. The sprite should be of type Image (although you can't easily enforce this in JavaScript when you define a function). The position is an object variable consisting of an x part and a y part. When you call this method, you have to provide this information. For example, you can draw the balloon sprite at position (100, 100) as follows:

```
Game.drawImage(Game.balloonSprite, { x : 100, y : 100 });
```

You use braces to define an object literal that has x and y components. As you can see, it's allowed to define an object in the instruction that calls a method. Alternatively, you can first define an object, store it in a variable, and then call the drawImage method using that variable:

```
var balloonPos = {
    x : 100,
    y : 100
};
Game.drawImage(Game.balloonSprite, balloonPos);
```

This code does exactly the same thing as the preceding call to drawImage, except it's much longer to write. You can simply put the drawImage method call in the draw method, and the balloon will be drawn at the desired position:

```
Game.draw = function () {
    Game.drawImage(Game.balloonSprite, { x : 100, y : 100 });
};
```

Figure 4-1 shows what the program's output looks like in the browser.

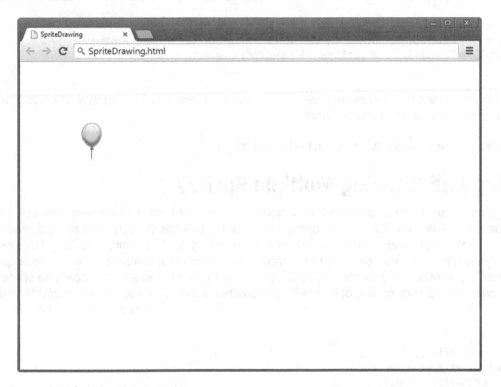

Figure 4-1. Output of the SpriteDrawing program

Again, note that if you tell the browser to draw a sprite at a given position, the *top-left* part of the sprite is drawn there.

Moving Sprites

Now that you're able to draw a sprite on the screen, you can use the game loop to make it move, just like you did with the square in the MovingSquare example in Chapter 3. Let's make a small extension of this program that changes the balloon's position based on the passed time. In order to do that, you have to store the balloon position somewhere. You need to calculate this position in the update method and draw the balloon at that position in the draw method. Therefore, you add a variable to the Game object that represents the position, as follows:

```
var Game = {
    canvas : undefined,
    canvasContext : undefined,
    balloonSprite : undefined,
    balloonPosition : { x : 0, y : 50 }
};
```

As you can see, you define the position as an object consisting of two variables (x and y) in the Game object. You can now add an instruction to the update method that modifies the x-position depending on the time passed, just as you did in the MovingSquare example. Here is the update method:

```
Game.update = function () {
    var d = new Date();
    Game.balloonPosition.x = d.getTime() % Game.canvas.width;
};
```

Now the only thing left to do is make sure you use the balloonPosition variable when you draw the balloon on the screen in the draw method:

```
Game.drawImage(Game.balloonSprite, Game.balloonPosition);
```

Loading and Drawing Multiple Sprites

Building games with only a plain white background is somewhat boring. You can make your game a bit more visually appealing by displaying a background sprite. This means you have to load another sprite in the start method and extend the draw method in order to draw it. The final version of this program is called FlyingSprite, and you can find the complete source code in the sample folder belonging to this chapter. If you open the program FlyingSprite in your browser, you see that now two sprites are drawn: a background and, on top of it, a balloon. To achieve this, you add another variable to contain the background sprite. Like the balloonSprite variable, this variable is part of the Game object:

```
var Game = {
    canvas : undefined,
    canvasContext : undefined,
    backgroundSprite : undefined,
    balloonSprite : undefined,
    balloonPosition : { x : 0, y : 50 }
};
```

Also, in the draw method, there are now two calls to the drawImage method instead of one:

```
Game.draw = function () {
    Game.drawImage(Game.backgroundSprite, { x : 0, y : 0 });
    Game.drawImage(Game.balloonSprite, Game.balloonPosition);
};
```

The order in which these methods are called is very important! Because you want the balloon to appear on top of the background, you *first* have to draw the background, and *then* you draw the balloon. If you did it the other way around, the background would be drawn over the balloon, and you wouldn't see it anymore (try it yourself). Figure 4-2 shows the output of the program.

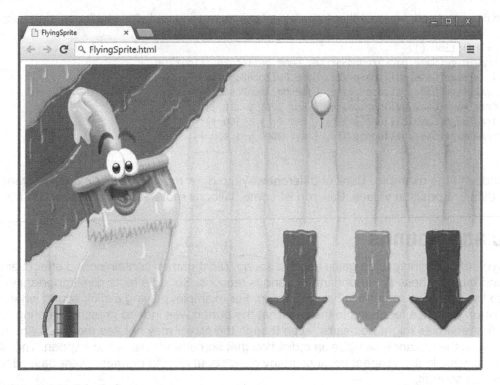

Figure 4-2. Output of the FlyingSprite program

Every time you want to draw a sprite on the screen, you add a call to the drawImage method in the draw method. You can draw a single sprite several times, in different positions on the screen. For instance, if you want to draw a few balloons at different positions over the background, you simply call drawImage for every balloon you want to draw and pass the desired position as a parameter, as follows:

```
Game.draw = function () {
    Game.drawImage(Game.backgroundSprite, { x : 0, y : 0 });
    Game.drawImage(Game.balloonSprite, { x : 0, y : 0 });
    Game.drawImage(Game.balloonSprite, { x : 100, y : 0 });
    Game.drawImage(Game.balloonSprite, { x : 200, y : 0 });
    Game.drawImage(Game.balloonSprite, { x : 0, y : 300 });
    Game.drawImage(Game.balloonSprite, { x : 200, y : 300 });
};
```

Again, pay attention to the order in which you draw the sprites.

You can also draw multiple moving sprites at the same time. For each balloon, you can define its own position variable, which is updated in the update method:

```
Game.update = function () {
    var d = new Date();
    Game.balloonPosition1.x = d.getTime() % Game.canvas.width;
    Game.balloonPosition2.x = (d.getTime() + 100) % Game.canvas.width;
    Game.balloonPosition3.x = (d.getTime() + 200) % Game.canvas.width;
};
```

And in the draw method, you use these positions to draw moving and static balloons at the same time:

```
Game.draw = function () {
    Game.drawImage(Game.backgroundSprite, Game.balloonPosition1);
    Game.drawImage(Game.balloonSprite, Game.balloonPosition2);
    Game.drawImage(Game.balloonSprite, Game.balloonPosition3);
    Game.drawImage(Game.balloonSprite, { x : 200, y : 0 });
    Game.drawImage(Game.balloonSprite, { x : 0, y : 300 });
    Game.drawImage(Game.balloonSprite, { x : 200, y : 300 });
};
```

Play around with the example. Think of different ways to draw moving balloons on the screen. Try a few different position values. Can you let some balloons move faster or slower than others?

Music and Sounds

Another type of commonly used game asset is *sound*. Most games contain sound effects and background music. These are important for various reasons. Sound effects give important cues to indicate to the user that something has happened. For example, playing a click sound when the user clicks a button provides feedback to the user that the button was indeed pressed. Hearing footsteps indicates that enemies might be nearby, even though the player may not see them yet. And hearing a bell ringing in the distance can give an indication that something is about to happen. The old game Myst was a classic in this respect because many cues about how to progress were passed to the player through sounds.

Atmospheric sound effects like dripping water, wind in the trees, and the sound of cars in the distance enhance the experience and give a feeling of being present in the game world. They make the environment more alive, even when nothing is actually happening on the screen.

> **Note** Music plays a crucial role in the way players experience the environment and the action. Music can be used to create tension, sadness, happiness, and many other emotions. However, dealing with music in games is a lot harder than it is in movies. In movies, it's clear what is going to happen, so the music can match perfectly. But in games, part of the action is under the player's control. Modern games use adaptive music that constantly changes according to how the game story evolves.
>
> If you want to implement more advanced handling of music and sound in your game, the basic JavaScript sound engine will not do. Use Web Audio (http://www.w3.org/TR/webaudio/) instead, which is a high-level library for processing and synthesizing audio supported by many modern browsers.

In JavaScript, it's very easy to play background music or sound effects. To use sound, you first need a sound file that you can play. In the FlyingSpriteWithSound program, you play the file snd_music.mp3, which serves as background music. Similar to storing and using sprites, you add a variable to the Game object in which you store the music data. So, the Game object is declared and initialized as follows:

```
var Game = {
    canvas : undefined,
    canvasContext : undefined,
    backgroundSprite : undefined,
    balloonSprite : undefined,
    balloonPosition : { x : 0, y : 50 },
    backgroundMusic : undefined
};
```

You need to add a few instructions to the start method in order to load a sound effect or background music. JavaScript provides a type that you can use as a blueprint for creating an object that represents a sound. This type is called Audio. You can create an object of that type and begin loading a sound as follows:

```
Game.backgroundMusic = new Audio();
Game.backgroundMusic.src = "snd_music.mp3";
```

As you can see, this works almost the same way as loading a sprite. Now you can call methods that are defined as a part of this object, and you can set member variables of the object. For example, the following instruction tells the browser to start playing the audio that is stored in the Game.backgroundMusic variable:

```
Game.backgroundMusic.play();
```

You want to reduce the volume of the background music so you can play (louder) sound effects over it later. Setting the volume is done with the following instruction:

```
Game.backgroundMusic.volume = 0.4;
```

The volume member variable is generally a value between 0 and 1, where 0 means no sound, and 1 plays back the sound at full volume.

Technically, there is no difference between background music and sound effects. Normally, background music is played at a lower volume; and many games loop the background music so that when the song ends, the audio is played from the beginning again. You see later how to do that. All the games you develop in this book use both types of sound (background music and sound effects) to make the games more exciting.

> **Note** You need to watch out for a few things when using sounds and music in your game. Sound can be annoying to some players, so if you do use sound effects or music, make sure there is a way for the player to turn them off. Also, don't force players to wait until a sound has finished playing before they can continue. You might have composed a great song that you want to play while the introduction screen is shown, but players don't launch your game to listen to your music—they want to play! The same principle holds for in-game video sequences. Always provide a way for the user to skip those (even if you got your favorite family member to provide the zombie sounds). Finally, loading sounds and music can take time, especially when the files are hosted on a web site. Try to use small sound files whenever possible.

What You Have Learned

In this chapter, you have learned:

- How to load game assets such as sprites and sounds into memory
- How to draw multiple sprites on the screen and move them around
- How to play background music and sound effects in your game

Part **II**

Creating Colorful Games

In this part, you develop a game called *Painter* (see Figure II-1). While you're developing this game, I also introduce a few new techniques that are very useful when programming games, such as organizing instructions in classes and methods, conditional instructions, iteration, and much more.

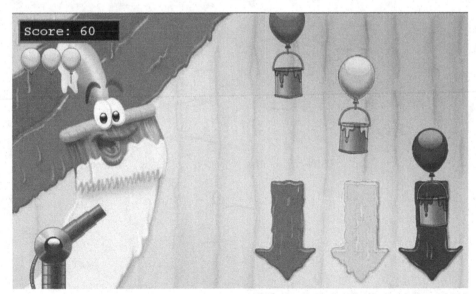

© Springer-Verlag Berlin Heidelberg 2013

Figure II-1. The Painter game

The goal of the Painter game is to collect three different colors of paint: red, green, and blue. The paint falls from the sky in cans that are kept floating by balloons, and you must make sure each can has the right color before it falls through the bottom of the screen. You can change the color of the paint by shooting a paint ball of the desired color at the falling can. You can select the color that you shoot by using the R, G, and B keys on the keyboard. You can shoot a paint ball by left-clicking in the game screen. By clicking further away from the paint cannon, you give the ball a higher velocity. The place where you click also determines the direction in which the cannon shoots. For each can that lands in the correct bin, you get 10 points. For each wrongly colored can, you lose a life (indicated by the yellow balloons at top left on the screen). You can run the final version of this game by downloading the example code zip file belonging to Chapter 12. Double-click the `Painter.html` file in the `PainterFinal` folder to start playing the game.

Chapter 5

Knowing What the Player Is Doing

In this chapter, you start to create a game called Painter. In this game, you need to show sprites that move on the screen. You've already seen a few examples of loading and displaying sprites. Also, you've seen that it's possible to use the current time information to change the position of a sprite. You build on these examples to begin creating Painter. Furthermore, you learn how to deal with player input in your game. You see how to retrieve what the player is doing and how the game world changes depending on that information. You start with a simple extension of the FlyingSprite program that draws a balloon at the position of the mouse pointer. The next chapter examines other types of input, such as keyboard and touch input.

A Sprite Following the Mouse Pointer

Now that you know how to display sprites on the screen, let's see if you can use player input to control a sprite's position. To do that, you have to find out the current position of the mouse. This section shows you how to retrieve this position and how to use it to draw a sprite that follows the mouse pointer.

Retrieving the Mouse Position

Have a look at the program Balloon1 in the book's samples. There isn't a lot of difference between it and the FlyingSprite program. In FlyingSprite, you calculate the position of the balloon by using the system time:

```
var d = new Date();
Game.balloonPosition.x = d.getTime() * 0.3 % Game.canvas.width;
```

The position you calculate is stored in the variable `balloonPosition`. Now you want to create a program where instead of being calculated based on the passed time, the balloon position is the same as the current mouse position. Getting the current mouse position is very easy using *events*.

In JavaScript, you can handle many different kinds of events. Examples of events are the following:

- The player moves the mouse.
- The player left-clicks.
- The player clicks a button.
- An HTML page has been loaded.
- A message is received from a network connection.
- A sprite has finished loading.

When such an event occurs, you can choose to execute instructions. For example, when the player moves the mouse, you can execute a few instructions that retrieve the new mouse position and that store it in a variable so you can use it to draw a sprite at that position. A few JavaScript objects can help you do that. For example, when you display an HTML page, the `document` variable gives you access to all the elements in the page. But, more important, this variable also lets you access the way the user interacts with the document by using the mouse, keyboard, or touch screen.

You've already used this variable in several ways. For example, here you use `document` to retrieve the canvas element from the HTML page:

```
Game.canvas = document.getElementById("myCanvas");
```

In addition to `getElementById`, the `document` object has a lot of other methods and member variables. For example, there is a member variable called `onmousemove` to which you can assign a value. This member variable doesn't refer to a numeric value or a string, but to a function/method. Whenever the mouse is moved, the browser calls that function. You can then write instructions in the function that handle the event in any way you wish. Because of that, these kinds of functions are called *event handlers*. Using event-handler functions is a very efficient way of dealing with input.

Another approach would be to put instructions in the game loop that retrieve the current mouse position or the keys that are currently pressed in each iteration. Although that would work, it would be a lot slower than using event handlers, because you would have to check for input at each iteration instead of only when the player is actually doing something.

An event-handler function has a specific header. It contains a single parameter that, when the function is called, contains an object providing information about the event. For example, here is an empty event-handler function:

```
function handleMouseMove(evt) {
    // do something here
}
```

As you can see, the function has a single parameter evt, which will contain information about the event that needs to be handled. You can now assign this function to the `onmousemove` variable:

```
document.onmousemove = handleMouseMove;
```

Now, every time the mouse is moved, the handleMouseMove function is called. You can put instructions in this function to extract the mouse position from the evt object. For example, this event-handler function retrieves the mouse's x-position and y-position and stores them in the variable balloonPosition:

```
function handleMouseMove(evt) {
    Game.balloonPosition = { x : evt.pageX, y : evt.pageY };
}
```

The pageX and pageY member variables of the evt object contain the position of the mouse relative to the page, meaning the top-left corner of the page has coordinates (0, 0). You can see a few examples of mouse positions in Figure 5-1: three of the corners are labeled with their respective positions as reported when running the program in a browser.

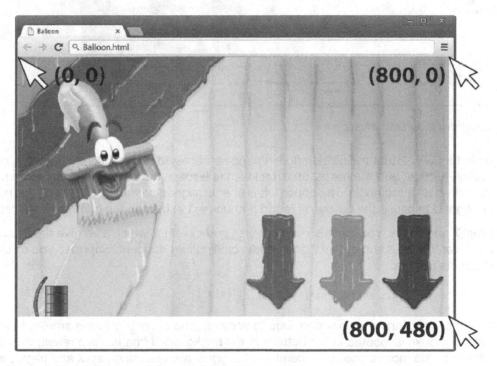

Figure 5-1. *Mouse positions for the upper-left, upper-right, and lower-right corners*

Because the Draw method simply draws the balloon at the mouse position, the balloon now follows the mouse. Figure 5-2 shows what that looks like. You can see the balloon drawn underneath the mouse pointer; it will track the pointer as you move it.

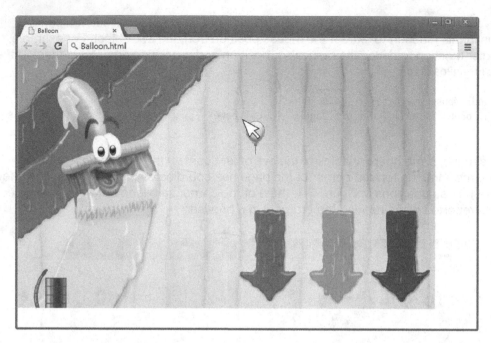

Figure 5-2. Screenshot of the Balloon1 program

You can see in Figure 5-2 that the balloon doesn't appear centered under the very tip of the pointer. There's a reason for that, and the next section tackles the issue in detail. For now, just remember that the sprite is treated as a rectangle. The upper-left corner is aligned with the pointer tip. The balloon appears misaligned because the balloon is round and doesn't extend to the corners of the rectangle.

Instead of pageX and pageY, you can also use clientX and clientY, which also give the mouse position. However, clientX and clientY don't take scrolling into account. Suppose you calculate the mouse position as follows:

```
Game.balloonPosition = { x : evt.clientX, y : evt.clientY };
```

Figure 5-3 shows what can now go wrong. Due to scrolling, the clientY value is smaller than 480, even though the mouse is located at the bottom of the background image. As a result, the balloon is no longer drawn at the mouse position. Therefore, I suggest always using pageX and pageY, and not clientX and clientY. In some cases, though, it may be useful to not take scrolling into account—for example, if you're developing one of those annoying ads that keeps appearing in the middle of the browser view even if the user tries to scroll past it.

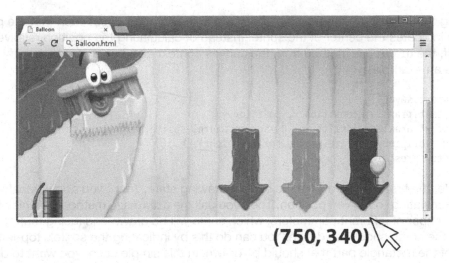

(750, 340)

Figure 5-3. The mouse pointer is at the bottom of the background sprite, but the mouse y-position is 340 (instead of 480) because clientY *doesn't take scrolling into account*

Changing the Origin of a Sprite

When you run the Balloon1 example, notice that the balloon is drawn such that the top-left corner of the sprite is at the current mouse position. When you draw a sprite at a certain position, the default behavior is that the top-left corner of the sprite is drawn at that position. If you execute the following instruction

```
Game.drawImage(someSprite, somePosition);
```

the sprite named someSprite is drawn on the screen such that its top-left corner is at position somePosition. You can also call the top-left corner of the sprite its *origin*. So, what if you want to change this origin? For example, suppose you would like to draw the center of the sprite someSprite at position somePosition. Well, you can calculate that by using the width and height variables of the Image type. Let's declare a variable called origin and store the center of the sprite in it:

```
var origin = { x : someSprite.width / 2, y : someSprite.height / 2 };
```

Now, if you want to draw the sprite someSprite with this different origin, you can do so as follows:

```
var pos = { x : somePosition.x - origin.x,
            y : somePosition.y - origin.y };
Game.drawImage(someSprite, pos);
```

By subtracting the origin from the position, the sprite is drawn at an offset such that the position
somePosition indicates the center of the sprite. Instead of calculating the position relative to the
origin yourself, the drawImage method from the canvas context also has a way to specify the origin
offset. Here is an example:

```
Game.canvasContext.save();
Game.canvasContext.translate(position.x, position.y);
Game.canvasContext.drawImage(sprite, 0, 0, sprite.width, sprite.height,
    -origin.x, -origin.y, sprite.width, sprite.height);
Game.canvasContext.restore();
```

In this example, the first step is to save the current drawing state. Then, you apply transformations.
You start by translating to a given position. Then you call the drawImage method, in which you have
to provide a number of different parameters: which sprite will be drawn and (using four parameters)
which part of the sprite should be drawn. You can do this by indicating the sprite's top-left coordinate
and the size of the rectangle part that should be drawn. In this simple case, you want to draw the
entire sprite, so the top-left coordinate is the point (0, 0). You draw a rectangle part that has the same
width and height as the entire sprite. This also shows that it's possible to use this feature to store
multiple sprites in a single image file while having to load that file into memory only once. Later in this
book, in Chapter 18, you see a nice way to do this and incorporate it into your game applications.

Next you can indicate a position offset. You can see in the previous code that you set this offset to
the negative origin values. In other words, you subtract the origin from the current position. That way,
the top-left coordinate is moved to the origin. Say you have a ball sprite with a width and height of 22
pixels. Suppose you want to draw this ball at position (0, 0), which is the top-left corner of the screen.
Depending on the origin you choose, the result is different. Figure 5-4 shows two examples of drawing
a ball sprite at position (0, 0) with two different origins. The left example has the origin of the ball in the
top-left corner, and the right example shows the ball with the origin at the center of the sprite.

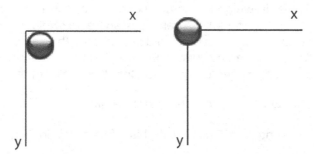

*Figure 5-4. Drawing a ball sprite at position (0, 0) with the origin at the top-left corner of the sprite (left) or the center of the
sprite (right)*

As you've probably noticed, subtracting one position from another is a bit cumbersome in JavaScript:

```
var pos = { x : somePosition.x - origin.x,
            y : somePosition.y - origin.y };
```

It would be much nicer if you could write something like this:

```
var pos = somePosition - origin;
```

Unfortunately, this isn't possible in JavaScript. Some programming languages (such as Java and C#) support operator overloading. This allows a programmer to define what should happen when, for example, two objects are "added" to each other using the plus operator. However, all is not lost. It's possible to define methods that perform these arithmetic operations on object literals such as the one defined above. Chapter 8 deals with this in more detail.

Now that you know how to draw a sprite at a different origin, you can, for example, draw a balloon such that its bottom center is attached to the mouse pointer. To see this in action, look at the Balloon2 program. You declare an additional member variable in which you store the origin of the balloon sprite:

```
var Game = {
    canvas : undefined,
    canvasContext : undefined,
    backgroundSprite : undefined,
    balloonSprite : undefined,
    mousePosition : { x : 0, y : 0 },
    balloonOrigin : { x : 0, y : 0 }
};
```

You can only calculate the origin once the sprite has been loaded. So, just to be sure, you calculate the origin in the draw method by using the following instruction:

```
Game.balloonOrigin = { x : Game.balloonSprite.width / 2,
                       y : Game.balloonSprite.height };
```

The origin is set to half the width of the sprite, but to the full height. In other words, this origin is the bottom center of the sprite, which is exactly what you want. Calculating the origin in the draw method isn't ideal; it would be preferable if you could calculate the origin only once, just after the image has been loaded. Later, you see a better way of doing this.

You can now extend the drawImage method in the Game object so that it supports drawing a sprite at a different origin. The only thing you need to do for that is add an extra position parameter and pass the x and y values in that parameter to the drawImage method of the canvas context. Here is the complete method:

```
Game.drawImage - function (sprite, position, origin) {
    Game.canvasContext.save();
    Game.canvasContext.translate(position.x, position.y);
    Game.canvasContext.drawImage(sprite, 0, 0, sprite.width, sprite.height,
       -origin.x, -origin.y, sprite.width, sprite.height);
    Game.canvasContext.restore();
};
```

In the draw method, you can now calculate the origin and pass it along to the drawImage method, as follows:

```
Game.draw = function () {
    Game.drawImage(Game.backgroundSprite, { x : 0, y : 0 }, { x : 0, y : 0 });
    Game.balloonOrigin = { x : Game.balloonSprite.width / 2,
                           y : Game.balloonSprite.height };
    Game.drawImage(Game.balloonSprite, Game.mousePosition, Game.balloonOrigin);
};
```

Using the Mouse Position to Rotate the Cannon Barrel

One of the features of the Painter game is that it contains a cannon barrel that rotates according to the mouse position. This cannon is controlled by the player in order to shoot paint balls. You can write the part of the program that does this, using the tools discussed in this chapter. You can see this working in the Painter1 example belonging to this chapter.

You have to declare a few member variables to make this possible. First, you need variables for storing the background and the cannon-barrel sprites. You also need to store the current mouse position, just like you did in the previous examples in this chapter. Then, because you rotate the cannon barrel, you need to store its position, its origin, and its current rotation. Finally, you need the canvas and the canvas context so you can draw game objects. As usual, all these variables are declared as members of the Game object:

```
var Game = {
    canvas : undefined,
    canvasContext : undefined,
    backgroundSprite : undefined,
    cannonBarrelSprite : undefined,
    mousePosition : { x : 0, y : 0 },
    cannonPosition : { x : 72, y : 405 },
    cannonOrigin : { x : 34, y : 34 },
    cannonRotation : 0
};
```

Both the position and the origin of the cannon barrel are given a value when the Game variable is defined. The position of the barrel is chosen such that it fits nicely on the cannon base that is already drawn on the background. The barrel image contains a circular part with the actual barrel attached to it. You want the barrel to rotate around the center of the circular part. That means you have to set this center as the origin. Because the circle part is at left on the sprite and the radius of this circle is half the height of the cannon-barrel sprite (which is 68 pixels high), you set the barrel origin to (34, 34), as you can see in the code.

To draw the cannon barrel at an angle, you need to apply a rotation when you draw the cannon-barrel sprite on the screen. This means you have to extend the drawImage method such that it can take rotation into account. Applying rotation is done through the rotate method that is part of the canvas context.

You also add a parameter to the drawImage method that lets you specify the angle at which the object should be rotated. This is what the new version of the drawImage method looks like:

```
Game.drawImage = function (sprite, position, rotation, origin) {
    Game.canvasContext.save();
    Game.canvasContext.translate(position.x, position.y);
    Game.canvasContext.rotate(rotation);
    Game.canvasContext.drawImage(sprite, 0, 0, sprite.width, sprite.height,
        -origin.x, -origin.y, sprite.width, sprite.height);
    Game.canvasContext.restore();
};
```

In the start method, you load the two sprites:

```
Game.backgroundSprite = new Image();
Game.backgroundSprite.src = "spr_background.jpg";
Game.cannonBarrelSprite = new Image();
Game.cannonBarrelSprite.src = "spr_cannon_barrel.png";
```

The next step is implementing the methods in the game loop. Until now, the update method has always been empty. Now you have a good reason to use it. In the update method, you update the game world, which in this case means you calculate the angle at which the cannon barrel should be drawn. How do you calculate this? Have a look at Figure 5-5.

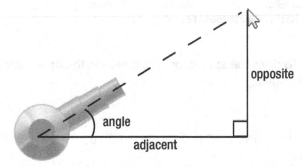

© Springer-Verlag Berlin Heidelberg 2013

Figure 5-5. *Calculating the angle of the barrel based on the mouse pointer position*

If you remember your math classes, you may recall that angles in triangles can be calculated with trigonometric functions. In this case, you can calculate the angle using the tangent function, which is given as follows:

$$tan(angle) = \frac{opposite}{adjacent}$$

In other words, the angle is given by

$$angle = arctan\left(\frac{opposite}{adjacent}\right)$$

You can calculate the length of the opposite and adjacent sides by calculating the difference between the current mouse position and the position of the cannon barrel, as follows:

```
var opposite = Game.mousePosition.y - Game.cannonPosition.y;
var adjacent = Game.mousePosition.x - Game.cannonPosition.x;
```

Now you have to calculate the arctangent using these values. How do you do this? Fortunately, JavaScript knows a Math object that can help. The Math object contains a number of useful mathematical functions, including trigonometric functions such as sine, cosine, and tangent, and their inverses arcsine, arccosine, and arctangent. Two functions in the Math object calculate the arctangent. The first version takes a single value as a parameter. You can't use this version in this case: when the mouse is directly over the barrel, a division by zero will occur because adjacent is zero.

For situations where the arctangent needs to be calculated while taking into account possible singularities such as this, there is an alternative arctangent method. The atan2 method takes opposite and adjacent lengths as separate parameters and returns the equivalent in radians of 90 degrees in this situation. You can use this method to calculate the angle, as follows:

```
Game.cannonRotation = Math.atan2(opposite, adjacent);
```

These instructions are all placed in update. Here is the complete method:

```
Game.update = function () {
    var opposite = Game.mousePosition.y - Game.cannonPosition.y;
    var adjacent = Game.mousePosition.x - Game.cannonPosition.x;
    Game.cannonRotation = Math.atan2(opposite, adjacent);
};
```

The only thing left to do is to draw the sprites on the screen in the draw method, at the correct position and at the correct angle:

```
Game.draw = function () {
    Game.clearCanvas();
    Game.drawImage(Game.backgroundSprite, { x : 0, y : 0 }, 0,
        { x : 0, y : 0 });
    Game.drawImage(Game.cannonBarrelSprite, Game.cannonPosition,
        Game.cannonRotation, Game.cannonOrigin);
};
```

What You Have Learned

In this chapter, you have learned:

- How to read the current mouse position using an event handler, and how to draw a sprite at the current mouse position
- How to draw a sprite at an angle
- How to change the angle at which a sprite is drawn based on the mouse position

Chapter **6**

Reacting to Player Input

In this chapter, you see how your game program can react to button presses. In order to do this, you need an instruction called if that executes an instruction (or a group of instructions) when a condition is met. You also learn to structure your code a bit more into objects and methods.

Objects in Games

Until now, all the example programs have had one big object called Game. This object consists of a number of variables for storing the canvas and its context, sprites, positions, and so on. This is what the Game object from the Painter1 example looks like:

```
var Game = {
    canvas : undefined,
    canvasContext : undefined,
    backgroundSprite : undefined,
    cannonBarrelSprite : undefined,
    mousePosition : { x : 0, y : 0 },
    cannonPosition : { x : 72, y : 405 },
    cannonOrigin : { x : 34, y : 34 },
    cannonRotation : 0
};
```

As you can see, it already contains quite a few variables, even for a simple program that only draws a background and a rotating cannon. As the games you develop become more complicated, this list of variables will grow, and as a result, the code will become harder for other developers to understand (and for you, when you don't look at the code for a few months). The problem is that you store everything in a single, big object called Game. Conceptually, this makes sense, because Game contains everything pertaining to the Painter game. However, the code will be easier to understand if you separate things a little.

If you look at the contents of the Game object, you can see that certain variables belong together in some way. For example, the canvas and canvasContext variables belong together because they both concern the canvas. Also, quite a few variables store information about the cannon, such as its

67

position or its rotation. You can group related variables into different objects to make the fact that these variables are related clearer in the code. For example, look at this example:

```
var Canvas2D = {
    canvas : undefined,
    canvasContext : undefined
};

var Game = {
    backgroundSprite : undefined,
};

var cannon = {
    cannonBarrelSprite : undefined,
    position : { x : 72, y : 405 },
    origin : { x : 34, y : 34 },
    rotation : 0
};

var Mouse = { position : { x : 0, y : 0 } };
```

As you can see, you now have a couple of different objects, each containing some of the variables that were before grouped in the Game object. Now it's much easier to see which variables belong to the cannon and which variables belong to the canvas. And the nice thing is that you can do the same thing for *methods*. For example, you can add the methods for clearing the canvas and drawing an image on it to the Canvas2D object, as follows:

```
Canvas2D.clear = function () {
    Canvas2D.canvasContext.clearRect(0, 0, this.canvas.width,
        this.canvas.height);
};

Canvas2D.drawImage = function (sprite, position, rotation, origin) {
    // canvas drawing code
};
```

Using different objects, as opposed to a single object that contains everything belonging to the game, makes your code a lot easier to read. Of course, this is only true if you distribute the variables over the objects in a *logical manner*. Even for simple games, there are a lot of ways in which you can organize code. All developers have their own style of doing this. As you read on, you'll discover that this book also follows a certain style. You may not agree with that style, or sometimes you might have approached a problem differently than we do in this book. That's okay. There is almost never a single correct solution for programming problems.

Going back to the distribution over objects, you can see that we named most objects beginning with an uppercase character (such as Canvas2D), but the cannon object starts with a lowercase character. We did this for a reason, which we discuss in more detail later. For now, let's just say that the objects that start with an uppercase character are useful for *any* game, but the objects whose names start with a lowercase letter are only used for a *particular* game. In this case, you can imagine that the Canvas2D object could be used in any HTML5 game, but the cannon object is only useful for the Painter game.

Loading Sprites

Now that you have different objects in your game, where do you load the sprites? You could load all the sprites in the start method of the Game object, but another option is to add a similar method to, for example, the cannon object and load the sprites belonging to the cannon there. Which approach is better?

There is something to say for loading the sprites belonging to the cannon object in an initialization method of that object. That way, you can clearly see from the code which sprites belong to what object. However, this also means that if you reuse the same image for different game objects, you have to load that sprite multiple times. And for games that run in a browser, this means the browser has to download the image file from a server, which can take time. A better option is to load all the sprites the game needs when the game is started. And to clearly separate the sprites from the rest of the program, you store them in an object called sprites. This object is declared at the top of the program as an empty object:

```
var sprites = {};
```

You fill this variable with sprites in the Game.start method. For each sprite you want to load, you create an Image object, and then set its source to the sprite location. Because you're already using quite a few different sprites, you load these sprites from another asset folder that contains all the sprites belonging to the Painter game. That way, you don't have to copy these image files for all the different examples in the book that use these sprites. These are the instructions that load the various sprites needed for the Painter2 example belonging to this chapter:

```
var spriteFolder = "../../assets/Painter/sprites/";
sprites.background = new Image();
sprites.background.src = spriteFolder + "spr_background.jpg";
sprites.cannon_barrel = new Image();
sprites.cannon_barrel.src = spriteFolder + "spr_cannon_barrel.png";
sprites.cannon_red = new Image();
sprites.cannon_red.src = spriteFolder + "spr_cannon_red.png";
sprites.cannon_green = new Image();
sprites.cannon_green.src = spriteFolder + "spr_cannon_green.png";
sprites.cannon_blue = new Image();
sprites.cannon_blue.src = spriteFolder + "spr_cannon_blue.png";
```

You use the + operator here to concatenate text. For example, the value of the expression spriteFolder + "spr_background.jpg" is "../../assets/Painter/sprites/spr_background.jpg". The sprite folder path looks a bit complicated. The ../../ bit means you're moving up two directories in the hierarchy. This is needed because the example directories Painter2 and Painter2a are not at the same level as the assets directory. You store these images in variables that are part of the sprites object. Later, you access that object when you need to retrieve sprites. The next step is handling the player's keypresses.

Handling a Key-Down Event

In the previous chapter, you saw how to use an event handler to read the current position of the mouse. In a very similar way, you can react to the event that the player holds down a key on the keyboard. Again, you do this by defining an event handler. You need to store the key that is held down so you can access it later and do something with that information. The easiest way to store which key was pressed is to use *key codes*. A key code is basically a number that represents a certain key. For example, the spacebar could be number 13, or the A key could be number 65. So, why use these particular numbers for these keys, and not other ones? Because *character code tables* are standardized, and different standards have emerged over the years.

In the 1970s, programmers thought $2^6 = 64$ symbols would be enough to represent all the possible symbols you would need: 26 characters, 10 numbers, and 28 punctuation marks (comma, semicolon, and so on). Although this meant there was no distinction between lowercase and uppercase characters, it wasn't a problem at the time.

In the 1980s, people used $2^7 = 128$ different symbols: 26 uppercase characters, 26 lowercase characters, 10 numbers, 33 punctuation marks, and 33 special characters (end-of-line, tabulation, beep, and so on). The order of these symbols was known as *ASCII*: the American Standard Code for Information Interchange. This was nice for the English language, but it wasn't sufficient for other languages such as French, German, Dutch, Spanish, and more.

As a result, in the 1990s, new code tables were constructed with $2^8 = 256$ symbols; the most common letters for various countries were represented as well. The symbols from 0–127 were the same as in ASCII, but symbols 128–255 were used for special characters belonging to a given language. Depending on the language (English, Russian, Indian, and so on), a different code table was used. The Western European code table was Latin1, for example. For Eastern Europe, another code table was used (Polish and Czech have many special accents for which there was no more room in the Latin1 table). Greek, Russian, Hebrew, and the Indian Devangari alphabet all had their own code tables. This was a reasonable way of dealing with the different languages, but things became complicated if you wanted to store text in different languages at the same time. Also, languages containing more than 128 symbols (such as Mandarin) were impossible to represent using this format.

At the beginning of the twenty-first century, the coding standard was extended again to a table containing $2^{16} = 65536$ different symbols. This table could easily contain all the alphabets in the world, including many different punctuation marks and other symbols. If you ever encounter an alien species, this table probably has room to represent the characters in the alien's language as well. The code table is called *Unicode*. The first 256 symbols of Unicode are the same symbols as the Latin1 code table.

Going back to the key code you want to store for the example, let's add a simple variable that contains the last pressed key:

```
var Keyboard = { keyDown : -1 };
```

When the variable is initialized, it contains a keyDown variable that contains the value -1. This value represents that the player *currently is not pressing any key*. When the player presses a key, you have to store the key code in the variable Keyboard.keyDown. You do so by writing an *event handler* that stores the currently pressed key. Here is what that event handler looks like:

```
function handleKeyDown(evt) {
    Keyboard.keyDown = evt.keyCode;
}
```

As you can see, the function gets an event as a parameter. That event object has a variable called keyCode, which contains the key code of the key the player is currently pressing.

You assign this event-handler function in Game.start, as follows:

```
document.onkeydown = handleKeyDown;
```

Now, every time the player presses a key, the key code is stored so that you can use it in your game. But what happens when the player releases the key? The Keyboard.keyDown value should be assigned -1 again, so you know the player currently isn't pressing any key. This is done with the *key up* event handler. Here are the header and body of that handler:

```
function handleKeyUp(evt) {
    Keyboard.keyDown = -1;
}
```

As you can see, it's very simple. The only thing you need to do is assign the value -1 to the keyDown variable in the Keyboard object. Finally, you assign this function in Game.start:

```
document.onkeyup = handleKeyUp;
```

Now you're ready to deal with keypresses in your game. Note that this way of dealing with keypresses is a bit limited. For example, there is no way to keep track of simultaneous keypresses, such as the player pressing the A and B keys at the same time. Later, in Chapter 13, you extend the Keyboard object to take this into account.

Conditional Execution

As a simple example of how you can use the Keyboard object to do something, let's make an extension of the Painter1 program that draws a colored ball on top of the cannon barrel. By pressing the R, G, or B key, the player can change the cannon color to red, green, or blue. Figure 6-1 shows a screenshot of the program.

Figure 6-1. A screenshot of the Painter2 program

You need to load three extra sprites, one for each colored ball. This is done with the following three instructions:

```
sprites.cannon_red = Game.loadSprite(spriteFolder + "spr_cannon_red.png");
sprites.cannon_green = Game.loadSprite(spriteFolder + "spr_cannon_green.png");
sprites.cannon_blue = Game.loadSprite(spriteFolder + "spr_cannon_blue.png");
```

You add an `initialize` method to the `cannon` object, in which you assign values to variables belonging to that object. This method is called from `Game.start`. That way, the cannon is initialized when the game starts:

```
Game.start = function () {
    Canvas2D.initialize("myCanvas");
    document.onkeydown = handleKeyDown;
    document.onkeyup = handleKeyUp;
    document.onmousemove = handleMouseMove;
    ...
    cannon.initialize();
    window.setTimeout(Game.mainLoop, 500);
};
```

In the `cannon.initialize` method, you assign values to the variables belonging to the cannon. This is the complete method:

```
cannon.initialize = function() {
    cannon.position = { x : 72, y : 405 };
    cannon.colorPosition =  { x : 55, y : 388 };
    cannon.origin = { x : 34, y : 34 };
    cannon.currentColor = sprites.cannon_red;
    cannon.rotation = 0;
};
```

As you can see, you have two position variables: one for the cannon barrel and one for the colored sphere. Furthermore, you add a variable that refers to the current color of the sphere that should be drawn. Initially, you assign the red sphere sprite to this variable.

In order to make a clear separation between the objects, you can also add a draw method to the cannon object. In this method, you draw the cannon barrel and the colored sphere on top of it:

```
cannon.draw = function () {
    Canvas2D.drawImage(sprites.cannon_barrel, cannon.position, cannon.rotation,
        cannon.origin);
    Canvas2D.drawImage(cannon.currentColor, cannon.colorPosition, 0,
        { x : 0, y :  0 });
};
```

This draw method is called from Game.draw as follows:

```
Game.draw = function () {
    Canvas2D.clear();
    Canvas2D.drawImage(sprites.background, { x : 0, y : 0 }, 0,
        { x : 0, y : 0 });
    cannon.draw();
};
```

That way, you can more easily see which drawing instructions belong to what object. Now that the preparatory work has been done, you can start handling the player's keypresses. Until now, all the instructions you've written had to be executed all the time. For example, the program always needs to draw the background sprite and the cannon barrel sprite. But now you encounter a situation where you need to execute instructions only if some condition is met. For example, you need to change the color of the ball to green *only if the player presses the G key*. This kind of instruction is called a *conditional instruction*, and it uses a new keyword: if.

With the if instruction, you can provide a condition and execute a block of instructions if this condition holds (in total, this is sometimes also referred to as a *branch*). Here are some examples of conditions:

- The player has pressed the G key.
- The number of seconds that have passed since the start of the game is larger than 1,000.
- The balloon sprite is exactly in the middle of the screen.
- The monster has eaten your character.

These conditions can either be *true* or *false*. A condition is an *expression*, because it has a value (it's either *true* or *false*). This value is also called a *Boolean* value. With an if instruction, you can execute a block of instructions if a condition is true. Take a look at this example if instruction:

```
if (Game.mousePosition.x > 200) {
    Canvas2D.drawImage(sprites.background, { x : 0, y : 0 }, 0,
        { x : 0, y : 0 });
}
```

The condition is always placed in parentheses. A block of instructions follows, enclosed by braces. In this example, the background is drawn only if the mouse's x-position is larger than 200. As a result, if you move the mouse too far to the left on the screen, the background isn't drawn. You can place multiple instructions between the braces if you want:

```
if (Game.mousePosition.x > 200) {
    Canvas2D.drawImage(sprites.background, { x : 0, y : 0 }, 0,
        { x : 0, y : 0 });
    cannon.draw();
}
```

If there is only one instruction, you may omit the braces to shorten the code a bit:

```
if (Game.mousePosition.x > 200)
    Canvas2D.drawImage(sprites.background, { x : 0, y : 0 }, 0,
        { x : 0, y : 0 });
```

In this example, you want to change the color of the cannon barrel only when the player presses the R, G, or B key. This means you have to check whether one of these keys is currently pressed. Using the Keyboard object, the condition that checks whether the R key is pressed is given as follows:

```
Keyboard.keyDown === 82
```

The === operator compares two values and returns true if they're the same or false otherwise. On the left side of this comparison operator is the value of the keyDown variable in the Keyboard object. On the right side is the key code that corresponds to the R key. You can now use it in an if instruction as follows, in the update method of cannon:

```
if (Keyboard.keyDown === 82)
    cannon.currentColor = sprites.cannon_red;
```

A slightly annoying thing is that you have to remember all these key codes in order to understand what is happening in the program. You can make life easier by defining a second variable called Keys that contains the most common key codes, as follows:

```
var Keys = {
    A: 65,    B: 66,    C: 67,    D: 68,    E: 69,    F: 70,
    G: 71,    H: 72,    I: 73,    J: 74,    K: 75,    L: 76,
    M: 77,    N: 78,    O: 79,    P: 80,    Q: 81,    R: 82,
    S: 83,    T: 84,    U: 85,    V: 86,    W: 87,    X: 88,
    Y: 89,    Z: 90
};
```

Now, if you want to know which number the key R has, you can simply access the variable Keys.R, and the if instruction becomes a lot clearer:

```
if (Keyboard.keyDown === Keys.R)
    cannon.currentColor = sprites.cannon_red;
```

Comparison Operators

The condition in the header of an if instruction is an expression that returns a truth value: *yes* or *no*. When the outcome of the expression is *yes*, the body of the if instruction is executed. In these conditions, you're allowed to use comparison operators. The following operators are available:

- **<**   Less than
- **<=** Less than or equal to
- **>**   Greater than
- **>=** Greater than or equal to
- **===** Equal to
- **!==** Not equal to

These operators may be used between any two numbers. On the left side and the right side of these operators, you may put constant values, variables, or complete expressions with addition, multiplication, or whatever you want. You test the equality of two values using a triple equals sign (===). This is very different from a single equals sign, which denotes an assignment. The difference between these two operators is very important:

x = 5; means: *assign* the value 5 to x.

x === 5 means: *is* x equal to 5?

Because you have seen single-equals and triple-equals operators, you might wonder if there is also a double-equals operator. There is. The double-equals operator also compares values, but if those values aren't of the same type, this operator converts one of the values such that the types match. Such a conversion sounds like it could be useful, but it leads to some strange behavior. Here are a few examples:

```
'' == '0'       // false
0 == ''         // true!
0 == '0'        // true!
```

The triple-equals operator would return false in all three cases because the types are different. Generally, it's best to avoid the double-equals operator. The triple-equals operator is much more predictable, which leads to fewer bugs and errors when you use it in your program.

> **Caution**   Chances are, you'll encounter the double-equals operator quite often in existing JavaScript libraries or code snippets. Programming habits are hard to change.

Logic Operators

In logical terms, a condition is also called a *predicate*. The operators that are used in logic to connect predicates (*and*, *or*, and *not*) can also be used in JavaScript. They have a special notation:

- && is the logical and operator.
- || is the logical *or* operator.
- ! is the logical *not* operator.

You can use these operators to check for complicated logical statements so that you can execute instructions only in very particular cases. For example, you can draw a "You win!" overlay only if the player has more than 10,000 points, the enemy has a life force of 0, and the player's life force is greater than 0:

```
if (playerPoints > 10000 && enemyLifeForce === 0 && playerLifeForce > 0)
    Canvas2D.drawimage(winningOverlay, { x : 0, y : 0 }, 0, { x : 0, y : 0 });
```

The Boolean Type

Expressions that use comparison operators or that connect other expressions with logical operators also have a type, just like expressions that use arithmetic operators. After all, the result of such an expression is a value: one of the two truth values *yes* or *no*. In logic, these values are called *true* and *false*. In JavaScript, these truth values are represented by the true and false keywords.

In addition to being used to express a condition in an if instruction, logical expressions can be applied in a lot of different situations. A logical expression is similar to an arithmetic expression, except that it has a different type. For example, you can store the result of a logical expression in a variable, pass it as a parameter, or use that result again in another expression.

The type of logical values is *Boolean*, named after the English mathematician and philosopher George Boole (1815–1864). Here is an example of a declaration and an assignment of a Boolean variable:

```
var test;
test = x > 3 && y < 5;
```

In this case, if x contains, for example, the value 6 and y contains the value 3, the Boolean expression x > 3 && y < 5 will evaluate to true and this value will be stored in the variable test. You can also store the Boolean values true and false directly in a variable:

```
var isAlive = false;
```

Boolean variables are extremely handy for storing the status of different objects in a game. For example, you can use a Boolean variable to store whether the player is still alive, whether the player is currently jumping, whether a level is finished, and so on. You can use Boolean variables as an expression in an if instruction:

```
if (isAlive)
    // do something
```

In this case, if the expression isAlive evaluates to true, the body of the if instruction is executed. You might think this code would generate a compiler error and you need to do a comparison of the Boolean variable, like this:

```
if (isAlive === true)
    // do something
```

However, this extra comparison isn't necessary. A conditional expression as in the if instruction *has to evaluate to* true or false. Because a Boolean variable already represents one of these two values, you don't need to perform the comparison. In fact, if the previous comparison was needed, you would also need to compare that outcome again with a Boolean value:

```
if ((isAlive === true) === true)
    // do something
```

And it gets worse:

```
if ((((((isAlive === true) === true) === true) === true) === true) === true)
    // do something
```

In summary, don't make things more complicated than they are. If the outcome is already a Boolean value, you don't have to compare it to anything.

You can use the Boolean type to store complex expressions that are either true or false. Let's look at a few additional examples:

```
var a = 12 > 5;
var b = a && 3 + 4 === 8;
var c = a || b;
if (!c)
    a = false;
```

Before you read on, try to determine the value of the variables a, b, and c after these instructions have been executed. In the first line, you declare and initialize a Boolean a. The truth value that is stored in this Boolean is evaluated from the expression 12 > 5, which evaluates to true. This value is then assigned to variable a. In the second line, you declare and initialize a new variable b, in which you store the result of a more complex expression. The first part of this expression is the variable a, which contains the value true. The second part of the expression is a comparison expression 3 + 4 === 8. This comparison is not true (3 + 4 doesn't equal 8), so this evaluates to false, and therefore the logical *and* also results in false. Therefore, the variable b contains the value false after this instruction executes.

The third instruction stores the result of the logical *or* operation on variables a and b in variable c. Because a contains the value true, the outcome of this operation is also true, and this outcome is assigned to c. Finally, there is an if instruction, which assigns the value false to variable a, but only if !c evaluates to true. In this case, c is true, so !c is false, which means the body of the if instruction is not executed. Therefore, after all the instructions are executed, a and c both contain the value true, and b contains the value false.

Doing these kinds of exercises shows that it's very easy to make logical mistakes. This process is similar to what you do when you debug your code. Step by step, you move through the instructions and determine the values of the variables at various stages. A single mix-up can cause something you assume to be true to evaluate to false!

Aiming the Barrel at the Mouse Pointer

In the previous sections, you've seen how to use the `if` instruction to check whether the player has pressed the R key. Now, suppose you want to update the angle of the cannon barrel only if the left mouse button is down. In order to handle mouse button presses, you need two more event handlers: one for handling the event that the user presses a mouse button, and another for handling the event that the user releases the mouse button. This is done in a way similar to pressing and releasing a key on the keyboard. Whenever a mouse button is pressed or released, the `which` variable in the event object tells you which button it was (1 is the left button, 2 is the middle button, 3 is the right button). You can add a Boolean variable to the `Mouse` object that indicates whether a mouse button is down. Let's do this for the left mouse button:

```
var Mouse = {
    position : { x : 0, y : 0 },
    leftDown : false
};
```

You also have to add the two handler functions that assign a value to the `leftDown` variable. Here are the two functions:

```
function handleMouseDown(evt) {
    if (evt.which === 1)
        Mouse.leftDown = true;
}

function handleMouseUp(evt) {
    if (evt.which === 1)
        Mouse.leftDown = false;
}
```

As you can see, you use the `if` instruction to find out whether the left mouse button was pressed or released. Depending on the truth value of the condition, you execute the body of the instruction. Of course, you need to assign these handlers to the appropriate variables in the document so they're called when a mouse button is pressed or released:

```
document.onmousedown = handleMouseDown;
document.onmouseup = handleMouseUp;
```

Now, in the `update` method of `cannon`, you update the cannon barrel angle only if the left mouse button is down:

```
if (Mouse.leftDown) {
    var opposite = Mouse.position.y - this.position.y;
    var adjacent = Mouse.position.x - this.position.x;
    cannon.rotation = Math.atan2(opposite, adjacent);
}
```

Suppose you want to have the angle reset to zero after the player releases the left mouse button. You could add another `if` instruction, like this:

```
if (!Mouse.leftDown)
    cannon.rotation = 0;
```

For more complex conditions, this kind of solution will become harder to understand. There is a nicer way of dealing with this situation: by using an `if` instruction with an *alternative*. The alternative instruction is executed when the condition in the `if` instruction is not true; you use the `else` keyword for that:

```
if (Mouse.leftDown) {
    var opposite = Mouse.position.y - this.position.y;
    var adjacent = Mouse.position.x - this.position.x;
    cannon.rotation = Math.atan2(opposite, adjacent);
} else
    cannon.rotation = 0;
```

This instruction does exactly the same thing as the previous two `if` instructions, but you only have to write the condition once. Execute the Painter2 program and see what it does. Note that the angle of the cannon barrel is zero as soon as you release the left mouse button.

The syntax of the `if` instruction with an alternative is represented by the syntax diagram in Figure 6-2. The body of an `if` instruction can consist of multiple instructions between braces because an instruction can also be a *block* of instructions, as defined in the syntax diagram in Figure 6-3.

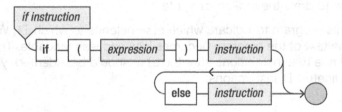

***Figure 6-2.** Syntax diagram of the `if` instruction*

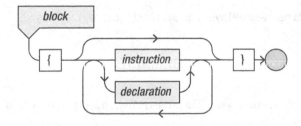

***Figure 6-3.** Syntax diagram of a block of instructions (which itself is in turn an instruction)*

A Number of Different Alternatives

When there are multiple categories of values, you can find out with `if` instructions which case you're dealing with. The second test is placed after the `else` of the first `if` instruction so that the second test is executed only when the first test fails. A third test could be placed after the `else` of the second `if` instruction, and so forth.

The following fragment determines within which age segment a player falls, so that you can draw different player sprites:

```
if (age < 4)
    Canvas2D.drawImage(sprites.babyPlayer, playerPosition, 0,
        { x : 0, y : 0 });
else if (age < 12)
        Canvas2D.drawImage(sprites.youngPlayer, playerPosition, 0,
            { x : 0, y : 0 });
    else if (age < 65)
            Canvas2D.drawImage(sprites.adultPlayer, playerPosition, 0,
                { x : 0, y : 0 });
        else
            Canvas2D.drawImage(sprites.oldPlayer, playerPosition, 0,
                { x : 0, y : 0 });
```

After every `else` (except the last one) is another `if` instruction. For babies, the `babyPlayer` sprite is drawn and the rest of the instructions are ignored (they're after the `else`, after all). Old players, on the other hand, go through all the tests (younger than 4? younger than 12? younger than 65?) before you conclude that you have to draw the `oldPlayer` sprite.

I used indentation in this program to indicate which `else` belongs to which `if`. When there are many different categories, the text of the program becomes less and less readable. Therefore, as an exception to the usual rule that instructions after the `else` should be indented, you can use a simpler layout with such complicated `if` instructions:

```
if (age < 4)
    Canvas2D.drawImage(sprites.babyPlayer, playerPosition, 0,
        { x : 0, y : 0 });
else if (age < 12)
    Canvas2D.drawImage(sprites.youngPlayer, playerPosition, 0,
        { x : 0, y : 0 });
else if (age < 65)
    Canvas2D.drawImage(sprites.adultPlayer, playerPosition, 0,
        { x : 0, y : 0 });
else
    Canvas2D.drawImage(sprites.oldPlayer, playerPosition, 0, { x : 0, y : 0 });
```

The additional advantage here is that using this layout, it's a lot easier to see which cases are handled by the instructions. You can also see that the example code uses multiple alternatives to handle the three different color cases in the update method of the cannon object:

```
if (Keyboard.keyDown === Keys.R)
    cannon.currentColor = sprites.cannon_red;
else if (Keyboard.keyDown === Keys.G)
    cannon.currentColor = sprites.cannon_green;
else if (Keyboard.keyDown === Keys.B)
    cannon.currentColor = sprites.cannon_blue;
```

Next to the if instruction, there is an instruction called switch that is better suited for dealing with many different alternatives. See Chapter 21 more information about how to use switch.

Toggling the Cannon Barrel's Behavior

As a final example of using the if instruction to handle mouse button presses, let's try to handle a mouse button *click* instead of a mouse button down. You know how to check with an if instruction whether the mouse button is currently down, but how do you find out whether the player has *clicked* (pressed the button while it was not previously pressed)? Look at the program Painter2a. In this program, the cannon barrel's rotation follows the mouse pointer after you click the left button. When you click again, the cannon stops following the mouse pointer.

The issue with this kind of *toggle* behavior is that you only know the current status of the mouse in the update method. This isn't enough information to determine when a click happens, because a click is partly defined by what happened the previous time you were in the update method. You can say that a player has clicked the mouse button if these two things happen:

- Currently, the mouse button is down.
- The mouse button was not down during the last call to the update method.

You add an extra Boolean variable leftPressed to the Mouse object, which hat indicates whether a mouse pressed occurred. You need to set this variable to true if you receive a mouse down event (covering the first item in the bullet list) and the variable Mouse.leftDown is not yet true (which corresponds to the second bullet item). This is what the extended handleMouseDown event handler looks like:

```
function handleMouseDown(evt) {
    if (evt.which === 1) {
        if (!Mouse.leftDown)
            Mouse.leftPressed = true;
        Mouse.leftDown = true;
    }
}
```

Here you also see an example of a *nested* if instruction, meaning the body of an if instruction contains one or more if instructions itself. You can now write the code needed to toggle the cannon barrel's behavior by writing an if instruction that checks whether the left mouse button has been pressed:

```
if (Mouse.leftPressed)
    cannon.calculateAngle = !cannon.calculateAngle;
```

In the body of the if instruction, you toggle the calculateAngle variable. This is a Boolean member variable of the cannon object. In order to get the toggling behavior, you use the logical *not* operator. The result of the *not* operation on the variable calculateAngle is stored again in the variable calculateAngle. So, if that variable contains the value true, you store in the same variable the value false and vice versa. The result is that the value of the calculateAngle variable toggles every time you execute that instruction.

You can now use that variable in another if instruction to determine whether you should update the angle:

```
if (cannon.calculateAngle) {
    var opposite = Mouse.position.y - this.position.y;
    var adjacent = Mouse.position.x - this.position.x;
    cannon.rotation = Math.atan2(opposite, adjacent);
} else
    cannon.rotation = 0;
```

In order to finalize this example, you need to do a bit of extra bookkeeping. Currently, the variable Mouse.leftPressed is never reset. So, after each execution of the game loop, you reset Mouse.leftPressed to false. You add a reset method to the Mouse object that does this, as follows:

```
Mouse.reset = function() {
    Mouse.leftPressed = false;
};
```

And finally, this method is called from the mainLoop method in the Game object:

```
Game.mainLoop = function() {
    Game.update();
    Game.draw();
    Mouse.reset();
    window.setTimeout(Game.mainLoop, 1000 / 60);
};
```

What You Have Learned

In this chapter, you have learned:

- How to react to mouse clicks and button presses using if instructions
- How to formulate conditions for these instructions using Boolean values
- How to use if instructions with different alternatives

Chapter 7

Basic Game Objects

In this chapter, you start organizing the source code of the Painter game a bit more. This is necessary because the source code of a game contains many lines of code. In the previous examples, you began grouping variables over different objects (such as `Canvas2D` or cannon). In this chapter, you continue structuring your code by using more objects and by splitting the code over separate files.

Using Separate JavaScript Files

One thing you've probably noticed is that your JavaScript file is becoming rather big. Having a single big file that contains all your code isn't ideal, because it makes it hard to find certain parts of the program. It makes more sense to split the code over multiple source files. A good way to do this is to split the different JavaScript objects over separate JavaScript files so each JavaScript file contains the code of one of the objects. The Painter3 example program contains the objects introduced in the previous chapters, but each object is described in its own JavaScript file. It's now much easier to navigate through the code and understand the structure of the program. You can even place these files into separate directories to indicate which objects belong together. For example, you can put both the `Keyboard` and `Mouse` JavaScript files in a directory called `input`. This way, it's clear that both these files contain code related to dealing with input.

Loading these separate JavaScript files in the browser is a little tricky. In the previous examples, you've seen the following line to load a JavaScript file:

```
<script src="FlyingSpriteWithSound.js"></script>
```

You would expect that you could load the JavaScript files used in the Painter3 program by just adding more of these `script` elements to the HTML file, as follows:

```
<script src="input/Keyboard.js"></script>
<script src="input/Mouse.js"></script>
<script src="Canvas2D.js"></script>
<script src="system/Keys.js"></script>
<script src="Painter.js"></script>
<script src="Cannon.js"></script>
```

Unfortunately, you run into trouble if you try to take this approach of adding more and more `script` elements. Because the JavaScript files are retrieved from a server somewhere, there is no way to know for sure which JavaScript file will be finished loading first. Suppose the first file the browser can load is `Painter.js`. The browser can't interpret the code in this file because the code *refers to code in other files* (such as the `Canvas2D` object). And this holds for other files as well. So, in order for this to work, you need to make sure the files are loaded in a certain order that *respects the existing dependencies between the files*. In other words: if file A needs file B, you need to load file B before file A.

In JavaScript, it's possible to modify HTML pages; so, in theory, you could add an additional script element to the HTML page, which would then start loading another JavaScript file. By using event handlers in a smart way, you could imagine writing JavaScript code that loads other JavaScript files in a predefined order. Instead of writing all this code yourself, you can also use code already written by others. This is another advantage of structuring code: it makes the code more useable for other applications.

For this book, I've chosen to use a dynamic script-loading tool called *LABjs* (http://labjs.com/). This is a very simple script that lets you load other JavaScript files dynamically and in a predefined order. Here is the code that loads all your JavaScript files in the right order using LABjs:

```
<script src="../LAB.min.js"></script>
<script>
    $LAB.script('input/Keyboard.js').wait()
        .script('input/Mouse.js').wait()
        .script('Canvas2D.js').wait()
        .script('system/Keys.js').wait()
        .script('Painter.js').wait()
        .script('Cannon.js').wait(function () {
            Game.start('mycanvas');
        });
</script>
```

As you can see, using LABjs is straightforward. You simply call a sequence of `script` and `wait` methods. The final `wait` method call gets as a parameter a function to be executed. Inside this function, you start the game. By changing the order of the `script` method calls, you can change the order in which the scripts are loaded. When you're developing games or other bigger JavaScript applications, it's very useful to use such a script because it makes developing and maintaining code much easier. For a complete example that shows loading different JavaScript files, see Painter3. Another improvement here is that I pass the name of the canvas element as a parameter to the `start` method. This way, the JavaScript game code can work with any canvas name.

You probably don't want to use such a method for the final (release) version of the game, because the browser will have to load many JavaScript files. At that point, it's preferable to use another program that combines all the JavaScript files into a single big file, which leads to much faster loading. Furthermore, it's common practice to perform some optimization on the structure of the code such that the script file size is as small as possible. This process is called *minification*. Chapter 30 discusses this in more detail.

Loading Game Assets the Wrong Way

Previously, I talked about the browser loading files in an arbitrary order because these files have to be retrieved from a server. The same rules apply to loading game assets such as sprites and sounds. This is the method you've used up until now to load game assets:

```
var sprite = new Image();
sprite.src = "someImageFile.png";
var anotherSprite = new Image();
anotherSprite.src = "anotherImageFile.png";
    // and so on
```

It seems straightforward. For each sprite you want to load you create an Image object and assign a value to its src variable. Setting the src variable to a certain value doesn't mean the image is immediately loaded. It simply tells the browser to start retrieving that image from the server. Depending on the speed of the Internet connection, this may take a while. If you try drawing the image too soon, the browser will stop the script because of an access error (trying to draw an image that is not yet loaded). In order to avoid this issue, this is how the sprites were loaded in the previous example:

```
sprites.background = new Image();
sprites.background.src = spriteFolder + "spr_background.jpg";
sprites.cannon_barrel = new Image();
sprites.cannon_barrel.src = spriteFolder + "spr_cannon_barrel.png";
sprites.cannon_red = new Image();
sprites.cannon_red.src = spriteFolder + "spr_cannon_red.png";
sprites.cannon_green = new Image();
sprites.cannon_green.src = spriteFolder + "spr_cannon_green.png";
sprites.cannon_blue = new Image();
sprites.cannon_blue.src = spriteFolder + "spr_cannon_blue.png";
cannon.initialize();
window.setTimeout(Game.mainLoop, 500);
```

Note the last line of code, in bold. After setting the src variables of all the Image objects, you tell the browser to wait 500 milliseconds before executing the main loop. That way, the browser should have enough time to load the sprites. But what if the Internet connection is too slow? Then 500 milliseconds might not be enough. Or what if the Internet connection is really fast? Then you're letting the player wait needlessly. In order to solve this issue, you need the program to wait until all the images have been loaded before executing the main loop. You will see how to do this properly with event-handler functions. But before that, let's talk a little bit more about methods and functions.

Methods and Functions

You've already seen and used quite a few different kinds of methods and functions. For example, there is a clear difference between the Canvas2D.drawImage method and the cannon.update method: the latter one doesn't have any parameters, whereas the first one does (the sprite, its position, its rotation, and its origin). Additionally, some functions/methods can have a *result value of an object* that can be used in the instruction that does the method call—for example, by storing the result in a variable:

```
var n = Math.random();
```

Here, you call the random function that is defined as a part of the Math object, and you store its result in the variable n. Apparently, random provides a result value that can be stored. The Canvas2D.drawImage method on the other hand doesn't provide a result that you can store in a variable. Of course, the method does have an effect of some sort, because it draws a sprite on the screen, which could also be considered a result of the method call. However, when I talk about the *result* of a method, I don't mean the method has some effect on an object. I mean the *method call* returns a value that can be stored in a variable. This is also called the *return value* of a method or function. In mathematics, it's common that a function has a result. A mathematical function $f(x) = x^2$ takes as parameter an x value and it returns its square as a result. You could write this mathematical function in JavaScript if you wanted to:

```
var square = function(x) {
    return x*x;
}
```

If you look at the header of this method, you see that it takes one parameter called x. Because the function returns a value, you can store that value in a variable:

```
var sx = square(10);
```

After this instruction is executed, the variable sx will contain the value 100. In the function body, you can indicate using the keyword return what the actual value is that the function returns. In the case of square, the function returns the outcome of the expression x*x. Note that executing the return instruction also terminates execution of the rest of the instructions in a function. Any instructions placed *after* the return instruction are not executed. For example, consider the following function:

```
var someFunction = function() {
    return 12;
    var tmp = 45;
}
```

In this example, the second instruction (var tmp = 45;) will never be executed because the instruction before it ends the function. This is a very handy feature of the return instruction, and you can use it to your advantage:

```
var squareRoot = function(x) {
    if (x < 0)
        return 0;
    // Calculate the square root, we are now sure that x >=0.
}
```

In this example, you use the return instruction as a safeguard against wrong input by the user of the method. You can't calculate the square root of a negative number, so you handle the case where x is negative before you do any calculations or raise any annoying, potentially hard-to-debug errors.

An example of a method that doesn't have a return value is cannon.handleInput. Because this method doesn't have a return value, you don't need to use the return keyword in the body of the method, although doing so can sometimes still be useful. For example, suppose you only want to change the color of the cannon if the mouse is in the left part of the screen. You can achieve that as follows:

```
cannon.handleInput = function () {
    if (Mouse.position.x > 10)
        return;
    if (Keyboard.keyDown === Keys.R)
        cannon.currentColor = sprites.cannon_red;
    else if (Keyboard.keyDown === Keys.G)
        // etc.
};
```

In this method, you first check if the mouse x-position is greater than 10. If that is the case, you execute the `return` instruction. Any instructions after that will then no longer be executed.

Notice that whenever a method with no return value is called, it has no result that can be stored in a variable. For example:

```
var what = cannon.handleInput();
```

Because `cannon.handleInput` doesn't have a return value, the variable `what` will have the value `undefined` after this instruction is executed.

If a method or function has a return value, this value doesn't necessarily have to be stored in a variable. You can also directly use it in an `if` instruction, as you do in the `cannon.handleInput` method:

```
if (Math.random() > 0.5)
    // do something
```

Here, the `Math.random` method returns a number and if that number is greater than 0.5, the body of the `if` instruction is executed. The difference between things that have a value and things that don't have a value is something you've seen before: it's the same difference you saw between *instructions* (which don't have a value) and *expressions* (which do have a value). So, this means `Math.random()` is an *expression*, whereas `cannon.handleInput();` is an *instruction*. A second difference between these two things is that expressions never end with a semicolon, and instructions always end with a semicolon, unless the instruction is a block.

DECLARATIONS VS. PARAMETERS

Declarations of variables have a lot in common with parameters that are written in the method header. In fact, those parameters also are declarations, but there are a few differences:

- Variables are declared in the body of the method; parameters are declared between the parentheses in the method header.
- Variables get a value by using an assignment instruction; parameters automatically get a value when the method is called.
- Variable declarations start with the word `var`; parameter declarations don't.
- Variable declarations end with a semicolon; parameter declarations don't.

Loading Game Assets the Right Way

In order to make sprite loading a little bit easier, let's add a method `loadSprite` to the Game object:

```
Game.loadSprite = function(imageName) {
    var image = new Image();
    image.src = imageName;
    return image;
}
```

The code for loading the different sprites now becomes much shorter:

```
var sprFolder = "../../assets/Painter/sprites/";
sprites.background = Game.loadSprite(sprFolder + "spr_background.jpg");
sprites.cannon_barrel = Game.loadSprite(sprFolder + "spr_cannon_barrel.png");
sprites.cannon_red = Game.loadSprite(sprFolder + "spr_cannon_red.png");
sprites.cannon_green = Game.loadSprite(sprFolder + "spr_cannon_green.png");
sprites.cannon_blue = Game.loadSprite(sprFolder + "spr_cannon_blue.png");
```

However, the problem of dealing with the time it takes to load sprites is not solved yet. In order to tackle this problem, the first thing you need to do is keep track of how many sprites you're loading. You do this by adding a variable to the Game object, called `spritesStillLoading`:

```
var Game = {
    spritesStillLoading : 0
};
```

Initially, this variable is set to the value 0. Every time you load a sprite, you increment the variable by 1. Logically, you do this in the `loadSprite` method:

```
Game.loadSprite = function(imageName) {
    var image = new Image();
    image.src = imageName;
    Game.spritesStillLoading += 1;
    return image;
}
```

So now, every time you load a sprite, the `spritesStillLoading` variable is incremented. Next you want to *decrement* this variable every time a sprite has finished loading. This can be done by using an event-handler function. You assign this function to the variable `onload` in the `image` object. In the body of that function, you decrement the variable. Here is the version of the `loadSprite` method that adds the event handler:

```
Game.loadSprite = function (imageName) {
    var image = new Image();
    image.src = imageName;
    Game.spritesStillLoading += 1;
    image.onload = function () {
        Game.spritesStillLoading -= 1;
    };
    return image;
};
```

Now the spritesStillLoading variable accurately represents how many sprites still have to be loaded. You can use this information to wait on starting the main loop until this variable contains the value 0. In order to do this, you create two loop methods: an asset-loading loop and a main game loop. In the asset-loading loop, you simply check if there are still sprites that have to be loaded. If that is the case, you call the asset-loading loop again. If all the sprites have been loaded, you call the main loop method. Here is the asset-loading loop method:

```
Game.assetLoadingLoop = function () {
    if (Game.spritesStillLoading > 0)
        window.setTimeout(Game.assetLoadingLoop, 1000 / 60);
    else {
        Game.initialize();
        Game.mainLoop();
    }
};
```

You use the if instruction to check whether the number of sprites still loading is larger than 0. If this is the case, you call the assetLoadingLoop method again after a short delay. Once all the sprites are loaded, the else part of the if instruction is executed. In this part, you call the initialize method in the Game object, and then the mainLoop method. In the initialize method, all the game objects are initialized (in this case, only the cannon object). It's useful to do this initialization step after all the sprites have been loaded, because the sprite data might be useful when initializing objects. For example, if you want to calculate the position of an overlay such that it's drawn in the center of the screen, you need to know the width and height of the sprite. This information is only available when the sprite has finished loading. For a complete overview, see the Painter3 example, which illustrates the new sprite-loading code.

Writing a More Efficient Game Loop

Until now, you've used the window.setTimeout method to create a running game loop. Although this code is fine, unfortunately it isn't very efficient. Most browsers provide a more efficient way to do this that is specifically targeted toward interactive drawing applications such as games. The problem is that not all browsers and versions use the same method name. The newer versions of the most commonly used browsers all use the window.requestAnimationFrame method. However, older versions of Firefox use window.mozRequestAnimationFrame, and older versions of Safari and Chrome use window.webkitRequestAnimationFrame. You want to deal with browser-specific code as little as possible, so let's come up with a way to use the faster method to run the game loop without having to know about the different methods that different browser makes and versions use. Because most browsers already use the window.requestAnimationFrame method, you can extend the definition of that method as follows:

```
window.requestAnimationFrame = window.requestAnimationFrame ||
    window.webkitRequestAnimationFrame || window.mozRequestAnimationFrame ||
    window.oRequestAnimationFrame || window.msRequestAnimationFrame ||
    function (callback) {
        window.setTimeout(callback, 1000 / 60);
    };
```

You use the || operator here to determine which method the `window.requestAnimationFrame` name refers to. If the first option isn't defined (for example, if you're dealing with an older browser), you check any of the older names. If none of the optimized game-loop methods are available, you let `requestAnimationFrame` point to a function that calls the `window.setTimeout` method. In JavaScript, the `window` variable is a container of the global namespace. This means that you can call the `requestAnimationFrame` method with or without the `window` variable in front of it. The call:

```
window.requestAnimationFrame(callbackFunction);
```

is equivalent to

```
requestAnimationFrame(callbackFunction);
```

The Painter3 example uses the optimized game-loop method to run the asset-loading loop as well as the game loop, as follows:

```
Game.assetLoadingLoop = function () {
    if (Game.spritesStillLoading > 0)
        window.requestAnimationFrame(Game.assetLoadingLoop);
    else {
        Game.initialize();
        Game.mainLoop();
    }
};
```

And similarly, here is the `mainLoop` method in the `Game` object:

```
Game.mainLoop = function () {
    Game.handleInput();
    Game.update();
    Game.draw();
    Mouse.reset();
    window.requestAnimationFrame(Game.mainLoop);
};
```

Browsers handling things differently is a major challenge for JavaScript developers, even though a lot of progress has been made toward standardization of how browsers execute JavaScript code. When you develop JavaScript games, you'll probably encounter these differences in browsers at some point. Therefore, always test your game on the most common browsers before releasing it!

Separating Generic Code from Game-Specific Code

Previously, you haven't made any distinction between code that can be used for many different games and code that is specific to a single game. Some parts of the code that you've written, such as the `Game.mainLoop` method, would probably be useful for other JavaScript games as well. The same goes for all the code you've written to load sprites. Now that you've seen a way to split code over different script files, you can use that to your advantage. By splitting generic code from code that is specific to Painter, it will be easier to reuse that generic code later. If you would like to reuse the sprite-loading code, you simply have to include the source file containing the code into your new game application, instead of sorting through the Painter game code to find what you need. Another reason to do this is to enable you to more quickly create similar games later. You might find yourself developing a game that is similar to a game you developed earlier. By organizing code in this way, you can produce your new game more rapidly while also not reinventing the wheel.

The Painter4 example creates a separate Game.js file that contains the Game object and a number of useful methods belonging to that object. The parts that are specific to Painter have been moved to the Painter.js file. In that file, you have a method for loading sprites as well as a method for initializing the game. Furthermore, a new file called PainterGameWorld.js handles the various objects in the game. In the previous versions of Painter, this game world consisted only of a background image and a cannon. In the next section, you add a *ball* to this game world. The Painter game world is then defined by an object that makes sure all the game objects are updated and drawn. This is part of the definition of the painterGameWorld object:

```
var painterGameWorld = {
};

painterGameWorld.handleInput = function (delta) {
    ball.handleInput(delta);
    cannon.handleInput(delta);
};

painterGameWorld.update = function (delta) {
    ball.update(delta);
    cannon.update(delta);
};

painterGameWorld.draw = function () {
    Canvas2D.drawImage(sprites.background, { x : 0, y : 0 }, 0,
        { x : 0, y : 0 });
    ball.draw();
    cannon.draw();
};
```

When you initialize the game, you initialize the game objects, and you tell the Game object that the object governing the game world is painterGameWorld, as follows:

```
Game.initialize = function () {
    cannon.initialize();
    ball.initialize();
    Game.gameWorld = painterGameWorld;
};
```

Inside the Game.mainLoop method, you now only have to make sure to call the right methods on the gameWorld variable (which refers to painterGameWorld):

```
Game.mainLoop = function () {
    Game.gameWorld.handleInput();
    Game.gameWorld.update();
    Canvas2D.clear();
```

```
        Game.gameWorld.draw();
        Mouse.reset();
        requestAnimationFrame(Game.mainLoop);
};
```

As a result, you have nicely separated the generic game code (in Game.js) and the game-specific code, which consists of loading the sprites and initializing the game (Painter.js) and updating and drawing the Painter game objects (PainterGameWorld.js). Any other game objects specific to Painter are each defined in their own script file (such as Cannon.js).

Adding a Ball to the Game World

In the previous sections, you saw how to make your JavaScript game applications more flexible and efficient by being able to load separate JavaScript files, by separating generic game code from Painter-specific code, by loading assets properly, and by creating a more efficient game loop. In this section, you extend the Painter game by adding a ball that is shot by the cannon object. For that, you add a ball object.

You set up the ball object in a fashion very similar to the cannon object. In the Painter4 example, you see a version of the Painter game that adds a ball to the game world (see Figure 7-1). The ball can be shot from the cannon by clicking anywhere in the game screen. Furthermore, the ball changes color together with the cannon. You can find the code that describes the ball object in the Ball.js file. Just like the cannon object, ball consists of a number of variables, such as a position, the current color of the ball, and the origin of the ball sprite. Because the ball moves, you also need to store its *velocity*. This velocity is a vector that defines how the position of the ball changes over time. For example, if the ball has a velocity of (0,1), then every second, the y-position of the ball increases by 1 pixel (meaning the ball falls down). Finally, the ball can be in two states: it's either flying through the air because it was shot from the cannon, or it's waiting to be shot (so it isn't moving). For that, you add to the ball object an extra Boolean variable called shooting. This is the complete definition of the structure of the ball object:

```
var ball = {
};

ball.initialize = function() {
    ball.position = { x : 65, y : 390 };
    ball.velocity =  { x : 0, y : 0 };
    ball.origin = { x : 0, y : 0 };
    ball.currentColor = sprites.ball_red;
    ball.shooting = false;
};
```

Figure 7-1. A screenshot of the Painter4 example that contains a cannon barrel and a flying ball

In the games you develop in this book, most of the objects have a position and a velocity. Because the book is only concerned with 2D games, both the position and the velocity are always variables that consists of an x and a y variable. When you update these game objects, you need to calculate the new position based on the velocity vector and the time that has passed. Later in this chapter, you see how to do that.

In order to be able to use the ball object, you need a few more sprites. In the Game.loadAssets method, you load the red, green, and blue ball sprites. Depending on the color of the cannon, you change the color of the ball later. This is the extended loadAssets method:

```
Game.loadAssets = function () {
    var loadSprite = function (sprite) {
        return Game.loadSprite("../../assets/Painter/sprites/" + sprite);
    };

    sprites.background = loadSprite("spr_background.jpg");
    sprites.cannon_barrel = loadSprite("spr_cannon_barrel.png");
    sprites.cannon_red = loadSprite("spr_cannon_red.png");
    sprites.cannon_green = loadSprite("spr_cannon_green.png");
    sprites.cannon_blue = loadSprite("spr_cannon_blue.png");
    sprites.ball_red = loadSprite("spr_ball_red.png");
    sprites.ball_green = loadSprite("spr_ball_green.png");
    sprites.ball_blue = loadSprite("spr_ball_blue.png");
};
```

Here you can see a nice way of making the sprite-loading calls more readable in JavaScript. You declare a local variable loadSprite that refers to a function. This function takes as a parameter a sprite image name and calls the Game.loadSprite method. As a parameter to that method, you pass along the folder path of the sprite plus the name of the sprite. Finally, the function returns the result of the Game.loadSprite method.

Creating the Ball

Let's get back to the ball object. In the initialize method of that object, you have to assign values to the member variables, just as in the case of the cannon object. When the game starts, the ball should not be moving. Therefore, you set the velocity of the ball to zero. Also, you initially set the ball to the zero position. That way, it's hidden behind the cannon, so when the ball isn't moving, you don't see it. You initially set the color of the ball to red, and you set the shooting member variable to false. Here is the complete method:

```
ball.initialize = function() {
    ball.position = { x : 0, y : 0 };
    ball.velocity =  { x : 0, y : 0 };
    ball.origin = { x : 0, y : 0 };
    ball.currentColor = sprites.ball_red;
    ball.shooting = false;
};
```

Next to the initialize method, you also add a reset method that resets the ball position and its shooting status:

```
ball.reset = function () {
    ball.position = { x : 0, y : 0 };
    ball.shooting = false;
};
```

When the ball flies outside of the screen after it has been shot from the cannon, you can reset it by calling this method. Furthermore, you add a draw method to the ball object. If the ball isn't shooting, you don't want the player to see it. So, you draw the ball sprite only if the ball is currently shooting:

```
ball.draw = function () {
    if (!ball.shooting)
        return;
    Canvas2D.drawImage(ball.currentColor, ball.position, ball.rotation,
        ball.origin);
};
```

You can see in the body of this method that you use the `return` keyword to draw the ball only if it isn't shooting. Inside the `painterGameWorld` object, you have to call the game-loop methods on the ball. For example, this is the `draw` method in `painterGameWorld`, from which the `ball.draw` method is called:

```
painterGameWorld.draw = function () {
    Canvas2D.drawImage(sprites.background, { x : 0, y : 0 }, 0,
        { x : 0, y : 0 });
    ball.draw();
    cannon.draw();
};
```

Note the order in which the game objects are drawn: first the background image, then the ball, and then the cannon.

Shooting the Ball

The player can click the left mouse button in the game screen to shoot a ball of paint. The speed of the ball and the direction in which it's moving are determined by the position where the player clicks. The ball should move in the direction of that position; and the further from the cannon a player clicks, the higher the speed of the ball. This is an intuitive way for the user to control the speed of the ball. Whenever you design a game, think carefully about how instructions from the user are received and what the most natural or efficient way is to process them.

In order to handle input, you add a `handleInput` method to the `ball` object. Inside this method, you can check whether the player clicks with the left button by using the `Mouse` object:

```
if (Mouse.leftPressed)
    // do something...
```

However, because there can be only a single ball in the air at any moment, you want to do something only if the ball isn't already in the air. This means you have to check the ball's shooting status. If the ball has already been shot, you don't have to handle the mouse click. So, you extend your `if` instruction with an extra condition that the ball currently isn't in the air:

```
if (Mouse.leftPressed && !ball.shooting)
    // do something...
```

As you can see, you're using two logical operators (`&&` and `!`) in conjunction. Because of the logical *not* (`!`) operator, the entire condition in the `if` instruction will evaluate to `true` only if the `shooting` variable has the value `false`: in other words, the ball is not currently shooting.

Inside the `if` instruction, you need to do a couple of things. You know the player has clicked somewhere and that the ball has to be shot from the cannon. The first thing you need to do is set the variable `shooting` to the correct value, because the status of the ball needs to be changed to "currently shooting":

```
ball.shooting = true;
```

Because the ball is now moving, you need to give it a *velocity*. This velocity is a vector in the direction of the place where the player clicked. You can calculate this direction by subtracting the ball position from the mouse position. Because the velocity has an x component and a y component, you need to do this for both dimensions:

```
ball.velocity.x = (Mouse.position.x - ball.position.x);
ball.velocity.y = (Mouse.position.y - ball.position.y);
```

Calculating the velocity in this way also gives the desired effect that when the user clicks further from the cannon, the velocity is greater, because then the difference between the mouse position and the ball position is also greater. However, if you were to play the game now, the ball would move a bit slowly. Therefore, you multiply this velocity with a constant value that gives the ball a velocity that is usable in the context of this game:

```
ball.velocity.x = (Mouse.position.x - ball.position.x) * 1.2;
ball.velocity.y = (Mouse.position.y - ball.position.y) * 1.2;
```

I chose the constant value of 1.2 after testing the gameplay with different values. Each game will have a number of these *gameplay parameters* that you'll need to tweak while play-testing the game to determine their optimal value. Finding the right values for these parameters is crucial for a balanced game that plays well, and you need to make sure the values you choose don't make the game overly easy or difficult. For example, if you chose a constant value of 0.3 instead of 1.2, the ball would move much more slowly. This would make the game much more difficult, and it might even make the game unplayable because the ball might never be able to reach the furthest can.

If you add the handleInput method to ball, it isn't automatically called. You need to do that explicitly in the painterGameWorld object. Therefore, you add an extra instruction to the handleInput method of that object:

```
painterGameWorld.handleInput = function () {
    ball.handleInput();
    cannon.handleInput();
};
```

Updating the Ball

A big advantage of grouping related variables and methods together in objects is that you can keep each object relatively small and clear. You can design objects that more or less reflect the various kinds of game objects in the game. In this case, you have an object for the cannon as well as for the ball. The goal is that each of these game objects deals with player input relevant for that object. You also want the game objects to update and draw themselves. That is the reason you added an update method and a draw method to ball, so you can call these methods in the game loop methods of painterGameWorld.

Inside ball.update, you need to define the ball's behavior. This behavior is different depending on whether the ball is currently shooting. This is the complete method:

```
ball.update = function (delta) {
    if (ball.shooting) {
        ball.velocity.x = ball.velocity.x * 0.99;
        ball.velocity.y = ball.velocity.y + 6;
        ball.position.x = ball.position.x + ball.velocity.x * delta;
        ball.position.y = ball.position.y + ball.velocity.y * delta;
    }
    else {
        if (cannon.currentColor === sprites.cannon_red)
            ball.currentColor = sprites.ball_red;
        else if (cannon.currentColor === sprites.cannon_green)
            ball.currentColor = sprites.ball_green;
        else
            ball.currentColor = sprites.ball_blue;
        ball.position = cannon.ballPosition();
        ball.position.x = ball.position.x - ball.currentColor.width / 2;
        ball.position.y = ball.position.y - ball.currentColor.height / 2;
    }
    if (painterGameWorld.isOutsideWorld(ball.position))
        ball.reset();
};
```

As you can see in the header of this method, it has one parameter called delta. This parameter is necessary because in order to calculate what the new position of the ball should be, you need to know how much time has passed since the previous call to update. This parameter might also be useful in the handleInput method of some game objects—for example, if you want to know the speed at which the player is moving the mouse, then you need to know how much time has passed. The Painter4 example extends every object that has game-loop methods (handleInput, update, draw) such that the time passed since the last update is passed along as a parameter.

But where do you calculate the value of delta? And how do you calculate it? In the example, you do this in the Game.mainLoop method:

```
Game.mainLoop = function () {
    var delta = 1 / 60;
    Game.gameWorld.handleInput(delta);
    Game.gameWorld.update(delta);
    Canvas2D.clear();
    Game.gameWorld.draw();
    Mouse.reset();
    requestAnimationFrame(Game.mainLoop);
};
```

Because you want the game loop to be executed 60 times per second, you calculate the delta value as follows:

```
var delta = 1 / 60;
```

This way of calculating the past time in a game loop is called a *fixed timestep*. If you have a very slow computer that is not able to execute the game loop 60 times per second, you still tell your game objects that only 1/60 of a second has passed since the last time, even though that may not be true. As a result, *game time* is different from *real time*. Another way to do it would be to calculate the *actual passed time* by accessing the system time. Here is how you do that:

```
var d = new Date();
var n = d.getTime();
```

The variable n now contains the number of milliseconds since January 1, 1970 (!). Every time you run the game loop, you could store this time and subtract the time you stored the previous time you went through the game loop. That would give you the real time that has passed. There is no fixed timestep in this case, because the passed time depends on the speed of the computer/device that is used, the priority of processes in the OS, whether the player is doing other tasks at the same time, and so on. Therefore, this approach to dealing with time in games is called *variable timestep*.

Variable timestep is especially useful in games where high frame rates are desirable: for example, in first-person shooters where camera motions can be quite fast because the camera is controlled directly by the player. In those cases, a variable timestep in combination with trying to call the game-loop methods as often as possible can result in smoother motions and a more pleasurable gaming experience. The disadvantage of variable timestep is that the time continues even if the player is temporarily doing something different (like opening a menu in the game or saving the game). Generally, players won't be very happy if they discover that while they were browsing their inventory, their character was killed in the game world. So, as a game developer, you need to fix such issues when using variable timestep.

Another example of when using variable timestep may interfere with the playability of the game is if the player switches to another application (or tab in a browser) temporarily. This happens quite often, especially when you're developing games that run in a browser. This is also one of the main reasons you use a fixed timestep in this book. When the player switches to another tab, the JavaScript code execution in the inactive tab is automatically paused until the player returns. When using a fixed timestep, the game simply continues where it was paused when the player reactivates the tab, because the game objects don't care about the real time that has passed, only about the fixed delta value.

Let's go back to the ball.update method. If you look at the body of the method, you can see that the first part consists of an if instruction. The condition of the if is that the ball.shooting variable should have the value true. So, if the ball is currently moving, the body of the if instruction is executed. This body again consists of four instructions. The first two instructions update the velocity, and the last two update the position. The first instruction updates the x direction of the velocity. You multiply the velocity with a value of 0.99, the effect of which is that the velocity slowly decreases. This is done to simulate air friction. The second instruction increases the y velocity in each update. This is done to simulate the effect that *gravity* has on the ball. Together, the velocity changes in the x and y directions result in plausible ball behavior. Of course, in the real world, the gravity is not 6. But then again, your real world doesn't consist of pixels, either. Physics in game worlds doesn't always accurately represent physics in the real world. When you want to incorporate some form of physics in your game (be it very simple or extremely complex), the most important part isn't that the physics is realistic, but that the *game is playable*. This is why in a strategy game, an airplane will move as fast as a soldier walking on the ground. If the game used realistic speeds for those two objects, it would result in an unplayable game.

The current position of the ball is updated by adding the velocity to its x and y components. Here are the instructions that do this:

```
ball.position.x = ball.position.x + ball.velocity.x * delta;
ball.position.y = ball.position.y + ball.velocity.y * delta;
```

As you can see, this is where the delta variable is used. You calculate the new position of the ball based on the velocity and the time that has passed since the last update. You multiply each velocity dimension with the value in the delta variable, and you add the result to the current position of the ball. That way, if you ever decide to use a higher or lower frame rate, the speed at which game objects move will not change.

> **Note** In the old days, computers were so slow that the concept of a fixed timestep didn't exist. Game developers assumed that everyone would be playing their game on an equally slow machine, so they called the game-loop methods as often as possible and simply updated the position of an object with a constant velocity factor. As a result, when computers became faster, these games became more and more difficult to play! Players don't like this. Therefore, always take the elapsed time into account when calculating things like velocities and positions.

If the ball isn't currently shooting, you're allowed to change its color. In this case, you do that by retrieving the current color of the cannon and changing the color of the ball accordingly. That way, you're sure the color of the ball always matches the color of the cannon. You need an if instruction to handle the different cases, as follows:

```
if (cannon.currentColor === sprites.cannon_red)
    ball.currentColor = sprites.ball_red;
else if (cannon.currentColor === sprites.cannon_green)
    ball.currentColor = sprites.ball_green;
else
    ball.currentColor = sprites.ball_blue;
```

You also update the position of the ball:

```
ball.position = cannon.ballPosition();
ball.position.x = ball.position.x - ball.currentColor.width / 2;
ball.position.y = ball.position.y - ball.currentColor.height / 2;
```

Why do you change the position? When the ball isn't in the air, the player can modify its shooting position by rotating the barrel of the cannon. Therefore, you need to calculate the correct ball position here, to ensure that it matches the current orientation of the cannon barrel. In order to do this, you add a new method called ballPosition to cannon, in which you calculate the position of the ball based on the barrel orientation. Using the sine and cosine functions, you calculate the new position as follows:

```
cannon.ballPosition = function() {
    var opp = Math.sin(cannon.rotation) * sprites.cannon_barrel.width * 0.6;
    var adj = Math.cos(cannon.rotation) * sprites.cannon_barrel.width * 0.6;
    return { x : cannon.position.x + adj, y : cannon.position.y + opp };
};
```

As you can see, you multiply the opposite and adjacent sides with a value of 0.6 so the ball is drawn a bit more than halfway up the rotated barrel. The method returns a new composite object that has x and y variables containing the desired x and y positions of the ball.

After you've retrieved the desired ball position, you subtract half of the width and height of the ball sprite from it. That way, the ball is drawn nicely in the middle of the cannon barrel.

The second part of the `ball.update` method also is an `if` instruction:

```
if (painterGameWorld.isOutsideWorld(ball.position))
    ball.reset();
```

This part of the method deals with the event that occurs when the ball goes outside the game world. In order to calculate if this is true, you add a method called `isOutsideWorld` to `painterGameWorld`. The goal of this method is to check whether a given position is outside the game world. You define the boundaries of the game world using a few simple rules. Remember that the top left of the screen is the origin. An object is outside the game world if its x-position is smaller than zero or larger than the width of the screen. An object is also outside the game world if its y-position is larger than the height of the screen. Note that I don't say an object is outside the game world if its y-position is smaller than zero. Why not? I chose to do this so it's possible for a player to shoot a ball in the air and let the ball be momentarily above the screen before falling down again. Often you see a similar effect in platform games, where a character can jump up and disappear partly outside the screen as opposed to falling through the bottom of the screen (which generally means instant death of the character).

If you look at the header of this method, you see that it expects one parameter, a position:

```
painterGameWorld.isOutsideWorld = function (position)
```

If you want to check whether a position is outside the screen, you need to know the width and height of the screen. In an HTML5 game such as Painter, this corresponds to the size of the *canvas*. Painter4 adds a variable called `size` to Game. When the `Game.start` method is called, the desired size of the screen is passed along as a parameter. Here is the extended `Game.start` method:

```
Game.start = function (canvasName, x, y) {
    Canvas2D.initialize(canvasName);
    Game.size = { x : x, y : y };
    Keyboard.initialize();
    Mouse.initialize();
    Game.loadAssets();
    Game.assetLoadingLoop();
};
```

In the isOutsideWorld method, you use the Game.size variable to determine whether a position is outside the game world. The body of the method consists of a single instruction using the keyword return to calculate a Boolean value. The logical *or* operation is used to cover the different cases in which the position is outside the game world:

```
return position.x < 0 || position.x > Game.size.x || position.y > Game.size.y;
```

As you can see, you don't mind if the y coordinate is smaller than zero. This allows you to have the ball end up above the screen and fall back in again.

Let's return to the ball.update method. The second if instruction calls the isOutsideWorld method in its condition; and if this method returns the value true, then the ball.reset method is executed. Or, in simpler terms: if the ball flies out of the screen, it's placed at the cannon, ready to be shot again by the player. Here you see another advantage of grouping instructions in methods: methods such as isOutsideWorld can be *reused* in different parts of the program, which saves development time and results in shorter, more readable programs. For example, isOutsideWorld will probably also be useful for the paint cans later in the game, to test whether they have fallen out of the screen.

Finally, you make sure to call the ball.update method in the painterGameWorld.update method:

```
painterGameWorld.update = function (delta) {
    ball.update(delta);
    cannon.update(delta);
};
```

When you run the Painter4 example, you can see that it's now possible to aim the cannon, choose a color, and shoot a ball. In the next chapter, you add paint cans to this game. But in order to do that, I have to introduce a new JavaScript programming concept: *prototypes*.

What You Have Learned

In this chapter, you have learned:

- How to separate code over different source files
- How to make the game loop more efficient
- The different kinds of methods/functions (with/without parameters, and with/without a return value)
- The difference between fixed and variable timestep
- How to add a flying ball to the game world

Game Object Types

In the previous chapters, you've seen how to create a game world that contains a few different game objects, such as a cannon and a ball. You've seen how to let game objects interact with each other. For example, the ball object updates its color according to the color of the cannon. In this chapter, you add falling paint cans to the game world. However, before you can do that, you have to reexamine how to create and manage objects in JavaScript. I introduce the class concept as a means to create multiple game objects of a certain type. Then, you apply the class concept to other parts of the Painter game application. Furthermore, you learn how to incorporate randomness in your games.

Creating Multiple Objects of the Same Type

Until now, you only needed one instance of each game object in Painter. There is only one cannon and one ball. The same holds for all the other objects in the JavaScript code. There is a single Game object, a single Keyboard object, a single Mouse object, and so on. You create these objects by declaring a variable referring to an empty or a composite object and adding useful methods to it. For example, here is how you create the ball object:

```
var ball = {
};

ball.initialize = function() {
    ball.position = { x : 0, y : 0 };
    // etc.
};

ball.handleInput = function (delta) {
    if (Mouse.leftPressed && !ball.shooting) {
        // do something
    }
};

// etc.
```

Suppose you want to be able to shoot three balls at the same time in the Painter game. If you did this the way you created objects until now, you would create two variables, ball2 and ball3, and copy the code you used for the ball object twice. This isn't a very nice solution, for several reasons. For one, copying code means you have to deal with version-management problems. For example, what if you find a bug in the update method code? You have to make sure you copy the improved code to the other ball objects. If you forget one copy, the bug is still there when you thought you solved it. Another problem is that this approach simply doesn't scale up very well. What happens if you want to extend the game such that the player can shoot 20 balls at the same time? Do you copy the code 20 times? Also note that the bigger your JavaScript files become, the longer it takes for the browser to download and interpret them. So, if you don't want your players waiting too long for scripts to load, it's better to avoid copying code. Finally, duplicated code looks ugly, clutters up your source code files, and makes it hard to find other sections of the code that you need, leading to excessive scrolling and a general reduction of your coding efficiency.

Fortunately, there is a very nice solution to this problem. It's a JavaScript programming construct called *prototypes*. Prototypes allow you to define a sort of blueprint for an object, including the variables and methods it contains. Once this prototype is defined, you can create objects using that prototype with a single line of code! You have already used something like this. Look at this line of code:

```
var image = new Image();
```

Here, you create an image object that uses the Image prototype to construct itself.

Defining a prototype is easy. Have a look at this example:

```
function Dog() {
}
Dog.prototype.bark = function () {
    console.log("woof!");
};
```

This creates a function called Dog. When this function is called in combination with the new keyword, an object is created. Each function in JavaScript has a *prototype* that contains information about what objects should look like that are created by calling the function together with the new keyword. This example defines a method called bark that is part of the prototype of Dog. The prototype word isn't just there for aesthetics. With it, you indicate that you're adding things to the prototype of Dog. Whenever you create a Dog object, only the things that are part of its prototype are part of the object. Here is how you create a new Dog object:

```
var lucy = new Dog();
```

Because lucy is created according to the prototype in the Dog function, the lucy object contains a method called bark:

```
lucy.bark(); // outputs "woof!" to the console
```

The nice thing is that you can now create lots of dogs that can bark, but you only have to define the bark method once:

```
var max = new Dog();
var zoe = new Dog();
var buster = new Dog();
max.bark();
zoe.bark();
buster.bark();
```

Of course, the goal of this book is not to show you how to become a dog breeder, but how to create games. And for games, the prototype concept is very powerful. It allows you to *separate the actual objects that are used in your game from how they should be constructed*.

As an exercise, let's apply the prototype principle to creating a ball object. In order to do this, you need to define a function. Let's call this function Ball, and let's add the initialize method to the prototype:

```
function Ball() {
}
Ball.prototype.initialize = function() {
    // ball object initialization here
};
```

In the initialize method, you have to define variables that are part of each ball object you create. The problem is, you didn't make an object yet—you only have a function and a prototype that contains an initialize method. So in the body of the initialize method, how do you refer to the object this method belongs to? In JavaScript, the this keyword is used for that purpose. In a method, this always refers to the object the method belongs to. Using that keyword, you can fill in the body of the initialize method:

```
Ball.prototype.initialize = function() {
    this.position = { x : 0, y : 0 };
    this.velocity =  { x : 0, y : 0 };
    this.origin = { x : 0, y : 0 };
    this.currentColor = sprites.ball_red;
    this.shooting = false;
};
```

You can now create as many balls as you want and initialize them:

```
var ball = new Ball();
var anotherBall = new Ball();
ball.initialize();
anotherBall.initialize();
```

Each time you create a new ball, any methods in the prototype are added to the object. When the initialize method is called on the ball object, this refers to ball. When it's called on anotherBall, this refers to anotherBall.

You can actually shorten the code you've written a little. Why add an `initialize` method when `Ball` itself already is a function that is called? You can simply perform the initialization in that function, as follows:

```
function Ball() {
    this.position = { x : 0, y : 0 };
    this.velocity =  { x : 0, y : 0 };
    this.origin = { x : 0, y : 0 };
    this.currentColor = sprites.ball_red;
    this.shooting = false;
}
```

Now when you create balls, they're initialized on creation:

```
var ball = new Ball();
var anotherBall = new Ball();
```

And since `Ball` is a function, you can even pass along parameters if you want to:

```
function Ball(pos) {
    this.position = pos;
    this.velocity =  { x : 0, y : 0 };
    this.origin = { x : 0, y : 0 };
    this.currentColor = sprites.ball_red;
    this.shooting = false;
}
var ball = new Ball({ x : 0, y : 0});
var anotherBall = new Ball({ x : 100, y : 100});
```

Because the `Ball` function is responsible for initializing (or *constructing*) the object, this function is also called the *constructor*. The constructor together with the methods defined in the prototype is called a *class*. When an object is created according to a class, you also say that the object has that class as a *type*. In the previous example, the `ball` object has as a type `Ball`, because it was created using the `Ball` constructor and its prototype. A class is a *blueprint* for an object, and as such it describes two things:

- The data that is contained within an object. In the case of balls, this data consists of a position, a velocity, an origin, the current color, and a variable indicating whether the ball is shooting. Generally, this data is initialized in the constructor.

- The methods that *manipulate* the data. In the `Ball` class, these methods are the game-loop methods (`handleInput`, `update`, `draw`, and `reset`).

You can very easily translate the game-loop methods as methods in the `Ball` prototype, simply by replacing `ball` with `this`. For example, here is the `handleInput` method:

```
Ball.prototype.handleInput = function (delta) {
    if (Mouse.leftPressed && !this.shooting) {
        this.shooting = true;
        this.velocity.x = (Mouse.position.x - this.position.x) * 1.2;
        this.velocity.y = (Mouse.position.y - this.position.y) * 1.2;
    }
};
```

Have a look at the Ball.js file in the Painter5 example belonging to this chapter. You can see the Ball class and all its methods. Note that I didn't add any functionality to the balls; I only applied the prototype principle to define the *blueprint for balls*.

The concept of classes and objects is extremely powerful. It forms the basis of the *object-oriented programming paradigm*. JavaScript is a very flexible language, in that it doesn't oblige you to use classes. You could write scripts using only functions if you wanted to (and this is what you've done until now). But because classes are such a powerful programming concept and are widely used in the (game) industry, this book exploits them as much as possible. By learning how to properly use classes, you can design much better software, in *any* programming language.

> **Note**   When programming games, you often have to make a trade-off between how long it takes to do something and how often you do it. In the case of Painter, if you're only ever going to create one or two balls, then it might not be worth going through the trouble of creating a class for the balls. However, it's often the case that things scale up slowly. Before you know it, you're copying and pasting dozens of lines of code because you didn't create an easier way to do it once. When you design your classes, consider the long-term gains of a proper design, even if that requires a short-term sacrifice such as having to do some extra programming work to make the class design more generic.

Constructing Game Objects as Part of the Game World

Now that you've seen how to create classes, you need to rethink where your game objects are constructed. Until now, game objects were declared as global variables, and as such, they were accessible everywhere. For example, this is how you create the cannon object:

```
var cannon = {
};
cannon.initialize = function() {
    cannon.position = { x : 72, y : 405 };
    cannon.colorPosition =  { x : 55, y : 388 };
    cannon.origin = { x : 34, y : 34 };
    cannon.currentColor = sprites.cannon_red;
    cannon.rotation = 0;
};
```

In the Painter5 example, this is the constructor of the Cannon class:

```
function Cannon() {
    this.position = { x : 72, y : 405 };
    this.colorPosition =  { x : 55, y : 388 };
    this.origin = { x : 34, y : 34 };
    this.currentColor = sprites.cannon_red;
    this.rotation = 0;
}
```

In the update method of the ball, you need to retrieve the current color of the cannon so you can update the ball's color. Here is how you did this in the previous chapter:

```
if (cannon.currentColor === sprites.cannon_red)
    ball.currentColor = sprites.ball_red;
else if (cannon.currentColor === sprites.cannon_green)
    ball.currentColor = sprites.ball_green;
else
    ball.currentColor = sprites.ball_blue;
```

When defining a class using the JavaScript prototype approach, you have to replace ball with this (because there is no named instance of an object). So the previous code is translated to

```
if (cannon.currentColor === sprites.cannon_red)
    this.currentColor = sprites.ball_red;
else if (cannon.currentColor === sprites.cannon_green)
    this.currentColor = sprites.ball_green;
else
    this.currentColor = sprites.ball_blue;
```

But how do you refer to the cannon object if cannons are also constructed using a class? This raises two questions:

- Where in the code are game objects constructed?
- How do you refer to these game objects if they aren't global variables?

Logically, game objects should be constructed when the game world is constructed. This is why the Painter5 example creates the game objects in the PainterGameWorld class (which before was the painterGameWorld object). Here is part of the constructor of that class:

```
function PainterGameWorld() {
    this.cannon = new Cannon();
    this.ball = new Ball();
    // create more game objects if needed
}
```

So, this answers the first question, but it raises another question. If game objects are created when the game world is created, where do you call the constructor of PainterGameWorld to create the game world? If you open the Game.js file, you see that there is yet another class defined using the prototype approach: Game_Singleton. This is its constructor:

```
function Game_Singleton() {
    this.size = undefined;
    this.spritesStillLoading = 0;
    this.gameWorld = undefined;
}
```

As you can see, this class is capable of constructing the Game object that was used in the previous chapter. The Game_Singleton class has an initialize method, where the game world object is created:

```
Game_Singleton.prototype.initialize = function () {
    this.gameWorld = new PainterGameWorld();
};
```

Okay, you've discovered where the game world is constructed. But where is the instance of the Game_Singleton object constructed? You need this instance in order to access the game world, which will in turn give you access to the game objects. If you look at the last line of the Game.js file, you see this instruction:

```
var Game = new Game_Singleton();
```

Finally an actual variable declaration! So through the variable Game, you can access the game world; and through that object, you can access the game objects that are part of the game world. For example, this is how you get to the cannon object:

```
Game.gameWorld.cannon
```

Why so complicated, you might ask? Why not simply declare each game object as a global variable like you did before? There are several reasons. First, by declaring many global variables in different places, your code becomes more difficult to reuse. Suppose you want to use parts of the code from Painter in another application that also uses balls and cannons. Now you have to sift through the code to find where global variables were declared and make sure they're useful for your application. It's much better to declare these variables in one place (such as the PainterGameWorld class) so these declarations are easier to find.

A second issue with using many global variables is that you're throwing away any structure or relationship that exists between variables. In the Painter game, it's clear that the cannon and the ball *are part of the game world*. Your code becomes easier to understand if you express that relationship explicitly by letting the game objects be part of the game-world object.

In general, it's a good idea to avoid global variables as much as possible. In the Painter game, the main global variable is Game. This variable consists of a tree structure containing the game world, which in turn contains the game objects, which in turn contain other variables (such as a position or a sprite).

Using the new structure where the Game object is a tree structure of other objects, you can now access the cannon object to retrieve the desired color of the ball, as follows:

```
if (Game.gameWorld.cannon.currentColor === sprites.cannon_red)
    this.currentColor = sprites.ball_red;
else if (Game.gameWorld.cannon.currentColor === sprites.cannon_green)
    this.currentColor = sprites.ball_green;
else
    this.currentColor = sprites.ball_blue;
```

Sometimes it can be useful to sketch the tree structure of game objects on paper, or create a diagram where you can put references with proper names later. As the games you develop become more complex, such a tree provides a useful overview of what object belongs where, and it saves you from having to re-create this tree mentally when working with the code.

Writing a Class with Multiple Instances

Now that you can construct multiple objects of the same type, let's add a few paint cans to the Painter game. These paint cans should be given a random color, and they should fall down from the top of the screen. Once they have fallen out of the bottom of the screen, you assign a new color to them and move them back to the top. For the player, it seems as though different paint cans are falling each time. Actually, you need only three paint-can objects that are reused. In the `PaintCan` class, you define what a paint can is and what its behavior is. Then, you can create multiple instances of this class. In the `PainterGameWorld` class, you store these instances in three different member variables, which are declared and initialized in the `PainterGameWorld` constructor:

```
function PainterGameWorld() {
    this.cannon = new Cannon();
    this.ball = new Ball();
    this.can1 = new PaintCan(450);
    this.can2 = new PaintCan(575);
    this.can3 = new PaintCan(700);
}
```

A difference between the `PaintCan` class and the `Ball` and `Cannon` classes is that paint cans have different positions. This is why you pass along a coordinate value as a parameter when the paint cans are constructed. This value indicates the desired x-position of the paint can. The y-position doesn't have to be provided, because it will be calculated based on the y-velocity of each paint can. In order to make things more interesting, you let the cans fall with different, random velocities. (How you do that is explained later in this chapter.) In order to calculate this velocity, you want to know the minimum velocity a paint can should have, so it doesn't fall too slowly. To do this, you add a member variable `minVelocity` that contains the value. As a result, this is the constructor of the `PaintCan` class:

```
function PaintCan(xPosition) {
    this.currentColor = sprites.can_red;
    this.velocity = new Vector2();
    this.position = new Vector2(xPosition, -200);
    this.origin = new Vector2();
    this.reset();
}
```

Just like the cannon and the ball, a paint can has a certain color. By default, you choose the red paint-can sprite. Initially, you set the y-position of the paint can such that it's drawn just outside the top of the screen, so that later in the game, you can see it fall. In the `PainterGameWorld` constructor, you call this constructor three times to create the three `PaintCan` objects, each with a different x-position.

Because the paint cans don't handle any input (only the ball and the cannon do this), you don't need a `handleInput` method for this class. However, the paint cans do need to be updated. One of the things you want to do is to have the paint cans fall at random moments and at random speeds. But how can you do this?

Dealing with Randomness in Games

One of the most important parts of the paint-can behavior is that some aspects of it should be *unpredictable*. You don't want every can falling at a predictable speed or time. You want to add a factor of *randomness* so that every time the player starts a new game, the game will be different. Of course, you also need to keep this randomness in control. You don't want one can to take three hours to fall from top to bottom while another can takes only one millisecond. The speed should be random, but within a *playable range of speeds*.

What does randomness actually mean? Generally, random events or values in games and other applications are managed by a *random-number generator*. In JavaScript, there is a `random` method that is part of the `Math` object. You might wonder: how does a computer generate a completely random number? Does randomness exist in reality? Isn't randomness just a manifestation of behavior that you can't yet fully predict and therefore call "random"? Well, let's not get too philosophical. In game worlds and computer programs, you *can* predict precisely what is going to happen, because a computer can only do exactly what you tell it to do. Therefore, strictly speaking, a computer isn't capable of producing a completely random number. One way to pretend that you can produce random numbers is by picking a number from a predefined, very large table of numbers. Because you aren't really producing random numbers, this is called a *pseudo-random number generator*. Most random-number generators can generate a number in a range, such as between 0 or 1, but they often can also generate an arbitrary number or a number in another range. Every number within the range has an equal chance of being generated. In statistics, such a distribution is called a *uniform distribution*.

Suppose that when you start a game, you begin generating "random" numbers by walking through the table. Because the number table doesn't change, every time you play the game, the same sequence of random numbers is generated. In order to avoid this problem, you can indicate in the beginning that you want to start at a *different* position in the table. The position where you start in the table is also called the *seed* of the random-number generator. Often, you take a value for the seed that is different every time you start the program, such as the current system time.

How do you use a random-number generator to create randomness in your game world? Suppose you want to spawn an enemy 75% of the times that a user steps through a door. In that case, you generate a random number between 0 and 1. If the number is less than or equal to 0.75, you spawn an enemy; otherwise you don't. Because of the uniform distribution, this will lead exactly to the behavior that you require. The following JavaScript code illustrates this:

```
var spawnEnemyProbability = Math.random();
if (spawnEnemyProbability >=0.75)
    // spawn an enemy
else
    // do something else
```

If you want to calculate a random speed between 0.5 and 1, you generate a random number between 0 and 1, divide this number by 2, and add 0.5:

```
var newSpeed = Math.random()/2 * 0.5;
```

Humans aren't really any better than computers at understanding "true" randomness. This is why your MP3 player in shuffle mode sometimes seems to keep playing the same songs over and over. You perceive naturally occurring streaks to be non-random when in fact they are random. This means programmers sometimes have to create a function that appears random to humans—even though it's not truly random.

In games, you have to deal very carefully with randomness. A wrongly designed mechanism to spawn random units may spawn units of a certain type more often for certain players, giving them an unfair (dis)advantage. Furthermore, when you design your games, make sure random events don't have too much influence over the outcome. For example, don't have the player roll a die after completing 80 levels of your highly challenging platform game and let the outcome of the roll determine whether the player dies.

Calculating a Random Velocity and Color

Each time a can falls, you want to create a random velocity and color for it. You can use the `Math.random` method to help you do this. Let's first look at creating a random velocity. For neatness, you do this in a separate method in the `PaintCan` class called `calculateRandomVelocity`. You can then call this method when you want to initialize the velocity of the can. Here you use the member variable `minVelocity` to define the minimum velocity that paint cans have when they fall. This variable is given an initial value in the `reset` method, which is called from the constructor:

```
PaintCan.prototype.reset = function () {
    this.moveToTop();
    this.minVelocity = 30;
};
```

You use this minimum velocity value when you calculate a random velocity, which you do in the `calculateRandomVelocity` method:

```
PaintCan.prototype.calculateRandomVelocity = function () {
    return { x : 0, y : Math.random() * 30 + this.minVelocity };
};
```

The method contains only a single instruction, which returns an object representing a velocity. The velocity in the x-direction is zero, because cans aren't moving horizontally—they only fall down. The y-velocity is calculated using the random-number generator. You multiply this random value by 30 and add the value stored in the member variable `minVelocity` in order to get a positive y-velocity between `minVelocity` and `minVelocity+30`.

To calculate a random color, you also use the random-number generator, but you want to choose among a few discrete options (red, green, or blue). The problem is that `Math.random` returns a real number between zero and one. What you would like is to generate a random *integer* number of 0, 1, or 2. Then you can handle the different cases using an `if` instruction. Fortunately, the `Math.floor` method can help. `Math.floor` returns the highest integer number that is less than the value passed along as a parameter. For example:

```
var a = Math.floor(12.34);    // a will contain the value 12
var b = Math.floor(199.9999); // b will contain the value 199
var c = Math.floor(-3.44);    // c will contain the value -4
```

This example combines `Math.random` and `Math.floor` to generate a random number that is 0, 1, or 2:

```
var randomval = Math.floor(Math.random() * 3);
```

Using this approach, you can calculate a random value and then use an `if` instruction to select a color for the paint can. This task is done by the `calculateRandomColor` method. Here is what the method looks like:

```
PaintCan.prototype.calculateRandomColor = function () {
    var randomval = Math.floor(Math.random() * 3);
    if (randomval == 0)
        return sprites.can_red;
    else if (randomval == 1)
        return sprites.can_green;
    else
        return sprites.can_blue;
};
```

Now that you've programmed these two methods for generating random values, you can use them when you define the behavior of the paint can.

Updating the Paint Can

The update method in the `PaintCan` class should do at least the following things:

- Set a randomly created velocity and color if the can currently is not yet falling
- Update the can position by adding the velocity to it
- Check whether the can has fallen completely, and reset it in that case

For the first task, you can use an `if` instruction to check whether the can currently is not moving (the velocity equals zero). Furthermore, you want to introduce a bit of unpredictability for when the can appears. In order to achieve that effect, you assign a random velocity and color only if some generated random number is smaller than a threshold of 0.01. Because of the uniform distribution, only in approximately 1 out of 100 random numbers will the number be smaller than 0.01. As a result, the body of the `if` instruction will only be executed sometimes, even when a can's velocity is zero. In the body of the `if` instruction, you use the two methods you defined earlier for generating a random velocity and a random color:

```
if (this.velocity.y === 0 && Math.random() < 0.01) {
    this.velocity = this.calculateRandomVelocity();
    this.currentColor = this.calculateRandomColor();
}
```

You also need to update the can position by adding the current velocity to it, again taking into account the elapsed game time, just as you did with the ball:

```
this.position.x = this.position.x + this.velocity.x * delta;
this.position.y = this.position.y + this.velocity.y * delta;
```

Now that you've initialized the can and updated its position, you need to handle the special cases. For the paint can, you have to check whether it has fallen outside the game world. If so, you need to reset it. The nice thing is that you already wrote a method to check whether a certain position is outside the game world: the isOutsideWorld method in the `PainterGameWorld` class. You can now use that method again to check whether the position of the can is outside the game world. If this is the case, you need to reset the can so it's placed at the top, outside the screen again. The complete if instruction then becomes

```
if (Game.gameWorld.isOutsideWorld(this.position))
    this.moveToTop();
```

Finally, in order to make the game a bit more challenging, you slightly increase the minimum velocity of the can each time you go through the update loop:

```
this.minVelocity = this.minVelocity + 0.01;
```

Because the minimum velocity slowly increases, the game becomes more difficult as time progresses.

Drawing the Cans on the Screen

To draw the paint cans on the screen, you add a draw method to the `PaintCan` class, which simply draws the paint-can sprite at the desired position. In the `PainterGameWorld` class, you call the handleInput, update, and draw methods on the different game objects. For example, the draw method in `PainterGameWorld` is as follows:

```
PainterGameWorld.prototype.draw = function () {
    Canvas2D.drawImage(sprites.background, { x : 0, y : 0 }, 0,
        { x : 0, y : 0 });
    this.ball.draw();
    this.cannon.draw();
    this.can1.draw();
    this.can2.draw();
    this.can3.draw();
};
```

All the code for the Painter5 example is available in the example folder belonging to this chapter. Figure 8-1 shows a screenshot of the Painter5 example, which now has three falling paint cans.

Figure 8-1. A screenshot of the Painter5 example with a cannon, a ball, and three falling paint cans

Representing Positions and Velocities as Vectors

You've seen that classes are a valuable concept because they define a structure for objects, as well as behavior to modify those objects through methods. This is particularly useful when you need multiple similar objects (such as three paint cans). Another area where classes can be very useful is for defining basic data structures and methods to manipulate these structures. A common structure that you've already seen is an object that represents a two-dimensional position or velocity vector:

```
var position = { x : 0, y : 0 };
var anotherPosition = { x : 35, y : 40 };
```

Unfortunately, the following instruction isn't allowed:

```
var sum = position + anotherPosition;
```

The reason is that the addition operator isn't defined for composite objects such as these. You can of course define a method that does this work for you. But a couple of other methods would be useful as well. For instance, it would be nice if you could subtract such vectors, multiply them, calculate their length, and so on. In order to do this, let's create a Vector2 class. Start by defining the constructor:

```
function Vector2(x, y) {
    this.x = x;
    this.y = y;
}
```

You can now create an object as follows:

```
var position = new Vector2(0,0);
```

It would be nice if somehow you could initialize a vector without having to pass both parameters all the time. One way to do this is to check whether x and/or y is undefined. If that is the case, you simply initialize the member variable to 0, as follows:

```
function Vector2(x, y) {
    if (typeof x === 'undefined')
        this.x = 0;
    else
        this.x = x;
    if (typeof y === 'undefined')
        this.y = 0;
    else
        this.y = y;
}
```

The typeof keyword is used in JavaScript to return the type of a variable. Here you use it to check whether x and y have a defined type. If that is the case, you assign the value passed as a parameter to the member variable. Otherwise, you assign the value 0. JavaScript knows a shorter version of writing down such if instructions. This is what the same method looks like, but shortened:

```
function Vector2(x, y) {
    this.x = typeof x !== 'undefined' ? x : 0;
    this.y = typeof y !== 'undefined' ? y : 0;
}
```

This code does exactly the same thing as the version with the full if instructions, but it's a lot shorter. In front of the question mark is the condition. Then, after the question mark, there are the two options for the values, separated by a colon. When using this shorter version, make sure your code is still readable. This book uses the shorter version only to check whether parameters are defined. This has advantages; for example, you can create Vector2 objects in various ways:

```
var position = new Vector2();             // create a vector (0, 0)
var anotherPosition = new Vector2(35, 40); // create a vector (35, 40)
var yetAnotherPosition = new Vector2(-1);  // create a vector (-1, 0)
```

Now you can add a few useful methods to the Vector2 class so it becomes easier to perform calculations with vectors. For example, the following method makes a copy of a vector:

```
Vector2.prototype.copy = function () {
    return new Vector2(this.x, this.y);
};
```

This is handy if you want to copy positions or velocities from different game objects. Also, comparing vectors is useful. The equals method does this for you:

```
Vector2.prototype.equals = function (obj) {
    return this.x === obj.x && this.y === obj.y;
};
```

You can also define a few basic operations such as adding, subtracting, multiplying, and dividing vectors. First, let's define a method for adding a vector to an existing vector:

```
Vector2.prototype.addTo = function (v) {
    this.x = this.x + v.x;
    this.y = this.y + v.y;
    return this;
};
```

You can use this method as follows:

```
var position = new Vector2(10, 10);        // create a vector (10, 10)
var anotherPosition = new Vector2(20, 20); // create a vector (20, 20)
position.addTo(anotherPosition);           // now represents the vector (30, 30)
```

The last instruction of the addTo method returns this. The reason is that you can do what's called *operator chaining*. Because the addTo method returns a vector as a result, you can call methods on that result. For example:

```
var position = new Vector2(10, 10);        // create a vector (10, 10)
var anotherPosition = new Vector2(20, 20); // create a vector (20, 20)
position.addTo(anotherPosition).addTo(anotherPosition);
// position now represents the vector (50, 50)
```

Depending on the type of the parameter that is passed to the addTo method, you can do something different. If the parameter is a number, you simply add that number to each element of the vector. If it's a vector, you perform the operation in the way already described. One way to do this is to use the typeof operator you've seen before, as follows:

```
Vector2.prototype.addTo = function (v) {
    if (typeof v === 'Vector2') {
        this.x = this.x + v.x;
        this.y = this.y + v.y;
    }
    else if (typeof v === 'Number') {
        this.x = this.x + v;
        this.y = this.y + v;
    }
    return this;
};
```

You use an if instruction to determine the type of the parameter that was passed, and you perform the addition operation accordingly. Another way of determining the type is to use the constructor variable, which is part of each object in JavaScript (just like prototype is part of each function). This is a version of the addTo method that uses the constructor variable instead of the typeof operator:

```
Vector2.prototype.addTo = function (v) {
    if (v.constructor === Vector2) {
        this.x = this.x + v.x;
        this.y = this.y + v.y;
    }
```

```
    else if (v.constructor === Number) {
        this.x = this.x + v;
        this.y = this.y + v;
    }
    return this;
};
```

The addTo method adds a vector to an existing vector. You can also define an add method that adds two vectors and returns a *new vector*. To do that, you can reuse the copy and addTo methods:

```
Vector2.prototype.add = function (v) {
    var result = this.copy();
    return result.addTo(v);
};
```

You can now do the following:

```
var position = new Vector2(10, 10);       // create a vector (10, 10)
var anotherPosition = new Vector2(20, 20); // create a vector (20, 20)
var sum = position.add(anotherPosition);   // creates a new vector (30, 30)
```

In this example, position and anotherPosition are unchanged in the third instruction. A new vector object is created that contains the sum of the values in the operand vectors.

Take a look at the Vector2.js file in the Painter6 example, where you can see the full definition of the Vector2 class. It defines the most common vector operations in this class, including the addition methods discussed in this section. As a result, using vectors in the Painter game is much easier.

You use the Vector2 type in all the game objects to represent positions and velocities. For example, this is the new constructor of the Ball class:

```
function Ball() {
    this.position = new Vector2();
    this.velocity =  new Vector2();
    this.origin = new Vector2();
    this.currentColor = sprites.ball_red;
    this.shooting = false;
}
```

Thanks to the methods in the Vector2 class, you can intuitively update the ball position according to its velocity, in a single line of code:

```
this.position.addTo(this.velocity.multiply(delta));
```

Default Values for Parameters

Before completing this chapter, let's have one more look at how the Vector2 constructor is defined:

```
function Vector2(x, y) {
    this.x = typeof x !== 'undefined' ? x : 0;
    this.y = typeof y !== 'undefined' ? y : 0;
}
```

Because of the assignment instructions inside the method body, you will still create a valid `Vector2` object even if you don't pass any parameters when you call the constructor method. If the parameters x and y are not defined, *default values* are used. You can use this situation to your advantage, because relying on default values can lead to much simpler code writing. To give an example, this is the instruction that draws the background image on the screen:

```
Canvas2D.drawImage(sprites.background, { x : 0, y : 0 }, 0, { x : 0, y : 0 });
```

You can make this method call much more compact, by letting the `drawImage` method automatically provide default values for the position, rotation and origin parameters:

```
Canvas2D_Singleton.prototype.drawImage = function (sprite, position,
                                                    rotation, origin) {
    position = typeof position !== 'undefined' ? position : Vector2.zero;
    rotation = typeof rotation !== 'undefined' ? rotation : 0;
    origin = typeof origin !== 'undefined' ? origin : Vector2.zero;
    // remaining drawing code here
    ...
}
```

Drawing the background is then done as follows:

```
Canvas2D.drawImage(sprites.background);
```

Although default values for parameters are very useful in creating compact code, make sure that you always provide documentation for your methods that specify what default values will be used if the caller of a method doesn't provide all parameters.

What You Have Learned

In this chapter, you have learned:

- How to define classes using the prototype mechanism
- How to create multiple instances of a type/class
- How to add randomness to your game to increase replayability

Colors and Collisions

By now, you've implemented quite a large part of the Painter game. You've seen how to define game object classes by using the prototype mechanism. By using these classes, you gain more control over how game objects are structured and how you can create game objects of a certain type. You separate these class definitions over different files. That way, when you need a cannon or a ball with the same behavior in a future game you're working on, you can simply copy these files and create instances of these game objects in your game.

When you look more closely at the definition of a class, you can see that a class defines the internal structure of an object (which variables it consists of) as well as methods that manipulate this object in some way. These methods can help define more precisely what the possibilities and limitations of an object are. For example, if someone wanted to reuse the Ball class, they wouldn't need a lot of detailed information about how a ball is structured. Simply creating an instance and calling the game-loop methods suffices to add a flying ball to the game. Generally, when you design a program, whether it's a game or a completely different kind of application, it's important to clearly define what is possible with objects of a certain class. Methods are one way to do that. This chapter shows you another way to define an object's possibilities: by defining *properties*. The chapter also introduces a type for representing colors and shows how to handle a collision between the ball and a paint can (if that happens, the paint can needs to change color).

A Different Way to Represent Colors

In the previous versions of Painter, you've dealt with colors rather practically. For example, in the Cannon class, you kept track of the current color by using the currentColor variable, which initially points to the red cannon sprite:

```
this.currentColor = sprites.cannon_red;
```

You did a similar thing in the Ball class, except you let the variable of the same name point to colored ball sprites. Although this works fine, it's slightly inconvenient when the color of a ball needs to change according to the color of the cannon:

```
if (Game.gameWorld.cannon.currentColor === sprites.cannon_red)
    this.currentColor = sprites.ball_red;
else if (Game.gameWorld.cannon.currentColor === sprites.cannon_green)
    this.currentColor = sprites.ball_green;
else
    this.currentColor = sprites.ball_blue;
```

In this if instruction, you need to handle all three different colors; furthermore, now the Ball class needs to have knowledge about the sprites that the Cannon class uses. Wouldn't it be better if you could define colors more uniformly and use that definition in all the game-object classes to represent different colors? Of course it would! Another reason to start unifying the usage of colors in your games now is that the current approach will take much longer to program if you ever decide to increase the number of possible colors in the game (to 4, 6, 10, or more).

The Painter7 example belonging to this chapter adds a Color.js JavaScript file. To define different colors, you use an approach similar to what you do to define different keys. This file defines a variable called Color. The Color variable contains a number of subvariables, each representing a different color. You could define colors as follows:

```
var Color = {
    red : 1,
    blue : 2,
    yellow : 3,
    green : 4,
    // and so on
}
```

However, this approach is not such a good solution. Using numbers to represent colors isn't a bad idea, but you shouldn't make up your own numbering scheme that no one else will know. There is already a standard for defining colors in HTML that uses integers expressed in *hexadecimal* form, and you can use that same standard. The advantage is that this approach is widely used, widely understood, and widely supported by tools (such as Adobe's Kuler, for example, at http://kuler.adobe.com).

In the HTML standard, you can define the colors of elements in a web page by using a hexadecimal representations. For example:

```
<body style="background: #0000FF">
That's a very nice background.
</body>
```

In this case, you indicate that the background color of the body should be the color *blue*. The hexadecimal representation lets you define colors in Red, Green, Blue (RGB) values, where *00* means the color component is absent, and *FF* means the color component is maximal.

The # sign isn't a part of the number, it's merely there to indicate to the browser that what follows is a hexadecimal number instead of a decimal number. So, the #0000FF hexadecimal number represents the color blue, #00FF00 is green, and #FF0000 is red. And of course, any blend or gradation of color components can be defined in a similar way. #808080 is gray, #800080 results in a purple color, and #FF00FF is magenta.

Here is a part of the Color variable:

```
var Color = {
    aliceBlue: "#F0F8FF",
    antiqueWhite: "#FAEBD7",
    aqua: "#00FFFF",
    aquamarine: "#7FFFD4",
    azure: "#F0FFFF",
    beige: "#F5F5DC",
    bisque: "#FFE4C4",
    black: "#000000",
    blanchedAlmond: "#FFEBCD",
    blue: "#0000FF",
    blueViolet: "#8A2BE2",
    brown: "#A52A2A",
    // and so on
}
```

For a more complete list of colors, see the Color.js file. You can now begin using these color definitions in your classes.

Controlled Data Access for Objects

Three game-object classes represent an object of a certain color: Cannon, Ball, and PaintCan. For simplicity, let's start with how you can modify the Cannon class to use the color definitions from the previous section. Until now, this is what the Cannon constructor has looked like:

```
function Cannon() {
    this.position = new Vector2(72, 405);
    this.colorPosition =  new Vector2(55, 388);
    this.origin = new Vector2(34, 34);
    this.currentColor = sprites.cannon_red;
    this.rotation = 0;
}
```

What you could do is add another member variable that gives the current color of the cannon. So, the new Cannon constructor would be as follows:

```
function Cannon() {
    this.position = new Vector2(72, 405);
    this.colorPosition =  new Vector2(55, 388);
    this.origin = new Vector2(34, 34);
    this.currentColor = sprites.cannon_red;
    this.color = Color.red;
    this.rotation = 0;
}
```

However, this isn't ideal. You now store redundant data, because the color information is represented by two variables. Furthermore, you might introduce bugs this way if you forget to change one of the two variables when the color of the cannon changes.

Another way to do it would be to not store a reference to the current sprite. This would be the constructor:

```
function Cannon() {
    this.position = new Vector2(72, 405);
    this.colorPosition =  new Vector2(55, 388);
    this.origin = new Vector2(34, 34);
    this.color = Color.red;
    this.rotation = 0;
}
```

This also isn't an ideal approach, because you would need to look up the correct sprite every time you call the draw method.

One solution is to define two methods that allow users of the Cannon class to retrieve and set the color information. You can then leave the constructor as is but add methods to read and write a color value. For example, you could add the following two methods to the Cannon prototype:

```
Cannon.prototype.getColor = function () {
    if (this.currentColor === sprites.cannon_red)
        return Color.red;
    else if (this.currentColor === sprites.cannon_green)
        return Color.green;
    else
        return Color.blue;
};
Cannon.prototype.setColor = function (value) {
    if (value === Color.red)
        this.currentColor = sprites.cannon_red;
    else if (value === Color.green)
        this.currentColor = sprites.cannon_green;
    else if (value === Color.blue)
        this.currentColor = sprites.cannon_blue;
};
```

Now the user of the Cannon class doesn't need to know that internally, you use a sprite to determine the current color of the cannon. The user can simply pass along a color definition to read or write the color of the cannon:

```
myCannon.setColor(Color.blue);
var cannonColor = myCannon.getColor();
```

Sometimes, programmers call these kinds of methods *getters* and *setters*. In many object-oriented programming languages, methods are the only way to access the data inside an object, so for each member variable that needs to be accessible outside of the class, programmers added a getter and a setter. JavaScript provides a feature that is relatively new to object-oriented programming languages: *properties*. A property is a replacement for a getter and a setter. It defines what happens when you retrieve data from an object and what happens when you assign a value to data inside an object.

Read-Only Properties

Following the prototype-based programming paradigm, you want to be able to add properties to classes. JavaScript has a handy method called `defineProperty` that allows you to do this. This method is part of an object, elusively called `Object`. `Object` has a couple of other useful methods as well, as you learn later. The `defineProperty` method expects three parameters:

- The prototype to which the property should be added (for example, `Cannon.prototype`)
- The name of the property (for example, `color`)
- An object containing at most two variables: `get` and `set`

The `get` and `set` variables each should point to a function that should be executed when the property is read or written. However, it's possible to define only a `get` or a `set` part. This can be useful if the property only reads information and can't change information. If a property only reads information, it's called a *read-only property*. Here is a simple example of a read-only property that you add to the Cannon class:

```
Object.defineProperty(Cannon.prototype, "center",
    {
        get: function () {
            return new Vector2(this.currentColor.width / 2,
                this.currentColor.height / 2);
        }
    });
```

As you can see, you provide three parameters to the `defineProperty` method: a prototype, a name, and an object. The name of this property is `center`. Its goal is to provide the center of the sprite representing the cannon. Because it isn't possible to change the value of the center, this property has only a get part. This is reflected in the object that is passed as the third parameter, which contains one variable, get, that points to a function. Here is how you can use this property:

```
var cannonCenter = cannon.center;
```

Easy, isn't it? Similarly, you can add a property that provides the height of the cannon, as follows:

```
Object.defineProperty(Cannon.prototype, "height",
    {
        get: function () {
            return this.currentColor.height;
        }
    });
```

You can even define a property `ballPosition` that calculates the position at which the ball should be:

```
Object.defineProperty(Cannon.prototype, "ballPosition",
    {
        get: function () {
            var opposite = Math.sin(this.rotation) *
                sprites.cannon_barrel.width * 0.6;
```

```
            var adjacent = Math.cos(this.rotation) *
                sprites.cannon_barrel.width * 0.6;
            return new Vector2(this.position.x + adjacent,
                this.position.y + opposite);
        }
    });
```

Just as you do with methods, you use the `this` keyword to refer to the object the property belongs to. The Painter7 example belonging to this chapter adds properties to different classes. For example, the `Ball` class also contains a `center` property. In combination with the handy methods you added to `Vector2`, you can now calculate the new position of the ball depending on the cannon rotation in a single line of code:

```
this.position = Game.gameWorld.cannon.ballPosition.subtractFrom(this.center);
```

The nice thing about defining classes, methods, and properties is that your code becomes shorter and much easier to understand. For example, you also add the following property to `Vector2`:

```
Object.defineProperty(Vector2, "zero",
    {
        get: function () {
            return new Vector2();
        }
    });
```

Now you have a very short way of creating a two-dimensional vector, as follows:

```
var position = Vector2.zero;
```

From now on, I use both properties and methods to define behavior and data access for objects. By defining useful properties and methods in your classes, the game code becomes generally shorter and much easier to read. For example, before you had classes with useful methods and properties, this is how you had to calculate the ball position:

```
this.position = Game.gameWorld.cannon.ballPosition();
this.position.x = this.position.x - this.currentColor.width / 2;
this.position.y = this.position.y - this.currentColor.height / 2;
```

The new way of doing this is much shorter, as you saw earlier in this section. This effect happens throughout the code in the games you develop in this book, and I encourage you to embrace the power that classes, methods, and properties provide!

Retrieving the Color of the Cannon

You define a new type called `Color` in this chapter. So let's use that type in combination with a property to read and write the color of the cannon. Depending on the sprite to which the `currentColor` variable points, you want to return a different color value. In order to achieve that, you add a property called `color` to the `Cannon` class. Inside the get part of that property, you use an if instruction to find out which color to return. Just as for a method that has a return value, you use the `return` keyword to indicate what value the property should return:

```
Object.defineProperty(Cannon.prototype, "color",
    {
        get: function () {
            if (this.currentColor === sprites.cannon_red)
                return Color.red;
            else if (this.currentColor === sprites.cannon_green)
                return Color.green;
            else
                return Color.blue;
        }
    });
```

You can now use this property to access the color of the cannon. For example, you can store it in a variable, like this:

```
var cannonColor = cannon.Color;
```

You also want to be able to assign a value to the cannon color. For that, you have to define the `set` part of the property. In that part, you need to modify the value of the `currentColor` variable. This value is provided when the property is used in another method. For example, it could be an instruction like this:

```
cannon.color = Color.Red;
```

Again, you use an `if` instruction to determine what the new value of the `currentColor` variable should be. The right side of the assignment is passed to the `set` part as a *parameter*. The complete property is then given as follows:

```
Object.defineProperty(Cannon.prototype, "color",
    {
        get: function () {;
            if (this.currentColor === sprites.cannon_red)
                return Color.red;
            else if (this.currentColor === sprites.cannon_green)
                return Color.green;
            else
                return Color.blue;
        },
        set: function (value) {
            if (value === Color.red)
                this.currentColor = sprites.cannon_red;
            else if (value === Color.green)
                this.currentColor = sprites.cannon_green;
            else if (value === Color.blue)
                this.currentColor = sprites.cannon_blue;
        }
    });
```

This is an example of a property that can be read from and written to. You add a `color` property to all the colored game-object types: `Cannon`, `Ball`, and `PaintCan`. The only difference in the code in the get and set parts is the sprites used to represent the colors. For example, this is the `color` property of the `Ball` class:

```
Object.defineProperty(Ball.prototype, "color",
    {
        get: function () {
            if (this.currentColor === sprites.ball_red)
                return Color.red;
            else if (this.currentColor === sprites.ball_green)
                return Color.green;
            else
                return Color.blue;
        },
        set: function (value) {
            if (value === Color.red)
                this.currentColor = sprites.ball_red;
            else if (value === Color.green)
                this.currentColor = sprites.ball_green;
            else if (value === Color.blue)
                this.currentColor = sprites.ball_blue;
        }
    });
```

Because you've defined these properties, you can now change the color of the ball depending on the color of the cannon very easily, in a single line of code:

```
this.color = Game.gameWorld.cannon.color;
```

Look at the Painter7 example to see how and where it uses properties to make the code easier to read. For some programmers, properties may look odd at first because they're used to getter and setter methods. However, properties do make more intuitive sense. They're a great way to reduce the complexity of lines of code.

Handling Collisions between the Ball and the Cans

The Painter7 example extends the game by handling collisions between the ball and the cans. If two objects collide, you have to handle this collision in the `update` method of one of the two objects. In this case, you can choose to handle collisions in the `Ball` class or in the `PaintCan` class. Painter7 handles the collision in the `PaintCan` class, because if you were to do it in the `Ball` class, you would need to repeat the same code three times, once for each paint can. By handling collisions in the `PaintCan` class, you get this behavior automatically, because each can checks for itself whether it collides with the ball.

Although collision checking can be done in many different ways, you use a very simple method here. You define that there is a collision between two objects if the distance between their centers is smaller than a certain value. The position of the center of the ball at any time in the game world is computed by adding the center of the ball sprite to the position of the ball. You can calculate the center of a paint can in a similar way. Because you added a few nice properties to calculate the center of game objects, let's use them to calculate the distance between the ball and a paint can, as follows:

```
var ball = Game.gameWorld.ball;
var distance = ball.position.add(ball.center).subtractFrom(this.position)
    .subtractFrom(this.center);
```

Now that you've calculated this vector, you have to check whether its length in both the x- and y-directions is smaller than some given value. If the absolute value of the x-component of the distance vector is smaller than the x-value of the center, it means the ball object is within the x range of the can. The same principle holds for the y-direction. If this holds for both the x- and y-components, you can say that the ball collides with the can. You can write an if instruction that checks this condition:

```
if (Math.abs(distance.x) < this.center.x &&
    Math.abs(distance.y) < this.center.y) {
    // handle the collision
}
```

You use the Math.abs method to calculate the absolute value of the distance components. If there is a collision between the ball and the can, you need to change the color of the can to the color of the ball.

Next, you have to reset the ball so it can be shot again. The following two instructions do exactly that:

```
this.color = ball.color;
ball.reset();
```

You can try out the Painter7 example to see that collisions between the ball and the paint cans are properly handled.

As you've probably noticed, the collision-detection method used here isn't very precise. In Chapter 26, you see a better way of dealing with collisions on a per-pixel level, although this does make your game run more slowly if you don't watch out.

> **Note**   In the end, simple lines of code like the ones written in this section make all the difference in the player experience. As you build up your game application, you'll find that sometimes the littlest thing to the player took the longest to program, and the biggest changes were achieved with only one or two lines!

What You Have Learned

In this chapter, you have learned:

- How to add properties to your classes
- How to handle basic collisions between game objects
- How to define game objects that have different colors

Chapter 10

Limited Lives

In this chapter, you make the Painter game more interesting by giving the player a limited number of lives. If players miss too many paint cans, they die. The chapter discusses how to deal with that and how to display the current number of lives to the player. In order to do the latter, you learn about a few programming constructs for repeating a group of instructions several times.

Maintaining the Number of Lives

To introduce some danger and incentive to work hard in the game, you would like to limit the number of paint cans of the wrong color that the player can allow to fall through the bottom of the screen. The Painter8 example adds this kind of behavior to the game and uses a limit of five.

The choice of a limit of five paint cans is one of many examples of the decisions you have to make as a game designer and developer. If you give the player only a single life, then the game will be too hard to play. Giving the player hundreds of lives removes the incentive for the player to play well. Determining such parameters often happens by play-testing the game and determining reasonable parameter values. In addition to testing the game yourself, you can also ask your friends or family to play your game to get some idea of what values to choose for these parameters.

In order to store the life limit, you add an extra member variable to the `PainterGameWorld` class:

```
this.lives = 5;
```

You initially set this value to 5 in the constructor of the `PainterGameWorld` class. Now you can update the value whenever a paint can falls outside the screen. You perform this check in the update method of the `PaintCan` class. Therefore, you have to add a few instructions in that method to deal with this. The only thing you need to do is check whether the color of the paint can is the same as its target color when it falls through the bottom of the screen. If that is the case, you have to decrement the lives counter in the `PainterGameWorld` class.

Before you can do this, you have to extend the PaintCan class so that PaintCan objects know that they need to have a target color when they fall out of the bottom of the screen. Painter8 passes along this target color as a parameter when you create the PaintCan objects in PainterGameWorld:

```
this.can1 = new PaintCan(450, Color.red);
this.can2 = new PaintCan(575, Color.green);
this.can3 = new PaintCan(700, Color.blue);
```

You store the target color in a variable in each paint can, as you can see in the constructor of PaintCan:

```
function PaintCan(xPosition, targetColor) {
    this.currentColor = sprites.can_red;
    this.velocity = Vector2.zero;
    this.position = new Vector2(xPosition, -200);
    this.origin = Vector2.zero;
    this.targetColor = targetColor;
    this.reset();
}
```

You can now extend the update method of PaintCan so that it handles the situation where the paint can falls outside the bottom of the screen. If that happens, you need to move the paint can back to the top of the screen. If the current color of the paint can doesn't match the target color, you decrease the number of lives by one:

```
if (Game.gameWorld.isOutsideWorld(this.position)) {
    if (this.color !== this.targetColor)
        Game.gameWorld.lives = Game.gameWorld.lives - 1;
    this.moveToTop();
}
```

You might want to decrease the number of lives by more than one at some point. In order to facilitate this, you can change the penalty into a variable:

```
var penalty = 1;
if (Game.gameWorld.isOutsideWorld(this.position)) {
    if (this.color !== this.targetColor)
        Game.gameWorld.lives = Game.gameWorld.lives - penalty;
    this.moveToTop();
}
```

This way, you can introduce steeper penalties if you want to, or dynamic penalties (first miss costs one life, second miss costs two, and so on). You could also imagine that sometimes a special paint can falls. If the player shoots that can with a ball of the right color, the penalty for mismatching paint-can colors temporarily becomes zero. Can you think of other ways in which you can deal with penalties in the Painter game?

Indicating the Number of Lives to the Player

Obviously, players would like to know how they're doing. So, you have to indicate somehow on the screen how many lives the player has left. In the Painter game, you do that by displaying a number of balloons in the upper-left corner of the screen. Using the knowledge you have, you could use an if instruction to do that:

```
if (lives === 5) {
    // Draw the balloon sprite 5 times in a row
} else if (lives === 4) {
    // Draw the balloon sprite 4 times in a row
} else if (lives === 3)
    // And so on...
```

This isn't a very nice solution. It leads to a lot of code, and you would have to copy the same instruction many times. Fortunately, there is a better solution: *iteration*.

Executing Instructions Multiple Times

Iteration in JavaScript is a way to repeat instructions a number of times. Have a look at the following code fragment:

```
var val = 10;
while (val >=3)
    val = val - 3;
```

The second instruction is called a while loop. This instruction consists of a kind of header (while (val >=3)) and a body (val = val - 3;), which is very similar to the structure of an if instruction. The header consists of the word while followed by a *condition* in parentheses. The body itself is an instruction. In this case, the instruction subtracts 3 from a variable. However, it could just as well have been another kind of instruction, such as calling a method or accessing a property. Figure 10-1 shows the syntax diagram of the while instruction.

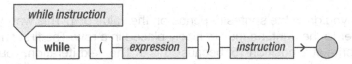

Figure 10-1. Syntax diagram of the while instruction

When the while instruction is executed, its body is executed multiple times. In fact, as long as the *condition* in the header yields true, the body will be executed. In this example, the condition is that the val variable contains a value that is 3 or greater. In the beginning, the variable contains the value 10, so it's certainly greater than 3. Therefore, the body of the while instruction is executed, after which the variable val contains the value 7. The condition is then evaluated again. The variable still is greater than 3, so the body is executed once more, after which the variable val contains the value 4. Again, the value is greater than 3, so the body is executed again, and val will contain the value 1.

At that point, the condition is evaluated, but it's no longer `true`. Therefore, the repeating instruction comes to an end. So, after this piece of code is executed, the variable `val` contains the value 1. In fact, what you've programmed here is integer division using the `while` instruction. Of course, in this case it's easier to simply use the following single line of code that achieves the same result:

```
var val = 10 % 3;
```

If you want to draw the player's number of lives on the screen, you can use a `while` instruction to do so quite efficiently:

```
var i = 0;
while (i < numberOfLives) {
    Canvas2D.drawImage(sprites.lives,
        new Vector2(i * sprites.lives.width + 15, 60));
    i = i + 1;
}
```

In this `while` instruction, the body is executed as long as the variable `i` contains a value less than `numberOfLives` (which is a variable you assume is declared and initialized to a certain value somewhere else). Every time the body is executed, you draw the sprite on the screen, and then you increment `i` by 1. The result is that you draw the sprite on the screen exactly `numberOfLives` times! So, you're using the variable `i` here as a *counter*.

Note   You start with `i` equal to zero and continue until `i` has reached the same value as `numberOfLives`. This means the body of the `while` instruction is executed for the values 0, 1, 2, 3, and 4 of `i`. As a result, the body is executed five times.

As you can see, the body of a `while` instruction may contain more than a single instruction. If the body contains more than one instruction, the instructions need to be placed between braces, just like with the `if` instruction.

The position at which you draw the sprites depends on the value of `i`. This way, you can draw each sprite a bit further to the right, so they're nicely placed in a row. The first time you execute the body, you draw the sprite at x-position 15, because `i` is 0. The next iteration, you draw the sprite at x-position `sprites.lives.width + 15`, the iteration after that at 2 * `sprites.lives.width + 15`, and so on. In this case, you use the counter not only to determine how often you execute instructions, but also to *change what the instructions do*. This is a very powerful feature of an iteration instruction such as `while`. Because of the looping behavior, a `while` instruction is also called a `while` *loop*. Figure 10-2 shows a screenshot of the Painter game where the number of lives is indicated at upper left on the screen.

Figure 10-2. The Painter game showing the player the remaining number of lives

A Shorter Notation for Incrementing Counters

Many while instructions, especially those that use a counter, have a body that contains an instruction for incrementing a variable. This can be done with the following instruction:

```
i = i + 1;
```

As a side note, especially because of these kinds of instructions, it's unwise to express the assignment as "is". The value of i can of course never be the same as i + 1, but the value of i *becomes* the old value of i, plus 1. These kinds of instructions are very common in programs, so a special, shorter notation exists that does exactly the same thing:

```
i++;
```

The ++ can be expressed as "is incremented." Because this operator is placed after the variable it operates on, the ++ operator is called a *postfix operator*. To increment a variable by more than 1, there is another notation

```
i += 2;
```

which means the same as

```
i = i + 2;
```

There is a similar notation for other basic arithmetic operations, for example:

```
i -= 12;    // this is the same as i = i - 12
i *= 0.99; // this is the same as i = i * 0.99
i /=5;     // this is the same as i = i / 5
i--;       // this is the same as i = i - 1
```

This notation is very useful, because it allows you to write shorter code. For example, the following code:

```
Game.gameWorld.lives = Game.gameWorld.lives - penalty;
```

...becomes:

```
Game.gameWorld.lives -= penalty;
```

When you look at the example code belonging to this chapter, you will see that this shorter notation is used in many different classes to make the code more compact.

A More Compact Looping Syntax

Many while instructions use a counting variable and therefore have the following structure:

```
var i;
i = begin value;
while (i < end value ) {
    // do something useful using i
    i++;
}
```

Because this kind of instruction is quite common, a more compact notation is available for it:

```
var i;
for (i = begin value ; i < end value ; i++ ) {
    // do something useful using i
}
```

The meaning of this instruction is exactly the same as the earlier while instruction. The advantage of using the for instruction in this case is that everything that has something to do with the counter is nicely grouped together in the header of the instruction. This reduces the chance of you forgetting the instruction to increment the counter (resulting in an endless loop). In the cases where "do something useful using i" consists of only a single instruction, you can leave out the braces, which makes the notation even more compact. Also, you can move the declaration of the variable i in the header of the for instruction. For example, look at the following code fragment:

```
for (var i = 0; i < this.lives; i++) {
    Canvas2D.drawImage(sprites.lives,
        new Vector2(i * sprites.lives.width + 15, 60));
}
```

This is a very compact instruction that increments the counter and draws the sprite at different positions. This instruction is equivalent to the following while instruction:

```
var i = 0;
while (i < this.lives) {
    Canvas2D.drawImage(sprites.lives,
        new Vector2(i * sprites.lives.width + 15, 60));
    i = i + 1;
}
```

And here's another example:

```
for (var i = this.lives - 1; i >=0; i--)
    Canvas2D.drawImage(sprites.lives,
        new Vector2(i * sprites.lives.width + 15, 60));
```

To which while instruction is this for instruction equivalent? Does it make a difference in practice whether you increase or decrease the counter in this case? Figure 10-3 contains the syntax diagram of the for instruction.

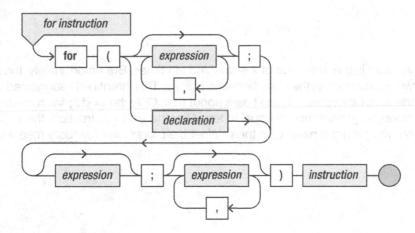

Figure 10-3. Syntax diagram of the for *instruction*

A Few Special Cases

There are a few special cases that you need to know about when dealing with while and for loops. The following subsections discuss these cases.

No Repeat at All

Sometimes the condition in the header of a while instruction is already false at the beginning. Look at the following code fragment:

```
var x = 1;
var y = 0;
while (x < y)
    x++;
```

In this case, the body of the while instruction isn't executed—not even once! Therefore, in this example, the variable x retains the value 1.

Infinite Repeat

One of the dangers of using while instructions (and, to a lesser extent, for instructions) is that they might never end, if you're not careful. You can easily write such an instruction:

```
while (1 + 1 === 2)
    x = x + 1;
```

In this case, the value of x is incremented without end. This is because the condition 1 + 1 === 2 always yields true, no matter what is done in the body of the instruction. This example is quite easy to avoid, but often a while instruction ends in an infinite loop because of a programming error. Consider the following example:

```
var x = 1;
var n = 0;
while (n < 10)
    x = x * 2;
    n = n + 1;
```

The intention of this code is that the value of x is doubled ten times. But unfortunately, the programmer forgot to put the two instructions in the body between braces. This intention is suggested by the layout of the program, but the script interpreter doesn't care about that. Only the x=x*2; instruction is repeated, so the value of n will never be greater than or equal to ten. After the while instruction, the instruction n=n+1; will be executed, but the program never gets there. What the programmer actually meant was

```
var x = 1;
var n = 0;
while (n < 10) {
    x = x * 2;
    n = n + 1;
}
```

It would be a pity if you had to throw away your computer or mobile device after it was put into a coma because you forgot to write braces around your while instruction. Fortunately, the operating system can stop the execution of a program by force, even if it hasn't finished. Even browsers nowadays can detect scripts that are running indefinitely, in which case the browser can stop the script execution. Once that's done, you can start to look for the cause of the program hanging. Although such hang-ups occur occasionally in programs, it's your job as a game programmer to make sure that once the game is publicly available, these kinds of programming errors have been removed from the game code. This is why proper testing is so important.

In general, if the program you wrote doesn't seem to do anything on startup, or if it hangs indefinitely, check out what is happening in the while instructions. A very common mistake is to forget to increment the counter variable, so the condition of the while instruction never becomes false and the while loop continues indefinitely. Many other programming errors may lead to an infinite loop. In fact, infinite loops are so common that a street in Cupertino, California has been named after them—and located on that street is Apple headquarters!

Nested Repeats

The body of a while instruction or a for instruction is an instruction. This instruction can be an assignment, a method call, a block of instructions delimited by braces, or another while or for loop. For example:

```
var x, y;
for (y=0; y<7; y++)
    for (x=0; x<y; x++)
        Canvas2D.drawImage(sprites.lives,
            new Vector2(x * sprites.lives.width, y * sprites.lives.height));
```

In this fragment, the variable y counts from 0 to 7. For each of these values of y, the body is executed, which consists of a for instruction. This second for instruction uses the counter x, which has as an upper limit the value of y. Therefore, in each progression of the outer for instruction, the inner for instruction goes on longer. The instruction that is repeated draws a yellow balloon sprite at the position calculated by using the values of the x and y counters. The result of this loop is a number of balloons placed in the shape of a triangle (see Figure 10-4).

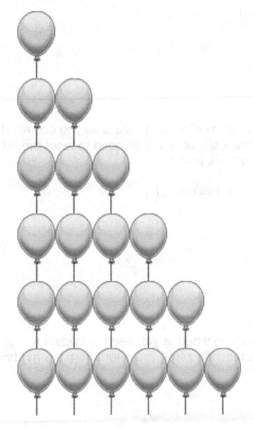

Figure 10-4. Balloons in a triangle shape

The first line in this shape contains zero balloons. The reason is that the value of y is still 0 at that point, which means the inner for instruction is executed zero times.

Restarting the Game

When the player has lost all their lives, the game is over. How do you deal with this? In the case of the Painter game, you would like to show a Game Over screen. The player can press the left mouse button, which will then restart the game. In order to add this to the game, you load an extra sprite when the game is started that represents the Game Over screen:

```
sprites.gameover = loadSprite("spr_gameover_click.png");
```

Now you can use an if instruction in each of the game-loop methods to determine what you should do. If the game is over, you don't want the cannon and the ball to handle input anymore; you simply want to listen if the player presses the mouse button. If that happens, you reset the game. So, the handleInput method in the PainterGameWorld class now contains the following instructions:

```
if (this.lives > 0) {
    this.ball.handleInput(delta);
    this.cannon.handleInput(delta);
}
else {
    if (Mouse.leftPressed)
        this.reset();
}
```

You add a reset method to the PainterGameWorld class so you can reset the game to its initial state. This means resetting all the game objects. You also need to reset the number of lives to five. Here is the full reset method in PainterGameWorld:

```
PainterGameWorld.prototype.reset = function () {
    this.lives = 5;
    this.cannon.reset();
    this.ball.reset();
    this.can1.reset();
    this.can2.reset();
    this.can3.reset();
};
```

For the update method, you only need to update the game objects if the game isn't over. Therefore, you first check with an if instruction whether you need to update the game objects. If not (in other words: the number of lives has reached zero), you return from the method:

```
if (this.lives <= 0)
    return;
this.ball.update(delta);
this.cannon.update(delta);
this.can1.update(delta);
this.can2.update(delta);
this.can3.update(delta);
```

Finally, in the draw method, you draw the game objects, and the Game Over screen if the player has no lives left. This results in the following structure:

```
PainterGameWorld.prototype.draw = function () {
    // draw the game world
    ...
    for (var i = 0; i < this.lives; i++) {
        Canvas2D.drawImage(sprites.lives,
            new Vector2(i * sprites.lives.width + 15, 60));
    }
    if (this.lives <= 0) {
        Canvas2D.drawImage(sprites.gameover,
            new Vector2(Game.size.x - sprites.gameover.width,
            Game.size.y - sprites.gameover.height).divideBy(2));
    }
};
```

You can see that you use the dimensions of the screen and the dimensions of the Game Over overlay to position it nicely in the center of the screen. Figure 10-5 shows a screenshot of the Game Over overlay drawn on top of the game world.

Figure 10-5. Game over!

In Figure 10-5, notice that the Game Over overlay doesn't completely hide the other objects and the background. The reason is that the Game Over sprite has some *transparent* pixels. Often, sprites have transparent parts so the sprites seem to be integrated parts of the game world. The balloon, the ball, the paint cans, and the cannon barrel all are partly transparent, which is why they seamlessly integrate into the game world. When designing sprites, you need to make sure the image has these transparency values set correctly. Although doing this right can be a lot of work, modern image-editing tools such as Adobe Photoshop give you many means to define transparency in images. Just be sure you save the image in a format that supports transparency, such as PNG.

> **Note**   You can use the (lack of) transparency of overlays to control what the player is seeing. In some cases, you might want things obscured (such as a "pause" screen in a time-sensitive game) or able to be seen (such as the Game Over screen in Painter).

What You Have Learned

In this chapter, you have learned:

- How to store and display the number of lives a player currently has
- How to repeat a group of instructions using the `while` or `for` instruction
- How to restart the game when the player has no lives remaining

11

Organizing Game Objects

You've seen in the previous chapters how you can use classes to group variables that belong together. This chapter looks at the similarities between the different types of game objects and how you can express these similarities in JavaScript.

Similarities between Game Objects

If you look at the different game objects in the Painter game, you can see that they have a lot of things in common. For example, the ball, the cannon, and the paint cans all use three sprites that represent each of the three different colors. Also, most objects in the game have a position and a velocity. Furthermore, all game objects need a method to draw them, some of the game objects have a method for handling input, some of them have an update method, and so on. Now, it isn't really a problem that these classes have similarities. The browser or the players of the game won't complain about that. However, it's a pity that you have to copy code all the time. To give an example, both `Ball` and the `PaintCan` class have width and height properties:

```
Object.defineProperty(Ball.prototype, "width",
    {
        get: function () {
            return this.currentColor.width;
        }
    });
Object.defineProperty(Ball.prototype, "height",
    {
        get: function () {
            return this.currentColor.height;
        }
    });
```

The code is exactly the same, but you have to copy it for both classes. And every time you want to add a different kind of game object, you probably need to copy these properties again. In this case, these properties are fortunately not that complicated, but in the application you're copying around a lot of other things as well. For example, most game object classes in the Painter game define the following member variables:

```
this.currentColor = some sprite;
this.velocity = Vector2.zero;
this.position = Vector2.zero;
this.origin = Vector2.zero;
this.rotation = 0;
```

The draw methods of the various game objects also look similar. For example, here are the draw methods of the Ball and the PaintCan classes:

```
Ball.prototype.draw = function () {
    if (!this.shooting)
        return;
    Canvas2D.drawImage(this.currentColor, this.position, this.rotation, 1,
        this.origin);
};
PaintCan.prototype.draw = function () {
    Canvas2D.drawImage(this.currentColor, this.position, this.rotation, 1,
        this.origin);
};
```

Again, the code is very similar in the different classes, and you copy it every time you make a new kind of game object. In general, it's better to avoid copying a lot of code. Why is that? Because if at some point you realize there is a mistake in that part of the code, you have to correct it everywhere you copied it to. In a small game like Painter, this isn't a big issue. But when you develop a commercial game with hundreds of different game-object classes, this becomes a serious maintenance problem. Furthermore, you don't always know how far a small game will go. If you aren't careful, you can end up copying a lot of code (and the bugs associated with it). As a game matures, it's a good idea to keep an eye out for where to optimize code, even if this means some extra work to find these duplications and consolidate them. For this particular situation, you need to think about how the different kinds of game objects are similar and whether you can group these similarities together, just as you grouped the member variables in the previous chapters.

Conceptually speaking, it's easy to say what is similar between balls, paint cans, and cannons: they're all *game objects*. Basically, they can all be drawn at a certain position; they all have a velocity (even the cannon, but its velocity is zero); and they all have a color that is red, green, or blue. Furthermore, most of them handle input of some kind and are updated.

Inheritance

Using prototypes in JavaScript, it's possible to group these similarities together in a sort of generic class and then define other classes that are a *special version* of this generic class. In object-oriented jargon, this is called *inheritance*, and it's a very powerful language feature. In JavaScript, inheritance is made possible by the prototype mechanism. Consider the following example:

```
function Vehicle() {
    this.numberOfWheels = 4;
    this.brand = "";
}
Vehicle.prototype.what = function() {
    return "nrOfWheels = " + this.numberOfWheels + ", brand = " + this.brand;
};
```

Here you have a very simple example of a class for representing vehicles (you can imagine that this could be useful for a traffic-simulation game). To keep things simple, a vehicle is defined by a number of wheels and a brand. The Vehicle class also has a method called what that returns a description of the vehicle. This could be useful if you wanted to create a website that presented a list of vehicles in a table. You can use this class as follows:

```
var v = new Vehicle();
v.brand = "volkswagen";
console.log(v.what()); // outputs "nrOfWheels = 4, brand = volkswagen"
```

There are different types of vehicles, such as cars, bikes, motorbikes, and so on. For some of these types, you would like to store additional information. For example, for a car, it could be useful to store whether it's a convertible; for the motorbike, how many cylinders it has; and so on. You can use the prototype-based inheritance mechanism in JavaScript to do that. Here is an example of a class called Car:

```
function Car(brand) {
    Vehicle.call(this);
    this.brand = brand;
    this.convertible = false;
}
Car.prototype = Object.create(Vehicle.prototype);
```

There are a couple of new things in this class declaration. At the bottom, you assign a value to the prototype object of Car. You do this by using the Object.create method. In this case, you make a copy of the prototype object of Vehicle, and you store that copy in the prototype object of Car. In other words, Car now has the same functionality as Vehicle, including the what method:

```
var c = new Car("mercedes");
console.log(c.what()); // outputs "nrOfWheels = 4, brand = mercedes"
```

In the constructor of Car is the following line:

```
Vehicle.call(this);
```

What happens here is that the Vehicle constructor is called, *using the same object* that is created when the Car constructor is invoked. In essence, you're telling the interpreter that the Car object (this) you're currently manipulating *is actually also a* Vehicle *object*. So you can see the two important aspects of inheritance:

- There is a relationship between objects (a Car object is also a Vehicle).

- A class that inherits from another class copies its functionality (Car objects have the same member variables, properties, and methods as Vehicle objects).

Because Car inherits from Vehicle, you also say that Car is a *subclass* or *derived class* of Vehicle, or that Vehicle is the *superclass*, or *parent class*, or *base class*, of Car. The inheritance relationship between classes is widely used; and in a good class design, it can be interpreted as "is a kind of." In this example, the relationship is clear: a car is a kind of vehicle. The other way around isn't always true. A vehicle isn't always a car. There could be other subclasses of Vehicle, for example:

```
function Motorbike(brand) {
    Vehicle.call(this);
    this.numberOfWheels = 2;
    this.brand = brand;
    this.cylinders = 4;
}
Motorbike.prototype = Object.create(Vehicle.prototype);
```

A motorbike is also a kind of vehicle. The Motorbike class inherits from Vehicle and adds its own custom member variable to indicate the number of cylinders. Figure 11-1 illustrates the hierarchy of classes. For a more expanded version of this hierarchy, see Figure 11-4.

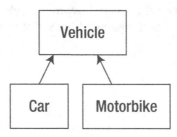

Figure 11-1. *Inheritance diagram of* Vehicle *and its subclasses*

Game Objects and Inheritance

The "is a kind of" relationship also holds for the game objects in the Painter game. A ball is a kind of game object, and so are the paint cans and the cannon. You can make this inheritance relationship explicit in the program by defining a generic class called ThreeColorGameObject and having your actual game-object classes inherit from that generic class. You can then put everything that defines what a three-color game object is in that class, and the ball, the cannon, and the paint can will be special versions of that class.

Let's look at this ThreeColorGameObject class in more detail. You put into this class the member variables that are commonly used by the different types of game objects in the game. You can define a basic skeleton of this class as follows:

```
function ThreeColorGameObject() {
    this.currentColor = undefined;
    this.velocity = Vector2.zero;
    this.position = Vector2.zero;
    this.origin = Vector2.zero;
    this.rotation = 0;
    this.visible = true;
}
```

Each class that inherits from ThreeColorGameObject will have a velocity, a position, an origin, a rotation, and so on. This is nice, because now you only define these member variables in one place, and they can be used in any class that inherits from ThreeColorGameObject.

One thing that is still missing in this constructor is a way to deal with the three different colors. In the case of Painter, each game-object type has three different sprites, each one representing a different color. When you define the ThreeColorGameObject class, you don't know yet which sprites to use, because they will depend on the final type of the game object (cannons use sprites other than balls or paint cans). In order to solve this, let's extend the constructor as follows:

```
function ThreeColorGameObject(sprColorRed, sprColorGreen, sprColorBlue) {
    this.colorRed = sprColorRed;
    this.colorGreen = sprColorGreen;
    this.colorBlue = sprColorBlue;
    this.currentColor = this.colorRed;
    this.velocity = Vector2.zero;
    this.position = Vector2.zero;
    this.origin = Vector2.zero;
    this.rotation = 0;
    this.visible = true;
}
```

Whenever you inherit from this class, you can define what the values of the member variables colorRed, colorGreen,and colorBlue should be.

Now you need to define the basic game-loop methods. The method for drawing the game object is straightforward. You probably noted that a member variable visible is added to the class. You can use this member variable to toggle the visibility of game objects. In the draw method, you draw the sprite on the screen only if the game object should be visible:

```
ThreeColorGameObject.prototype.draw = function () {
    if (!this.visible)
        return;
    Canvas2D.drawImage(this.currentColor, this.position, this.rotation, 1,
        this.origin);
};
```

The update method of the class contains a single instruction that updates the current position of the game object:

```
ThreeColorGameObject.prototype.update = function (delta) {
    this.position.addTo(this.velocity.multiply(delta));
};
```

Finally, you add a few convenient properties for getting and setting the color, and retrieving the dimensions of the object. For example, this is the property for reading and writing the object's color:

```
Object.defineProperty(ThreeColorGameObject.prototype, "color",
    {
        get: function () {
            if (this.currentColor === this.colorRed)
                return Color.red;
            else if (this.currentColor === this.colorGreen)
                return Color.green;
            else
                return Color.blue;
        },
        set: function (value) {
            if (value === Color.red)
                this.currentColor = this.colorRed;
            else if (value === Color.green)
                this.currentColor = this.colorGreen;
            else if (value === Color.blue)
                this.currentColor = this.colorBlue;
        }
    });
```

As you can see, you use the colored sprite member variables here. Any class that inherits from ThreeColorGameObject also now has this property. This saves you a lot of code copying! For the complete ThreeColorGameObject class, see the Painter9 example belonging to this chapter.

Cannon as a Subclass of ThreeColorGameObject

Now that you've created a very basic class for colored game objects, you can reuse this basic behavior for the actual game objects in your game by *inheriting* from this class. Let's first look at the Cannon class. Because you've defined the basic ThreeColorGameObject class, you can create the Cannon class as a subclass of that class, as follows:

```
function Cannon() {
    // to do...
}
Cannon.prototype = Object.create(ThreeColorGameObject.prototype);
```

You create the Cannon.prototype object by making a copy of the ThreeColorGameObject.prototype object. You still need to write the code in the constructor method, though.

Because Cannon inherits from ThreeColorGameObject, you need to call the constructor of the ThreeColorGameObject class. This constructor expects three parameters. Because you're creating a Cannon object, you want to pass the colored cannon sprites to that constructor. Fortunately, you can pass along these sprites in the call method, as follows:

```
ThreeColorGameObject.call(this, sprites.cannon_red, sprites.cannon_green,
    sprites.cannon_blue);
```

Second, you set the position and the origin of the cannon, just as you did in the original Cannon class:

```
this.position = new Vector2(72, 405);
this.origin = new Vector2(34, 34);
```

The rest of the work (assigning the three color sprites and initializing the other member variables) is done for you in the ThreeColorGameObject constructor! Note that it's important to first call the constructor of the superclass before setting the member variables in the subclass. Otherwise, the position and origin values you choose for the cannon will be reset to zero when the ThreeColorGameObject constructor is called.

Now that the new version of the Cannon class has been defined, you can start adding properties and methods to the class, just as you did before. For example, here is the handleInput method:

```
Cannon.prototype.handleInput = function (delta) {
    if (Keyboard.down(Keys.R))
        this.currentColor = this.colorRed;
    else if (Keyboard.down(Keys.G))
        this.currentColor = this.colorGreen;
    else if (Keyboard.down(Keys.B))
        this.currentColor = this.colorBlue;
    var opposite = Mouse.position.y - this.position.y;
    var adjacent = Mouse.position.x - this.position.x;
    this.rotation = Math.atan2(opposite, adjacent);
};
```

As you can see, you can access member variables such as currentColor and rotation without any problem. Because Cannon inherits from ThreeColorGameObject, it contains the same member variables, properties, and methods.

Overriding Methods from the Superclass

In addition to adding new methods and properties, you can also choose to *replace* a method in the Cannon class. For example, ThreeColorGameObject has the following draw method:

```
ThreeColorGameObject.prototype.draw = function () {
    if (!this.visible)
        return;
    Canvas2D.drawImage(this.currentColor, this.position,
        this.rotation, 1, this.origin);
};
```

For cannons, this method doesn't do exactly what you want. You want to draw the color of the cannon, but you also want to draw the cannon barrel. Replacing a method is very easy. You simply redefine the method as a part of the Cannon prototype:

```
Cannon.prototype.draw = function () {
    if (!this.visible)
        return;
    var colorPosition = this.position.subtract(this.size.divideBy(2));
    Canvas2D.drawImage(sprites.cannon_barrel, this.position, this.rotation, 1,
        this.origin);
    Canvas2D.drawImage(this.currentColor, colorPosition);
};
```

In object-oriented jargon, when you replace a method inherited from the superclass in the subclass, you say that you *override* the method. In this case, you override the draw method from ThreeColorGameObject. Similarly, if you wanted to, you could override a property, or even remove properties and methods by letting them refer to undefined. Once a Cannon object has been created, you have the full flexibility that JavaScript offers to modify that object.

> **Note**   Even though you're overriding a method in this example, JavaScript doesn't use an override keyword as is common in other languages such as Java or C#.

If you take a look at the Cannon.js file in the Painter9 example belonging to this chapter, you can see that the Cannon class definition is much smaller and easier to read than in the previous version, because all the generic game-object members are placed in the ThreeColorGameObject class. Organizing your code in different classes and subclasses helps to reduce code copying and results in generally cleaner designs. There is a caveat, however: your class structure (which class inherits from which other class) must be correct. Remember that classes should only inherit from other classes if there is a "is a kind of" relationship between the classes. To illustrate this, suppose you would like to add an indicator at the top of the screen that shows which color the ball currently is. You could make a class for that and let it inherit from the Cannon class because it needs to handle input in a similar way:

```
function ColorIndicator() {
    Cannon.call(this, ...);
    // etc.
}
```

However, this is a very bad idea. A color indicator is certainly not a kind of cannon, and designing your classes this way makes it very unclear to other developers what the classes are used for. Furthermore, the color indicator would also have a rotation, which doesn't make any sense. Class-inheritance diagrams should be logical and easy to understand. Every time you write a class that inherits from another class, ask yourself whether that class really "is a kind of" the class that you inherit from. If it isn't, then you have to rethink your design.

The Ball Class

You define the new Ball class in a fashion very similar to the Cannon class. Just as in the Cannon class, you inherit from the ThreeColorGameObject class. The only difference is that you have to add an extra member variable that indicates whether the ball is currently shooting:

```
function Ball() {
    ThreeColorGameObject.call(this, sprites.ball_red, sprites.ball_green,
        sprites.ball_blue);
    this.shooting = false;
    this.reset();
}
Ball.prototype = Object.create(ThreeColorGameObject.prototype);
```

When a Ball instance is created, you need to call the ThreeColorGameObject constructor, just as you did with the Cannon class. In this case, you pass along the ball sprites as parameters. In addition, you need to give the shooting variable an initial value of false, and you reset the ball by calling the reset method.

The Ball class clearly illustrates what happens when you inherit from another class. Each Ball instance consists of a part that has been inherited from ThreeColorGameObject and a part that is defined in the Ball class. Figure 11-2 shows what the memory looks like for a Ball object without using inheritance. Figure 11-3 also shows a Ball instance, but using the inheritance mechanism introduced in this chapter.

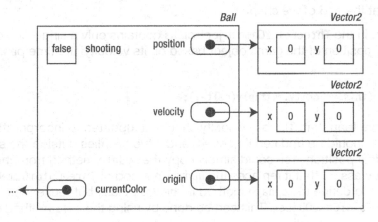

Figure 11-2. Overview of the memory used by an instance of the Ball class (no inheritance)

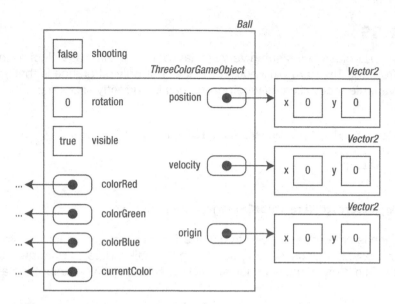

Figure 11-3. An instance of the `Ball` *class (which inherits from* `ThreeColorGameObject`)

You might be a bit puzzled by these two figures and the structures they present. Later, this chapter discusses memory structure in a bit more detail. For now, assume that complicated objects consisting of multiple member variables (such as `Cannon` or `Ball` instances) are stored differently than simple numbers or Booleans. What that means and how you should properly deal with it in your code are covered at the end of the chapter.

The `update` method in the `ThreeColorGameObject` class contains only a single line of code that calculates the new position of the game object based on its velocity, the time passed, and its current position:

```
this.position.addTo(this.velocity.multiply(delta));
```

Balls should do more than that. The ball velocity should be updated to incorporate drag and gravity; the color of the ball should be updated if needed; and if the ball flies outside the screen, it should be reset to its original position. You could simply copy the `update` method from the previous version of the `Ball` class so that it replaces the `update` method of `ThreeColorGameObject`. A slightly nicer way to do it is to define the `update` method in the `Ball` class but reuse the original `update` method from `ThreeColorGameObject`. This can be done by using the `call` method in a way very similar to how you used it to call the constructor of the superclass. Here is the new version of the `Ball.update` method:

```
Ball.prototype.update = function (delta) {
    ThreeColorGameObject.prototype.update.call(this, delta);
    if (this.shooting) {
        this.velocity.x *= 0.99;
        this.velocity.y += 6;
    }
}
```

```
else {
    this.color = Game.gameWorld.cannon.color;
    this.position = Game.gameWorld.cannon.ballPosition
        .subtractFrom(this.center);
}
if (Game.gameWorld.isOutsideWorld(this.position))
    this.reset();
};
```

Look at the first instruction in this method. You're accessing the prototype object of ThreeColorGameObject, which contains an update function. You call this update function while passing the this object, so the Ball object is updated, but according to the update method defined in ThreeColorGameObject. Finally, you pass the delta parameter to that call. The nice thing is that this approach allows you to separate different parts of (in this case) the updating process. Any game object with a position and velocity will need to update its position based on its velocity in each iteration of the game loop. You define this behavior in the update method of ThreeColorGameObject so you can reuse it for any class that inherits from ThreeColorGameObject!

Polymorphism

Because of the inheritance mechanism, you don't always have to know to what type of object a variable is pointing to. Consider the following declaration and initialization:

```
var someKindOfGameObject = new Cannon();
```

And somewhere else in the code, you do this:

```
someKindOfGameObject.update(delta);
```

Now suppose you change the declaration and initialization, as follows:

```
var someKindOfGameObject = new Ball();
```

Do you need to change the call to the update method? No, you don't, because the way the game-loop methods are being called is defined in the ThreeColorGameObject class. When you call the update method on the someKindOfGameObject variable, it doesn't matter which game object it actually refers to. The only thing that is important is that the update method is defined and that it expects a single parameter: the time passed since the last update call. Because the interpreter keeps track of which object it is, the right version of the update method is called automatically.

This effect is called *polymorphism*, and it comes in very handy sometimes. Polymorphism allows you to better separate code. Suppose a game company wants to release an extension of its game. For example, it might want to introduce a few new enemies, or skills that a player can learn. The company can provide these extensions as subclasses of generic Enemy and Skill classes. The actual game code will then use these objects without having to know which particular skill or enemy it's dealing with. It simply calls the methods that were defined in the generic classes.

Hierarchies of Classes

You've seen several examples in this chapter of classes inheriting from a base game-object class. A class should inherit from another class only if the relationship between these two classes can be described as "is a kind of." For example: a `Ball` is a kind of `ThreeColorGameObject`. In fact, the hierarchy doesn't end there. You could write another class that inherits from the `Ball` class, such as `BouncingBall`, which could be a special version of a standard ball that bounces off paint cans instead of only colliding with them. And you could make another class `BouncingElasticBall` that inherits from `BouncingBall`, which is a ball that deforms according to its elastic properties when it bounces against a paint can. Every time you inherit from a class, you get the data (encoded in member variables) and the behavior (encoded in methods and properties) from the base class for free.

Commercial games have a class hierarchy of different game objects with many different levels. Going back to the traffic-simulation example at the beginning of this chapter, you can imagine a very complicated hierarchy of all kinds of different vehicles. Figure 11-4 shows an example of such a hierarchy. The figure uses arrows to indicate an inheritance relation between classes.

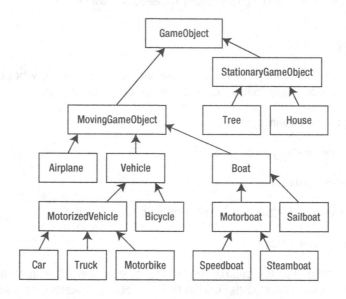

© Springer-Verlag Berlin Heidelberg 2013

Figure 11-4. A complex hierarchy of game objects in a traffic-simulation game

At the very base of the inheritance tree is a `GameObject` class. This class contains only very basic information such as the position or the velocity of the game object. For each subclass, new members (variables, methods, or properties) can be added, which are relevant for the particular class and its subclasses. For example, the variable `numberOfWheels` typically belongs in the `Vehicle` class and not in `MovingGameObject` (because boats don't have wheels). The variable `flightAltitude` belongs in the `Airplane` class, and the variable `bellIsWorking` belongs in the `Bicycle` class.

When you determine the way your classes are structured, you have to make many decisions. There isn't a single best hierarchy; and, depending on the application, one hierarchy might be more useful than another. For instance, this example first divides the `MovingGameObject` class according to the medium the object uses to displace itself: land, air, or water. After that, the classes are divided in different subclasses: motorized or not motorized. You could choose to do this the other way around. For some classes, it isn't entirely clear where in the hierarchy they belong: do you say that a motorbike is a special type of bike (one with a motor)? Or is it a special kind of motorized vehicle (one with only two wheels)?

What is important is that the relationship between the classes themselves is clear. A sailboat is a boat, but a boat isn't always a sailboat. A bicycle is a vehicle, but not every vehicle is a bicycle.

Values vs. References

Before you finish this chapter, let's see how objects and variables are dealt with in memory. When dealing with basic types such as numbers or Booleans, the variables are directly associated with a place in memory. For example, look at the following declaration and initialization:

```
var i = 12;
```

After this instruction has been executed, the memory looks as depicted in Figure 11-5.

Figure 11-5. Memory usage of a number variable

Now you can create a new variable j and store the value of variable i in that variable:

```
var j = i;
```

Figure 11-6 shows what the memory looks like after executing this instruction.

Figure 11-6. Memory usage after declaring and initializing two number variables

If you assign another value to the j variable, for example by executing the instruction j = 24, the resulting memory usage is shown in Figure 11-7.

Figure 11-7. Memory usage after changing the value of the j variable

Now let's look at what happens when you use variables of a more complicated type, such as the Cannon class. Consider the following code:

```
var cannon1 = new Cannon();
var cannon2 = cannon1;
```

Looking at the previous example using the number type, you would expect that there are now two Cannon objects in memory: one stored in the variable cannon1, and one stored in cannon2. However, this isn't the case! Actually, both cannon1 and cannon2 *refer to the same object*. After the first instruction (creating the Cannon object), the memory is shown in Figure 11-8.

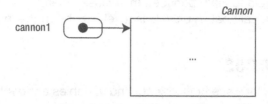

© Springer-Verlag Berlin Heidelberg 2013

Figure 11-8. A Cannon object in memory

Here, you see that there is a big difference between how basic types such as numbers and Booleans are represented in memory as opposed to more complicated types such as the Cannon class. In JavaScript, all objects that aren't primitive types, such as numbers, Booleans, and characters, are stored as *references* as opposed to values. This means a variable such as cannon1 doesn't directly contain the Cannon object, but it contains *a reference to it*. Figure 11-8 indicate that cannon1 is a reference by representing it as a block containing an arrow to an object. If you now declare the cannon2 variable and assign the value of cannon1 to it, you can see the new situation in Figure 11-9.

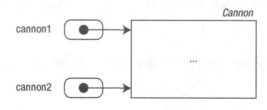

© Springer-Verlag Berlin Heidelberg 2013

Figure 11-9. Two variables that refer to the same object

The result is that if you change the color of the cannon as follows

```
cannon2.color = Color.red;
```

then the expression cannon1.color will be Color.red, because both cannon1 and cannon2 refer to the same object! This also has an effect on how objects are passed around in methods. For example, the constructor method of ThreeColorGameObject expects three sprites as a parameter. Because sprites aren't a basic type in JavaScript, you're actually passing references to these sprites. In theory, this means you could modify the sprites in the ThreeColorGameObject constructor. Passing basic types such as numbers as parameters to methods happens *by value*, so changing the value in the method has no effect. Consider the following function

```
function square(f) {
    f = f * f;
}
```

and now the following instructions:

```
var someNumber = 10;
square(someNumber);
```

After executing these instructions, the value of someNumber still is 10 (and not 100). Why is this? Because when the square function is called, the number parameter is passed *by value*. The variable f is a local variable in the method that initially contains the value of the someNumber variable. In the method, the local variable f is changed to contain f * f, but this doesn't change the someNumber variable, because it's another location in memory. Because non-primitive objects are passed by *reference*, the following example will result in a changed value of the object passed as a parameter:

```
function square(obj) {
    obj.f = obj.f * obj.f;
}

var myObject = { f : 10 };
square(myObject);
// myObject.f now contains the value 100.
```

Whenever a JavaScript script is running, there are a number of references and values in memory. For example, if you look at Figures 11-2 and 11-3, you see that the Ball objects contain both values and references to other objects (such as Vector2 objects or Image objects).

Null and Undefined

Whenever you declare a variable in JavaScript, initially its value is set to undefined:

```
var someVariable;
console.log(someVariable); // will print 'undefined'.
```

In JavaScript, you can also indicate that a variable is defined but currently doesn't refer to any object. This is done by using the null keyword:

```
var anotherCannon = null;
```

Because you haven't yet created an object (using the new keyword), the memory looks like what is depicted in Figure 11-10.

anotherCannon (null)

Figure 11-10. A variable pointing to null

So, indicating that a variable isn't yet pointing to anything is done by assigning null to it. It's even possible to check in a JavaScript program whether a variable is pointing to an object or not, like this:

```
if (anotherCannon === null)
    anotherCannon = new Cannon();
```

In this example, you check whether the variable is equal to null (not pointing to an object). If so, you create a Cannon instance using the new keyword, after which the situation in memory is changed again (see Figure 11-11).

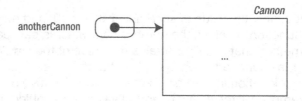

Figure 11-11. Final situation in memory

It's up to you to decide when you would like to use null and undefined. Not all programmers do this the same way. We suggest that you use undefined to indicate that a variable doesn't exist and null to indicate that the variable exists but doesn't yet refer to any object.

What You Have Learned

In this chapter, you have learned:

- How to use inheritance to structure related classes in a hierarchy
- How to override methods in a subclass to provide specific behavior for that class
- How to call methods from the superclass, such as the constructor method
- The meaning of null and undefined

12

Chapter

Finishing the Painter Game

In this chapter, you finish the Painter game by adding a few extra features such as motion effects, sounds, and music, and maintaining and displaying a score. Finally, you learn about characters and strings in a bit more detail.

Adding Motion Effects

In order to make the game more visually appealing, you can introduce a nice rotational effect in the movement of the paint cans to simulate the effect of wind and friction on the falling motion. The Painter10 program that belongs to this chapter is the final version of the game with this motion effect added to the cans. Adding such an effect isn't complicated. Thanks to the work you did in the previous chapter, only a single line needs to be added to the update method of the PaintCan class. Because PaintCan is a subclass of ThreeColorGameObject, it already has a rotation member variable, which is automatically taken into account when the sprite is drawn on the screen!

In order to achieve the motion effect, you use the Math.sin method. By letting the value depend on the current position of the can, you get different values depending on that position. You then use this value to apply a *rotation* on the sprite. This is the line of code you add to the PaintCan.update method:

```
this.rotation = Math.sin(this.position.y / 50) * 0.05;
```

This instruction uses the y-coordinate of the paint-can position to get different rotation values. Furthermore, you divide it by 50 to get a nice slow movement; and you multiply the outcome by 0.05 to reduce the amplitude of the sine so the rotation looks more or less realistic. If you like, you can try out different values and see how they affect the behavior of the paint cans.

CREATING SPRITES

Even if you're not an artist, it helps to be able to make simple sprites yourself. It enables you to quickly make a prototype of the game—and maybe find out there also is an artist inside you. To create sprites, you first need good tools. Most artists use a painting program like Adobe Photoshop or a vector drawing program like Adobe Illustrator, but others work with such simple tools as Microsoft Paint or the more extensive and free GIMP. Every tool requires practice. Work your way through some tutorials, and make sure you get some insight into the many different features. Often, the things you want can be achieved in an easy way.

Preferably, create very large images of your game objects and then scale them down to the required size. The advantages are that you can change the required size in your game later and that you get rid of aliasing effects due to images being represented by pixels. When scaling images, anti-aliasing techniques blend the colors so the image remains smooth. If you keep the outside of the game object in the image transparent, then, when you scale, the border pixels will automatically become partially transparent. Only if you want to create the classic pixel style should you create the sprites in the actual size required.

Finally, look around on the web. There are lots of sprites that you can use for free. Make sure to check the license terms so the pack of sprites you're using are legal for what you're building. You can then use them as a basis for your own sprites. But in the end, realize that the quality of your game increases significantly when you work with an experienced artist.

Adding Sounds and Music

Another way to make the game more enjoyable is to add some sound. This game uses both background music and sound effects. In order to make dealing with sounds a bit easier in JavaScript, you add a Sound class that allows you to play back and loop sounds. Here is the constructor of that class:

```
function Sound(sound, looping) {
    this.looping = typeof looping !== 'undefined' ? looping : false;
    this.snd = new Audio();
    if (this.snd.canPlayType("audio/ogg")) {
        this.snd.src = sound + ".ogg";
    } else if (this.snd.canPlayType("audio/mpeg")) {
        this.snd.src = sound + ".mp3";
    } else // we cannot play audio in this browser
        this.snd = null;
}
```

Because not all browsers are capable of playing all different kinds of music, you added an if instruction that loads different sound types depending on which type the browser can play. Similar to creating Image objects (for representing sprites), you create an Audio object and initialize its source to the sound file that needs to be loaded. In addition to the sound file, you add a looping variable that indicates whether the sound should be looped. In general, background music should be looped; sound effects (such as firing a paint ball) shouldn't.

In addition to the constructor, you add a method called play. In this method, you load the sound, and you set an attribute called autoplay to true. The result of this is that the sound will immediately start playing after it's loaded. If the sound doesn't need to loop, you're done and can return from the method. If you do require the sound to loop, you need to reload and play the sound again after it has finished playing. The Audio type allows you to attach functions to so-called *events*. When an event occurs, the function you attached is executed. Examples are the event that the audio has started playing, or the event that the audio has finished playing.

This book uses events and event handling very little. A number of JavaScript concepts rely on them, though. For example, keyboard presses and mouse actions all generate events that you should handle in your games. In this case, you want to execute a function when the audio has finished playing. Here is the complete play method:

```
Sound.prototype.play = function () {
    if (this.snd === null)
        return;
    this.snd.load();
    this.snd.autoplay = true;
    if (!this.looping)
        return;
    this.snd.addEventListener('ended', function () {
        this.load();
        this.autoplay = true;
    }, false);
};
```

Finally, you add a property to change the volume of a sound that is playing. This is particularly useful, because generally you want sound effects to be louder than background music. In some games, these volumes can be changed by the player (later in the book, you see how to do that). Whenever you introduce sound in your game, make sure to always provide volume or at least mute controls. Games without the ability to mute sounds will suffer the wrath of annoyed users via reviews! Here is the volume property, which is straightforward:

```
Object.defineProperty(Sound.prototype, "volume",
    {
        get: function () {
            return this.snd.volume;
        },
        set: function (value) {
            this.snd.volume = value;
        }
    });
```

In Painter.js, the file where you load all the assets, you load sounds and store them in a variable, just as you did for sprites:

```
var sounds = {};
```

And here is how you load the relevant sounds, using the Sound class that you just created:

```
var loadSound = function (sound, looping) {
    return new Sound("../../assets/Painter/sounds/" + sound, looping);
};

sounds.music = loadSound("snd_music");
sounds.collect_points = loadSound("snd_collect_points");
sounds.shoot_paint = loadSound("snd_shoot_paint");
```

Now it's very easy to play sounds during the game. For example, when the game is initialized, you begin playing the background music at a low volume, as follows:

```
sounds.music.volume = 0.3;
sounds.music.play();
```

You also want to play sound effects. For example, when the player shoots a ball, they want to hear it! So, you play this sound effect when they start shooting the ball. This is dealt with in the handleInput method of the Ball class:

```
Ball.prototype.handleInput = function (delta) {
    if (Mouse.leftPressed && !this.shooting) {
        this.shooting = true;
        this.velocity = Mouse.position.subtract(this.position)
            .multiplyWith(1.2);
        sounds.shoot_paint.play();
    }
};
```

Similarly, you also play a sound when a paint can of the correct color falls out of the screen.

Maintaining a Score

Scores are often a very effective way to motivate players to continue playing. *High scores* work especially well in that regard, because they introduce a competitive factor into the game: you want to be better than AAA or XYZ (many early arcade games allowed only three characters for each name in the high-score list, leading to very imaginative names). High scores are so motivating that third-party systems exist to incorporate them into games. These systems let users compare themselves against thousands of other players around the world. In the Painter game, you keep it simple and add a member variable score to the PainterGameWorld class in which to store the current score:

```
function PainterGameWorld() {
    this.cannon = new Cannon();
    this.ball = new Ball();
    this.can1 = new PaintCan(450, Color.red);
    this.can2 = new PaintCan(575, Color.green);
    this.can3 = new PaintCan(700, Color.blue);
    this.score = 0;
    this.lives = 5;
}
```

The player starts with a score of zero. Each time a paint can falls outside the screen, the score is updated. If a can of the correct color falls out of the screen, 10 points are added to the score. If a can isn't the right color, the player loses a life.

The score is a part of what is called the *economy* of a game. The game's economy basically describes the different costs and merits in the game and how they interact. When you make your own game, it's always useful to think about its economy. What do things cost, and what are the gains of executing different actions as a player? And are these two things in balance with each other?

You update the score in the `PaintCan` class, where you can check whether the can falls outside the screen. If so, you check whether it has the right color and update the score and the number of player lives accordingly. Then you move the `PaintCan` object to the top so that it can fall again:

```
if (Game.gameWorld.isOutsideWorld(this.position)) {
    if (this.color === this.targetColor) {
        Game.gameWorld.score += 10;
        sounds.collect_points.play();
    }
    else
        Game.gameWorld.lives -= 1;
    this.moveToTop();
}
```

Finally, whenever a can of the right color falls off the screen, you play a sound.

A More Complete Canvas2D Class

In addition to drawing the sprites on the screen, you also want to draw the current score on the screen (otherwise it wouldn't make much sense to maintain it). Until now, you've only drawn images on the canvas. The HTML5 canvas element also allows text to be drawn on it. In order to draw text, you extend the `Canvas2D_Singleton` class.

While you're modifying the canvas drawing class, you want to do something else as well. Now that you've organized all your variables into objects, which can be created using classes, which can inherit from other classes, this is a good moment to think about what information is supposed to be changed where. For example, you probably only want to change the `canvas` and `canvasContext` variables in the `Canvas2D_Singleton` class. You don't need to access these variables in, for instance, the `Cannon` class. In the `Cannon` class, you only want to use the high-level behavior that is provided through the methods in the canvas drawing class.

Unfortunately, there is no way in JavaScript to directly control access to variables. An evil programmer could write the following line of code somewhere in their program:

```
Canvas2D.canvas = null;
```

After executing this line of code, nothing can be drawn on the screen! Of course, no sane programmer would write something like that on purpose, but it's a good idea to be as clear as possible to users of your classes about what data they're supposed to change and what data is internal to the class and shouldn't be modified. One way to do this is to add something to the name of any variable that is supposed to be internal. This book adds an underscore to all variables that are internal and shouldn't be changed outside the class they're a member of. For example, here is the modified constructor of the `Canvas2D_Singleton` class that follows this rule:

```
function Canvas2D_Singleton() {
    this._canvas = null;
    this._canvasContext = null;
}
```

You also add a new method to the class, `drawText`, which can be used to draw text on the screen at a certain position. The `drawText` method is very similar to the `drawImage` method. In both cases, you use the canvas context to perform a transformation before drawing the text. This allows you to draw text at any desired position on the canvas. Furthermore, you can change the color of the text and the text alignment (left, center, or right). Look at the Painter10 example belonging to this chapter to see the body of this method.

Drawing text on the screen is now easy using this method. For example, this draws some green text at upper left on the screen:

```
Canvas2D.drawText("Hello, how are you doing?", Vector2.zero, Color.green);
```

Characters and Strings

A sequence of characters is called a *string* in most programming languages, including JavaScript. Just like numbers or Booleans, strings are primitive types in JavaScript. Strings are also *immutable*. This means once a string is created, it can't be changed. Of course, it's still possible to *replace* the string with another string. For example:

```
var name = "Patrick";
name = "Arjan";
```

In JavaScript, strings are delimited by single or double quote characters. If you start a string with a double quote, it should end with a double quote. So, this isn't allowed:

```
var country = 'The Netherlands";
```

When you assign a string to a variable, the string is called a *constant*. In addition to string values, constant values can be numbers, Boolean values, `undefined`, or `null`, as expressed in the syntax diagram in Figure 12-1.

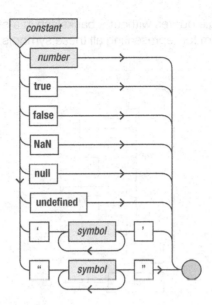

Figure 12-1. The syntax diagram for constant values

Using Single and Double Quotes

When using string values and combining them with other variables, you have to be careful which type of quotes you use (if any). If you forget the quotes, you're not writing text or characters anymore, but a piece of a JavaScript program! There is a big difference between

- The string "hello" and the variable name hello
- The string '123' and the value 123
- The string value '+' and the operator +

Special Characters

Special characters, simply because they're *special*, are not always easy to indicate using a single character between quotes. So, a number of special symbols have special notations using the backslash symbol, as follows:

- '\n' for the end-of-line symbol
- '\t' for the tabulation symbol

This introduces a new problem: how to indicate the backslash character itself. The backslash character is indicated using the *double backslash*. In a similar way, the backslash symbol is used to represent the character for the single and double quotes themselves:

- '\\' for the backslash symbol
- '\'' or "'" for the single quote character
- "\"" or '"' for the double quote character

As you can see, you may use single quotes without a backslash in a string delimited by double quotes, and vice versa. The syntax diagram for representing all these symbols is given in Figure 12-2.

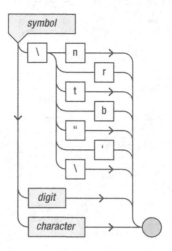

Figure 12-2. The syntax diagram for symbols

String Operations

In the Painter game, you use string values in combination with the drawText method to draw text of a certain color in a desired font somewhere on the screen. In this case, you want to write the current score at upper left on the screen. The score is maintained in a member variable called score. This variable is increased or decreased in the update method of PaintCan. How can you construct the text that should be printed on the screen, given that part of this text (the score) is changing all the time? The solution is called *string concatenation*, which means gluing one piece of text after another. In JavaScript (and in many other programming languages), this is done using the plus sign. For example, the expression "Hi, my name is " + "Arjan" results in the string "Hi, my name is Arjan". In this case, you concatenate two pieces of text. It's also possible to concatenate a piece of text and a number. For example, the expression "Score: " + 200 results in the string "Score: 200". Instead of using a constant, you can use a variable. So if the variable score contains the value 175, then the expression "Score: " + score evaluates to "Score: 175". By writing this expression as a parameter of the drawText method, you always draw the current score on the screen. The final call to the drawText method then becomes (see the PainterGameWorld class)

```
Canvas2D.drawText("Score: " + this.score, new Vector2(20, 22), Color.white);
```

Watch out: concatenation only makes sense when you're dealing with text. For example, it isn't possible to "concatenate" two numbers: the expression 1 + 2 results in 3, not 12. Of course, you can concatenate numbers *represented as text*: "1" + "2" results in "12". Making the distinction between text and numbers is done by using single or double quotes.

In fact, what is secretly done in the expression "Score: " + 200 is a *type conversion* or *cast*. The numerical value 200 is automatically cast to the string "200" before being concatenated to the other string.

If you want to convert a string value to a numerical value, things get a bit more complicated. This isn't an easy operation for the interpreter to perform, because not all strings can be converted to a numerical value. For this, JavaScript has a few useful built-in functions. For example, this is how you can transform a string into an integer number:

```
var x = parseInt("10");
```

If the string passed as a parameter isn't a whole number, the result of the `parseInt` function is the integer portion of the number:

```
var y = parseInt("3.14"); // y will contain the value 3
```

To parse numbers with decimals, JavaScript has the `parseFloat` function:

```
y = parseFloat("3.14"); // y will contain the value 3.14
```

If the string doesn't contain a valid number, the result of trying to parse it using one of these two functions is the constant NaN (not a number; see also Figure 12-1).

A Few Final Remarks

Congratulations—you've completed your first game! Figure 12-3 contains a screenshot of the final game. While developing this game, you've learned about a lot of important concepts. In the next game, you expand on the work you've already done. In the meantime, don't forget to play the game! You'll notice that it becomes really difficult after a few minutes, because the paint cans come down faster and faster.

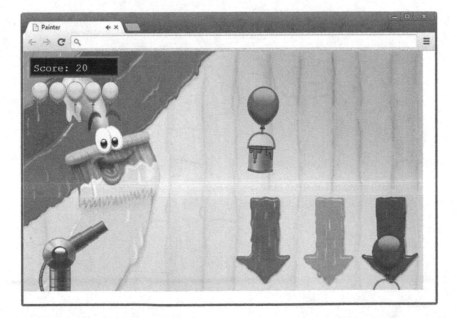

Figure 12-3. Screenshot of the final version of Painter

WHO PLAYS GAMES?

You might think that games are primarily played by young males, but that isn't true at all. A huge percentage of people play games. In 2013 in the United States there were 183 million active gamers, which is more than half the total population (including babies). They play games on many different devices. 36% of the games play games on their smart phone and 25% play games on their wireless device (source: the Entertainment Software Association (ESA), 2013).

If you develop a game, you'd better first think about the audience you want for it. Games for young kids are different from games for middle-aged women. The games should have different kinds of gameplay, different visual styles, and different goals.

Although console games tend to take place in large 3D worlds, casual games on websites and mobile devices are often 2D and are limited in size. Also, console games are designed such that they can (and need to be) played for hours and hours, whereas casual games are often designed to be playable in sessions of just a few minutes. There are also many types of *serious games*, which are games that are used to train of professionals such as firefighters, mayors, and doctors.

Realize that the games you like aren't necessarily the games your target audience likes.

What You Have Learned

In this chapter, you have learned:

- How to add music and sound effects to your game
- How to maintain and display a score
- How to use strings to represent and work with text

Part III

Jewel Jam

Jewel Jam is a puzzle game in which you try to find combinations of jewels (see Figure III-1). Watch out, though: the jewel cart is slowly moving away. Once this cart is off the screen, your time is up! The playing board consists of ten rows and five columns. The jewels on the playing field differ according to three properties: color (red, blue, or yellow), shape (diamond, sphere, or ellipse), and number (one, two, or three jewels).

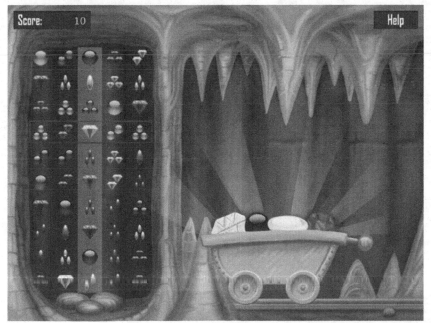

© Springer-Verlag Berlin Heidelberg 2013

Figure III-1. The Jewel Jam game

The player can shift rows to the left or to the right using the mouse or the touch screen (if the game is played on a phone or a tablet). The goal is to find matching combinations of three adjacent jewels in the middle column. A combination of three jewels is valid if each of the properties is either the same for all objects or different for all objects. For example, a yellow single-diamond object, a blue single-diamond object, and a red single-diamond object form a valid combination, because the color is different for each object and the shape and number are the same for all objects. A yellow sphere object, a yellow double-diamond object, and a yellow triple-ellipse object also form a valid combination, because all three objects have the same color, a different shape, and a different number. The combination yellow diamond, red double sphere, and blue double ellipse is not valid, because although the color and the shape are different for each object, the number for the diamond object is different from the other two. The combination yellow diamond, red double sphere, and blue triple ellipse, on the other hand, is valid.

Once the player has found a valid combination by shifting the rows around, they press the space bar, the jewels that form the combination disappear, the remaining jewels fall to fill the empty slots, and three new jewels fall from the top of the screen. When there are two or three combinations at the same time in the middle column when the player presses the space bar, extra points are awarded and an overlay is shown on the screen to indicate that a double or triple combination was made.

In the following chapters, you develop this game. If you want to play the complete version to get a feel for how the game works, run the example belonging to Chapter 17!

Chapter 13

Adapting to Different Devices

This chapter deals with adapting games to different devices. Until now, you've been developing examples that will only work on devices that have a keyboard and a mouse, such as laptop or desktop machines. One of the nice things about JavaScript programs is that they also run on smartphones and tablets, which currently is a booming market. Making your games run on such platforms will result in a lot of extra players for your games. In order to play games on smartphones or tablets, you need to handle touch input, in a way very similar to dealing with keyboard and mouse input.

Another thing you need to take care of is the variety of screen sizes on the devices for which you want to make games. This chapter shows you how to create games that automatically adapt to any screen size, whether it's a huge 24-inch desktop monitor or a tiny smartphone screen.

Allowing the Canvas to Change Size

The first thing you need to do to allow for automatic screen-size adaptation is place the canvas element in such a way that the canvas automatically scales to the size of the page. Once that is done, you can retrieve the size of the canvas, compare it with the actual size of the game screen, and perform a scaling operation. In Painter, this is how you placed the canvas element on the HTML page:

```
<div id="gameArea">
    <canvas id="mycanvas" width="800" height="480"> </canvas>
</div>
```

As you can see, you define a div element called gameArea. In this div element is a single canvas element. In order to let the canvas element scale automatically, you need to set its width and height to 100% of the browser window width and height. That way, when the browser window changes size, the canvas element is resized as well. Furthermore, you make the page you're displaying as clean as possible (no margins). In order to do this, you use *style sheets*. Style sheets are a nice way to define what elements of a web page should look like. Different HTML pages can then use the same style sheet to ensure a uniform design. This is the style sheet for the example games:

```
html, body {
    margin: 0;
}
#gameArea {
    position: absolute;
}

#mycanvas {
    position: absolute;
    width: 100%;
    height: 100%;
}
```

Discussing what is possible with style sheets in depth isn't in the scope of this book, but if you want to learn more about that, you can read either *Beginning CSS Web Development* (Apress, 2006) by Simon Collision or *HTML and CSS* by Jon Ducket (Wiley, 2011).

In this particular example, you do a couple of things. First, you define that the html and body elements don't have a margin. That way, the canvas can fully fill the screen if you want it to. Then, you define that things that are called gameArea and mycanvas are positioned absolutely on the page. This way, these elements are always placed at their desired position, regardless of what other elements are in the HTML page. Finally, you indicate that mycanvas has a width and height of 100% of the screen. As a result, the canvas now fills the entire display of the browser, and it automatically scales to different resolutions.

> **Note**   Having the canvas fill the entire browser display isn't necessarily the best solution for all setups. In some cases, if might be hard for users to interact with elements on the very edge of their browser window without accidentally clicking outside the browser. In those cases, you could consider adding a margin.

Setting the Native Game Size

Now that the canvas automatically scales to the size of the browser window, you no longer can use the canvas resolution as the native game resolution. If you did that, you would have to recalculate all the game object positions whenever the canvas was resized. A better way to do this is to define a native game size. Then, when you draw the objects, you scale their position and size such that it matches the actual canvas size.

The first step is being able to indicate what the native game size should be. You can do this when you call the Game.start method. You extend this method such that it accepts two extra parameters to define the width and height of the game, and then call it from the HTML page:

```
Game.start('gameArea', 'mycanvas', 1440, 1080);
```

The native resolution of the Jewel Jam game is big (1440 × 1080), so scaling is definitely necessary if you want the game to run properly on all smartphones and tablets. You also pass along the name of the div element containing the canvas. The reason is that you change the margin of this div so the game is displayed nicely in the middle of the screen, in case the screen ratio differs from the game-size ratio (see Figure 13-1).

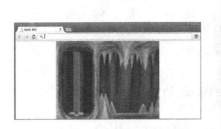
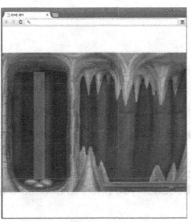
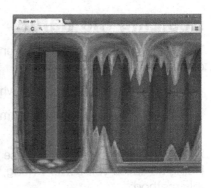

Figure 13-1. You have to make sure the game screen is always nicely displayed in the middle of the browser window!

In the Game.start method, you store the size of the game in a member variable _size. You also define a read-only property size to access that member variable. This way, you indicate to the users of the Game class that they aren't supposed to change the native size of the game while the game is running. You pass along the identifiers for the game area and the canvas to the Canvas2D.initialize method, because you have to do the legwork of scaling and positioning the sprites in the methods belonging to Canvas2D. This is the complete Game.start method:

```
Game_Singleton.prototype.start = function (divName, canvasName, x, y) {
    this._size = new Vector2(x, y);
    Canvas2D.initialize(divName, canvasName);
    this.loadAssets();
    this.assetLoadingLoop();
};
```

In Canvas2D, you store a reference to the div element so you can use that to change margins later. You retrieve that element the same way you retrieved the canvas element:

```
this._canvas = document.getElementById(canvasName);
this._div = document.getElementById(divName);
```

You need to calculate the scaling factor to apply every time the browser window is resized. You can do this by attaching an event-handler function, as follows:

```
window.onresize = Canvas2D_Singleton.prototype.resize;
```

Now, whenever the window is resized, the `resize` method is called. Finally, you explicitly call the `resize` method:

```
this.resize();
```

By calling this method, the right scale is calculated according to the browser window size when the game is started.

Resizing the Game

The `resize` method is called whenever the window is resized. When that happens, you need to calculate two things:

- The desired scale at which the sprites should be drawn
- The margins of the game area, in order to draw the game nicely in the middle of the browser window

Before you start calculating these things, store the `canvas` and `div` elements in two local variables. Doing so saves you some writing, because you need to access these elements quite often in this method:

```
var gameCanvas = Canvas2D._canvas;
var gameArea = Canvas2D._div;
```

Now you calculate the ratio of the native game size:

```
var widthToHeight = Game.size.x / Game.size.y;
```

The next step is calculating the browser window ratio. You first retrieve the size of the browser window by accessing the `innerWidth` and `innerHeight` variables. Once you have those, you can calculate the browser window ratio:

```
var newWidth = window.innerWidth;
var newHeight = window.innerHeight;
var newWidthToHeight = newWidth / newHeight;
```

You don't want the game screen to look squished or elongated, so you have to make sure the ratio doesn't change when the window size is changed. When the new ratio is bigger than the native game-size ratio, it means the browser window is too wide. Therefore, you need to recalculate the width in order to correct the ratio, as follows:

```
if (newWidthToHeight > widthToHeight) {
    newWidth = newHeight * widthToHeight;
}
```

The other case is that the new ratio is smaller, meaning the browser window is too high. In that case, you need to recalculate the height:

```
newHeight = newWidth / widthToHeight;
```

Now that you've calculated the correct width and height, you first change gameArea div so it has this height and width. You do that as follows, simply by editing the style of the element:

```
gameArea.style.width = newWidth + 'px';
gameArea.style.height = newHeight + 'px';
```

In order to display the gameArea element in the middle of the screen, you also define margins, as follows:

```
gameArea.style.marginTop = (window.innerHeight - newHeight) / 2 + 'px';
gameArea.style.marginLeft = (window.innerWidth - newWidth) / 2 + 'px';
gameArea.style.marginBottom = (window.innerHeight - newHeight) / 2 + 'px';
gameArea.style.marginRight = (window.innerWidth - newWidth) / 2 + 'px';
```

You divide the difference between the new width and height and the actual width and height by 2 and set those values as the margins. For example, if the desired game screen width is 800 but the window is actually 900 pixels wide, you create a margin of 50 pixels on each side so that the element is drawn in the middle of the screen. Finally, you change the size of the canvas so that it has the desired width and height (and thus the correct ratio):

```
gameCanvas.width = newWidth;
gameCanvas.height = newHeight;
```

The scale at which the sprites should be drawn can now be calculated easily. You define a property that does this for you:

```
Object.defineProperty(Canvas2D_Singleton.prototype, "scale",
    {
        get: function () {
            return new Vector2(this._canvas.width / Game.size.x,
                this._canvas.height / Game.size.y);
        }
    });
```

When you draw an image, you simply apply this scale before you perform the drawing operation. This is done by adding a few lines of code to the Canvas2D.drawImage method—one line for retrieving the scale, and one for applying it:

```
var canvasScale = this.scale;
this._canvasContext.scale(canvasScale.x, canvasScale.y);
```

Do the same thing in the Canvas2D.drawText method. For the complete code, look at the *JewelJam1* example belonging to this chapter.

Redesigning Mouse-Input Handling

After doing all this, you've moved around the div and canvas elements quite a bit. In the Painter game, you assumed that the canvas was always drawn at top left on the screen. Here, this is no longer the case. If you want to detect mouse clicks on the screen, you need to take the position of the canvas on the screen into account when calculating the local position of the mouse on the game screen. Furthermore, because you applied a scale, you also need to scale the mouse position accordingly.

This is a good opportunity to have another look at the way the input-handling classes Mouse and Keyboard are designed. One thing you never properly implemented was dealing with keyboard or mouse-button up and down versus keyboard or mouse button *presses*. Furthermore, in the Mouse class, you only considered left button presses; and in the Keyboard class, only a single key could be pressed at the same time. You can use the power of object-oriented programming through JavaScript's prototype system to design a better solution.

The first step is creating a simple class that can store the state of a button (regardless of whether it's a key or a mouse button). Let's call this class ButtonState. The ButtonState class is very simple and only has two (boolean) member variables: one to indicate if the button is down, and another to indicate if the button is pressed. Here is the complete class:

```
function ButtonState() {
    this.down = false;
    this.pressed = false;
}
```

Now you use ButtonState instances in the Mouse class to represent the states of the left, middle, and right mouse buttons. This is what the new constructor of Mouse looks like:

```
function Mouse_Singleton() {
    this._position = Vector2.zero;
    this._left = new ButtonState();
    this._middle = new ButtonState();
    this._right = new ButtonState();
    document.onmousemove = handleMouseMove;
    document.onmousedown = handleMouseDown;
    document.onmouseup = handleMouseUp;
}
```

As you can see, you have member variables for the buttons next to the member variables associated with each position. You add read-only properties to access these variables. For example, if you want to check whether the middle mouse button is down, you can do that with the following simple line of code:

```
if (Mouse.middle.down)
    // do something
```

In the event-handler functions, you're changing the values of the member variables. In the handleMouseMove event-handler function, you have to calculate the mouse position. This is also the place where you make sure the mouse position is scaled and moved according to the scale and offset applied to the canvas. Here is the complete handleMouseMove function:

```
function handleMouseMove(evt) {
    var canvasScale = Canvas2D.scale;
    var canvasOffset = Canvas2D.offset;
    var mx = (evt.pageX - canvasOffset.x) / canvasScale.x;
    var my = (evt.pageY - canvasOffset.y) / canvasScale.y;
    Mouse._position = new Vector2(mx, my);
}
```

Now, whenever the mouse is moved, the mouse position is calculated correctly. The next thing you need to do is handle mouse-button down and up events. A mouse button is pressed only if the button is currently down when it wasn't in the previous game loop iteration. For the left mouse button, here is how you express this:

```
if (evt.which === 1) {
    if (!Mouse._left.down)
        Mouse._left.pressed = true;
    Mouse._left.down = true;
}
```

The evt.which value indicates whether you're dealing with the left (1), middle (2), or right (3) mouse button. Have a look at the *JewelJam1* example for the complete handleMouseDown event-handler function. In the handleMouseUp event handler, you set the down variable to false again. Here is the complete function:

```
function handleMouseUp(evt) {
    handleMouseMove(evt);

    if (evt.which === 1)
        Mouse._left.down = false;
    else if (evt.which === 2)
        Mouse._middle.down = false;
    else if (evt.which === 3)
        Mouse._right.down = false;
}
```

You can see that you call the handleMouseMove function here as well. This is done to make sure the mouse position is available when you press a mouse button. If you omit this line, and the player starts the game and presses a mouse button without having moved the mouse, the game will try to handle a mouse-button press without having position information. This is why you call the handleMouseMove function in both the handleMouseDown and handleMouseUp functions (although probably the latter isn't required).

Finally, at the end of each game-loop iteration, the Mouse object is reset. The only thing you need to do here is set the pressed variables to false again:

```
Mouse_Singleton.prototype.reset = function () {
    this._left.pressed = false;
    this._middle.pressed = false;
    this._right.pressed = false;
};
```

By setting the pressed variables to false after each game-loop iteration, you make sure a mouse or key press is handled only once.

Arrays

You can also redesign keyboard input handling now that you have this ButtonState class—but before you do that, let's introduce another concept you need, called an *array*. An array is basically a numbered list. Have a look at the following examples:

```
var emptyArray = [];
var intArray = [4, 8, 15, 16, 23, 42];
```

Here you see two declarations and initializations of array variables. The first declaration is an empty array (no elements). The second variable, intArray, refers to an array of length 6. You can access the elements in the array by their index, where the first element in the array has index 0:

```
var v = intArray[0]; // contains the value 4
var v2 = intArray[4]; // contains the value 23
```

You use square brackets to access elements in the array. You can also modify the values in the array using the same square brackets:

```
intArray[1] = 13; // intArray now is [4, 13, 15, 16, 23, 42]
```

It's also possible to add an element to the array:

```
intArray.push(-3); // intArray now is [4, 13, 15, 16, 23, 42, -3]
```

Finally, each array has a length variable that you can access to retrieve the length:

```
var l = intArray.length; // contains the value 7
```

You can use arrays in combination with for loops to do interesting things. Here's an example:

```
for (var i = 0; i < intArray.length; i++) {
    intArray[i] += 10;
}
```

This walks through all the elements in the array and adds 10 to each. So, after this code is executed, `intArray` refers to [14, 23, 25, 26, 33, 52, 7].

In addition to initializing an array in the way you just saw, there is another way to create an array, as follows:

```
var anotherArray = new Array(3);
```

This example creates an array of size 3, which you can then fill:

```
anotherArray[0] = "hello";
```

You can even create multidimensional arrays in JavaScript. For example:

```
var tictactoe = new Array(3);
tictactoe[0] = ['x', 'o', ' '];
tictactoe[1] = [' ', 'x', 'o'];
tictactoe[2] = [' ', 'o', 'x'];
```

So, elements of arrays can also be arrays. These kinds of grid structures are especially useful when representing a playing field in games such as chess. Because arrays are stored as references (just like instances of classes), representing a grid using such a two-dimensional array is computationally not very efficient. There is a simple way to represent a grid using a one-dimensional array, as follows:

```
var rows = 10, cols = 15;
var myGrid = new Array(rows * cols);
```

Accessing the element at row i and column j can now be done as follows:

```
var elem = myGrid[i * cols + j];
```

Figure 13-2 shows another part of the expression syntax diagram, with the syntax for specifying an array. The next chapter talks more in detail about using arrays to represent structures and grids in games.

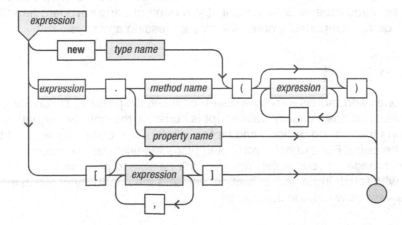

Figure 13-2. Partial syntax diagram of expressions

Handling Keyboard Input Using Arrays

Let's see how you can use arrays to deal with keypresses more efficiently. Because you now have the ButtonState class, you can use it to handle keyboard input as well and store a ButtonState instance for each key state. So, in the constructor of Keyboard_Singleton, create an array that contains all the possible key states, as follows:

```
this._keyStates = [];
for (var i = 0; i < 256; ++i)
    this._keyStates.push(new ButtonState());
```

Now you can set the down status of a key whenever a key down is detected, as follows:

```
function handleKeyDown(evt) {
    var code = evt.keyCode;
    if (code < 0 || code > 255)
        return;
    if (!Keyboard._keyStates[code].down)
        Keyboard._keyStates[code].pressed = true;
    Keyboard._keyStates[code].down = true;
}
```

As you can see, you handle key downs and keypresses just as you did in the case of the mouse buttons. The following two methods added to Keyboard_Singleton make detecting whether a key is pressed or down very easy:

```
Keyboard_Singleton.prototype.pressed = function (key) {
    return this._keyStates[key].pressed;
};
Keyboard_Singleton.prototype.down = function (key) {
    return this._keyStates[key].down;
};
```

You don't need the keyboard in the *JewelJam* game, because all interaction takes place with the mouse or the touch screen. A later example uses the keyboard once more. This also means you can basically ignore any keyboard events that occur. If you don't put any keyboard handling in the game-loop methods, the game completely ignores the player pressing any keys.

Touchscreen Input

Because smartphones and tablets also have a web browser, it's possible to run JavaScript applications on these devices. Actually, JavaScript is currently the only cross-platform way to develop applications that run on desktop and laptop machines, mobile phones, and tablets without having to rewrite the code. For example, you could place the final Painter example on a server and then access the web page on your tablet. You wouldn't be able to play the game, though, because you haven't dealt with touch input. In this section, you add the capability of touch input to games. Fortunately, this is very easy to do in JavaScript!

Before you can start writing JavaScript code, you need to take care of a few things in the HTML page. The reason is that tablets and smartphone devices define default touch behavior on web pages, such as the ability to scroll or zoom in a web page. Those interactions would interfere with playing the game, so you want to switch them off. This can be done in the header of the HTML file by adding the following tag to the header:

```
<meta name="viewport" content="width=device-width, initial-scale=1.0, user-scalable=no">
```

The *viewport* in HTML defines the section of the page that is in view. For example, when you navigate to a page and it zooms in automatically on one portion, this is done by modifying the size of the viewport. In the meta tag, you can define the properties of the viewport. This example tells the browser three things: the width of the viewport is the same as the width of the device, the scale of the page is 1 when the page is first viewed, and the user can't scale the page. As a result, all touch interactions to change the positioning or scaling of the HTML page are switched off.

Now you can start writing the JavaScript code to handle touch events. The way touch input works in JavaScript is that every time the user touches the screen, a touchstart event is generated, and a unique identifier is assigned to that touch. When the user touches the screen with another finger, another touchstart event occurs with a new, unique identifier. When the user moves a finger on the screen, a touchmove event is generated, and the unique identifier of the finger that is moving can be obtained from the event. Similarly, when the user stops touching the screen, a touchend event is generated, and again the identifier of the finger that has stopped touching the screen can be retrieved from the event.

To handle touches, create a class Touch_Singleton and the associated single instance Touch, similar to the way you created the Keyboard and Mouse objects. In the constructor of the class, you create an array where you store each touch and the related information. In addition, you store whether each touch is a press or not. A touch press means in the previous game-loop iteration the finger was not touching the screen, but in the current iteration it is. Furthermore, you have to attach the event-handler functions. Here is the complete constructor method:

```
function Touch_Singleton() {
    this._touches = [];
    this._touchPresses = [];
    document.addEventListener('touchstart', handleTouchStart, false);
    document.addEventListener('touchend', handleTouchEnd, false);
    document.addEventListener('touchcancel', handleTouchEnd, false);
    document.addEventListener('touchleave', handleTouchEnd, false);
    document.body.addEventListener('touchmove', handleTouchMove, false);
}
```

Dealing with touches is relatively new for browsers (as opposed to keyboard and mouse input). As a result, not all browsers use the same terminology. This is why you need to add event listeners for different varieties of touchend events. However, in the end, you deal with three types of events: touchstart, touchmove, and touchend. Each of them gets its own event-handler function.

When a user starts touching the screen, the handleTouchStart function is called. In that function, you simply store the touch event in the _touches array so you can retrieve the data later if needed. However, it's possible that the user may start touching the screen with multiple fingers at the same time. Therefore, the event contains an array of new touches. You can access that array with the variable changedTouches. For each element in that array, you add the touch event data to the _touches array. Because these are new touches, you also add true values to the _touchPresses variable. This is the complete method:

```
function handleTouchStart(evt) {
    evt.preventDefault();
    var touches = evt.changedTouches;
    for (var i = 0; i < touches.length; i++) {
        Touch._touches.push(touches[i]);
        Touch._touchPresses.push(true);
    }
}
```

Note that the first instruction in this function is evt.preventDefault();. This method call makes sure the touch event isn't used for default behavior (such as scrolling). You also place that instruction in the other touch event-handler functions. In handleTouchEnd, you need to remove the touch from both the arrays in your class. For that, you have to search through the array to find the data belonging to the particular touch ID. To make this a bit easier, you add a method getTouchIndexFromId to your class that finds the index in the array for you. Later, you can call this method to find where the touch is stored in the array, and then remove that element.

In the method, you walk through all the elements in the array using a for loop. When you find the touch that matches the identifier of the touch data you're looking for, you return that data. If the touch data can't be found, you return the value -1. Here is the complete method:

```
Touch_Singleton.prototype.getTouchIndexFromId = function (id) {
    for (var i = 0, l = this._touches.length; i < l; ++i) {
        if (this._touches[i].identifier === id)
            return i;
    }
    return -1;
};
```

In the handleTouchEnd function, you walk through the changedTouches variable with a for loop. For each touch, you find the corresponding index and remove the touch from the two arrays (_touches and _touchPresses). Removing an element from an array is done with the splice method. This method takes an index and a number: the index indicates where the element should be removed, and the second parameter indicates how many elements should be removed. Here is an example:

```
var myArray = [2, 56, 12, 4];
myArray.splice(0,1); // myArray now contains [56, 12, 4]
myArray.splice(1,2); // myArray now contains [56]
```

Here is the full handleTouchEnd function:

```
function handleTouchEnd(evt) {
    evt.preventDefault();
    var touches = evt.changedTouches;
    for (var i = 0; i < touches.length; ++i) {
```

```
        var id = Touch.getTouchIndexFromId(touches[i].identifier);
        Touch._touches.splice(id, 1);
        Touch._touchPresses.splice(id, 1);

    }
}
```

Finally, in handleTouchMove, you have to update the touch information for the touches that have changed. This means you have to replace an element in the array. The splice method accepts a third parameter in which you can indicate a replacement element. Have a look at the code belonging to this chapter to see the implementation of the handleTouchMove event-handler function.

Making Dealing with Touch Input Easier

You've seen how touch input is handled in JavaScript. You can add a few more methods to the Touch_Singleton class to make it easier to use in games. First is a simple method for retrieving the position of a touch with a given index:

```
Touch_Singleton.prototype.getPosition = function (index) {
    var canvasScale = Canvas2D.scale;
    var canvasOffset = Canvas2D.offset;
    var mx = (this._touches[index].pageX - canvasOffset.x) / canvasScale.x;
    var my = (this._touches[index].pageY - canvasOffset.y) / canvasScale.y;
    return new Vector2(mx, my);
};
```

Note that you have to apply the same position and scale correction as for the mouse position. The pageX and pageY variables in the touch event provide the coordinates where the player is touching the screen.

It would also be useful to check whether you're touching a certain area of the screen. For that, you can add a class called Rectangle to the *JewelJam1* example. This is a very simple class, similar to Vector2, for representing a rectangle. You can also add a few simple methods to check whether two rectangles intersect (useful for collision checking) and whether a rectangle contains a certain position. Check out the Rectangle.js file to see how to structure this class.

You can use rectangles to define portions of the screen. The containsTouch method checks whether there is a touch in a rectangle provided as a parameter to the method:

```
Touch_Singleton.prototype.containsTouch = function (rect) {
    for (var i = 0, l = this._touches.length; i < l; ++i) {
        if (rect.contains(this.getPosition(i)))
            return true;
    }
    return false;
};
```

In the method body is a for loop that checks, for each touch in the array, whether its position falls inside the rectangle. You reuse the getPosition method defined earlier. Depending on the outcome, the method returns either true or false. Also add the following property to Touch:

```
Object.defineProperty(Touch_Singleton.prototype, "isTouchDevice",
    {
        get: function () {
            return ('ontouchstart' in window) || (navigator.msMaxTouchPoints > 0);
        }
    });
```

This is a very simple property for checking whether you're currently dealing with a touch device. Not all browsers detect this the same way, so that is a good reason to encapsulate it in a method or property. That way, you only have to deal with these differences between browsers once. Afterward, you access the Touch.isTouchDevice property, and you're done.

Adding Touch Input to Painter

It would be a pity not to add touch to the Painter game now that you have this nice Touch object. The example code belonging to this chapter has a version of Painter with touch input. Look at the example code, in particular the Cannon.js file, where touch input has been added. In the touch interface, you can tap the colored ball in the cannon barrel to switch to a different color. Tapping outside the cannon aims the cannon. Releasing the touch afterward shoots the ball.

To separate touch-input handling from mouse-input handling, you can rewrite the handleInput method as follows:

```
Cannon.prototype.handleInput = function (delta) {
    if (Touch.isTouchDevice)
        this.handleInputTouch(delta);
    else
        this.handleInputMouse(delta);
};
```

Now you write two separate methods for handling touch and mouse input. This is what the handleInputTouch method looks like:

```
Cannon.prototype.handleInputTouch = function (delta) {
    var rect = this.colorSelectRectangle;
    if (Touch.containsTouchPress(rect)) {
        if (this.currentColor === this.colorRed)
            this.currentColor = this.colorGreen;
        else if (this.currentColor === this.colorGreen)
            this.currentColor = this.colorBlue;
        else
            this.currentColor = this.colorRed;
```

```
    } else if (Touch.touching && !Touch.containsTouch(rect)) {
        var opposite = Touch.position.y - this.position.y;
        var adjacent = Touch.position.x - this.position.x;
        this.rotation = Math.atan2(opposite, adjacent);
    }
};
```

First you retrieve the rectangle that represents the part of the cannon you can touch to select a different color. You add a simple property for calculating this rectangle. Then you check whether the rectangle contains a touch press. If that is the case, you change the color. By using an if instruction, you can easily cycle through the three colors.

If the player is touching the screen somewhere, but not inside the rectangle, you change the aim of the cannon to be directed at that position. Also check out the Ball class to see how it handles touch input! Finally, another nice thing to do is load different sprites depending on whether the application is running on a tablet or on a desktop computer:

```
if (Touch.isTouchDevice)
    sprites.gameover = loadSprite("spr_gameover_tap.png");
else
    sprites.gameover = loadSprite("spr_gameover_click.png");
```

When the game is running on a touch device, the overlay has the text "Tap to continue"; otherwise it says "Click to continue".

Note   Many modern laptops contain both a touch screen and a keyboard, and it's not always obvious how to automatically determine whether a player wants to use touch or keyboard input. Players might want to use the touch screen for some games, and the keyboard for others. One possible solution is to accept both inputs at the same time. Another solution is to let the player make his own choice of input method through a menu setting.

What You Have Learned

In this chapter, you have learned:

- How to automatically adapt the dimensions of the game screen according to different devices
- How to automatically correct the mouse position according to the dimensions of the game screen
- What an array is and how to use one
- How to use a touch interface to control what is happening in the game

Chapter 14

Game Objects in a Structure

In the previous chapter, you saw how you can use arrays to represent lists of things. For example, you used an array to keep track of the locations where the player is touching the touch screen, or how many keys the player is currently pressing on the keyboard.

Arrays can be used in a lot of other situations as well. You can use them to store more complicated objects such as the ball or the paint cans in the Painter game. In general, it's useful to provide some structure to the game objects, instead of simply having them all declared as member variables in the game world. Many games place their game objects in some kind of game hierarchy. For example, you could have a game object Car that consists of other game objects such as wheels, a transmission system, a motor, windows, seats, and so on. Each of these objects can in turn consist of smaller game objects, and so on.

In some cases, game objects have to adhere to a certain structure in the game world. Many board or puzzle games have this requirement. These games impose a set of rules that binds the playing pieces to certain positions or configurations on the playing board. For example, in a chess game, the pieces can only be placed (meaningfully) on the white and black squares on the playing board. You aren't allowed to place your queen halfway between two squares. In computer games, these kinds of restrictions are easier to enforce: you just have to make sure the position where you place your game object is a valid one. In this chapter, you see how to incorporate hierarchies and structures into computer games.

Game Objects in a Grid

Often, board games and puzzle games are based on placing objects in some kind of grid. There are many examples of such games: Chess, Tetris, Tic-Tac-Toe, Sudoku, Candy Crush, and many more. Often the goal in these games is to modify the configuration of the grid in some way to achieve points. In Tetris, completely filled rows have to be constructed; and in Sudoku, numerical properties must hold for rows, columns, and subgrids. The game *JewelJam* also uses a grid structure. The question is, how do you represent these kinds of grid-like structures in your games?

First let's look at a simplified case where you want to draw a background sprite and, on top of that, a grid of ten rows times five columns, where each location in the grid is filled with a sprite. The program that does this is called *JewelJam2*, and you can find it in the example code folder belonging to this chapter.

Creating a Grid of Sprites

The previous chapter showed how to create arrays. Let's put this feature to use in the next example to create a two-dimensional playing field. The program *JewelJam2* contains the instructions to create a game world consisting of a grid of sprites that can be manipulated. In this particular example, you don't store the actual sprites in the grid, but rather an *integer number that represents them*. That way, you can choose which sprite to draw depending on that number, and perhaps even do calculations using the numbers in the grid. You load three jewel sprites together with the background sprite when you start the game:

```
Game.loadAssets = function () {
    var loadSprite = function (sprite) {
        return Game.loadSprite("../assets/sprites/" + sprite);
    };
    sprites.background = loadSprite("spr_background.jpg");
    sprites.single_jewel1 = loadSprite("spr_single_jewel1.png");
    sprites.single_jewel2 = loadSprite("spr_single_jewel2.png");
    sprites.single_jewel3 = loadSprite("spr_single_jewel3.png");
};
```

In the `JewelJamGameWorld` class, you create an array that represents the two-dimensional playing field. In the previous chapter, you saw how to use a one-dimensional array to represent a two-dimensional grid:

```
var myGrid = new Array(rows * cols);
var someElement = myGrid[i * cols + j];
```

So, let's create such a grid in the `JewelJamGameWorld` class:

```
this.rows = 10;
this.columns = 5;
this.grid = new Array(this.rows * this.columns);
```

To make things a bit easier when accessing this grid, define the following two methods for getting and setting values in the grid:

```
JewelJamGameWorld.prototype.setGridValue = function (x, y, value) {
    var index = y * this.columns + x;
    this.grid[index] = value;
};
JewelJamGameWorld.prototype.getGridValue = function (x, y) {
    var index = y * this.columns + x;
    return this.grid[index];
};
```

As you can see, you simply apply the trick explained in the previous chapter. Initially, you fill the grid randomly with one of the three jewel sprites you loaded. You could do this as follows:

```
for (var i = 0; i < this.rows * this.columns; i++) {
    var randomval = Math.floor(Math.random() * 3) + 1;
    if (randomval === 1)
        this.grid[i] = sprites.single_jewel1;
    else if (randomval === 2)
        this.grid[i] = sprites.single_jewel2;
    else
        this.grid[i] = sprites.single_jewel3;
}
```

The first instruction in the body of the for loop generates a random number from the set {1, 2, 3}. In that instruction, you use Math.random to get a value between 0 and 1, you multiply that value by 3 (to get a value between 0 and 3), and then you round it down and add 1 to get a value between 1 and 3. Depending on the value of the random number, you select a different sprite in an if instruction. You store a reference to the sprite in the grid array.

There is a nice way in JavaScript to shorten this code, because JavaScript allows you to access the member variables of an object by using an array-like syntax. For example, suppose you've defined the following object:

```
var person = {
    name : "Arjan",
    gender : "male",
    married : true
};
```

You can access the member variables in the regular way, as follows:

```
person.name = "John";
```

There is an instruction that is equivalent. It looks like this:

```
person["name"] = "John";
```

So, when accessing member variables of objects, you can use the regular syntax, or you can access the members as an array that is indexed with strings. Why is this useful, you ask? Well, strings can be concatenated, so you can write some clever code that selects different sprites based on the randomly generated number. Here is the same for loop as before, but now you use this feature to write shorter code—which easily accommodates a four or more jewel types!

```
for (var i = 0; i < this.rows * this.columns; i++) {
    var randomval = Math.floor(Math.random() * 3) + 1;
    this.grid[i] = sprites["single_jewel" + randomval];
}
```

Drawing the Grid

Now that you have a grid of randomly chosen jewel sprites, you're ready to draw the grid on the screen. The challenge here is that you need to calculate the position at which each jewel should be drawn. This position depends on the row and column index of the jewel you want to draw. So, you use a nested for loop to go through all the rows and columns and then draw the jewel at each row and column index. To retrieve the jewel, you use the getGridValue method that you defined earlier. Here is the complete draw method:

```
JewelJamGameWorld.prototype.draw = function (delta) {
    Canvas2D.drawImage(sprites.background);
    for (var row = 0; row < this.rows; row++) {
        for (var col = 0; col < this.columns; col++) {
            var position = new Vector2(85 + col * 85, 150 + row * 85);
            Canvas2D.drawImage(this.getGridValue(col, row), position);
        }
    }
};
```

In this code, you can see the advantage of using a grid. By using the indices, you can calculate the position of the sprite in a very convenient way. The whole grid should be drawn at an offset of (85, 150), so you add 85 to the *x*-coordinate and 150 to the *y*-coordinate of the local position variable. To calculate the actual position of the sprite, you multiply the indices by 85 (the width and height of the sprite) to get the final position. The offset value can be stored in a configuration variable at the start of the script. That way, if different levels use different background sprites, you only need to update that variable instead of having to go through the drawing code to update the offsets. Later, you see another way to deal with this. Figure 14-1 shows a screenshot of the *JewelJam2* example.

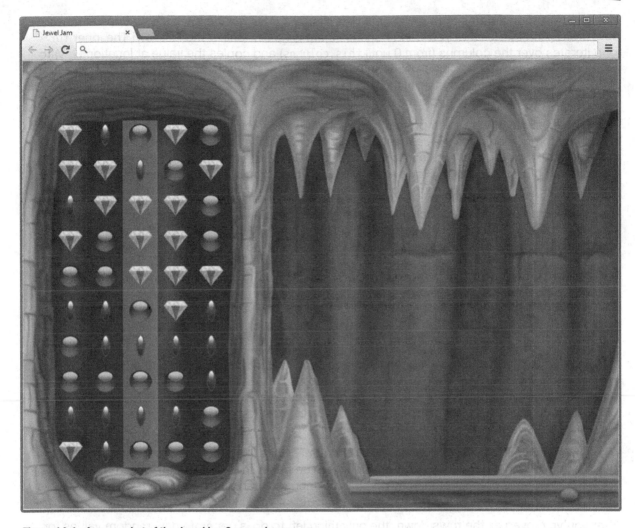

Figure 14-1. A screenshot of the JewelJam2 example program

Grid Operations

Because you've organized part of the game world in a grid, you can now use for loops in a smart way to add *behavior* to the grid. In this example, you add a feature that moves each row down one row. This means the last row disappears and you need to generate new (random) values for the first row. Let's add a method called moveRowDown that does this. What does it mean to "move down" a row? Basically, you simply have to copy the values in the row at index y to the row at index y + 1. Let's put this in a for loop:

```
for (var y = 1; y < this.rows - 1; y++) {
    for (var x = 0; x < this.columns; x++) {
        this.setGridValue(x, y + 1, this.getGridValue(x, y));
    }
}
```

The outer for loop iterates from row 0 until this.rows - 1. This means the last row doesn't move downward. And this is what you want, because there is no row below the last row! The inner for loop iterates over the columns (from 0 until this.columns) and copies the value at location (x, y) to location (x, y + 1). After this inner for loop has finished, the contents of row y have been copied to row y + 1. However, if you try to run this for loop, you'll notice that it doesn't have the behavior you want: the contents of the first row are copied to all the rows below it! How is this possible?

This is an example of why it's important to think through how loops work. The problem in this case is that you forgot that loops are *sequential*. Let's look at what is happening. The first time you enter the loop, you copy the contents of row 0 to row 1. The second time you enter the loop, you copy the contents of row 1 to row 2. However, row 1 was already replaced by the contents of row 0 the previous time you entered the loop, so you're copying (indirectly) the contents of row 0 to row 2!

How can you solve this issue? Actually, you only have to make a simple change to the algorithm. Instead of starting with row 0 and continuing until you reach the last row, you start with the last row and continue upward until you reach the first row. The modified algorithm looks like this:

```
for (var y = this.rows - 2; y >=0; y--) {
    for (var x = 0; x < this.columns; x++) {
        this.setGridValue(x, y + 1, this.getGridValue(x, y));
    }
}
```

In this case, you start with the row at index 8 and copy its contents to the row at index 9. After that, you copy row 7 to row 8, and so on. Unlike the previous version of the algorithm, this approach works, because you work from the bottom upward and only make modifications to rows that you no longer have to consider: once you've copied the values from row 7 to row 8, you don't look at row 8 anymore in the remainder of the algorithm.

When you use loops in your programs, you'll encounter bugs like those just described. The best thing to do when that happens is to draw a diagram on paper to see what is happening, and write out what the loop is doing, iteration by iteration. A debugger can also be helpful, because it allows you to stop the code in any place and check the values of variables.

After you've moved all the rows down, the only thing left to do is generate new random values for the first row. This can be done with a single for instruction that retrieves a random number for each item in the row:

```
for (x = 0; x < this.columns; x++) {
    var randomval = Math.floor(Math.random() * 3) + 1;
    this.setGridValue(x, 0, sprites["single_jewel" + randomval]);
}
```

More Possibilities with Grids

In order to get acquainted with how multidimensional arrays work, you can try to program some other grid operations on your own. For example, can you write a method void removeRow(int i) that removes a row at a given index and creates new values for the top row? Can you write a method that performs a round-robin operation on the rows (all rows move down, and the last row becomes the first row)? How about moving rows up? Or moving columns? It's possible to create many different operations on a grid like this. These operations can be useful for many different games. For example, removing a row from a grid is an operation that is used a lot in *Tetris* games. A game like *Bejeweled* needs operations that can remove a number of items from a row or a column and fill the grid again.

In addition to the operations you can perform on grids, you also have to think about the items the grid contains. In this example, you used a two-dimensional grid containing references to sprites. For more complicated games, it's useful to have a grid of *game objects* instead, so you can add more behavior and interaction to the objects that are part of the grid.

Hierarchy of Game Objects

This section shows you how to create a hierarchy of game objects. You start by defining a very basic GameObject class, and you add code that supports putting game objects into hierarchies.

Anatomy of a Game Object

Most games have quite a complicated structure of game objects. First there might be a background consisting of various layers of moving objects (mountains, air, trees, and so on). Then there are objects moving around that the player can interact with. These objects may be enemies of the player, so they need some level of intelligence; they can also be more static, such as power-ups, trees, doors, or ladders.

Sometimes objects don't even have a physical appearance in the shape of a sprite. For example, the player's current score could also be a game object, but rather than having a sprite associated with it, a font display the current score somewhere. Or imagine a game where an invisible enemy has to be defeated, and its position can only be seen by the effect it has on its surroundings. Other game objects are even more complex: game objects that consist of other game objects.

Suppose you have a game object that represents a house. It might consist of many other game objects, such as a door, stairs, windows, and a kitchen (which itself, in turn, consists of different game objects).

In the case of puzzle games, the grid that represents the playing field could also be considered a game object that consists of a grid of other game objects. Given these different types of game objects and the relations between them, you can say that game objects generally form part of a *hierarchy*. This hierarchy can be completely flat, as in the first example game, Painter; but the Jewel Jam game explained in the following chapters has a complicated hierarchy of game objects.

Many games use a hierarchy of game objects. Especially in 3D games, such a hierarchy is very important because of the complexity of three-dimensional environments. Objects in 3D games are normally represented not by sprites, but by one or more 3D models. The advantage of a hierarchy is that these objects can be grouped together, so that if you pick up a vase that contains a scroll with magic writing on it, the scroll moves along with the vase. Such hierarchies are also called *scene graphs* because they present the scene (the environment) as a graph-like structure.

In the Painter game, the basic type of game object is represented by the ThreeColorGameObject class. It's clear that not all game objects have three possible colors, a current position, and a current velocity. Until now, this is how you've represented game objects, simply because it was sufficient for the basic examples you were working on. If you want to develop bigger, more complicated games, you have to let go of the basic premise that a game object is a three-colored sprite. But then, what is a game object? In a sense, a game object can be anything you want. So you could define the following class to represent a game object:

```
function GameObject() {
}
```

Okay, this may be going a bit too far. For now, let's assume that any game object has a position and a velocity, but how the game object appears (if it appears) is something you don't yet deal with. Furthermore, you want to be able to set a visibility flag so you can choose not to draw certain game objects. So, let's create a generic GameObject class with these three member variables:

```
function GameObject() {
    this.position = Vector2.zero;
    this.velocity = Vector2.zero;
    this._visible = true;
}
```

If you want to have a game object that is represented by a sprite, you can inherit from this base class and add the necessary member variables.

You also add the main game-loop methods: handleInput, update, and draw. Because you don't know yet how the game object should handle input and how it should be drawn on the screen, you leave these two methods empty. In the update method, just as you did in the ThreeColorGameObject class, you update the current position of the game object according to its velocity and the elapsed time:

```
GameObject.prototype.update = function (delta) {
    this.position.addTo(this.velocity.multiply(delta));
};
```

Relations between Game Objects

If you want to establish a certain hierarchy between game objects, you need to identify which game object *is a part of* which other game object. In terms of hierarchies, this means you need to establish that a game object can have a *parent game object*. For the game object itself, it's very useful to know who the parent is. Therefore, the GameObject class needs a member variable that refers to the parent of the game object:

```
this.parent = null;
```

For example, imagine an object called playingField that contains all the jewels that are part of the playing field. The playingField object can then be considered the *parent* of these jewels. But not all game objects have a parent. For example, the root object doesn't have a parent. How can you indicate that a game object doesn't have a parent? You need to set the value of the parent member variable to "nothing"—in JavaScript programming terms, to null.

Now that you've added a parent to the game-object class, you have to deal with a few administrative hassles in order to make sure the parent-child relationship between game objects is properly maintained; but you get back to that later. Because of the hierarchy of game objects, you need to make decisions about a few thing.

Local vs. Global Positions

As you know, each game object has a variable containing its position. Until now, each game object was directly positioned in the game world. Although this approach works fine, it may not be the ideal solution. Consider the playing field game object. In order to align the playing field to the background sprite, you want to place it at position (85,150). However, all the child objects (the jewels in the grid) probably also have this same position offset of (85,150). In fact, you had to apply this offset to all the items in the grid in the previous example:

```
var position = new Vector2(85 + col * 85, 150 + row * 85);
Canvas2D.drawImage(this.getGridValue(col, row), position);
```

Although it's a bit of work to apply that offset to all game objects that are children of the playing field object, it's doable. It becomes more problematic once the child objects become more complicated and have child objects themselves that also need to be positioned correctly. And what happens if you change the position of the playing field? You would have to update the position of all the game objects that hang under it. There is a better way to do this: you have to differentiate between *local and world positions*. The *world position* of a game object is its absolute *x*- and *y*-coordinates in the game world. The *local position* of a game object is its position with respect to the position of the parent game object. So, do you need to store both these positions in each game object? No: you only need to store the *local position*. You can calculate the world position by adding the local position of the game object to the world position of the parent. If there is no parent, then the local position is the same as the world position. You can add a property to the GameObject class that does this work for you:

```
Object.defineProperty(GameObject.prototype, "worldPosition",
    {
        get: function () {
            if (this.parent !== null)
                return this.parent.worldPosition.addTo(this.position);
            else
                return this.position.copy();
        }
    });
```

Using this property, you can now obtain both the local position of the game object (which is stored in the position member variable) and the world position, which is accessed through the worldPosition property. As you can see, you calculate the world position by adding the local position to the world position of the parent. The world position of the parent is, in turn, calculated by taking its local position and adding it to the world position of its parent. This goes on until you reach a game object that doesn't have a parent, in which case the world position is a copy of the local position. As an example, the world position of a jewel is calculated by adding the (local) position of the root object, the local position of the playing field object plus its own local position. This is exactly the behavior you get when you access its worldPosition property. It may seem strange that you're calling the worldPosition property in the worldPosition property itself, but this is perfectly valid JavaScript code. In fact, you're using a programming technique called *recursion* (you'll learn more about that later).

Layers of Game Objects

When you want to draw a game object, you can use the worldPosition property as a convenient way to find out where to draw the game object on the screen. The only problem is that you don't have any idea of order in which the game objects in the hierarchy should be drawn. Looking at the Jewel Jam game, you clearly want the background to be drawn before the playing field is drawn; otherwise, the player will only see the background.

It would be nice if you could indicate somehow as part of the game object when it should be drawn. One way to do this is to introduce *layers*. You can assign a layer to each game object, and the layer it's assigned determines when the object should be drawn. You can represent these layers in a very simple way by using integers. Lower layer numbers indicate that the object will be drawn earlier. So, you can assign layer 0 to the background sprite game object and layer 1 to the playing field game object, making sure the background is drawn before the playing field. Storing a layer is done directly in a member variable belonging to the GameObject class:

```
this.layer = 0;
```

A minor drawback of using layers is that there is no guarantee about the order in which objects in the same layer are drawn. So, if you want one object to always be drawn after another, that object must be in a higher layer.

For a complete view of the GameObject class, see the code in the *JewelJam3* example. Of course, simply adding a layer member variable to the GameObject class isn't enough: you have to *do something* with this information. The next section looks at a few different game-object subclasses. One of these is the GameObjectList class, which consists of multiple other game objects. In this class, you see how the layer variable can be used to draw the objects in the right order.

Different Kinds of Game Objects

This section introduces a few useful game objects that are all defined as subclasses of GameObject. You start by defining a simple sprite-based game object. Then you move on to lists and grids of game objects.

A Sprite Game Object

One of the most commonly appearing game objects is a sprite with a position and a velocity. Because the position and velocity are two member variables available already in the GameObject class, you can inherit from this class and then add a member variable to store the sprite and a member variable to store the origin of the sprite. In the constructor of this class, you have to pass the sprite as a parameter, Because you're inheriting, you have to call the constructor of the base class so that the GameObject part of the object is constructed as well. This constructor expects a parameter denoting the layer. Finally, you have to replace/override the draw method. This method is empty in GameObject, because you decided game objects don't necessarily have a sprite attached to them. In the overridden draw method, you draw the sprite on the screen, and you use the `worldPosition` property to calculate the actual position of the sprite on the screen. Here is a simplified version of the `SpriteGameObject` class:

```
function SpriteGameObject(sprite, layer) {
    GameObject.call(this, layer);
    this.sprite = sprite;
    this.origin = Vector2.zero;
}

SpriteGameObject.prototype = Object.create(GameObject.prototype);

SpriteGameObject.prototype.draw = function () {
    if (!this.visible)
        return;
    Canvas2D.drawImage(this.sprite, this.worldPosition, 0, 1, this.origin);
};
```

Have a look at the complete version of the class in the *JewelJam3* example code. That version adds a few useful properties such as a property for retrieving the width of the sprite game object.

A List of Game Objects

The next type of game object consists of a list of other game objects. This is a very useful type, because it allows you to create hierarchical structures of game objects. For example, the *root* game object needs to be a list of other game objects, because it contains the background sprite game object as well as the playing field. To represent a game object containing a list of other game objects, you use a class called `GameObjectList`. This class inherits from the `GameObject` class, so a list of game objects is, itself, also a game object. This way, you can treat it as a normal game object and give it a position, a velocity, a drawing layer, or a parent game object. Furthermore, a game object in the list can itself be a list of other game objects. This design of the `GameObjectList` class allows you to define hierarchical structures of game objects. To manage a list of game objects, you need to add an array member variable that contains the (child) game objects. Here is the complete constructor of `GameObjectList`:

```
function GameObjectList(layer) {
    GameObject.call(this, layer);
    this._gameObjects = [];
}
```

One of the goals of the `GameObjectList` class is to take care of the game objects in its list. This means, if you call the `draw` method of a `GameObjectList` instance, this instance draws all the game objects that are in its list. The same procedure needs to be followed if the `handleInput` method is called or if the `update` method is called. Here is the update method defined in `GameObjectList`:

```
GameObjectList.prototype.update = function (delta) {
    for (var i = 0, l = this._gameObjects.length; i < l; ++i)
        this._gameObjects[i].update(delta);
};
```

So, GameObjectList itself doesn't define any behavior; it simply manages the behavior of the game objects it contains. For the update method, you don't care about the order in which the game objects update themselves. For the draw method, you do care, because you want to draw the game objects with the lowest layer numbers first. The most robust way to do this is to sort the list of game objects at the beginning of each call to the draw method. After that, you can use a for loop to draw the game objects one after the other, according to their ordering in the list. The body of the draw method looks something like this:

```
if (!this.visible)
    return;
// sort the list of game objects
...
for (var i = 0, l = this._gameObjects.length; i < l; ++i)
    this._gameObjects[i].draw();
```

Because sorting can be quite complex, you do it not when you draw the game objects (which has to happen 60 times per second), but when you add game objects to the list. That way, you only sort the list of game objects when necessary. Sorting an array in JavaScript is really easy. Arrays have a sort function you can call. For example:

```
var myArray = ["named", "must", "your", "fear", "be", "before", "banish", "it", "you", "can"];
myArray.sort();
/* myArray now refers to ["banish", "be", "before", "can", "fear", "it", "must", "named", "you",
"your"]; */
```

By default, the sort function sorts an array alphabetically. However, what happens if you have an array that contains more complex things than strings, such as game objects? In that case, you can provide sort with a sorting function as a parameter. This function should indicate the ordering of any two objects in the array. You can write this function yourself. For example, here is a call to the sort function that orders the game objects according to their layer:

```
this._gameObjects.sort(function (a, b) {
        return a.layer - b.layer;
    });
```

When the sorting function returns a positive number, a is "larger" than b and should be placed after b, and vice versa. You can write a method called add that adds a game object to the list and then sorts the list. This method also assigns the game-object list as the parent of the game object you add. Here is the complete method:

```
GameObjectList.prototype.add = function (gameobject) {
    this._gameObjects.push(gameobject);
    gameobject.parent = this;
    this._gameObjects.sort(function (a, b) {
        return a.layer - b.layer;
    });
};
```

Because you ensure that the game objects are added at the right positions, the draw method simply consists of a for loop:

```
GameObjectList.prototype.draw = function () {
    if (!this.visible)
        return;
    for (var i = 0, l = this._gameObjects.length; i < l; ++i)
        this._gameObjects[i].draw();
};
```

This way, your drawing operation stays very efficient because you don't sort the list of game objects every time! There is a slight disadvantage to doing it this way, though. Consider the following code fragment:

```
var obj1 = new SpriteGameObject(spr, 1);
var obj2 = new SpriteGameObject(spr, 2);
var objects = new GameObjectList(0);
objects.add(obj1);
objects.add(obj2);
obj2.layer = 0;
```

This fragment creates two sprite game objects and adds them to a list of game objects. The add method call makes sure they're added at the right position (in this case, the order of adding happens to coincide with the layer ordering). However, after that you change the layer index of object obj2, but the list of game objects isn't changed, meaning obj1 will still be drawn before obj2. As a result, it's possible to break the system. In this case, clear documentation that instructs the developer not to do such nasty things is highly recommended! You could, for example, add a warning comment above the definition of the add method in which you tell the user that only the current layer values of the objects are taken into account. Another option is to add a comment to the layer variable declaration that says when the layer is changed, the drawing order isn't automatically updated. A better, more robust way to deal with this is to add a property through which the layer is changed, which automatically sorts the drawing order of the parent the object belongs to.

For the sake of completeness, the GameObjectList class also contains a few other useful methods. The clear method removes all game objects from the list. The remove method removes an object from the list; and because the object isn't part of the list anymore, its parent is set to null.

You can now profit from the layered drawing mechanism you've created, as well as the hierarchical structure. To make your code clearer, you can define a few different layers as a variable (see JewelJam.js for the complete code):

```
var ID = {};
...
ID.layer_background = 1;
ID.layer_objects = 20;
```

Now take a look at the following code fragment:

```
function JewelJamGameWorld(layer) {
    GameObjectList.call(this, layer);
    this.add(new SpriteGameObject(sprites.background, ID.layer_background));
    var rows = 10, columns = 5;
    var grid = new JewelGrid(rows, columns, ID.layer_objects);
    grid.position = new Vector2(85, 150);
    grid.cellWidth = 85;
    grid.cellHeight = 85;
    this.add(grid);
    for (var i = 0; i < rows * columns; i++) {
        grid.add(new Jewel());
    }
}

JewelJamGameWorld.prototype = Object.create(GameObjectList.prototype);
```

This is part of the code needed to re-create the hierarchy of the Jewel Jam game. The JewelJameGameWorld class inherits from GameObjectList. As a result, you can add game objects to the game world using the add method!

First you add a sprite game object that represents the background. You assign the layer ID.layer_background to this object. Then, you create a JewelGrid at the ID.layer_objects layer (discussed later in more detail). Finally, you fill this grid with Jewel objects. This way, you create a hierarchy of related game objects that are automatically drawn in the right order! Furthermore, because you dealt with calling the other game-loop methods as well, you don't have to think about this anymore when you create the hierarchy.

A Grid of Game Objects

Just as you created a class GameObjectList to represent a list of game objects, you can also create a class GameObjectGrid to represent a *grid* of game objects. There is, however, a big conceptual difference between these two classes. For one thing, the GameObjectList class says nothing about the positions of the game objects it contains. On the other hand, GameObjectGrid relates all the game objects to a grid, which in turn means they all have a position on the grid. But each game object also has a position member variable.

Positions seem to be stored in duplicate, but in fact the positions of game objects in the world aren't necessarily always the same as the positions where they belong on the grid. The positions dictated by the grid can be considered *anchor positions* of the game objects (the positions where they belong). The *actual* positions of the game objects can be different, though. By using the anchor position in combination with the actual game-object position, you can achieve nice motion effects, where game objects move smoothly over the grid while still belonging to certain grid positions. An example of a game where this kind of effect is used quite a lot is *Tetris*: the player can move the blocks to different positions on the grid, but because the grid anchor position is different from the actual game-object position, the blocks move smoothly. If you run the *JewelJam3* example, you can also see a demonstration of this effect if you drag one of the rows to the left or to the right using your mouse or your finger (on a device with a touch screen).

Because you can use a regular array to represent two-dimensional structures, the GameObjectGrid class is a subclass of GameObjectList. You need to do a few additional things to make the GameObjectGrid class behave the way you want it to. First, you need to be able to calculate anchor positions, which means you need to know the size of a single element (*cell*) in the grid. Therefore, you also add two member variables to store the size of a single cell in the grid. In addition, you store the number of desired rows and columns in a member variable. These values have to be passed to the constructor as a parameter when a GameObjectGrid instance is created. This is the complete constructor method:

```
function GameObjectGrid(rows, columns, layer) {
    GameObjectList.call(this, layer);
    this.cellWidth = 0;
    this.cellHeight = 0;
    this._rows = rows;
    this._columns = columns;
}
GameObjectGrid.prototype = Object.create(GameObjectList.prototype);
```

Also, add two properties to the class so you can read the number of rows and columns:

```
Object.defineProperty(GameObjectGrid.prototype, "rows", {
    get: function () {
        return this._rows;
    }
});
Object.defineProperty(GameObjectGrid.prototype, "columns", {
    get: function () {
        return this._columns;
    }
});
```

Because you inherited from GameObjectList, you already have a method for adding a game object. However, you need to do things slightly differently in this class. Because the game objects are placed in a (flat) grid, the drawing order isn't really important anymore. When you add a game object, you don't want to sort the array. Furthermore, you want to set the position of the game object to its desired position in the grid. To do this, you override the add method from GameObjectList as follows:

```
GameObjectGrid.prototype.add = function (gameobject) {
    var row = Math.floor(this._gameObjects.length / this._columns);
    var col = this._gameObjects.length % this._columns;
    this._gameObjects.push(gamcobject);
    gameobject.parent = this;
    gameobject.position = new Vector2(col * this.cellWidth, row * this.cellHeight);
};
```

As you can see in this example, you calculate the row and column indices from the target location in the array. Then you push the game object on the array, set its parent, and, using the calculated row and column indices, determine its position. For convenience, add another method that allows you to add a game object at a specific row and column index in the grid:

```
GameObjectGrid.prototype.addAt = function (gameobject, col, row) {
    this._gameObjects[row * this._columns + col] = gameobject;
    gameobject.parent = this;
    gameobject.position = new Vector2(col * this.cellWidth, row * this.cellHeight);
};
```

A Grid of Jewels

For the Jewel Jam game, you want to perform a couple of basic operations on the grid, including shifting the elements in a row to the left or to the right. For example, when the player drags the third row in the grid to the left, all elements except the leftmost one should shift to the left, and the leftmost element becomes the rightmost one. Because this kind of operation isn't something you need in every game that uses a grid, let's create a class `JewelGrid` that inherits from `GameObjectGrid`, and then add the operations you need to that class. Here is the constructor method of the `JewelGrid` class:

```
function JewelGrid(rows, columns, layer) {
    GameObjectGrid.call(this, rows, columns, layer);
    this.dragging = false;
    this._dragRow = 0;
    this._draggingLastX = 0;
    this._touchIndex = 0;
}
JewelGrid.prototype = Object.create(GameObjectGrid.prototype);
```

It includes a few member variables you need for storing information related to the dragging that the user is doing. You see more detail later when you learn how to obtain this dragging behavior.

You shift the columns in a row to the left by storing the first element in a temporary object, moving the other objects one column to the left, and finally placing the element stored in the temporary object in the last column. You can add a method `shiftRowLeft` that does exactly this. Because the method is applied to only one row, you have to pass the row index as a parameter. The complete method is as follows:

```
JewelGrid.prototype.shiftRowLeft = function (selectedRow) {
    var firstObj = this.at(0, selectedRow);
    var positionOffset = firstObj.position.x;
    for (var x = 0; x < this._columns - 1; x++) {
        this._gameObjects[selectedRow * this._columns + x]
            = this._gameObjects[selectedRow * this._columns + x + 1];
    }
    this._gameObjects[selectedRow * this._columns + (this._columns - 1)] = firstObj;
    firstObj.position = new Vector2(this._columns * this.cellWidth + positionOffset,
        selectedRow * this.cellHeight);
};
```

In addition to moving the leftmost element to the rightmost column and shifting all the other elements, you change the position of the object that was changed from being the leftmost object to the rightmost object. You take into account any existing position offset of the first element by storing it in a local variable before you perform the shifting operation and then adding that offset to the new position. The result of this positional change is a nice motion effect, as you'll see later. The method shiftRowRight is similar to this method; see the example code for *JewelJam3*.

You also want to add a method that gives you the anchor position in the grid for any game object. This method will be useful later. As a parameter, this method expects a game object, and it returns a Vector2 object containing the anchor position. Here is the complete method:

```
GameObjectGrid.prototype.getAnchorPosition = function (gameobject) {
    var l = this._gameObjects.length;
    for (var i = 0; i < l; i++)
        if (this._gameObjects[i] === gameobject) {
            var row = Math.floor(i / this.columns);
            var col = i % this.columns;
            return new Vector2(col * this.cellWidth, row * this.cellHeight);
        }
    return Vector2.zero;
};
```

This method uses a for instruction to look for the game object that was passed as a parameter. Once this object has been found, you calculate its anchor position based on the row and column indices in the grid, together with the cell size. If the object wasn't found, you return the zero vector (Vector2.Zero). Because this method is useful for almost all grids, you add it to the GameObjectGrid class.

Moving Smoothly on the Grid

To make objects move smoothly on the grid, you can use the velocity and position member variables that are part of the GameObject class. You use the anchor position retrieved from the GameObjectGrid instance to calculate the velocity of the game object belonging at that position. The effect is that when the game object isn't exactly at the anchor position, it automatically starts moving toward that position.

To do this, you introduce another class called Jewel, which represents a game object in the grid (in this case, a kind of jewel). This game object is a subclass of SpriteGameObject. In the constructor of this class, you randomly select one of the three jewel sprites, as follows:

```
function Jewel(layer) {
    var randomval = Math.floor(Math.random() * 3) + 1;
    var spr = sprites["single_jewel" + randomval];
    SpriteGameObject.call(this, spr, layer);
}
```

The only other thing you need to change in this game object is the update method, because drawing the sprite is already properly handled in the base class. What needs to be done in the update method? First you need to call the original version of the update method so the position of the object is always updated according to its velocity:

```
SpriteGameObject.prototype.update.call(this, delta);
```

Then you need to find out the anchor position of this game object. You can do this by calling getAnchorPosition from the parent (which normally should be a JewelGrid instance):

```
var anchor = this.parent.getAnchorPosition(this);
```

And finally, you modify the velocity of the game object so it moves toward the anchor position:

```
this.velocity = anchor.subtractFrom(this.position).multiplyWith(15);
```

As you can see, you calculate the velocity by taking the difference between the target position (which is the anchor position) and the current position. To get a faster motion effect, you multiply this value by 15. When the game object's position is updated, this velocity is added to the position vector, and as a result the game object moves toward the target position. For the complete Jewel class, see the *JewelJam3* example.

Dragging Rows in the Grid

The final thing you do in this chapter is add dragging behavior to the grid so the player can move rows to the left and to the right. You define the dragging behavior in two steps. First you determine what the new position of the elements in the row should be, depending on where the player is dragging with the mouse or their finger. Then, depending on how far the player has dragged the row, you shift elements to the left or to the right.

You define this dragging behavior for both mouse and touch input. Therefore, you split the handleInput method into two parts, each defined in a specific method for the type of input:

```
JewelGrid.prototype.handleInput = function (delta) {
    if (Touch.isTouchDevice)
        this.handleInputTouch(delta);
    else
        this.handleInputMouse(delta);
};
```

Because the dragging behavior is specific to the Jewel Jam game, you handle the input in JewelGrid. Let's look at mouse dragging behavior first. You need to detect that the player has started dragging in the grid. This is only possible if the left mouse button is down and the player isn't yet dragging. If that is the case, you need to determine whether the player is dragging in the grid or outside it. In the latter case, you don't need to do anything. In the former case, you need to store some information related to where the player is dragging. Here is the complete code:

```
if (Mouse.left.down && !this.dragging) {
    var rect = new Rectangle(this.worldPosition.x, this.worldPosition.y, this.columns *
        this.cellHeight, this.rows * this.cellWidth);
    if (Mouse.containsMouseDown(rect)) {
        this.dragging = true;
        this._dragRow = Math.floor((Mouse.position.y - this.worldPosition.y) / this.cellHeight);
        this._draggingLastX = Mouse.position.x - this.worldPosition.x;
    }
}
```

You use the dragging variable to keep track of whether the player is dragging. If the player has started dragging, you calculate which row the player is dragging, and you store that in the _dragRow member variable. Finally, you calculate the *local x-position* in the grid of where the mouse currently is dragging. This will be useful later when you reposition all the jewels according to how much the player has dragged.

Next you check the second case, where the player isn't dragging. If that is the case, you set the dragging variable to false:

```
if (!Mouse.left.down) {
    this.dragging = false;
}
```

Now that you've performed the preparatory step to determine whether the player is dragging, you need to take action if the player is indeed dragging. The first step is to reposition the jewels according to how much the player has dragged the row to the left or right. Calculate the new position of the mouse:

```
var newpos = Mouse.position.x - this.worldPosition.x;
```

Then reposition each jewel in the row by adding the difference between the new position and the last dragging position to the *x*-coordinate of each jewel:

```
for (var i = 0; i < this.columns; i++) {
    var currObj = this.at(i, this._dragRow);
    currObj.position.x += (newpos - this._draggingLastX);
}
```

Now you check whether you need to shift a row to the left or to the right. You first check whether the leftmost object has been dragged more than half the width of the cell to the left. You can determine whether the player is dragging to the left by checking whether newpos is smaller than the last *x*-position while dragging. If that is the case, you shift the row to the left:

```
var firstObj = this.at(0, this._dragRow);
if (firstObj.position.x < -this.cellWidth / 2 && newpos - this._draggingLastX < 0)
    this.shiftRowLeft(this._dragRow);
```

Similarly, you check whether the rightmost object has been dragged more than half the cell width to the right. If that is the case, you shift the row to the right:

```
var lastObj = this.at(this.columns - 1, this._dragRow);
if (lastObj.position.x > (this.columns - 1) * this.cellWidth + this.cellWidth / 2 &&
    newpos - this._draggingLastX > 0)
    this.shiftRowRight(this._dragRow);
```

Finally, you update the last dragging position so it contains the newly calculated one. That way, you can perform the same dragging and shifting operations in the next call to update:

```
this._draggingLastX = newpos;
```

The way you handle touch dragging is very similar to mouse dragging. You need to do a little extra administrative work. For one thing, you need to keep track of the finger that is currently dragging in the grid. You store the touch index belonging to this finger in a member variable when the player starts dragging:

```
this._touchIndex = Touch.getIndexInRect(rect);
```

You can then retrieve the position of the finger by using the touch index that you stored:

```
pos = Touch.getPosition(this._touchIndex);
```

Then you do exactly the same thing you did to handle the mouse dragging. For the complete code to handle the touch and mouse dragging, see the JewelGrid class in the *JewelJam3* example.

Creating the Game Objects

Now that you've defined all these different types of game objects, you can create them as part of the game world. You've already briefly seen how to do that. First you add a background image:

```
this.add(new SpriteGameObject(sprites.background, ID.layer_background));
```

Then you create a grid to contain the jewels:

```
var rows = 10, columns = 5;
var grid = new JewelGrid(rows, columns, ID.layer_objects);
grid.position = new Vector2(85, 150);
grid.cellWidth = 85;
grid.cellHeight = 85;
this.add(grid);
```

Finally, you fill the grid with Jewel objects using a for loop:

```
for (var i = 0; i < rows * columns; i++) {
    grid.add(new Jewel());
}
```

Because of the hierarchy of game objects that you created, the game-loop calls are automatically propagated to all the game objects in the hierarchy. Another nice thing you can do because of this hierarchical structure is modify the position of a parent object, after which the child objects are automatically moved accordingly. For example, try to place the grid object at another position:

```
grid.position = new Vector2(300, 100);
```

The result of this change is shown in Figure 14-2. As you can see, all the child objects are moved, and the row-dragging mechanism works just as before. Here you see the true power of placing game objects in such a hierarchy: you have a lot of control over how the objects are placed on the screen. You could even go completely crazy and give the grid a velocity so it moves around the screen!

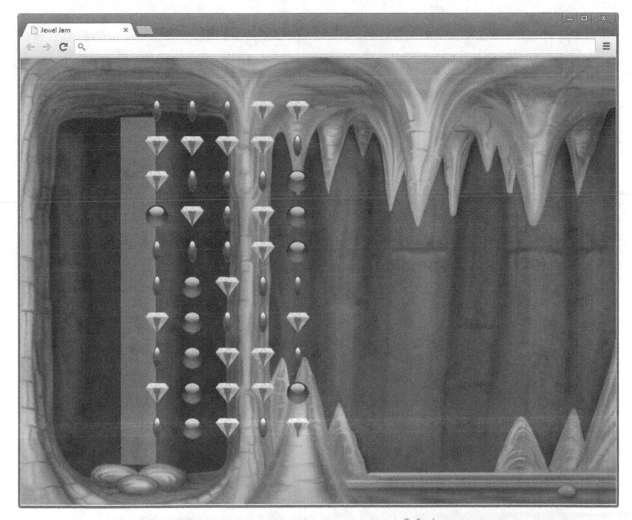

Figure 14-2. Moving the playing field to another position

What You Have Learned

In this chapter, you have learned:

- How to organize game objects in a scene graph

- How to create structured collections of game objects, such as grids and lists

- The difference between local and global positions

- How to make the scene graph an integral part of the game by using it to draw and update the game objects

- How to define dragging behavior for both mouse and touch input

Chapter **15**

Gameplay Programming

This chapter looks into the gameplay programming of the Jewel Jam game. First it talks about interaction between game objects. Then it introduces a few new game objects that are used in the game. Finally, you tackle the main gameplay element of this game: finding combinations of jewels and handling them properly.

Interaction between Game Objects

This section looks at how game objects communicate with each other. Before game objects can do that, you first need a way for these objects to *find* each other.

The previous chapter presented the game world as a hierarchy of game objects. Each of these game objects may process user input and may exhibit some kind of behavior. For example, the jewel grid game object checks whether the player has dragged one of the rows in the grid and performs a row-shifting operation if needed. This is a typical example of how many game objects in games are designed. They process input from the player, and they react to it, which in turn can influence other game objects (such as the positions of jewels on the grid). In the Painter game, you saw that the ball and the paint cans interact with each other in a similar fashion. In more complicated games, many different game objects interact with each other.

The challenge is, how do these game objects find each other? In the case of the Painter game, the PainterGameWorld class has member variables that refer to each of the game objects. This isn't a very good solution, because it makes the game world completely dependent on the game it's a part of. In the Jewel Jam game world, you only have a hierarchy of GameObject instances, which makes it much more complicated to find a particular game object.

You should design your classes in such a way that they can be used in many different games. In the last version of the game Jewel Jam, there was very little interaction between the game objects, so you could get away with a simple design. This won't work anymore now. For example, the jewel grid needs to be able to find the object that represent the player's score so that it can update this score when the player makes a valid combination of jewels. The grid also needs to find the moving jewel cart so that it can move the cart back to the left when it's required. To do these things, you need a way to find objects in the game world without making the game world rely on code specific to the game.

Assigning Identifiers to Game Objects

When you want to find game objects, it's helpful to assign *identifiers* to them. Not all objects need identifiers; generally only the ones that interact with other objects do. You use the same kind of identifiers that you used for layers earlier. For example, here you can see a few identifiers that will be useful for the Jewel Jam game:

```
ID.title = 1;
ID.help_frame = 2;
ID.jewel_cart = 3;
ID.grid = 4;
ID.game_over = 5;
ID.score = 6;
ID.double_timer = 7;
ID.triple_timer = 8;
```

All you need to do is extend the game object classes so that you can assign an identifier to game objects. Let's start with the GameObject class. In this class, you add a member variable to store an identifier, and you add a parameter to the GameObject constructor method so that you can associate an ID with an object when it's created:

```
function GameObject(layer, id) {
    this.layer = typeof layer !== 'undefined' ? layer : 0;
    this.id = typeof id !== 'undefined' ? id : 0;
    this.parent = null;
    this.position = Vector2.zero;
    this.velocity = Vector2.zero;
    this._visible = true;
}
```

Because not all objects need an ID (or a layer), you assign default values to these variables in case the parameters aren't defined.

Because all game objects inherit from the GameObject class, they also have an identifier. In many cases, you have to update the constructor of the GameObject subclasses so they pass along the identifier to the constructor of the base (GameObject) class. For example, the updated SpriteGameObject constructor is as follows:

```
function SpriteGameObject(sprite, layer, id) {
    GameObject.call(this, layer, id);
    this.sprite = sprite;
    this.origin = Vector2.zero;
}
```

Most of the GameObject subclasses are updated in this way. Take a look at the JewelJam4 example to see how this is done for all the different game object types.

Finding Game Objects

Although assigning identifiers to game objects may be a good idea, it's only useful if you also provide a way to *find* these game objects. To see how this can be done, let's add a method find to the GameObjectList class that looks through the list of game objects to see if any of them have the requested identifier. If the game object is found, the method returns a reference to this game object; otherwise, it returns null. The header of the method is as follows:

```
GameObjectList.prototype.find = function (id)
```

The only thing you have to do now is write the *algorithm* that examines the game objects in the list and returns the game object matching the identifier, if it's contained in the list. You use a for instruction to do this (although you could use a while instruction to do the same thing). In the for loop, you check whether the current game object's identifier matches the requested identifier that is passed as a parameter to the method. If so, you return that object. If you didn't return from the method in the body of the for loop, it means none of the game objects in the list had the requested ID, so the method returns null. The body of the find method then becomes

```
for (var i = 0, l = this._gameObjects.length; i < l; i++) {
    if (this._gameObjects[i].id === id)
        return this._gameObjects[i];
}
return null;
```

Note that once the return instruction is executed, you return immediately from the method. This means the remaining game objects aren't checked anymore. Furthermore, you don't check whether game objects have duplicate IDs. If multiple game objects carry the same ID, this method returns the first one it finds.

Recursion

There is one thing you haven't taken into account. It is, of course, possible that one or more of the game objects in the list is itself of the type GameObjectList. If that game object contained a game object with the ID you seek, then the method from the previous section wouldn't find it, because that method only checks the game objects that are stored in the list of the current object (this). How can you solve this? First you need to check whether an object is an instance of a certain type. For that, you can use the instanceof keyword:

```
if (someObject instanceof GameObjectList)
    // do something
```

Before the `instanceof` keyword, you put the object to be checked; and after the keyword you place the type. If the object is of the given type, then the expression yields `true`. If not, the result is `false`. Therefore, you can use it in an `if` instruction as in the previous example. If you know the object is of type `GameObjectList`, you can try to find the game object you're looking for in the game-object list represented by that object. The following code does exactly that:

```
for (var i = 0, l = this._gameObjects.length; i < l; ++i) {
    if (this._gameObjects[i].id === id)
        return this._gameObjects[i];
    if (this._gameObjects[i] instanceof GameObjectList) {
        var list = this._gameObjects[i]._gameObjects;
        for (var i2 = 0, l2 = list.length; i2 < l2; ++i) {
            if (list[i2].id === id)
                return list[i2];
        }
    }
}
return null;
```

So, now you check for each game object to determine whether it's of type `GameObjectList`. If so, you traverse that list's _gameObjects variable and look for the game object in there.

Are you finished now? Well, not really. What if one of the game objects in `list` is of type `GameObjectList`? It means you have to add another layer that checks whether one of the game objects in *that* list perhaps corresponds to the ID you're looking for. But one of those game objects could also be of type `GameObjectList`. Obviously, this approach isn't ideal. However, you can do something to avoid this kind of infinite-search problem. Why not use the `find` method again? Look at the following code:

```
for (var i = 0, l = this._gameObjects.length; i < l; ++i) {
    if (this._gameObjects[i].id === id)
        return this._gameObjects[i];
    if (this._gameObjects[i] instanceof GameObjectList) {
        var obj = this._gameObjects[i].find(id);
        if (obj !== null)
            return obj;
    }
}
return null;
```

This code may look a bit strange. You're actually calling the method that you're currently writing. Why does this work? Think about what is happening when the `find` method is called on an object. If the game object you're looking for is in the list, then this method returns that object. Furthermore, the method calls the `find` method on every object that is also of type `GameObjectList`. If none of those method calls finds the object, the method returns `null`. And each of the `find` method calls also calls the `find` method on the objects that belong to it that are of type `GameObjectList`. This big tree of `find` method calls ends when you reach the bottom of the game-object hierarchy. In other words, at some point there are no more lists: only game objects. Then the results of all the `find` method calls (each of which is either null or a game object) are sent back through the return values. Finally, the first caller of the method gets the object (if it was found somewhere in the tree), or null if no object carrying the requested ID was found. This kind of search strategy is also called *depth first*, because you call the find method on the child object before examining the rest of the objects in the list.

When a method calls itself, this is called *recursion*. Recursion is a very powerful tool, because it allows you to perform these kinds of complicated search algorithms without having to write a lot of code. However, watch out with recursion, because you could end up writing a method that calls itself indefinitely. Suppose you want to use recursion to compute the product of two (positive) integers by adding them up:

```
function product(a, b) {
    return b + product(a-1, b);
}
```

This code doesn't check that the product should return 0 if a equals zero. So, the method calls itself indefinitely, resulting in an endless loop, similar to what can happen if you forget to increment the counter in the while instruction. The correct version of this recursive method is, of course

```
function product(a, b) {
    if (a === 0)
        return 0;
    else
        return b + product(a-1, b);
}
```

The key is that the recursive method should have a *termination condition* somewhere, so that in some cases, the method doesn't call itself but does something else. In this example, the termination condition is a === 0. If that happens, the method doesn't call itself, but returns 0 (which is correct, because any number multiplied by 0 results in 0).

Accessing the Game World

Although you can look for a game object with a particular ID in a GameObjectList instance, you need access to the object representing the game world. The variable that refers to this object is a member variable of the Game class. So, whenever you want to look for a particular object, you can call the find method on the Game.gameWorld object, because that object also inherits from GameObjectList. Although you only have a single game world in both the Painter and Jewel Jam games, this is certainly not the case for more complicated games. Each level in a game could be a separate game world. Even a single level could contain several different game worlds. So, it's wise to prepare yourself so the classes you write will also be useful in these cases.

In order to do this, you rely on the parent-child relationship that is encoded into the generic GameObject class. For each game object, you can assume that if you get to the root of the hierarchy that the game object belongs to, this root is the game world of that particular game object.

Therefore, you can easily retrieve the game world by walking through the list of parents to get to the root. You add a property called root to the GameObject class that does this, and it relies on recursion:

```
Object.defineProperty(GameObject.prototype, "root",
    {
        get: function () {
            if (this.parent === null)
                return this;
            else
                return this.parent.root;
        }
    });
```

The code in the property is very simple. If your current parent isn't null (meaning you have a parent), you ask that parent for the root game object. If the parent is null, it means the game object you're currently manipulating is at the root of the hierarchy, meaning it's the game world. In that case, you return the current object.

Now that you've created an easy way for game objects to find each other, the following sections introduce a couple of game-object types that are needed for the Jewel Jam game.

The Jewel Class

In order to prepare the Jewel class a bit more for the game in which it will be used, you need to change a couple of things in this class. The biggest change is that you want to introduce more variety in the sorts of jewels this object can represent. Basically, there are three variations: the jewel's shape can vary, the color of the jewel can vary, and the number of jewels can vary (one, two or three jewels). So, a jewel can have three kinds of properties (shape, color, and number). Also, for each property, there are three variations: three different shapes, three different colors, and three different numbers. In total, that means there are 3 × 3 × 3 = 27 possible jewel configurations (see also Figure 15-1).

Figure 15-1. An overview of the different jewel types used in the Jewel Jam game

Instead of creating 27 different image files, you can store all the different varieties in a single image file (again, see Figure 15-1 for the image). Storing multiple images in a single image file can be beneficial for several reason. First, it provides a way for the artist to group related images together in one file; and, second, it's much more efficient in terms of memory usage and loading speed to load a single file and draw parts of that file instead of loading all the images separately.

The ordering of the jewels in the image file is important in this case, as you see later. When you create a Jewel instance, you randomly choose which jewel to represent by storing a random number between 0 and 26 (to cover the 27 varieties) in a member variable variation. Therefore, the Jewel constructor becomes

```
function Jewel(layer, id) {
    SpriteGameObject.call(this, sprites.jewels, layer, id);
    this.variation = Math.floor(Math.random() * 27);
}
```

Because the Jewel class knows which sprite it's going to use, you pass the sprite (sprites.jewels) directly to the base class constructor.

Now the only thing that needs to be modified is the draw method. You don't want to draw the entire sprite, but only a part of it: the part that contains the jewel this object represents. For this, you first have to extend the Canvas2D.drawImage method, because it needs to be able to draw only part of a sprite. Fortunately, this is straightforward to do. The drawImage method of the HTML5 canvas element has four parameters with which you can specify the part of the sprite you want to draw. To indicate which part of the sprite you want to draw, you use a Rectangle object. The header of the Canvas2D.drawImage method is as follows:

```
Canvas2D_Singleton.prototype.drawImage = function (sprite, position, rotation,
    scale, origin, sourceRect)
```

The last parameter of the method is the rectangle that defines which part of the source image should be drawn. In the method body, you use the member variables of this Rectangle object as follows:

```
this._canvasContext.drawImage(sprite, sourceRect.x, sourceRect.y,
    sourceRect.width, sourceRect.height, -origin.x * scale, -origin.y * scale,
    sourceRect.width * scale, sourceRect.height * scale);
```

The second through fifth parameters indicate what part of the image should be drawn. The last two parameters indicate the width and height of the projection of that image on the canvas. You multiply the width and height of the rectangle by the scale, so that the image drawn can be scaled by the user if desired. Because you're scaling the sprite, you also need to scale the origin, which happens in the third code line.

In the draw method of the Jewel class, you need to determine which part of the jewel sprite you want to draw depending on the value of the variation member variable:

```
var imagePart = new Rectangle(this.variation * this.height, 0, this.height,
    this.height);
```

Here the segment you want to draw is a square shape that has the same width and height as the height of the original sprite. The position of the rectangle (given by the first two parameters in the Rectangle constructor) is calculated by multiplying the height of the sprite by the variation index.

As a result, the higher the variation index, the further to the right the rectangle is moved. Finally, a call to the Canvas2D.drawImage method draws the jewel on the screen. Here is the complete draw method:

```
Jewel.prototype.draw = function () {
    if (!this.visible)
        return;
    var imagePart = new Rectangle(this.variation * this.height, 0,
        this.height, this.height);
    Canvas2D.drawImage(this.sprite, this.worldPosition, 0, 1, this.origin,
        imagePart);
};
```

Maintaining the Current Score

The next step in making this game more interesting is to add a few game objects that relate to the way the game is played and how rewards are handed to the player. In this game, you express the reward given to the player as a number of points: the *score*. Every time the player finds a valid combination of jewels, the player gains 10 points. This current score should be stored in a variable or an object. Also, the score should be written on the screen, so the player knows how many points they've obtained.

Now you see another advantage of not specifically assuming that every game object is represented by a sprite. The score game object uses a *font* to display itself on the screen. To make this even more generic, you first introduce a class called Label, which simply writes some text on the screen at a certain position. This class is very similar to the SpriteGameObject class, except that you draw text on the screen instead of a sprite. In order to do that, you need to store the text to be written and the font that is used. You also store other text properties, such as the alignment of the text and the size of the font. Here is the constructor of Label:

```
function Label(fontname, fontsize, layer, id) {
    GameObject.call(this, layer, id);

    this.color = Color.black;
    this.origin = Vector2.zero;
    this._fontname = typeof fontname !== 'undefined' ?
        fontname : "Courier New";
    this._fontsize = typeof fontsize !== 'undefined' ? fontsize : "20px";
    this._contents = "";
    this._align = "left";
    this._size = Vector2.zero;
}
```

The last member variable you assign a value to in the constructor is _size. Knowing the size (height and width in pixels) of the text can be very useful for drawing the text at the right spot. Because you can only calculate the size of the text when you know what the text is, you initially set this value to Vector2.zero.

How do you calculate the size of text? There isn't really an easy way to do this in HTML. This code uses a simple trick: you dynamically add the text to the HTML page, calculate its size when it's drawn, and remove it again. Here is the function that does this work for you:

```
function calculateTextSize(fontname, fontsize, text) {
    var div = document.createElement("div");
    div.style.position = "absolute";
    div.style.left = -1000;
    div.style.top = -1000;
    document.body.appendChild(div);
    text = typeof text !== 'undefined' ? text : "M";
    div.style.fontSize = "" + fontsize;
    div.style.fontFamily = fontname;
    div.innerHTML = text;
    var size = new Vector2(div.offsetWidth, div.offsetHeight);
    document.body.removeChild(div);
    return size;
}
```

You first create a div element, in which you place the text. You set the position of the element to (-1000, 1000) so that it's drawn outside of the screen. You place the text and calculate its size, which you then store in a Vector2 object. This object is returned as a result of this function. Although this isn't a very neat way of solving the problem, it's very easy to do and works fine. When you program, sometimes these quick and dirty hacks are acceptable, but be careful not to use them all the time. In this case, you have no choice because there is no alternative way to do this in HTML.

In the Label class, you calculate the size of the text when the text content is set. This is done in the text property:

```
Object.defineProperty(Label.prototype, "text",
    {
        get: function () {
            return this._contents;
        },
        set: function (value) {
            this._contents = value;
            this._size = calculateTextSize(this._fontname, this._fontsize,
                value);
        }
    });
```

The Label class also needs a draw method in order to draw the text on the screen. Drawing text on the screen is done by calling the Canvas2D.drawText method. You use the *world position* of the text label when drawing the text, so that text-based game objects can also be part of the hierarchy. Here is the complete draw method:

```
Label.prototype.draw = function () {
    if (!this.visible)
        return;
    Canvas2D.drawText(this._contents, this.worldPosition, this.origin,
        this.color, this._align, this._fontname, this._fontsize);
};
```

Now you define a `ScoreGameObject` class that inherits from the `Label` class. The score is represented by the text content. The nice thing is that JavaScript will automatically transform an integer number into text when drawing. So, you simply set the text to 0:

```
function ScoreGameObject(fontName, fontSize, layer, id) {
    Label.call(this, fontName, fontSize, layer, id);
    this.text = 0;
    this._align = "right";
}
ScoreGameObject.prototype = Object.create(Label.prototype);
```

You also add a `score` property that lets you retrieve or modify the current score:

```
Object.defineProperty(ScoreGameObject.prototype, "score",
    {
        get: function () {
            return this._contents;
        },
        set: function (value) {
            if (value >=0)
                this.text = value;
        }
    });
```

Finally, you add a `reset` method, so that when the game is over, you can call this method to reset the score to zero:

```
ScoreGameObject.prototype.reset = function () {
    this.text = 0;
};
```

Now that you have this class, you can simply create an instance of it and add it to the game world. Place these instructions in the `JewelJamGameWorld` class, and add a frame overlay on which you can draw the current score. These instructions do all the work:

```
var scoreFrame = new SpriteGameObject(sprites.frame_score, ID.layer_overlays);
scoreFrame.position = new Vector2(20, 20);
this.add(scoreFrame);

var score = new ScoreGameObject("Segoe UI Mono", "40px", ID.layer_overlays_1,
    ID.score);
score.position = new Vector2(270, 35);
score.color = Color.white;
this.add(score);
```

You assign the score game object to the layer ID.layer_overlays, so it's drawn on top of the background and the score frame. You also choose appropriate positions for the frame and the score. Finally, you assign an ID ID.score to the score game object, so that other objects can retrieve it when needed.

A Moving Jewel Cart

To make the game a bit more exciting, you can add a feeling of pressure for the player. In the Jewel Jam game, this is done by drawing a jewel cart that slowly moves off the screen. Once the jewel cart is outside the screen, the game is over. Every time the player finds a correct combination of jewels, the jewel cart moves back a little.

The jewel cart is represented in the JewelCart class. You define a couple of things in it. First, you define how much the jewel cart should be moved back when the player finds a correct combination. This is stored in the push member variable. You also want to set a minimal x-position, so the jewel cart will never be drawn over the playing field. This you do in the minxpos variable. You add a pushCart method that can be called when the player finds a correct combination of jewels. Because the class already inherits most of its features from SpriteGameObject, the class is rather small. Have a look at the JewelJam4 example to see the code for the class.

You add an instance of this class to the game world as follows:

```
var jewelCart = new JewelCart(sprites.jewelcart, ID.layer_objects, ID.jewel_cart);
jewelCart.position = new Vector2(410, 230);
jewelCart.minxpos = 410;
this.add(jewelCart);
```

The jewel cart object also gets an ID, so you can find it later when it needs to be pushed. You also set its position and its minimal x-position to appropriate values. If you look at the JewelCart.js file, you see that you assign a positive x-velocity to the cart. Because JewelCart is a subclass of SpriteGameObject, which in turn is a subclass of GameObject, the update method updates the cart position according to its velocity (assuming this method is called from somewhere else). Figure 15-2 shows a screenshot of the game with the new game objects (jewels, score, and jewel cart).

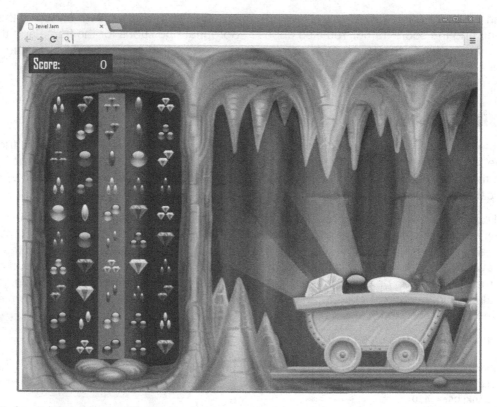

Figure 15-2. A screenshot of the JewelJam4 example

Dealing With Combinations of Jewels

Whenever a player has constructed a valid combination in the middle column by dragging rows, the game checks whether the combination is valid. If so, the game adds points to the score, pushes the jewel cart back, removes the combination of jewels from the grid, and adds new jewels. The JewelGrid class has a handleInput method where the row dragging is handled. In the update method of that class, you need to determine whether the player has made a valid combination of jewels.

Finding Valid Combinations

In the update method, you need to check for all groups of three adjacent jewels in the middle column to see if they form a valid combination. To help do that, you add a method isValidCombination, which has the following header:

```
JewelGrid.prototype.isValidCombination = function (a, b, c)
```

This method takes three Jewel objects, and it returns a Boolean value indicating whether the three jewels form a valid combination. So now the question is, how can you evaluate whether three jewels form a valid combination? Recall that a valid combination means for each property (color, shape, number), all three jewels should have either the same or a different value. In order to make things a bit easier, let's *encode* each jewel by using three integers from 0 to 2. Let's say the first integer represents the color (yellow, blue, or red), the second integer the shape (diamond, oval, or round), and the last integer the number of jewels (one, two, or three). Using this encoding scheme, you can, for example, encode the blue oval-shaped single jewel as (1,0,0). The yellow round single jewel is defined as (0,2,0), and the red oval-shaped triple jewel is defined as (2,1,2).

> **Note** Humans would probably try to find valid combinations of jewels in a different way, by simply looking at the row that was just shifted and the rows above and below. A computer can run periodic checks in the main loop to check all combinations of three in the center column, even if the player hasn't touched it, as is done here. Computers can do that, so programmers write it that way; but if you're new to programming, it may take you some time to get used to thinking this way.

Now let's see if you can use this encoding scheme to find valid combinations of three jewels (let's call them jewels A, B, and C). For each jewel, you have to compare the color, the shape, and the number. Each of these properties has to be either the same for all jewels, or different for all jewels. For example, if A has encoding value 0 for the color, B has value 0, and C also has value 0, then the condition holds for the color, because all three jewels have the same color (yellow). The same is true if the jewels all are blue (A-color = 1, B-color = 1, C-color = 1) or red (A-color = 2, B-color = 2, C-color = 2). Finally, the condition holds if all their colors are different: there is an ordering of A-color, B-color, and C-color that yields 0, 1, and 2. If you look at the sum of these different combinations, you see an interesting property: $0 + 0 + 0 = 0$, $1 + 1 + 1 = 3$, $2 + 2 + 2 = 6$, and $0 + 1 + 2 = 3$. In other words: *the sum is divisible by three*. Also, it happens that any of the other possible combinations of values is *not* divisible by three. Therefore, you can say that for each property (color, shape, and number), *the sum of the encoding values of each jewel must be divisible by three.* If this sum is represented by a variable sum, then in JavaScript code the condition sum % 3 === 0 must hold! So, if you calculate this sum for each property and determine that it's divisible by three, you have found a valid combination of three jewels. As you can see, sometimes basic mathematics can be very useful for writing efficient code. The alternative in this case would be to write a large number of if instructions that handle the different cases, which would most certainly result in slower code.

The only thing left to do is to retrieve the encoding from each jewel. As of now, you have a single number: the offset of the jewel in the sprite. This is a number from 0 to 26. If you look again at Figure 15-1, you see that the first nine jewels are yellow, the following nine are blue, and the last nine are red. Therefore, if you divide the variation variable by 9, you get a value between 0 and 2 that represents the color! The rest of that division is a number from 0 to 8. If you divide that number by 3, you again get a number from 0 to 2 that represents the shape. The rest of that division is a number from 0 to 2, and it represents the number of jewels. By using this concept, you can construct an algorithm that calculates these values for each property and that checks whether the sum of the properties is divisible by 3. Look at the following algorithm:

```
var curra = a.variation;
var currb = b.variation;
var currc = c.variation;
var divider = 9;
```

```
for (var i = 0; i < 3; i += 1) {
    if ((Math.floor(curra / divider) + Math.floor(currb / divider)
        + Math.floor(currc / divider)) % 3 !== 0)
        return false;
    curra = curra % divider;
    currb = currb % divider;
    currc = currc % divider;
    divider = Math.floor(divider / 3);
}
return true;
```

First you retrieve the value that represents which jewel you're dealing with, using the variation member variable of each jewel. Then you define a divider number that is equal to 9 (you first divide by 9). You next define a for instruction that runs three times. In the body of the for instruction, you place a condition that the sum of the three variation indices divided by divider should be divisible by 3. If this isn't the case, you return false because the combination condition doesn't hold for one of the properties. You assign the rest of the division by the divider to each of the variables containing the current variation index. You then divide the divider by 3. If you exit the for instruction, it means in all cases that the condition in the if instruction was true, meaning you found a valid combination. Because you found a valid combination, you return the value true.

Removing Jewels from the Grid

In the update method, you can now use the isValidCombination method to determine whether a valid combination exists. For this, you use a while instruction that evaluates all sequences of three jewels in the middle column:

```
var middleCol = Math.floor(this._columns / 2);
var i = 0;
while (i < this._rows - 2) {
    if (this.isValidCombination(this.at(middleCol, i),
        this.at(middleCol, i + 1), this.at(middleCol, i + 2))) {
        // do something
    }
    else
        i++;
}
```

When you find a valid combination, you need to remove these jewels from the grid and insert new jewels. To do this, you define a method called removeJewel, which removes a jewel from the grid and inserts a new one. To create a nice "falling down" motion, you place these jewels in different positions above the grid. You pass the desired y-location as a parameter to the removeJewel method so it knows where the new jewel should be located. The complete method then becomes

```
JewelGrid.prototype.removeJewel = function (x, y, newYPosition) {
    for (var row = y; row > 0; row -= 1)
        this._gameObjects[row * this._columns + x] =
            this._gameObjects[(row - 1) * this._columns + x];
```

```
    var jewel = new Jewel();
    this.addAt(jewel, x, 0);
    jewel.position.y = newYPosition;
};
```

In the update method, you call removeJewel three times to remove the three jewels that form a valid combination:

```
this.removeJewel(middleCol, i, -this.cellHeight);
this.removeJewel(middleCol, i + 1, -this.cellHeight * 2);
this.removeJewel(middleCol, i + 2, -this.cellHeight * 3);
```

As the grid is updated, the position difference between the jewel objects and their target location on the grid results in the desired falling effect. Finally, because introducing new jewels may mean there is a new valid combination of three jewels, you reset the counter i to zero with the instruction i = 0;.

Updating Other Game Objects

Now that the grid has been updated, you can focus on the other game objects that need to be updated. The first game object that needs to be updated is score, because the score should be increased if you handle a valid combination. You use the find method to retrieve the score object, and you add 10 points to the score, as follows:

```
var score = this.root.find(ID.score);
score.score += 10;
```

Also, because you found a valid combination, you push back the jewel cart:

```
var jewelCart = this.root.find(ID.jewel_cart);
jewelCart.pushCart();
```

For the complete program, see the JewelJam4 example belonging to this chapter.

What You Have Learned

In this chapter, you have learned:

- How to organize game objects and assign IDs to them
- How to program gameplay aspects and interaction between game objects
- How to detect valid combinations of jewels in the Jewel Jam game

Chapter **16**

Game States

In the previous chapter, you programmed the main gameplay elements of the Jewel Jam game. However, the game as it stands is far from complete. For example, nothing happens when the jewel cart disappears from the screen. Also, when you start the program, the game immediately begins without any warning. What is still needed is a way to incorporate menus and overlays in the game so the player can change settings, get help, or start playing the game. When the player is, for example, in a menu screen, the type of interaction with the game is very different from when the player is solving a level or trying to survive as long as possible. When programming a game, you have to think about how to incorporate these different *game states* and switch between them.

Modern games have many different game states, such as menus, maps, inventories, splash screens, intro movies, and much more. This chapter shows how to add different game states to the Jewel Jam game. Because this game isn't yet very complicated, you can get away with using a few simple extensions to your current classes. However, game-state management needs to be handled properly if you want to build a commercial game. In Chapter 20, this book discusses a software design using classes that can handle game states in a very nice and generic way.

Adding a Title Screen

One of the first things you can do to make a game more complete is add a title screen. The title screen allows the player to get ready to play the game instead of being immediately launched into it. You can extend the JewelJamGameWorld class so that it loads and displays a title screen consisting of a single image. You create a SpriteGameObject instance for that, assign it the ID ID.title, and add it to the game world:

```
var titleScreen = new SpriteGameObject(sprites.title, ID.layer_overlays_2,
    ID.title);
this.add(titleScreen);
```

You assign the layer ID.layer_overlays_2 so you can be sure the title is drawn on top of everything. But you have to do a little extra work to properly handle input and update the game world, because you want the game to start only when the title screen is no longer visible. You can do that by adding a few instructions to the handleInput method to distinguish between two states: the state in which you show the title screen and the state in which you're playing the game:

```
var titleScreen = this.root.find(ID.title);
if (titleScreen.visible) {
    if (Mouse.left.pressed || Touch.isPressing)
        titleScreen.visible = false;
    return;
}
GameObjectList.prototype.handleInput.call(this, delta);
```

Looking at the if instructions, you can see that if the title screen is visible, you react only when the player presses the left mouse button or touches the screen. In that case, you set the title screen's visibility flag to false so it isn't drawn anymore. After this, you return from the method, so whenever the title screen is visible, the only thing the game reacts to is player pressing the left mouse button or touching the screen. If the title screen isn't visible, you call the handleInput method on all the game objects in the game world: in other words, the game reacts to the player as it should when the player is playing the game.

You follow very much the same procedure for the update method, where you update the game world only if the title isn't visible:

```
var titleScreen = this.root.find(ID.title);
if (titleScreen.visible)
    return;
GameObjectList.prototype.update.call(this, delta);
```

When a player starts the game, they now see a title screen before the game starts (see Figure 16-1). You aren't done yet. In the next section, you add a simple button GUI element that shows a help frame.

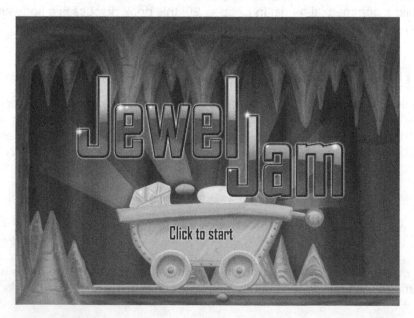

Figure 16-1. The Jewel Jam title screen

Adding a Button to Show a Help Frame

This section explains how to add a button to a game, which you use to display a help frame. To do that, you add another class, Button, to the program. You inherit from the SpriteGameObject class and add some simple behavior that checks whether the player pressed a button. In the Button class, you declare a boolean member variable that indicates whether the button was pressed. Then you override the handleInput method to check whether the player has clicked the left mouse button or has touched the button on the screen. If the mouse or touching position is within the boundaries of the sprite at that time, you know the player has pressed the button, and you set the value of the member variable to true. How can you check whether the mouse position is within the boundaries of the sprite? By using the Rectangle class. As a first step, you construct a Rectangle object that encompasses the sprite. The position of this rectangle should be the world position of the sprite minus its origin. The width and height of the rectangle are the same as the width and height of the sprite. For convenience, let's add a property to SpriteGameObject called boundingBox that calculates this rectangle for you:

```
Object.defineProperty(SpriteGameObject.prototype, "boundingBox",
    {
        get: function () {
            var leftTop = this.worldPosition.subtractFrom(this.origin);
            return new Rectangle(leftTop.x, leftTop.y, this.width,
                this.height);
        }
    });
```

You have to use the world position here, because you want to check whether the mouse pointer or the touch is within the sprite at its actual, world position. You add a simple method contains to Rectangle, which checks whether a point is inside the rectangle:

```
Rectangle.prototype.contains = function (v) {
    v = typeof v !== 'undefined' ? v : new Vector2();
    return (v.x >=this.left && v.x <= this.right &&
        v.y >=this.top && v.y <= this.bottom);
};
```

The first line of this code checks whether the parameter v has been defined. If it hasn't, you simply assign it the zero vector. You then check whether the x value lies between the left and right side of the rectangle and the y value lies between the top and bottom.

You also add methods to the Mouse and Touch classes that can help solve your problem easily. For example, this is the method for checking whether the player pressed the left mouse button within a given rectangle:

```
Mouse_Singleton.prototype.containsMousePress = function (rect) {
    return this._left.pressed && rect.contains(this._position);
};
```

In the Button class, you use these methods to determine whether the button is down and/or pressed. Here is the handleInput method of Button:

```
Button.prototype.handleInput = function (delta) {
    var boundingBox = this.boundingBox;
    this.pressed = this.visible && (Touch.containsTouchPress(boundingBox) ||
        Mouse.containsMousePress(boundingBox));
    this.down = this.visible && (Touch.containsTouch(boundingBox) ||
        Mouse.containsMouseDown(boundingBox));
};
```

Now that you have a button class, you can add a help button to the game world (see the JewelJamGameWorld class):

```
this.helpButton = new Button(sprites.button_help, ID.layer_overlays);
this.helpButton.position = new Vector2(1268, 20);
this.add(this.helpButton);
```

Because you want to display a help frame when the player presses the help button, you also add a help frame to the game world. You set its visibility flag to false so it isn't yet visible:

```
var helpFrame = new SpriteGameObject(sprites.frame_help, ID.layer_overlays,
    ID.help_frame);
helpFrame.position = new Vector2(636, 120);
helpFrame.visible = false;
this.add(helpFrame);
```

Now you have to make sure that when the player presses the help button, the help frame visibility is toggled. You can do this using the following if instruction in the handleInput method of the JewelJamGameWorld class:

```
var helpFrame = this.root.find(ID.help_frame);
if (this.helpButton.pressed) {
    helpFrame.visible = !helpFrame.visible;
}
```

Notice that the instruction in the if body is a toggle. It's basically a shorter way of writing.

```
if (helpFrame.visible)
    helpFrame.visible = false;
else
    helpFrame.visible = true;
```

When the help frame is visible, you want to be able to remove it by pressing the left mouse button or by touching the screen. So, the final if instruction is slightly more complicated:

```
var helpFrame = this.root.find(ID.help_frame);
if (this.helpButton.pressed ||
    (helpFrame.visible && (Mouse.left.pressed || Touch.isPressing))) {
    helpFrame.visible = !helpFrame.visible;
}
```

Finally, you have to make sure the game isn't updated when the help frame is displayed. You can do that in the update method by updating the game objects only if the help frame isn't visible:

```
var helpFrame = this.root.find(ID.help_frame);
if (!helpFrame.visible)
    GameObjectList.prototype.update.call(this, delta);
```

One more thing you have to take care of is that by pressing the help button, the player pauses the game. If you keep showing the jewel grid, this provides the player with a means to gain extra time to try to find jewel combinations. Of course, this isn't what you want! Fortunately, in the current class structure, this is very easy to solve. Add the following two lines to the update method:

```
var grid = this.root.find(ID.grid);
grid.visible = !helpFrame.visible;
```

These lines ensure that whenever the help frame is visible, the grid isn't, and vice versa. Figure 16-2 shows the game when the help frame is displayed.

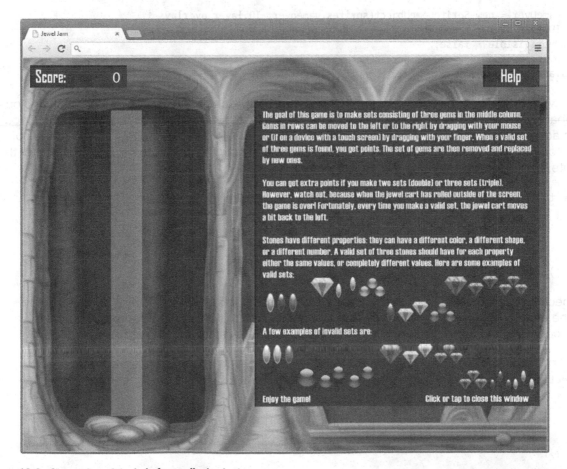

Figure 16-2. Screenshot of the help frame display in the game

Overlays

A very common way of presenting information to the player is to use *overlays*. Overlays are basically images that can be displayed on top of the game world to present information or to provide a user interface such as a menu, a mini map, status information, and more. The help frame introduced in the previous section is another example of an overlay.

Overlays can present an entirely new game state (such as a "game over" overlay), or they can supplement the game world by providing information to the player. For example, many strategy games provide information about the number of units selected, available resources, ongoing building processes, items gathered, and so on. These kinds of overlays are generally always on the screen, and together they're called the *heads-up display* (HUD). Jewel Jam has a very basic HUD: it consists of a frame that displays the current score, and a help button the user can press to view a frame with help information.

Next to the HUD, you want to show a "game over" overlay when the jewel cart moves offscreen. You add this overlay to the game world, and set its visibility to `false`:

```
var gameOver = new SpriteGameObject(sprites.gameover, ID.layer_overlays_1,
    ID.game_over);
gameOver.visible = false;
gameOver.position = gameOver.screenCenter;
this.add(gameOver);
```

You want to position the overlay nicely in the middle of the screen. Because this is something you'll probably use often, let's add a few useful properties to `SpriteGameObject` to deal with it. First, you can add a property that calculates the position of the sprite if you want to draw it in the center of the screen. This is relatively easy to calculate, once you know the size of the screen, the size of the sprite, and its origin. Here is the complete property:

```
Object.defineProperty(SpriteGameObject.prototype, "screenCenter",
    {
        get: function () {
            return Game.size.subtract(this.size).divideBy(2).addTo(this.origin);
        }
    });
```

Especially in the case of HUD elements, you sometimes don't want to display a sprite squarely in the middle; instead, for example, you may want it in the middle at the bottom of the screen. To accommodate these kinds of situations, you can add the following two properties to `SpriteGameObject`:

```
Object.defineProperty(SpriteGameObject.prototype, "screenCenterX",
    {
        get: function () {
            return (Game.size.x - this.width) / 2 + this.origin.x;
        }
    });
```

```
Object.defineProperty(SpriteGameObject.prototype, "screenCenterY",
    {
        get: function () {
            return (Game.size.y - this.height) / 2 + this.origin.y;
        }
    });
```

Now let's extend JewelJamGameWorld to display the "game over" overlay when needed. First you add a method that checks whether the jewel cart is outside the screen:

```
JewelJamGameWorld.prototype.gameOver = function () {
    var jewelCart = this.root.find(ID.jewel_cart);
    return jewelCart.position.x > Game.size.x;
};
```

You can then use this method in the handleInput method so the player can press the left mouse button or touch the screen to restart the game:

```
if (this.gameOver()) {
    if (Mouse.left.pressed || Touch.isPressing)
        this.reset();
    return;
}
```

You override the reset method because you need to do a little extra work when the game restarts. Notably, you have to set the visibility of some of the overlays to false so they aren't shown on the screen when the game restarts. Apart from that, you simply call the reset method from the base class so that all game objects in the game world are reset:

```
JewelJamGameWorld.prototype.reset = function () {
    GameObjectList.prototype.reset.call(this);
    var gameOver = this.root.find(ID.game_over);
    gameOver.visible = false;
    var titleScreen = this.root.find(ID.title);
    titleScreen.visible = false;
    var helpFrame = this.root.find(ID.help_frame);
    helpFrame.visible = false;
};
```

Now there is only one thing left to do. If the game is over, you have to set the visibility of the "game over" overlay to true. You do this in the update method of JewelJamGameWorld:

```
var gameOver = this.root.find(ID.game_over);
if (this.gameOver()) {
    gameOver.visible = true;
}
```

Figure 16-3 shows a screenshot of the "game over" state.

Figure 16-3. Too bad ...

DESIGNING GAMES

Although on game-development teams the programmer normally isn't responsible for the design of the game, it's still very useful to have a basic understanding of this process. The programmer must turn the game design into code and must be able to advise the designer about what will work and what will be difficult to achieve. For this collaboration to be successful, everyone has to speak the same language.

Designing a game primarily consists of defining the game mechanics, the setting of the game, and the game levels. Game mechanics involve such things are the rules of the game, the way players control the game, goals and challenges, and the reward structure. Psychology and educational science play an important role here. They help you to understand how players get in the flow (the mood in which they're fully committed to playing the game); how goals, challenges, and rewards can support each other; and how to vary and adapt the game's difficulty.

The game's setting deals with the story, the characters, and the virtual world in which the game takes place. A good story can be a strong motivator for players, and discovering the story while playing can be a very satisfying task. Characters need to evoke empathy from the player to give meaning to the tasks that must be performed. And the game world enhances these aspects and adapts the game to certain demographics.

Level design is sometimes done by special level designers, but in smaller teams it's often the responsibility of the game designer. Careful level design leads to a good learning curve. It keeps the player challenged and motivated, and it should result in pleasant surprises.

Many books have been written about game design, and you're strongly encouraged to read some of them. You can also find lots of information on all aspects of game development on sites like www.gamasutra.com. Finally, Chapters 30 and 31 of this book talk about game production and publishing.

What You Have Learned

In this chapter, you have learned:

- How to add an HUD and overlays to the game
- How to define a simple button that shows a frame
- How to deal with a few different game states such as a title screen and a "game over" state

Chapter **17**

Finishing the Jewel Jam Game

In this chapter, you finish the Jewel Jam game. As a first step, you give the player extra points when multiple combinations of three jewels happen. Second, you add a nice visual effect by showing glitters on the jewels in the game. Finally, you add sound and music.

Extra Points for Multiple Combinations

You want to give the player extra points when multiple combinations occur. Whenever the player makes a combination of three jewels, new random jewels are added to the playing field. These jewels can form new combinations. In addition, new combinations can be formed by jewels falling down. You award the player extra points in cases where there are two or three combinations. In order to do that, you have to count how many combinations a player finds. You do this in the JewelGrid class, by introducing an extra variable nrCombis:

```
var nrCombis = 0;
```

Every time you find a valid combination, you increment this variable. Now you can use an if instruction to check when you should award extra points:

```
if (nrCombis === 2) {
    score.score += 50;
}
else if (nrCombis >= 3) {
    score.score += 100;
}
```

You also want to show the player a message that they got extra points in the case of a double or triple combination. To do so, you can show an overlay for a couple of seconds. As a first step, let's load two overlays for that and add them to the game world in the `JewelJamGameWorld` class:

```
var doubleOverlay = new SpriteGameObject(sprites.double, ID.layer_overlays);
doubleOverlay.position = new Vector2(800, 400);
this.add(doubleOverlay);
var tripleOverlay = new SpriteGameObject(sprites.triple, ID.layer_overlays);
tripleOverlay.position = new Vector2(800, 400);
this.add(tripleOverlay);
```

As soon as the player gets multiple combinations, you want to show this overlay on the screen for a couple of seconds. In order to be able to do that, you first need to understand a bit more about how you deal with time in games.

Time in Games

Time is a very important concept in games. For example, it's used to measure how fast a player executes a task, to update positions of objects according to their velocity, to keep track of the last time the player beat an enemy, to determine whether it's currently day or night in the game, and so on. To accommodate these things, a game engine generally contains many classes to deal with different aspects of time. Because time is so important in games, game-loop methods such as `handleInput` and `update` always have a parameter `delta` that indicates how much time has passed since the last game-loop iteration. The game time doesn't have to be the same as the time in the real world. In the game, time can go three times as fast, or ten times as slow, or whatever the game designer wants. For example, a game designer could decide that in a simulation game, time at night goes much faster because not much happens at night. The game time begins only after the game has started. Furthermore, the game time can be interrupted. For example, if the player switches to another tab in the browser, the game time is paused because the browser stops executing the script (whereas real time continues).

When the game starts, the game time is zero: zero hours, zero minutes, and zero seconds have passed. Every time the game-loop methods are executed, you get as a parameter a real number indicating how much time has passed. The examples in this book follow the *fixed timestep* paradigm, meaning you assume a fixed number of game-loop iterations per second, regardless of how fast or slow the machine is. You can see this when you look at this line of code in the `Game` object:

```
var delta = 1 / 60;
```

So, even if the game loop is running less often than 60 times per second, all the objects in the game behave as though the game loop is running exactly 60 times per second. The advantage of this approach is that user interruptions (such as switching to another tab) simply pause the game time so that when the user comes back, they can continue to play like nothing happened. The downside is that on very slow computers, the game may slow down considerably.

Another option is to use real time. That way, it doesn't matter what the speed of the computer is (or whether the player switches to another tab): the game always continues. When using real time, it's also possible to call the game-loop methods more often than 60 times per second. The interruption problem can be solved by keeping track of whether the game is paused. Basically, you need to maintain a time offset that increases while the game is paused. Many first-person shooters follow this strategy because in those kinds of games, it's crucial to have a high framerate so the player can interact naturally with the game world. And with first-person shooters, chances are the players are completely involved in the game, and they wouldn't dream of interrupting the game to read the news or play a Sudoku!

Controlling the Visibility of a Game Object

In this section you create a class that controls the visibility of a game object based on a timer. Let's call this class `VisibilityTimer`. The idea of this class is that you can assign it a target game object, for which visibility is set to `false` by default; when you start the timer, the target object becomes visible until the timer has reached its maximum value. You can connect such a timer to an overlay in order to show that overlay on the screen for a while. Take a look at the `JewelJamFinal` program belonging to this chapter; it contains a file called `VisibilityTimer.js` that includes the complete `VisibilityTimer` class.

A visibility timer object needs to keep track of a couple of things. For one, you need to store the target object whose visibility you want to control. You also store how much time in total this object should be visible, for when the timer is started. Finally, when the timer is running you have to maintain how time is left before it stops. This value is updated every time the `update` method is called. Therefore, the `VisibilityTimer` class inherits from the `GameObject` class.

When the timer is created, you assume it isn't running, so the time left is set to 0. You also set the total time that the timer should run to 1 second:

```
function VisibilityTimer(target, layer, id) {
    GameObject.call(this, layer, id);
    this._target = target;
    this._timeLeft = 0;
    this.totalTime = 1;
}
```

In the update method, you then subtract the elapsed game time in seconds from the `_timeLeft` variable. If this variable contains a value less than zero, you set the target visibility to `false`:

```
VisibilityTimer.prototype.update = function (delta) {
    if (this._timeLeft > 0) {
        this._timeLeft -= delta;
        this._target.visible = true;
    } else
        this._target.visible = false;
};
```

Finally, you add a method called `startVisible` that assigns the total time to the `_timeLeft` variable and sets the targets visibility status to true.

Now you can use the VisibilityTimer class to control the visibility of the double and triple combination overlays in the Jewel Jam game. When you create overlay objects, you also create VisibilityTimer instances with these overlays as their target:

```
var doubleOverlay = new SpriteGameObject(sprites.double, ID.layer_overlays);
doubleOverlay.position = new Vector2(800, 400);
var doubleTimer = new VisibilityTimer(doubleOverlay, ID.layer_overlays, ID.double_timer);
this.add(doubleOverlay);
this.add(doubleTimer);

var tripleOverlay = new SpriteGameObject(sprites.triple, ID.layer_overlays);
tripleOverlay.position = new Vector2(800, 400);
var tripleTimer = new VisibilityTimer(tripleOverlay, ID.layer_overlays, ID.triple_timer);
this.add(tripleOverlay);
this.add(tripleTimer);
```

When two or three combinations of jewels occur, you start the visibility timer of that particular overlay. For example, this is what the code looks like for the double combination (see the update method of the JewelGrid class):

```
if (nrCombis === 2) {
    score.score += 50;
    var doubleTimer = this.root.find(ID.double_timer);
    doubleTimer.startVisible();
}
```

You can see the timer in action by running the JewelJamFinal program available with this chapter.

A Field of Glitters

In this section, you add some eye candy to the game. Currently, the jewels are sprites displayed on the screen. Let's add a nice visual effect to them: glitters. You can do this in a generic way by designating a rectangle on the screen in which the glitters are drawn at random positions. You also want to be able to indicate how *dense* this rectangle of glitters is. Then you can create rectangles of different sizes and attach them to game objects. Figure 17-1 shows the areas on the screen where you would like to add glitters. Later in the chapter, Figure 17-2 shows the final output that will be shown to the player.

Figure 17-1. The rectangles indicate where you would like to add glitters in the game

The Constructor

Let's create a GlitterField class that allows you to add glitters to game objects. This class inherits from the GameObject class, so you can easily attach it to the scene graph. The constructor of the GlitterField class has several parameters. Here is the header and part of the body of the constructor:

```
function GlitterField(density, width, height, layer, id) {
    GameObject.call(this, layer, id);
    this.width = width;
    this.height = height;
    // To do: initialize the glitter field
}
```

The first parameter is the density of the glitter field. This indicates how many glitters can be visible at the same time. Then you have the width and height parameters, which indicate the size of the rectangle. Finally, the layer and id parameters are passed to the base constructor. In the body of the constructor, you store the width and height of the glitter field in member variables.

Adding Glitters

A glitter field is a rectangle containing multiple glitters, depending on the desired density. Therefore, you need an array to maintain where these glitters should be drawn. This is done in the member variable `positions`, which is an array that is initialized in the constructor:

```
this.positions = [];
```

You fill this list with a number of randomly generated positions. To randomly generate a position within the field, you can add a method `createRandomPosition` that does this work for you. The method is straightforward; you simply generate a random position within the glitter rectangle:

```
GlitterField.prototype.createRandomPosition = function () {
    return new Vector2(Math.random() * this.width, Math.random() *
        this.height);
};
```

To fill the `position` array with random values, you use a `for` instruction:

```
for (var i = 0; i < density; i++) {
    this.positions.push(this.createRandomPosition());
}
```

To draw the glitters, you need more than just a position. You want to add a visual effect that lets the glitters appear and disappear smoothly. You achieve that by drawing them at a scale that first increases and then decreases. This means you also need to maintain the current scale for each of the glitters you're drawing. You do this in another array of variables called `scales`, which is also initialized in the constructor:

```
this.scales = [];
```

Every time you add a new position to the `positions` array, you also add a scale of 0 to the `scales` array. So the final `for` instruction becomes

```
for (var i = 0; i < density; i++) {
    this.positions.push(this.createRandomPosition());
    this.scales.push(0);
}
```

Updating the Glitter Field

In the constructor, you set the scale for each glitter to 0. The result is that when the glitters are drawn, they aren't visible to the player. In the `update` method, you increase and decrease this scale again until it returns to zero. When that happens, you generate another random position for that glitter so it appears elsewhere. Add the following two member variables to the `GlitterField` class:

```
this._scaleMax = 1;
this._scaleStep = 0.05;
```

The first variable specifies the maximum scale for the glitters (1 is the original size). The second variable, _scaleStep, indicates *how fast* the scale should increase or decrease.

You don't want to begin increasing each glitter's scale at the same time—you want the glitters to appear randomly. So, in the update method, you iterate through all the glitter positions and scales in the list and, depending on the value of a random number, start increasing the scale:

```
for (var i = 0; i < this.scales.length; i += 1) {
    if (this.scales[i] === 0 && Math.random() < 0.01)
        this.scales[i] += this._scaleStep;
}
```

You only begin increasing the scale if it's zero and the random number value is smaller than 0.01. This ensures that not all of the scales increase immediately. When a scale isn't zero anymore, you increase it:

```
else if (this.scales[i] !== 0) {
    this.scales[i] += this._scaleStep;
    // more code to come here
}
```

You can't infinitely increase the scale—you want to decrease it again. But how do you know if you should increase or decrease the scale? You don't know in the update method whether you're in the increasing part of the slope or the decreasing part. You can use a trick here: let the scale run from zero to *two times the maximum scale*, and then, in the draw method, calculate the real scale from that value (zero to maximum scale means increasing scale, and maximum scale to two times the maximum scale means decreasing scale). In the update method, you add an if instruction to deal with the situation when the scale is larger than twice the maximum scale:

```
if (this.scales[i] >=this._scaleMax * 2) {
    this.scales[i] = 0;
    this.positions[i] = this.createRandomPosition();
}
```

When that happens, you reset the scale to zero and generate a new random position for a new glitter.

Drawing the Glitter Field

In the draw method of the glitter field, you have to draw all the glitters on the screen at the desired scale. You want to draw these glitters with their origin at the center, because otherwise the scaling animation won't give the desired result. So, you calculate this origin once at the beginning of the method call:

```
var origin = new Vector2(sprites.glitter.width / 2,
    sprites.glitter.height / 2);
```

Then you add a for instruction that traverses all the glitter scales and positions. You still need to calculate the real scale value based on the scale value stored in the array in the update method. If that value is between zero and the maximum scale, you don't have to do anything (scale is increasing). If the value is between the maximum scale and twice the maximum scale, you need to convert that value into a decreasing scale. This is done using the following instructions:

```
var scale = this.scales[i];
if (this.scales[i] > this._scaleMax)
    scale = this._scaleMax * 2 - this.scales[i];
```

Each glitter should be drawn with respect to the world position of the glitter field. Therefore, you calculate a glitter position as follows:

```
var pos = this.worldPosition. addTo(this.positions[i]);
```

The only thing left to do is to draw the glitter at the desired position, with the desired scale, using the drawImage method from Canvas2D:

```
Canvas2D.drawImage(sprites.glitter, pos, 0, scale, origin);
```

For the complete GlitterField class, look at the JewelJamFinal program belonging to this chapter.

Adding Glitters to Game Objects

Now that you've made the generic GlitterField class, you can add a few simple extensions to your game objects to add glitters to them. You want to do this with tastefully and not blind the player, adding some glitters to the jewel grid as well as the moving jewel cart.

You want the glitter to appear as a rectangle on top of the jewel grid. To do that neatly, you store the jewel grid and the accompanying glitter field in a separate GameObjectList instance. You can then assign a position to that instance once, and the glitter field and jewel grid will be drawn at that position. First you create this instance, called playingField:

```
var playingField = new GameObjectList(ID.layer_objects);
playingField.position = new Vector2(85, 150);
this.add(playingField);
```

Then you create the grid, just as you did in the previous versions of the game. However, now you add it to the playingField list instead of directly to the game world:

```
var rows = 10, columns = 5;
var grid = new JewelGrid(rows, columns, ID.layer_objects, ID.grid);
grid.cellWidth = 85;
grid.cellHeight = 85;
grid.reset();
playingField.add(grid);
```

Finally, you add a `GlitterField` instance to the playing field, as follows:

```
playingField.add(new GlitterField(2, columns * grid.cellWidth,
    rows * grid.cellHeight, ID.layer_overlays_1));
```

Note that you place the glitter field in the overlay layer, so it's drawn on top of the jewel grid.

Let's also add a few glitters to the jewel cart. This example does that a little differently, to show you the various possibilities for attaching game objects to other game objects. In the case of the jewel cart, you introduce to the `JewelCart` class an additional member variable called `glitters`. This variable refers to the `GlitterField` instance associated with the jewel cart:

```
this.glitters = new GlitterField(2, 435, 75);
```

You assign the glitter field an appropriate density, width, and height. Because you want the glitter field to be drawn depending on the position of the cart, you make the cart the parent of the glitter field:

```
this.glitters.parent = this;
```

Finally, you give the glitter field a local position with respect to the cart so the glitters are drawn at the right spot (around the top of the cart where the shiny jewels are):

```
this.glitters.position = new Vector2(275, 475);
```

The only thing left to do is make sure the glitters are actually drawn. For this, you need to extend the `draw` method and explicitly call the `draw` method of the glitter field after the cart has been drawn. Here is the complete method:

```
JewelCart.prototype.draw = function () {
    SpriteGameObject.prototype.draw.call(this);
    this.glitters.draw();
};
```

For the complete `JewelCart` class, see the `JewelJamFinal` example. Play around with the parameter settings of the glitter fields. You can see the effect of changing the density, scale, and scale-step variables. Figure 17-2 goes a little overboard!

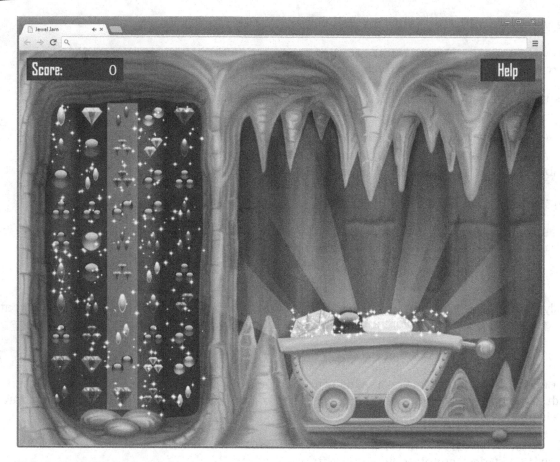

Figure 17-2. *A screenshot of very shiny jewels*

Adding Music and Sound Effects

Just like in the Painter game, you want to add music and sound effects to the game to make it more attractive. As you've seen, playing music and sounds is very easy in JavaScript. You can use the Sound class that you created earlier for Painter. This is another good example of reusing code: you created the Sound class once, and you're using it for all the games in this book!

Many of the classes designed for Jewel Jam will be useful for the other games in this book. When you start building your own games, you'll probably end up with a collection of similar classes that you use. When building games, it's a good idea to think ahead. What classes can you reuse for other projects you're working on? What is the best way to design a class so you might be able to use it again later? As you develop more and more classes, it may be useful to keep a list of these classes that you can reuse. You can then quickly scan the list as you develop new items and implement things you might not have thought of.

When the game is started, you begin playing the background music as soon as the assets are loaded, as follows:

```
sounds.music.volume = 0.3;
sounds.music.play();
```

And when you get a valid combination of jewels (single, double, or triple), you play different sound effects (see the JewelGrid class):

```
if (nrCombis === 1) {
    sounds.combi.play();
}
else if (nrCombis === 2) {
    score.score += 50;
    var doubleTimer = this.root.find(ID.double_timer);
    doubleTimer.startVisible();
    sounds.double.play();
}
else if (nrCombis >=3) {
    score.score += 100;
    var tripleTimer = this.root.find(ID.triple_timer);
    tripleTimer.startVisible();
    sounds.triple.play();
}
```

Finally, you play a sound when the game is over (see the JewelJamGameWorld class):

```
var gameOver = this.root.find(ID.game_over);
if (this.gameOver() && !gameOver.visible) {
    gameOver.visible = true;
    sounds.gameover.play();
    return;
}
```

This completes the Jewel Jam game. You can play the game by running the JewelJamFinal application belonging to this chapter. As an exercise, see if you're able to extend the game yourself with new features. For example, you could add extra animation effects when a combination of jewels is made. Or how about adding a leaderboard/high-score list? In any case, happy jewel hunting!

LEADERBOARDS

Why do games contain leaderboards and high-score lists? Early games didn't have them because there was no semi-permanent storage available in the game consoles. So, nothing could be remembered between playing sessions. That was also the reason there was no Save Game option, which in turn had an important effect on game mechanics: a player always had to start again from the beginning, even if they were experienced.

Once storage became available, designers started to introduce leaderboards. Being better than somebody else always gives a feeling of satisfaction, and it adds an important goal for the player. But this only makes sense if multiple people are playing the game on the same device. If you're the sole player, the only thing you can do is try to beat yourself. Fortunately, nowadays computers and game consoles are connected to the Internet. As a result, you can store leaderboards online and compete with the whole world.

But this adds an additional problem: a goal is only interesting when it's reachable. Being the best player among a couple of millions is unreachable for most people. So, worldwide leaderboards can actually reduce player satisfaction. To remedy this, games often introduce sub-leaderboards. For example, you see a leaderboard that is restricted to your own country or to scores reached this week. You can also see how you rank among your friends. Carefully designing your game's scoring system and the way such scores are shown on leaderboards can make a crucial difference in the satisfaction it gives to your players.

What You Have Learned

In this chapter, you have learned:

- How to build a timer to display overlays for a short time
- How to create a field of glitters and attach it to game objects
- How to play sound effects and music in the Jewel Jam game

Part IV

Penguin Pairs

In this part of the book, you develop the game *Penguin Pairs* (see Figure IV-1). I introduce a few new techniques for programming games, such as sprite sheets, better game-state management, storing game data between sessions, and more.

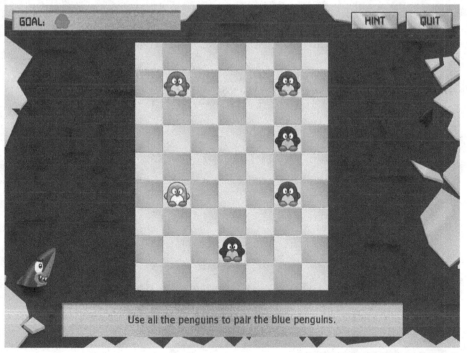

Figure IV-1. The Penguin Pairs game

Penguin Pairs is a puzzle game in which the goal is to make pairs of penguins of the same color. The player can move penguins by clicking or tapping them and selecting the direction in which the penguin should move. A penguin moves until it's stopped by another character in the game (this can be a penguin, a seal, a shark, or an iceberg) or it drops from the playing field, in which case it falls into the water and is eaten by hungry sharks. Throughout the different levels of the game, you introduce new gameplay elements to keep the game exciting. For example, there is a special penguin that can match any other penguin, penguins can get stuck in a hole (meaning they can't move), and penguin-eating sharks can be placed on the board. You can run the final version of this game by trying the example program belonging to Chapter 23. Open the `PenguinPairs.html` file in your browser, and you can immediately start playing.

Chapter **18**

Sprite Sheets

In this chapter, you start building the first elements of the Penguin Pairs game. This game is quite a bit more complicated than the previous games. You can see this by looking at the number of game **assets** it uses. Just as you did in the Jewel Jam game, you use Images containing several different sprites. This technique is used in many games. In the Jewel Jam game, you used it to store a strip of jewels in a single sprite. However, using strips isn't always a good idea. Especially when an image contains many different sprites in a strip, the strip may become too long for the graphics hardware to handle. This can be solved by storing sprites in a *sheet* instead, consisting of multiple rows and columns. Figure 18-1 shows an example of such a sprite sheet.

Figure 18-1. Example of a sheet of sprites (four columns and two rows)

Overview of the Example Program

To test the loading and displaying of a sheet of sprites, let's create a simple example program called PenguinPairs1. This example project shows a background and then draw a penguin (or seal) from the sprite sheet on top of the background. Using the left and right arrows keys, you can select which part of the sheet should be shown.

To get started more easily, you can copy a few classes from the previous game. First you need the GameObject class and the GameObjectList class. You also need the basic classes you wrote for programming games, such as Keyboard, Touch, Mouse, Game, Canvas2D, Vector, and so on. You modify the SpriteGameObject class so it can deal sheets of sprites. Just as in the Jewel Jam game, a class represents the game world; in this case, the class is called PenguinPairsGameWorld. In the constructor method of that class, you load a background image:

```
this.add(new SpriteGameObject(sprites.background_level, ID.layer_background));
```

You also add the penguin sprite to the game world and position it somewhere in the middle of the screen:

```
this.penguin = new SpriteGameObject(sprites.penguin, ID.layer_objects);
this.penguin.position = new Vector2(500, 420);
this.add(this.penguin);
```

Loading a Sprite Sheet

In the Jewel Jam game, a SpriteGameObject instance keeps a reference to the sprite, which is represented by an object of type Image. To deal with sprite sheets, you create a new class called SpriteSheet that you use instead of an Image object directly. You add specific functionality to this class that allows you to maintain the number of rows and columns in the sheet and that can select a different element of the sheet to be drawn. In the loadAssets method, both the background and penguin sprites are loaded; and you use the SpriteSheet class there, as you can see in the body of the loadAssets method:

```
Game.loadAssets = function () {
    var loadSprite = function (sprite) {
        return new SpriteSheet("../assets/sprites/" + sprite);
    };
    sprites.background_level = loadSprite("spr_background_level.jpg");
    sprites.penguin = loadSprite("spr_penguin@4x2.png");
};
```

The name of the penguin sprite (spr_penguin@4x2.png) is peculiar. This is because you use a trick in the SpriteSheet class that lets you specify the dimensions of the sprite sheet in the *file name*. In this case, the penguin sprite has four columns and two rows. The SpriteSheet constructor analyzes the name of the sprite and determines the dimensions accordingly. There are three possibilities:

- *The image is a single sprite*: In that case, no definition is provided at the end of the file name. For example: spr_wall.png.

- *The image is a strip of sprites*: In that case, you provide a single integer number behind the @ character. For example: spr_field@2.png.

- *The image is a sheet of sprites*: Both dimensions (columns and rows) are provided in the file name. For example: spr_penguin@4x2.png.

Note   If you download example code or open source code and related assets, you may find naming conventions for files similar to those used in this chapter. These naming conventions may seem arbitrary, but they may be programmatically based. Be sure to analyze any new code for the type of trick used here. Renaming files might seem harmless, but it could break more than you thought.

In a SpriteSheet instance, you have to load the image as you did before, and you have to store some information about the sprite sheet that it represents. First you load the Image and store a reference to it in the SpriteSheet instance:

```
Game._spritesStillLoading += 1;
Game._totalSprites += 1;

this._image = new Image();
this._image.src = imageName;
this._image.onload = function () {
    Game._spritesStillLoading -= 1;
};
```

This code first sets two status variables in the Game object so you can keep track of how many sprites are still loading and how many sprites there are in total. Then you create an Image instance, set its source, and define the onload event handler, very similar to what you did for the previous games.

You also need to store the number of rows and columns in the sprite sheet. You extract this information from the file name, but let's set both of these things to 1 by default:

```
this._sheetColumns = 1;
this._sheetRows = 1;
```

To retrieve the actual values for these variables, you need to extract them from the string that is passed as a parameter to the constructor. JavaScript has a very handy method called split that splits a string into little pieces. As a parameter, the split method takes a delimiter character, and it returns an array of strings. Here are a few examples of what split can do:

```
var s1 = "abcabcabc";
var s2 = "spring,summer,autumn,winter";
var s3 = "game";
var result = s1.split('c'); /* result now contains a 3 item array,
                               ["ab", "ab", "ab"] */
result = s2.split(',');      /* result now contains a 4 item array,
                               ["spring", "summer", "autumn", "winter"] */
result = s2.split(',');      /* result now contains a 1 item array, ["game"] */
```

The first thing you need to do with the file name is remove the path information from it. In order to do that, you split up the string, using a slash (/) as the delimiter. You then take the final element from the array, which should contain the full file name:

```
var pathSplit = imageName.split('/');
var fileName = pathSplit[pathSplit.length - 1];
```

The next step is removing the file extension. This means you have to call the split method using a period (.) as the delimiter. The first element in the array will contain the file name without an extension:

```
var fileNameNoExt = fileName.split('.')[0];
```

Then you split the file name without an extension using @-as a delimiter, as follows:

```
var fileSplit = fileNameNoExt.split("@");
```

The fileSplit variable refers to an array. If @-doesn't appear in the string, the number of elements in the fileSplit variable is 1 (the original string). If the number of elements in the array is greater than 1, you know that the file name contains information about the dimensions of the sheet. You also know, in that case, that the *last element* of the array contains that information. The last element is split again using the x character as the delimiter. All this is expressed in the following if instruction:

```
if (fileSplit.length <= 1)
    return;
var colRow = fileSplit[fileSplit.length - 1].split("x");
// deal with the sheet dimension data
```

Now there are two possibilities. The colRow array contains either one or two elements. In both cases, you know that the first element in the array represents the number of columns in the sheet, so you simply store it in the _sheetColumns variable:

```
this._sheetColumns = colRow[0];
```

If the length is two, you also need to store the second string element, in the _sheetRows variable:

```
if (colRow.length === 2)
    this._sheetRows = colRow[1];
```

Yet another possibility is that the array contains more than two elements. You don't handle that situation here (in that case, you only store the number of columns). In the SpriteGameObject class, you assume that you store a reference to a SpriteSheet instead of an Image. The sprite sheet should be passed as a parameter when the SpriteGameObject instance is created, very similar to what you did before. You also store the current sheet index. This number indicates which element from the sprite sheet the SpriteGameObject should draw. Here is the complete constructor:

```
function SpriteGameObject(sprite, layer, id) {
    GameObject.call(this, layer, id);
    this.sprite = sprite;
    this.origin = Vector2.zero;
    this._sheetIndex = 0;
}
```

> **Note**   You have seen how to analyze string contents by using, among others, the split method.
> There are many more ways to manipulate string data in JavaScript. For a more complete overview, visit
> www.w3schools.com/js/js_strings.asp, which is an excellent tutorial on JavaScript strings.

Managing the Sprite Sheet

You have already seen in the Jewel Jam game how to deal with a strip of sprites. You had to change the draw method to draw only part of the sprite. Here you need to do some extra administrative work to make sure the sprite sheet behaves the way it should. The first thing to do is add to the SpriteSheet class a width property and a height property that take into account the column and row numbers of the sprite sheet:

```
Object.defineProperty(SpriteSheet.prototype, "width",
    {
        get: function () {
            return this._image.width / this._sheetColumns;
        }
    });

Object.defineProperty(SpriteSheet.prototype, "height",
    {
        get: function () {
            return this._image.height / this._sheetRows;
        }
    });
```

Also, you add a property that computes the number of elements in the sheet, which is defined as the number of rows multiplied by the number of columns:

```
Object.defineProperty(SpriteSheet.prototype, "nrSheetElements",
    {
        get: function () {
            return this._sheetRows * this._sheetColumns;
        }
    });
```

You can also add a few more useful properties to SpriteSheet. Have a look at the PenguinPairs1 example belonging to the chapter to see the full SpriteSheet class.

The next step is being able to draw one of the elements in the sprite sheet. This is done in the draw method of the SpriteSheet class. This method expects a few parameters, notably the position at which the element should be drawn, its origin, and which element should be drawn. The latter is expressed by an index in the sprite sheet, and it's passed as the sheetIndex parameter. As a first step, you need to convert this index value to column and row indices in the sheet. You calculate the column index as follows:

```
var columnIndex = sheetIndex % this._sheetColumns;
```

Basically, you can see the sheet index as a value that passes through all the elements in the sheet from left to right, top to bottom. By applying the modulus operator on the sheet index, you "throw away" the rows that come before the row the element is in, which leaves you with the column index. Similarly, you calculate the row index by dividing the sheet index by the number of columns:

```
var rowIndex = Math.floor(sheetIndex / this._sheetColumns) % this._sheetRows;
```

Just to be sure the index falls within the range of rows, you perform a modulus operation by the number of rows. Now you can construct the rectangle that indicates the part of the sprite that should be drawn, using the width and height properties:

```
var imagePart = new Rectangle(columnIndex * this.width, rowIndex * this.height,
    this.width, this.height);
```

Finally, you draw the sprite part on the screen, as follows:

```
Canvas2D.drawImage(this._image, position, 0, 1, origin, imagePart, mirror);
```

The SpriteGameObject class is now straightforward. First you add a few useful properties for retrieving the width and height of the sprite:

```
Object.defineProperty(SpriteGameObject.prototype, "width",
    {
        get: function () {
            return this.sprite.width;
        }
    });
Object.defineProperty(SpriteGameObject.prototype, "height",
    {
        get: function () {
            return this.sprite.height;
        }
    });
```

You also add a property to read or write the current sheet index of the sprite game object. The selected element should be within the bounds of the possible element indices. You check this in the set part of the property:

```
Object.defineProperty(SpriteGameObject.prototype, "sheetIndex",
    {
        get: function () {
            return this._sheetIndex;
        },
```

```
        set: function (value) {
            if (value >=0 && value < this.sprite.nrSheetElements)
                this._sheetIndex = value;
        }
    });
```

Look at the `SpriteGameObject.js` file in the `PenguinPairs1` example to see a few other examples of properties you can add. The final method of `SpriteGameObject` is `draw`, which is simple because most of the work has already been done in the `SpriteSheet` class:

```
SpriteGameObject.prototype.draw = function () {
    if (this._visible)
        this.sprite.draw(this.worldPosition, this.origin, this._sheetIndex);
};
```

Finalizing the Example

In the `PenguinPairs1` example, you draw a background and a penguin on the screen (see Figure 18-2). To test your new `SpriteGameObject` class, modify the currently selected sheet index by pressing the left and right arrow buttons. This is done easily in the `PenguinPairsGameWorld` class:

```
if (Keyboard.pressed(Keys.left))
    this.penguin.sheetIndex--;
else if (Keyboard.pressed(Keys.right))
    this.penguin.sheetIndex++;
```

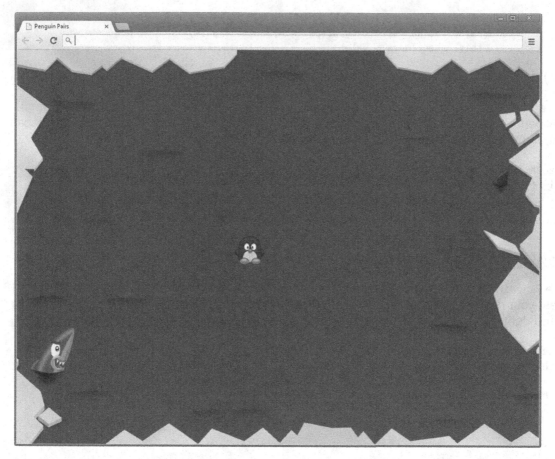

Figure 18-2. A screenshot of the PenguinPairs1 example program. That shark looks hungry, and that penguin looks tasty!

Because you handle all the sprite-sheet aspects in the SpriteSheet class, it's straightforward to draw the penguin exactly in the middle of the screen, as follows:

```
this.penguin.position = this.penguin.screenCenter;
```

This will work for any sprite sheet of any dimension! Try the PenguinPairs1 program, and play around with the code to see how it works.

What You Have Learned

In this chapter, you have learned:

- How to use the split method to analyze strings
- How to handle sprite sheets in games

Chapter 19

Menus and Settings

In the Jewel Jam game, you saw a few basic examples of adding GUI elements to a game such as a button or a frame. In this chapter, you add a few more GUI elements to the Penguin Pairs game, such as an on/off button and a slider button. You also see how to read and store game settings, such as music volume and whether hints are allowed.

Setting Up the Menu

When thinking about menus, you may think of a pull-down menu (like File or Edit) or buttons at the top of an application. Menus can be flexible, though, especially in games, where a menu is often designed in the style of the game and may in many cases cover part of the screen or even the entire screen. As an example, let's see how you can define a basic *options* menu screen containing two controls: one for switching hints on or off, and one for controlling the volume of the music. First you need to draw the elements surrounding these controls. You add a background to the menu and then add a text label to describe the Hints control. You use the Label class from the Jewel Jam game for that. You define the text that should be drawn and place it at the appropriate position (the following code is taken from PenguinPairsGameWorld):

```
var background = new SpriteGameObject(sprites.background_options,
    ID.layer_background);
this.add(background);
var onOffLabel = new Label("Arial", "60px", ID.layer_overlays);
onOffLabel.text = "Hints";
onOffLabel.position = new Vector2(150, 360);
onOffLabel.color = Color.darkBlue;
this.add(onOffLabel);
```

Similarly, you add a text label for the music volume controller. For the complete code, see the PenguinPairs2 example belonging to this chapter.

Adding an On/off Button

The next step is adding an on/off button that shows a hint (or doesn't) during game play. Later in the chapter, you see how the value of this button is used. Just as you did for the Button class in the Jewel Jam game, you make a special class for on/off buttons, called (not surprisingly) OnOffButton. The class is a subclass of SpriteGameObject, and it expects a *sprite strip* containing two sprites: one for the *off* state and one for the *on* state (see Figure 19-1).

© Springer-Verlag Berlin Heidelberg 2013

Figure 19-1. The sprite strip used for the on/off button

An important aspect of the button is that you need to be able to read and set whether it's on or off. Because the button is based on a sprite strip of length two, you can define that the button is in the *off* state if the sheet index is 0, and that it's in the *on* state if the sheet index equals 1. You can then add a boolean property that gets and sets this value. Here is the definition of that property:

```
Object.defineProperty(OnOffButton.prototype, "on",
    {
        get: function () {
            return this.sheetIndex === 1;
        },
        set: function (value) {
            if (value)
                this.sheetIndex = 1;
            else
                this.sheetIndex = 0;
        }
    });
```

Finally, you need to handle mouse clicks on the button to toggle its on and off states. Similar to what you did in the Button class, you check in the handleInput method whether the left mouse button was pressed and whether the mouse position is within the bounding box of the button. For touch input, you follow a similar procedure. If the player has pressed the button, you need to modify the sheet index. If the sheet index is 0, it should become 1, and vice versa. Here is the complete handleInput method:

```
OnOffButton.prototype.handleInput = function (delta) {
    if (!this.visible)
        return;
    if (Touch.containsTouchPress(this.boundingBox) ||
        Mouse.containsMousePress(this.boundingBox))
        this.sheetIndex = 1 - this.sheetIndex;
};
```

Note that you only handle input if the button is visible. In the `PenguinPairsGameWorld` class, you add an `OnOffButton` instance to the game world, at the desired position:

```
this.onOffButton = new OnOffButton(sprites.button_offon, ID.layer_overlays);
this.onOffButton.position = new Vector2(650, 340);
this.onOffButton.on = GameSettings.hints;
this.add(this.onOffButton);
```

In this example, you're using a variable `GameSettings`, in which you store any settings related to the game. In this case, you maintain a setting that indicates whether you should show a hint on the screen. Later, the chapter discusses this in more detail.

Adding a Slider Button

Next you add a second kind of GUI control: a slider. This slider will control the volume of the background music in the game. It consists of two sprites: a back sprite that represents the bar, and a front sprite that represents the actual slider. Therefore, the `Slider` class inherits from `GameObjectList`. Because the back sprite has a border, you need to take that into account when you move or draw the slider. Therefore, you also define left and right margins that define the border width on the left and right side of the back sprite. You also position the slider slightly lower than the back sprite, to account for the top border. The complete constructor is as follows:

```
function Slider(sliderback, sliderfront, layer) {
    GameObjectList.call(this, layer);
    this.dragging = false;
    this.draggingId = -1;
    this.leftmargin = 5;
    this.rightmargin = 7;

    this.back = new SpriteGameObject(sliderback);
    this.front = new SpriteGameObject(sliderfront, 1);
    this.front.position = new Vector2(this.leftmargin, 8);
    this.add(this.back);
    this.add(this.front);
}
```

As you can see, you also set a Boolean variable `dragging` to `false` and a variable `draggingId` to -1. You need these variable to keep track of when the player is dragging the slider and what the touch ID is so you update the slider position when needed, even when the mouse pointer / touch position isn't within the boundaries of the back sprite.

The next step is adding a property `value` that allows you to retrieve and set the value of the slider. You want a value of 0 to indicate that the slider is fully moved to the left, and a value of 1 to indicate the fully right position of the slider. You can calculate the current value by looking at the position of the *front* sprite, and seeing how much it's moved to the right. Therefore, the following line of code calculates the slider value from the slider position:

```
return (this.front.position.x - this.back.position.x - this.leftmargin) /
    (this.back.width - this.front.width - this.leftmargin - this.rightmargin);
```

In the upper part of the fraction, you calculate how far to the right the front sprite has been moved. You calculate this locally to the back position plus the left margin. You then divide this by the total length that the slider can move. This return instruction forms the get part of the value property. For the set part of the property, you need to convert a value between zero and one to the front slider x-position. This amounts to rewriting the previous formula such that the front x-position is the unknown, which is then calculated as follows:

```
var newxpos = value * (this.back.width - this.front.width - this.leftmargin -
    this.rightmargin) + this.back.position.x + this.leftmargin;
```

All that remains to be done is to create the new front position vector with the correct x-position:

```
this.front.position = new Vector2(newxpos, this.front.position.y);
```

Now that you have a way to set and get the slider value, you need to write the code to handle player input. Similar to what you did in previous classes, you deal with touch and mouse input separately. For each type of input, you add a specific method, which you then call from the handleInput method:

```
Slider.prototype.handleInput = function (delta) {
    GameObjectList.prototype.handleInput.call(this, delta);
    if (Touch.isTouchDevice) {
        this.handleInputTouch(delta);
    } else {
        this.handleInputMouse(delta);
    }
};
```

You still need to deal with touch input to drag the slider to a new position. The first step is checking whether the player is currently touching the screen. If that isn't the case, you simply reset the dragging status variables to their initial values, and you're done:

```
if (!Touch.isTouching) {
    this.dragging = false;
    this.draggingId = -1;
    return;
}
```

If instructions are executed that are written after this if instruction, you know the player is touching the screen.

You need to check whether the player is actually touching the button. If that is the case, you assign new values to the dragging status variables:

```
if (Touch.containsTouch(this.back.boundingBox)) {
    this.draggingId = Touch.getIndexInRect(this.back.boundingBox);
    this.dragging = true;
}
```

The final step is updating the slider position if the player is currently dragging. The first step is retrieving the position where the player is touching the screen:

```
var touchPos = Touch.getPosition(this.draggingId);
```

Next you calculate what the *x*-position of the slider should be. Because the touch position is in world coordinates, you subtract the world position of the back sprite from it to get the local position of the slider. You also subtract half the width of the slider from that number, so the place where the player is touching the screen is in the center of the slider. This is calculated using the following expression:

```
touchPos.x - this.back.worldPosition.x - this.front.width / 2
```

You need to do a little more work, though, because you have to make sure the slider can't move outside of its range. You therefore need to clamp the slider position within a certain range. In JavaScript you can augment objects with extra methods on the fly, so let's add a method to the `Math` object that can perform this clamping operation:

```
Math.clamp = function (value, min, max) {
    if (value < min)
        return min;
    else if (value > max)
        return max;
    else
        return value;
};
```

Now you use that method to calculate the clamped value of the slider, and you store it as the slider's new *x*-position:

```
this.front.position.x = Math.clamp(touchPos.x - this.back.worldPosition.x -
    this.front.width / 2, this.back.position.x + this.leftmargin,
    this.back.position.x + this.back.width - this.front.width -
    this.rightmargin);
```

This completes the code to handle touch input.

You deal with mouse input in a very similar way. Have a look at the `Slider` class to see the complete `handleInputTouch` and `handleInputMouse` methods.

Inside the `PenguinPairs` class, you add a slider to the game world:

```
this.musicSlider = new Slider(sprites.slider_bar, sprites.slider_button,
    ID.layer_overlays);
this.musicSlider.position = new Vector2(650, 500);
this.add(this.musicSlider);
```

You can then use the `value` property in that class to set the slider bar to match the current volume of the background music with a single line of code:

```
this.musicSlider.value = sounds.music.volume;
```

Finally, in the `update` method of the `PenguinPairsGameWorld` class, you retrieve the current value of the slider and use it to update the volume of the background music:

```
sounds.music.volume = this.musicSlider.value;
```

> **Note** Most games contain some menu screens. With these screens, the player can set options, choose levels, watch achievements, and pause the game. Creating all these additional screens can be a lot of work that doesn't contribute to the actual game play, so developers tend to put less effort into them. But that is a very wrong decision.
>
> An artist once said, "Your game is as good as its worst screen." If one of the menu screens has poor quality, the player will get the feeling the game is unfinished and the developer didn't put enough effort into it. So make sure all your menu screens look beautiful and are easy to use and navigate.
>
> Think carefully about what you put in these screens. You might be tempted to create options for everything: the difficulty of the game, the music to play, the color of the background, and so on. But remember, you're the person who should create the game, not the player. You or your artist should determine what gives the most interesting game play and the most compelling visual style, not the user.
>
> Try to avoid options as much as possible. For example, should a player really set the difficulty? Can't you adapt the difficulty automatically by monitoring the player's progress? And do you really need a level-selection screen? Can't you simply remember where the player was the last time, and immediately continue there? Keep your interface as simple as possible!

Reading and Storing Game Settings

Having the slider control the volume of the background music isn't complicated. Now, suppose you want an on/off button to control whether the player can press a button to view a hint. Where should you store this option information? In this example, it's stores in a special variable called `GameSettings`. You declare this variable in the same place where you declare the `sprites` and `sounds` variables—the `PenguinPairs.js` file:

```
var GameSettings = {
    hints: true
};
```

This variable is now accessible everywhere. Note, however, that it isn't persistent across game plays: if you close the game and open it in the browser later, the variable defaults to its original settings. In Chapter 21, you see a way to maintain data across different game plays.

In the options menu, you make sure the value of this variable is always the same as the state of the Hints button. This is done in the update method of PenguinPairsGameWorld, and you use the on property that you added to the button:

GameSettings.hints = this.onOffButton.on;

This completes the options menu. Figure 19-2 shows what it looks like.

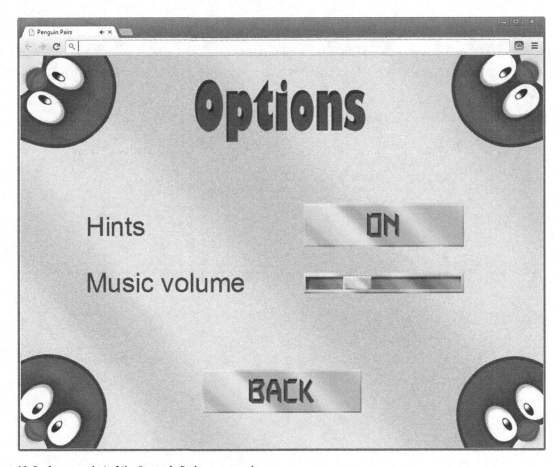

Figure 19-2. A screenshot of the PenguinPairs2 example

What You Have Learned

In this chapter, you have learned:

- How to create a menu with a variety of buttons and sliders
- How to retrieve the values of buttons and sliders and translate that information into game settings

Chapter 20

Game State Management

Normally, you don't immediately start playing when a game application starts. For example, in the Jewel Jam game, you see a title screen before playing. More complicated games have menus for options, menus for selecting different levels, screens to display the high score after finishing a level, a menu to select different characters and attributes, and so on. In Jewel Jam, adding a title screen wasn't that difficult, because the title screen itself had very little interaction. However, when you look at the example in the previous chapter, you can see that building a screen with a few options and controls can result in quite a lot of code. You can imagine that when you add more menus and screens to the game, it's going to be a pain to manage which objects belong to which screen and when they should be drawn or updated.

Generally, these different menus and screens are called *game states*. In some programs, they're called *scenes*, and the object responsible for managing the scenes is the *director*. Sometimes a distinction is made between game *modes* and game *states*. In that case, things like menus, the main playing screen, and so on are game *modes*, whereas "level finished" and "game over" are game *states*.

This book follows a simplified paradigm and calls everything *game states*. To deal with these different game states, you need a *manager*. In this chapter, you develop the main classes needed for such a structure and see how you can use it to display different menus and switch between them while keeping the code cleanly separated.

Basics of Managing Game States

When you want to deal properly with game states, you need to make sure of the following:

- Game states should be run completely independently. In other words, you don't want to have to deal with the options menu screen or the "game over" screen while you're in the game-playing state.

- There should be an easy way to define game states, find game states, and switch between them. That way, when the player presses the Options button in the title screen, you can easily switch to the options menu state.

In the examples you've seen until now, there was always some kind of game world class; it was called `PainterGameWorld`, `JewelJamGameWorld`, or `PenguinPairsGameWorld`, depending on the game you were building. Looking at it from the view of game states, each of these worlds represents a single (playing) game state. You need to define such a class for each different state. The nice thing is that you already have a lot of code in place that helps you do this. The `GameObjectList` class is particularly useful because it represents a list of game objects, which is a sufficient basis for representing a game state. In the previous games, the classes that represented the game world inherited from the `GameObjectList` class. In the remaining examples in this book, classes that represent a *game state* will also inherit from `GameObjectList`. So, if you have an options menu, a title screen, a level-selection screen, and a help menu, you make a separate class for each of these game states. The only thing you still need to provide is a way to manage the various game states in the game. You do this by creating a *game-state manager*.

The Game-State Manager

In this section, you create a class called `GameStateManager`. Because there should be only a single game-state manager in a game, you follow the *singleton design pattern*, where the class is called `GameStateManager_Singleton`, and you store the (single) instance in a global variable `GameStateManager`, just as you did for classes such as `Canvas2D` and `Game`:

```
var GameStateManager = new GameStateManager_Singleton();
```

You set up this class in such a way that it allows you to store different game states (that is, different `GameObjectList` instances), that you can select what the current game state is, and that the manager then automatically calls the game-loop methods on the currently active game state.

To store the various game states, you need an array. You also define an additional variable to keep track of the currently active game state. As a result, this is the constructor of the game-state manager:

```
function GameStateManager_Singleton() {
    this._gameStates = [];
    this._currentGameState = null;
}
```

Now you need to define a method that adds a game state to the array. In that method, you use push to add an element to the end of array. You also set the currently active game state to the state you just added. Here is the complete add method:

```
GameStateManager_Singleton.prototype.add = function (gamestate) {
    this._gameStates.push(gamestate);
    this._currentGameState = gamestate;
    return this._gameStates.length - 1;
};
```

As you can see when you look at the last instruction in the method, you return the *index* of the game state in the array. You do this because later it will provide you with a simple way to find the game state you added. You store this index as an identifier value in the ID variable. For example, adding a title menu state and storing its ID after you add it can be done in a single line of code, as follows:

```
ID.game_state_title = GameStateManager.add(new TitleMenuState());
```

Because the game-state identifier corresponds exactly to the index of the game state in the array, you can write a very simple get method that retrieves a game state, given an ID:

```
GameStateManager_Singleton.prototype.get = function (id) {
    if (id < 0 || id >=this._gameStates.length)
        return null;
    else
        return this._gameStates[id];
};
```

Switching to another game state is also straightforward. This is done by calling the switchTo method:

```
GameStateManager_Singleton.prototype.switchTo = function (id) {
    this._currentGameState = this.get(id);
};
```

Handling the different game-loop methods is quite simple. You have to call them on the currently active game state. For example, the handleInput method of GameStateManager is as follows:

```
GameStateManager_Singleton.prototype.handleInput = function (delta) {
    if (this._currentGameState !== null)
        this._currentGameState.handleInput(delta);
};
```

You follow a similar procedure for the other game-loop methods. To make the game-state manager an integral part of the game, you call its game-loop methods in the Game.mainLoop method:

```
Game_Singleton.prototype.mainLoop = function () {
    var delta = 1 / 60;
    GameStateManager.handleInput(delta);
    GameStateManager.update(delta);
    Canvas2D.clear();
    GameStateManager.draw();

    Keyboard.reset();
    Mouse.reset();
    Touch.reset();

    requestAnimationFrame(Game.mainLoop);
};
```

Adding States and Switching Between Them

Now that you have your game-state manager, you can start adding different states to it. A very basic game state is the title menu state. In the PenguinPairs3 example, you added a class TitleMenuState to the application that represents this state. Because this state contains a couple of different game objects, you let it inherit from the GameObjectList class. In the constructor of this class, you add the game objects that are required for this state: a background and three buttons. You can reuse the Button class that you developed earlier for the Jewel Jam game. Here is the constructor of TitleMenuState:

```
function TitleMenuState(layer) {
    GameObjectList.call(this, layer);

    this.add(new SpriteGameObject(sprites.background_title,
        ID.layer_background));

    this.playButton = new Button(sprites.button_play, ID.layer_overlays);
    this.playButton.position = new Vector2(415, 540);
    this.add(this.playButton);

    this.optionsButton = new Button(sprites.button_options, ID.layer_overlays);
    this.optionsButton.position = new Vector2(415, 650);
    this.add(this.optionsButton);

    this.helpButton = new Button(sprites.button_help, ID.layer_overlays);
    this.helpButton.position = new Vector2(415, 760);
    this.add(this.helpButton);
}
```

Because you need to do something when a button is pressed, you have to override the handleInput method. In that method, you check whether each of the buttons is pressed, and if so, you switch to another state. For instance, if the player presses the Play Game button, you need to switch to the level menu:

```
if (this.playButton.pressed)
    GameStateManager.switchTo(ID.game_state_levelselect);
```

You add similar alternatives for the other two buttons. Now the title menu state is basically done. In the PenguinPairs class, the only thing you need to do is make an instance of TitleMenuState and add it to the game-state manager. You do the same thing for all the other states in the game. After that you set the current state to be the title menu, so the player sees the title menu when the game starts:

```
ID.game_state_title = GameStateManager.add(new TitleMenuState());
ID.game_state_help = GameStateManager.add(new HelpState());
ID.game_state_options = GameStateManager.add(new OptionsMenuState());
ID.game_state_levelselect = GameStateManager.add(new LevelMenuState());

// the current game state is the title screen
GameStateManager.switchTo(ID.game_state_title);
```

The help and option menu states are set up in a fashion similar to `TitleMenuState`. In the class constructor, you add your game objects to the game world, and you override the `handleInput` method to switch between states. For example, both the help and option menu states contain a Back button that returns you to the title screen:

```
if (this.backButton.pressed)
    GameStateManager.switchTo(ID.game_state_title);
```

Have a look at the `HelpState` and `OptionsMenuState` classes in the `PenguinPairs3` example to get an idea of how the different states are set up and how you switch between states.

The Level Menu State

A slightly more complicated game state is the level menu. You want the player to be able to select a level from a grid of level buttons. You want to be able to display three different states with these level buttons, because a level can be locked, unlocked but not yet solved by the player, or solved. In order for this to work, you require some sort of persistent storage across game plays, as discussed in the next chapter. For each of the different states of a level button, you use a different sprite. Because you can't yet play the game in its current version, you simply show the "locked" status for each level.

Before you can create the `LevelMenuState` class, you add a class called `LevelButton` that inherits from `GameObjectList`. In the `LevelButton` class, you keep track of two things: whether the button is pressed, and the level index the button refers to:

```
function LevelButton(levelIndex, layer, id) {
    GameObjectList.call(this, layer, id);
    this.pressed = false;
    this.levelIndex = levelIndex;
    // to do: create the button sprites
}
```

Because the button has three different states, you load three sprites, one for each state. If a player has finished a level, the button should show a colored penguin. Because there are a couple of differently colored penguins, you select a colored button by varying the sheet index depending on the level index:

```
this._levelSolved = new SpriteGameObject(sprites.level_solved,
    ID.layer_overlays);
this._levelUnsolved = new SpriteGameObject(sprites.level_unsolved,
    ID.layer_overlays);
this._levelLocked = new SpriteGameObject(sprites.level_locked,
    ID.layer_overlays_2);
this.add(this._levelSolved);
this.add(this._levelUnsolved);
this.add(this._levelLocked);

this._levelSolved.sheetIndex = levelIndex;
```

Finally, you add a text label drawn on the belly of the penguin, so the player can see which level each button refers to:

```
var textLabel = new Label("Arial", "20px", ID.layer_overlays_1);
textLabel.text = levelIndex + 1;
textLabel.position = new Vector2(this._levelSolved.width - textLabel.width,
    this._levelSolved.height - textLabel.height + 50).divideBy(2);
textLabel.color = Color.black;
this.add(textLabel);
```

In the handleInput method, you check whether the button has been pressed. In case of mouse input, the mouse position should be within the bounding box of the sprite, and the player must have pressed the left mouse button. If you're dealing with a touch interface, the player's finger should have pressed within the area of the button on the screen. Finally, the player only can press the button it if is visible. Here is the complete handleInput method:

```
LevelButton.prototype.handleInput = function (delta) {
    if (Touch.isTouchDevice)
        this.pressed = this.visible &&
            Touch.containsTouchPress(this._levelLocked.boundingBox);
    else
        this.pressed = this.visible && Mouse.left.pressed &&
            this._levelLocked.boundingBox.contains(Mouse.position);
};
```

If you look at the LevelButton class in the PenguinPairs3 example, it also includes width and height properties, which you need when you place the level buttons on the screen.

Now that you have a basic LevelButton class, you can add the level buttons in the LevelMenuState class. In this example, you add 12 level buttons to the menu using a for instruction. Depending on the value of the counter variable (i), you calculate the row and column to which the button belongs. This information, together with the width and the height of a level button, helps you calculate the final position of each level button:

```
this.levelButtons = [];

for (var i = 0; i < 12; i += 1) {
    var row = Math.floor(i / 5);
    var column = i % 5;
    var level = new LevelButton(i, ID.layer_overlays);
    level.position = new Vector2(column * (level.width + 30) + 155,
        row * (level.height + 5) + 230);
    this.add(level);
    this.levelButtons.push(level);
}
```

Because later you have to check whether each button has been pressed, you not only add the buttons to the game state, but also store a reference to each button in an array called levelButtons. This array comes in handy when you want to determine whether the player has clicked one of the level buttons. You check this in a method called getSelectedLevel. This method, which is in the LevelMenuState class, iterates over all the level buttons in the array and returns the level index belonging to the first button that was pressed. If the player didn't press any button, the method returns −1. Here is the complete method:

```
LevelMenuState.prototype.getSelectedLevel = function () {
    for (var i = 0, j = this.levelButtons.length; i < j; i += 1) {
        if (this.levelButtons[i].pressed)
            return this.levelButtons[i].levelIndex;
    }
    return -1;
};
```

You can then use this method in the handleInput method:

```
LevelMenuState.prototype.handleInput = function (delta) {
    GameObjectList.prototype.handleInput.call(this, delta);

    var selectedLevel = this.getSelectedLevel();
    if (selectedLevel != -1) {
        // start playing the level
    }
    else if (this.back.pressed)
        GameStateManager.switchTo(ID.game_state_title);
};
```

As you can see, adding different states to a game and switching between them isn't very hard, as long as you think about the design of the software beforehand. By thinking in advance about which classes are needed and how the functionality of your game should be split up between them, you can save yourself a lot of time later. In the next chapter, you further extend this example by creating the actual levels. Figure 20-1 shows a screenshot of the level menu state.

Figure 20-1. The level menu screen in Penguin Pairs

Dealing with Errors

Before you finish this chapter, let's talk a little more about dealing with errors in JavaScript. Particularly when games get more complex, you need to think about what happens when an error occurs. To give a concrete example, in the get method of the GameStateManager class, you return a game state only if the identifier passed as a parameter falls in the range of the elements in the array:

```
GameStateManager_Singleton.prototype.get = function (id) {
    if (id < 0 || id >=this._gameStates.length)
        return null;
    else
        return this._gameStates[id];
};
```

You do this because otherwise, the user of the game-state manager could accidentally access the array outside its range. However, the way you do it here probably isn't the most robust approach. For one thing, when the index is too large or too small, you return null. This means the code using this method needs to be aware that the method might return null. As a result, that same code has to check this in an if instruction, to make sure you aren't trying to call a method on a null reference. Another problem is that you don't avoid all array out-of-range mistakes this way. For example:

```
var oops = GameStateManager.get(3.4);
```

Of course, arrays can only be accessed using integer values, so if you don't handle passing non-integer numbers, the program will crash. This can be avoided by accessing the array as follows:

```
return this._gameStates[Math.floor(id)];
```

But is this really what you want? If a user tries to access element 3.4 in the array (which obviously doesn't exist), do you want to return an object, meaning you pretend the object at index 3.4 exists? Perhaps it's better to let the user know that this isn't possible, and stop the execution of the method.

There are other examples of situations that merit a proper way to handle errors. Sometimes these situations occur not because of a bug in the program, but because something happened that is out of the programmer's control. For example, perhaps the player of your game has the excellent idea to disable the network adapter during the setup of an online game. Or, because of a virus wreaking havoc on the server, some files that you expected to be there are corrupted. If you depend on software developed by other companies, a new release could break your code because specs have been changed. There are several ways to deal with these types of errors. One way is to do nothing and let the program crash. This is a cheap solution for the game developer (initially, at least), but it doesn't result in a very robust, user-friendly game. You could also maintain a list of error codes. If an error occurs, the method would then return this error code, and the user would need to sift through a large document detailing each error code and how to solve it. Yet another way is to not report the error at all and try to work around it in the program. Although this sometimes is a good solution, in many cases you simply can't work around an error. For example, if the network connection suddenly is lost in a mass multiplayer online game, there isn't much you can do but report this to the player.

Most applications, including games, deal with errors by using *exceptions*. An exception is *thrown* by a method, and the caller of the method has to deal with it. For example, look at the following method definition:

```
GameStateManager_Singleton.prototype.get = function (id) {
    if (id < 0 || id >=this._gameStates.length)
        throw "game state id out of range";
    else if (Math.floor(id) !== id)
        throw "game state id should be an integer number";
    else
        return this._gameStates[id];
};
```

This code handles a variety of cases before actually accessing the array. If id is out of range or isn't an integer number (in other words, the floor function of the number doesn't return the number itself), the method stops execution and throws an exception (which in this case is a string value). To do something with the error, you can call the get function in a try-catch block:

```
try {
    var myGameState = GameStateManager.get(someId);
    // do something with the game state
} catch (e) {
    console.log("Error: " + e);
}
```

As you can see, the method call that may throw an exception is in the body of a try instruction. If there is an exception, the program continues in the body of the catch part. If there is no exception, then the catch body isn't executed.

In the catch part, the exception is caught. Behind the word catch is a parameter that contains the object being thrown. In the previous example, the get method can throw a string that contains the error message. This isn't the best way to do it. More complex programs generally define a hierarchy of exception classes. An instance of such a class can contain information such as the time at which the exception occurred and in which method, the parameter values of that method, a custom error message, and so on. Different classes can then be used to represent different types of errors. Because the games in this book are simple, they don't touch on handling errors this way. But it's a good idea to think about how you want to deal with errors in your games, and perhaps exceptions can help you do it in a more robust way.

Let's go back to the try instruction. You can place multiple instructions in the body of that instruction. But as soon as an exception occurs, the execution is halted and the body of the catch is executed. The remaining instructions after the try may therefore assume that there was no exception if they're executed.

The bodies of the try and the catch part need to be between braces, even if there is only a single instruction in the body. This is a bit illogical, given that the braces may be omitted in, for example, if and while instructions.

After the catch part, it's possible to place a finally part, which is executed whether an exception of a certain kind is caught or not. For example:

```
try {
    openServerConnection(ipAddress);
    // communicate with the server
    ...
}
catch (e) {
    console.log("Error while communicating with the server: " + e);
finally {
    // always close the server connection
    closeServerConnection();
}
```

In this example, the `finally` part saves you from copying code. Regardless of whether there was an error while communicating with the server, you need to close the connection when you're done.

To conclude, Figure 20-2 shows a syntax diagram for the expressions related to exceptions. Try to think of other examples in the games you've seen until now where exceptions could be useful.

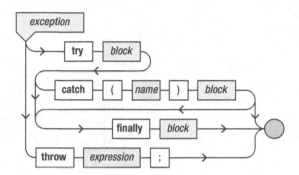

Figure 20-2. Syntax diagram of expressions related to exceptions

What You Have Learned

In this chapter, you have learned:

- How to define different game states using a game-state manager
- How to switch between game states depending on the player's actions
- How to properly deal with errors in games by using exceptions

Chapter 21

Storing and Recalling Game Data

Many games consist of different levels. Especially in casual games such as puzzles and maze games, a game may have several hundreds of levels. Until now, your games have relied on randomness to keep the gameplay interesting. Although randomness is a powerful tool to achieve replayability, in a lot of cases game designers want more control over how a game progresses. This control is generally achieved by designing *levels*. Each level is its own game world in which the player has to achieve some sort of objective.

With the tools you've seen until now, you can imagine that for each level in a game you can write a specific class in which you fill that specific level with game objects and add the behavior you want. This approach has a few disadvantages. The most important disadvantage is that you're mixing the *game logic* (gameplay, win condition, and so on), with the *game content*. This means every time you want to add another level to the game, you have to write a new class, which leads to a lot of classes that need to be retrieved when a game is loaded in the browser. Furthermore, if a game designer wants to add a level to a game that you built, the designer needs in-depth knowledge of how your code works. And any mistake the designer makes in writing the code will result in bugs or crashes in your game.

A much better approach is to store level information separately from the actual game code. While the game is loading, this level information is retrieved. Ideally, the information needs to be stored in a simple format that non-programmers can understand and work with. That way, levels can be designed by someone without that person having to know how the game converts the data into playable game levels. JavaScript is a very suitable language for representing structured information. This is so easy primarily because of the object literals you can define in JavaScript. Have a look at the following example:

```
var ticTacToeSaveGame = {
    scorePlayerX : 2,
    scorePlayerO : 1,
    currentStatus : ["x x",
                     "oox",
                     "o  "],
    turn : "x"
}
```

This variable describes a *Tic Tac Toe* game status for two players. The first player has won two games, and the second player only one. The current state of the game is stored in an array of strings. Finally, the player who places the *x* marks has their turn. By editing this variable, you can very easily change the score or the current state of the game. You could even decide to make the board bigger, by adding columns and rows to the `currentStatus` variable. All this can be done without knowing how the *Tic Tac Toe* game actually works. A game designer could edit data structured in this way, and the game could read the data from such a variable and let the player continue their game. Furthermore, because of JavaScript object literals, the format is relatively easy to understand, even for someone with little or no programming experience. Finally, as a game gets bigger, so will the team that develops the game. By separating out level design as well as things introduced earlier (such as sprite sheets), you allow non-programmers who excel at tasks such as game design and graphics design to help you more effectively create awesome games.

You can deal with the different levels in Penguin Pairs in a similar fashion. In this chapter, you see how to build such a level-loading scheme into your games. Another thing you look at is storing and recalling the state of the game over different sessions. Games such as Painter and Jewel Jam don't retain any information from previous times when the player played the game, which in those games doesn't really matter. However, in the case of Penguin Pairs it does matter, because you don't want the player to have to start all over every time the game is launched. If the player finishes a level, the browser should remember that the next time the player launches the game, so the player can continue where they left off.

Structure of a Level

Let's first look at what kind of things can be in a level in the Penguin Pairs game. First, there is some kind of background image. Let's assume that this background is fixed when you load the level, so there is no need to store any information about it in the text file.

In the level are a number of different animals such as penguins, seals, and sharks. There are also icebergs, background blocks that penguins can move on, and a few more things. You want to store all this information in a structured variable. One possibility would be to store every object's position and type, but that would make the variable complicated. Another possibility is to divide the level into small blocks, also called *tiles*. Every block has a certain type (this could be a penguin, a playing field tile, a transparent tile, a penguin, and so on). A tile can be represented by a single character, and you can store the structure of the level in a variable just as you did with the *Tic Tac Toe* example:

```
var myLevel = {
    tiles :                 ["#.......#",
                             "#...r...#",
                             "#.......#",
                             "#.     .#",
                             "#.     .#",
                             "#.     .#",
                             "#.......#",
                             "#...r...#",
                             "#.......#"]
};
```

In this level definition, a number of different blocks are defined. An iceberg (wall) tile is defined by the # sign, a penguin by an r character, a background tile by a . character, and an empty tile by a space character. Now you can write a method that uses this information to create the tiles and store them somewhere (probably in a GameObjectGrid instance). This means you need different types of tiles: a normal tile on which a penguin can stand, a transparent background tile, and a wall (iceberg) tile with which a penguin can collide.

The Tile Class

To get things started, let's first write a basic Tile class. This class is a subclass of the SpriteGameObject class. For now, you don't consider more complicated items in the level such as penguins, seals, and sharks. You only look at background (transparent) tiles, normal tiles, and wall (iceberg) tiles. Let's introduce a variable to represent these different varieties of tiles:

```
var TileType = {
    normal: 0,
    background: 1,
    wall: 2
};
```

The Tile class is a basic extension of SpriteGameObject. In the constructor, you declare a member variable type to store the type of tile that an instance represents:

```
function Tile(sprite, layer) {
    SpriteGameObject.call(this, sprite, layer);
    this.type = TileType.normal;
}
```

To accommodate transparent tiles, you override the draw method to draw the sprite only if the tile isn't a background tile:

```
Tile.prototype.draw = function () {
    if (this.type === TileType.background)
        return;
    SpriteGameObject.prototype.draw.call(this);
};
```

When you load the level, you create a tile for each character and store it in a grid structure such as GameObjectGrid.

Other Level Information

In addition to the tiles, you need to store a few other things in the levelData variable:

- Whether the level is locked
- Whether the level has been solved by the player
- A hint for the level

- The number of pairs to be made
- The location and direction of the hint arrow

So, you can define a complete level in a variable as follows:

```
var myLevel = {
    locked :                true,
    solved :                false,
    hint  :                 "Don't let the penguins fall in the water!",
    nrPairs  :              1,
    hint_arrow_x :          3,
    hint_arrow_y :          1,
    hint_arrow_direction :  2,
    tiles :                 ["#.......#",
                             "#...r...#",
                             "#.......#",
                             "#.     .#",
                             "#.     .#",
                             "#.     .#",
                             "#.......#",
                             "#...r...#",
                             "#.......#"]
};
```

You need to define such a variable for every level. It makes sense to store all these levels in an *array*. Because the level information needs to be available from everywhere, you store the level information in a *global variable*. Generally, global variables should be avoided when possible, for several reasons:

- The global namespace will get cluttered with lots of global variables, potentially slowing down script execution.
- Conflicts can occur if two different JavaScript files happen to use the same global variables.
- Your source code become less clear to read, because it's difficult to keep an overview of which data is used where.

In this case, you use a global variable because the level data needs to be accessible everywhere. However, you can do a few things to make sure it's clear that you're using a global variable. One thing you do is write the variable name in capital letters to stress that it's different from other, normal variables. You also explicitly attach the variable to the global domain (which is called window in JavaScript). Here is the variable initialization:

```
window.LEVELS = [];
```

The only thing you need to do now is fill this variable with the level information. For each level, you add an entry to the array using the push method:

```
window.LEVELS.push({
    locked :                false,
    solved :                false,
    hint  :                 "Click on a penguin and select the arrow to let
                             it move towards the other penguin.",
```

```
    nrPairs  :                      1,
    hint_arrow_x :                   4,
    hint_arrow_y :                   3,
    hint_arrow_direction :           3,
    tiles :                         ["#########",
                                     "#.......#",
                                     "#...r...#",
                                     "#.......#",
                                     "#.......#",
                                     "#.......#",
                                     "#...r...#",
                                     "#.......#",
                                     "#########"]
});
```

This example is the first level. As you can see, the locked status of the first level is set to false so the player is allowed to play this level. The locked status of all the other levels is set to true. When the player finishes a level, you update this status. The levels are defined in the levels.js file. This is a JavaScript file, but it's located in the assets folder of the PenguinPairs4 example, because this data is more an *asset* than code. Also, this way a designer can work in the assets folder and change sprites and level data without having to look at the game-running code.

The Playing State

In the previous chapter, you saw how to create multiple game states such as a title screen, a level-choice menu, and an options menu. In this section, you add a *playing state*. The playing state basically consists of a list of levels, each represented by its own game world. For states such as the title screen and the options menu, you could create a subclass of GameObjectList. However, here that doesn't make a lot of sense, because the playing state needs to switch between game worlds. Therefore, you aren't going to inherit from GameObjectList. But you do want to define game-loop methods such as update and draw. You can slightly change the software design to accommodate this by introducing a new class, IGameLoopObject. The only thing this class does is provide the definition of the methods that any object part of the game loop should have. Here is the complete class:

```
function IGameLoopObject() {
}

IGameLoopObject.prototype.handleInput = function (delta) {};
IGameLoopObject.prototype.update = function (delta) {};
IGameLoopObject.prototype.draw = function () {};
IGameLoopObject.prototype.reset = function () {};
```

This class is called IGameLoopObject instead of, for instance, GameLoopObject because such classes are generally called *interfaces* in software design. Interfaces are very useful because they provide programmers with information about the kinds of methods (or properties) that can be expected when a class *implements that interface* (in other words, inherits from the interface class). Quite a few programming languages have a special programming construct that lets you create these interfaces. This isn't the case for JavaScript, but you can still use the concept to achieve the same results.

The `IGameLoopObject` interface forms the basis of all objects that have game-loop methods. You can change the existing classes in the example to follow this approach. For example, the `GameObject` class now also inherits from `IGameLoopObject`:

```
function GameObject(layer, id) {
    IGameLoopObject.call(this);

    // initialize the game object...
}
GameObject.prototype = Object.create(IGameLoopObject.prototype);
```

Have a look at the classes in the `PenguinPairs4` example to see how the `IGameLoopObject` class in integrated into the program design. As you can see, the example adds a `PlayingState` class that also inherits from `IGameLoopObject`:

```
function PlayingState() {
    IGameLoopObject.call(this);

    // initialize the playing state...
}
PlayingState.prototype = Object.create(IGameLoopObject.prototype);
```

Creating the Levels in the Playing State

In this section, you create the levels in the game from the data stored in the global `windows.LEVELS` variable. To represent a level, you create a `Level` class that inherits from `GameObjectList`. For each level that needs to be created, you create a `Level` instance and fill it according to the data in the global `LEVELS` variable. In the `PlayingState` constructor, you initialize an array in which you store all these instances. You also store the level the player is currently playing:

```
this.currentLevelIndex = -1;
this.levels = [];
```

Then you call a method `loadLevels`, which is responsible for creating the `Level` instances from the level data:

```
this.loadLevels();
```

In the `loadLevels` method, you place a `for` loop in which you create `Level` instances. In the `Level` constructor, you translate the level data into actual game objects that are part of each level:

```
PlayingState.prototype.loadLevels = function () {
    for (var currLevel = 0; currLevel < window.LEVELS.length; currLevel++)
        this.levels.push(new Level(currLevel));
};
```

Creating the Level Instances

In the Level constructor, you have to create the different game objects belonging to that level. As a first step, you retrieve the level data and store it in a variable called levelData:

```
function Level(levelIndex) {
    GameObjectList.call(this);
    var levelData = window.LEVELS[levelIndex];
    this.levelIndex = levelIndex;

    // to do: fill this level with game objects according to the level data
}
```

You also need to keep track of animals such as the penguins and seals. You do this in a separate array so you can look them up quickly later. The same holds for the sharks that are present in some of the levels:

```
this.animals = [];
this.sharks = [];
```

Now you can start creating game objects to fill the game world. First you add a background image to the game world:

```
this.add(new SpriteGameObject(sprites.background_level, ID.layer_background));
```

Then you read the width and height of the level. You can determine those by retrieving the length of the tiles array as well as the length of a single string in that array:

```
var width = levelData.tiles[0].length;
var height = levelData.tiles.length;
```

You then create a GameObjectList instance to contain the playing field, just as you did in the Jewel Jam game. You position this playing field in such a way that it's nicely centered on the screen:

```
var playingField = new GameObjectList(ID.layer_objects);
playingField.position = new Vector2((Game.size.x - width * 73) / 2, 100);
this.add(playingField);
```

Now you need to retrieve the tile information from the levelData variable. You reuse the GameObjectGrid class to represent a grid of tiles. To read all the tiles, you use a nested for instruction. Have a look at the following lines of code:

```
var tileField = new GameObjectGrid(height, width, ID.layer_objects, ID.tiles);
tileField.cellHeight = 72;
tileField.cellWidth = 73;
for (var row = 0; row < height; row++) {
    for (var col = 0; col < width; col++) {
        // handle the tile 'levelData.tiles[row][col]' here
    }
}
```

You first create a `GameObjectGrid` instance and set the width and height of a cell in that grid to a given size. Then you start reading the characters containing the tile information.

Now, depending on the character you get from the expression `levelData.tiles[row][col]`, you need to create different kinds of game objects and add them to the grid. You could use an `if` instruction for that:

```
if (levelData.tiles[row][col] === '.')
    // create an empty tile
else if (levelData.tiles[row][col] === ' ')
    // create a background tile
else if (levelData.tiles[row][col] === 'r')
    // create a penguin tile
//... and so on
```

In principle, this code would work. But every time, you have to write a complex condition. It's easy to make a mistake such as misspelling the variable name or forgetting to include brackets. There is another option that allows you to write this in a slightly cleaner way. JavaScript offers a special kind of instruction for handling cases: `switch`.

> **Note**   When defining levels in a text-based format, you have to decide what kind of object each character represents. These decisions influence the work of both level designers, who have to enter the characters in the level data files, and developers, who have to write the code to interpret that level data. This shows how important documentation is, even during active development. A "cheat sheet" is nice to have so that when you write this code, you don't have to remember all the ideas you had for level design. Such a cheat sheet is also useful if you work with a designer, to make sure you're both on the same page.

Using `switch` to Handle Alternatives

The `switch` instruction allows you to specify alternatives, and the instructions that should be executed for each alternative. For example, the previous `if` instruction with multiple alternatives can be rewritten as a `switch` instruction as follows:

```
switch(levelData.tiles[row][col]) {
    case '.': // create an empty tile
            break;
    case ' ': // create a background tile
            break;
    case 'r': // create a penguin tile
            break;
}
```

The switch instruction has a few handy properties that make it very useful for handling different alternatives. Have a look at the following code example:

```
if (x === 1)
    one();
else if (x === 2) {
    two();
    alsoTwo();
} else if (x === 3 || x === 4)
    threeOrFour();
else
    more();
```

You can rewrite this with a switch instruction as follows:

```
switch(x) {
    case 1:  one();
             break;
    case 2:  two();
             alsoTwo();
             break;
    case 3:
    case 4:  threeOrFour();
             break;
    default: more();
             break;
}
```

When a switch instruction is executed, the expression between the parentheses is calculated. Then the instructions after the word case and the particular value are executed. If there is no case that corresponds to the value, the instructions after the default keyword are executed. The values behind the different cases need to be constant values (numbers, characters, strings between double quotes, or variables declared as constant).

The break Instruction

If you aren't careful, the switch instruction will execute not only the instruction behind the relevant case but also the instructions behind the other cases. You can prevent this by placing the special break instruction after each case. The break instruction basically means, "Stop executing the switch, while, or for instruction you're currently in." If there was no break instruction in the previous example, then in the case x === 2, the methods two and alsoTwo would be called, and also the methods threeOrFour and more.

In some cases this behavior is useful, so that, in a sense, the different cases flow through each other. You have to watch out when doing this, though, because it can lead to errors—for instance, if a programmer forgot to place a break instruction somewhere, this would lead to very strange behavior. When you use the switch instruction, do it in such a way that cases are always separated by break instructions. The only exception is when you write multiple case labels in front of a group of instructions, as you did in the example with cases 3 and 4. The syntax of the switch instruction is part of the *instruction* syntax diagram. Figure 21-1 shows the part of that diagram belonging to the switch instruction.

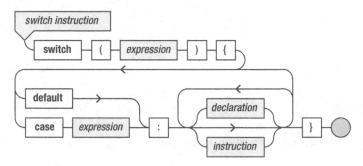

Figure 21-1. *Syntax diagram for the* switch *instruction*

Loading Different Kinds of Tiles

You can use the switch instruction to load all the different tiles and game objects. For each character in the levelData.tiles variable, you need to perform a different task. For example, when the character "." is read, you need to create a normal playing-field tile. The following instructions do that:

```
t = new Tile(sprites.field, ID.layer_objects);
t.sheetIndex = row + col % 2;
tileField.addAt(t, col, row);
break;
```

The sprite used for the tile is a strip consisting of two different sprites. By switching the sheet index using the formula row + col % 2, you get an alternating checkerboard pattern, as you can see by running the example program belonging to this chapter. Another example is adding a transparent background tile:

```
t = new Tile(sprites.wall, ID.layer_objects);
t.type = TileType.background;
tileField.addAt(t, col, row);
break;
```

Although the background sprite is invisible, you still load a sprite belonging to this tile. Why is that? Because the Tile class inherits from the SpriteGameObject class, which requires a sprite. Of course, another option would be to modify the SpriteGameObject class so that it can deal with a sprite that is null. However, in this case, you follow the simple solution of providing a sprite, even if the player will never see it. When you have to place a penguin, two things need to be done:

- Place a normal tile.
- Place a penguin.

Because penguins need to move around on the playing board and you need to interact with them, you create a class Animal to represent an animal such as a penguin or a seal. Later in this section, you see what this class looks like. To keep track of which animals are in the game, you maintain an array as a member variable of the Level class, as you've seen before:

```
this.animals = [];
```

In the switch instruction, you then create a normal tile and a penguin, as follows:

```
t = new Tile(sprites.field, ID.layer_objects);
t.sheetIndex = row + col % 2;
tileField.addAt(t, col, row);
var animalSprite = sprites.penguin;
if (levelData.tiles[row][col] === levelData.tiles[row][col].toUpperCase())
    animalSprite = sprites.penguin_boxed;
var p = new Animal(levelData.tiles[row][col], animalSprite, ID.layer_objects_1);
p.position = t.position.copy();
p.initialPosition = t.position.copy();
playingField.add(p);
this.animals.push(p);
break;
```

You're doing a couple of other things as well. For instance, you want there to be a difference between normal animals and boxed animals (animals that can't move). You make this distinction by using either uppercase or lowercase characters. JavaScript knows a method toUpperCase that converts a character to its uppercase variant. You use that method in the condition of an if instruction to determine the name of the asset that should be used. After creating the Animal object, you set its position to the position of the tile you created so it's placed correctly. You also set a variable called initialPosition to that same value. You do this so that if the player gets stuck and presses the Retry button, you know the original position of each animal in the level.

In the Animal constructor, you pass the character along as a parameter. You do this so that in the constructor, you can decide which element of the strip should be selected. You can also check the character to find out whether you're dealing with a boxed animal. The boxed status is stored in a Boolean member variable of the Animal class:

```
this.boxed = (color === color.toUpperCase());
```

In the next instruction, you use a method called indexOf in a smart way to calculate the animal you want to show, depending on the character passed as a parameter. The indexOf method checks the first index of a character in a string. For example:

```
"game".indexOf('a') // returns 1
"over".indexOf('x') // returns -1
"penguin pairs".indexOf('n') // returns 2
```

Here is how you use that method to calculate the animal's sheet index:

```
this.sheetIndex = "brgyopmx".indexOf(color.toLowerCase());
```

You convert the character to lowercase so the instruction works for both normal and boxed penguins. To complete the Animal class, you add a few convenient methods to check whether you're dealing with a special case such as a multicolored penguin, an empty box, or a seal. For the complete Animal class, see the example program PenguinPairs4 belonging to this chapter.

Finally, you also have sharks in the Penguin Pairs game. Sharks are relatively simple animals, and they can't be controlled by the player (very much as in real life!). Therefore, rather than the Animal class, you use SpriteGameObject for them, which contains everything you need. You follow a procedure similar to that for the penguins. You create a tile and a shark, and store the sharks in an array so you can easily find them later:

```
t = new Tile(sprites.field);
t.sheetIndex = row + col % 2;
tileField.addAt(t, col, row);
var s = new SpriteGameObject(sprites.shark, ID.layer_objects_1);
s.position = t.position.copy();
playingField.add(s);
this.sharks.push(s);
break;
```

Now that you've dealt with all these different cases in the switch instruction, you can load each level. Have a look at the Level class in the example to see the complete level-creation process. Figure 21-2 shows a screenshot of one of the levels after it's been loaded.

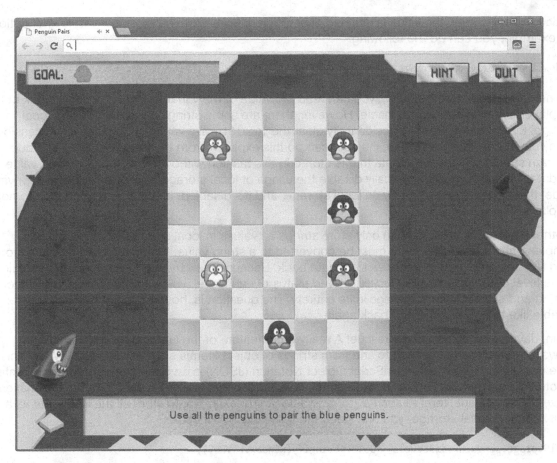

Figure 21-2. One of the levels in the Penguin Pairs game

Maintaining the Player's Progress

To complete this chapter, this section shows you a nice way to keep track of the player's progress over different sessions. You want the game to remember where the player was when they last played the game. There are several ways to do this. One way would be to let the player do this job and simply open all the levels to the player by default. This is a solution, but it doesn't really motivate the player to solve each level in sequence. Another way would be to use a database on a server that could be accessed by a JavaScript application. You could then store player information on that server and keep track of the player that way. This would work, but it's also not ideal because you would need to have a server up and running in addition to your JavaScript application. The third option is to use a feature introduced in HTML5 called *HTML5 web storage*.

HTML5 web storage provides a way to store information in two different ways, using two different variables. If you assign something to the variable code.sessionStorage, this information is retained until the tab where the application is running is closed. If you assign a value to the variable `window.localStorage`, the value is retained over different sessions. The latter is a very useful option. For example, you can do the following:

```
window.localStorage.playerName = "Bridget";
```

The next time you start the game, you can read the value of the variable and surprise (or freak out) the player by remembering her name. However, there are some strings attached to using local storage. First, it's very easy to accidentally clear the `localStorage` variable, because it's accessible to any JavaScript program. Also, the user can do this explicitly from the browser menu, so your program should never rely on data that is stored in this fashion without a backup or default value for the data. Modern browsers typically disable the usage of local storage when they operate in private mode. If your game relies heavily on local storage, and it's disabled, it might be a good idea to notify the player in some way.

Another limitation is that you can only store *strings* as values in local storage. That means any complex data you want to store must be converted to a string value. When you read the data, you need to parse the string and convert the data back. Because the `windows.LEVELS` variable contains all the level data, including the locked/solved status of each level, you want to convert this object to a string and store it in local storage in its entirety. The question is, how do you convert a complex variable like that to a string and back again?

Again, JavaScript comes to the rescue! A really great feature of the language is that JavaScript allows for seamless conversion to and from strings of object literals such as `windows.LEVELS`. This is done using the JSON object. JavaScript Object Notation (JSON) is an open standard for representing structured objects as strings, much like XML. JavaScript has a few useful methods for automatically converting an object literal to such a string and back. For example, to store all the level data as a JSON string in local storage, you only need the following line of code:

```
localStorage.penguinPairsLevels = JSON.stringify(window.LEVELS);
```

Going from a JSON string to an object literal is just as easy:

```
window.LEVELS = JSON.parse(localStorage.penguinPairsLevels);
```

In the `Level` class, you add two methods, `loadLevelsStatus` and `writeLevelsStatus`, that read and write the level information from and to the local storage. You add a few checks in these methods to make sure local storage is actually available (which it only is in newer browsers). Here are both method definitions:

```
PlayingState.prototype.loadLevelsStatus = function () {
    if (localStorage && localStorage.penguinPairsLevels) {
        window.LEVELS = JSON.parse(localStorage.penguinPairsLevels);
    }
};
PlayingState.prototype.writeLevelsStatus = function () {
    if (!localStorage)
        return;
    localStorage.penguinPairsLevels = JSON.stringify(window.LEVELS);
};
```

You call the loadLevelsStatus method in the constructor of PlayingState so the updated level information is used from local storage when the game starts. Whenever the player finishes a level, you call the writeLevelsStatus method. That way, the next time the player starts the game, the game will remember which levels the player has already completed.

An an exercise, try to extend the PenguinPairs4 example by storing more information. For example, currently the game doesn't remember the player's preferences for the music volume or whether hints should be shown. Can you create a version of the game that retains this information over different sessions?

THE CURSE OF SAVED GAMES

Most games contain a mechanism that lets the player save their progress. This is normally used in one of three ways: to continue playing later, to return to a previous save point when the player fails later in the game, or to exploit alternative strategies or storylines. These possibilities all sound reasonable, but they also introduce problems; when you design a game, you must carefully consider when (and how) to allow the player to save and load the game state.

For example, in older first-person shooters, all enemies were at fixed locations in the game world. A common strategy among players became to save a game, run into a room to see where the enemies were (which led to instant death), load the saved game, and, armed with the information about the location of the enemies, carefully clean out the room. This made the game a lot easier to play, but it was definitely not the intention of the creators. This can be partially remedied by making it difficult to save a game or to load a saved game. Other games only allow saves at particular save points. Some even make reaching a save point part of the challenge. But this can lead to frustration because the player may have to replay sections of the game over and over if there is one very difficult spot. The most interesting games are the ones where you never have to return to save points because you never really fail, but this is extremely difficult to design.

So think carefully about your saving mechanism. When will you allow saves? How many different saves will you allow? How does saving work in the game? How does the player load a saved game? Does it cost the player something to save or load a game? All these decisions will influence the gameplay and player satisfaction.

What You Have Learned

In this chapter, you have learned:

- How to create a tile-based game world
- How to use the switch instruction to handle different cases
- How to retrieve and store level-status data using local storage

Chapter 22

Pairing the Penguins

In this chapter, you program the main gameplay for the Penguin Pairs game. You learn how to move penguins around on the board and what to do when a penguin collides with another game object such as a shark or another penguin.

Selecting Penguins

Before you can move penguins around, you need to be able to *select* a penguin. When you click an animal such as a penguin or a seal, four arrows should appear that allow you to control the direction in which the animal should move. To display these arrows and handle the input, you'll can add a class called AnimalSelector. Because the animal selector contains four arrows, it inherits from the GameObjectList class. You also want to add a nice visual effect so that when the player moves the mouse over one of the arrows, it becomes darker. You can achieve this effect by adding a class Arrow that contains two sprites: one for the regular arrow and one for the arrow image when you hover over it. The Arrow class should also be able to show an arrow in any of the four possible directions.

The Arrow Class

You could have a single arrow image and rotate it depending on the desired direction, but this example keeps things simple by using an image that contains the arrow pointing in all four directions (see Figure 22-1). Therefore, when you load the sprite, the *sheet index* indicates which arrow to show. For the hover status, you load another sprite containing the same arrow images, in the same order, but darker.

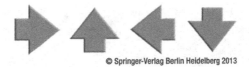

Figure 22-1. The sprite containing the four arrows, each pointing in a different direction

> **Note**   There is no particular reason I chose to use two sprites to implement the hover status. You could also place the eight arrow images on a single sprite sheet and use that instead of the two sprite sheets used here.

Because an Arrow instance more or less reacts like a button, it inherits from the Button class. In the constructor, you first create the superclass part of the instance by calling the constructor of the superclass. This loads the first arrow image. Then you define a second sprite, arrowHover, that contains the arrow image when you hover over it. By default, this sprite isn't visible, so you set its visibility status to false. You also set the parent of that sprite to be the Arrow instance, so that it's drawn in the right position. Here is the complete constructor:

```
function Arrow(sheetIndex, layer, id) {
    Button.call(this, sprites.arrow, layer, id);
    this.sheetIndex = sheetIndex;
    this.arrowHover = new SpriteGameObject(sprites.arrow_hover);
    this.arrowHover.sheetIndex = sheetIndex;
    this.arrowHover.visible = false;
    this.arrowHover.parent = this;
}
```

The sheet index that is passed as a parameter to the Arrow constructor is passed along to the actual sprites so the correct arrow direction is selected.

In the handleInput method, you check whether the hover sprite should be visible by calculating whether the mouse position is inside the bounding box of the arrow sprite. You only need to do this if the game isn't running on a touch device, so you incorporate that condition when calculating the visibility status:

```
Arrow.prototype.handleInput = function (delta) {
    Button.prototype.handleInput.call(this, delta);
    this.arrowHover.visible = !Touch.isTouchDevice &&
        this.boundingBox.contains(Mouse.position);
};
```

Finally, you override the draw method so you can add a line to draw the hover sprite as well:

```
Arrow.prototype.draw = function () {
    Button.prototype.draw.call(this);
    this.arrowHover.draw();
};
```

The Animal Selector

The animal selector uses the Arrow class to display four arrows when the player clicks an animal (see Figure 22-2). These four arrows are stored as member variables in the AnimalSelector class. Because the selector controls a particular animal, you also have to keep track of which one it controls. Therefore, you also add a member variable selectedAnimal, which contains a reference to the target animal. In the constructor method, you create the four Arrow objects and position them appropriately as follows:

```
function AnimalSelector(layer, id) {
    GameObjectList.call(this, layer, id);
    this._arrowright = new Arrow(0);
    this._arrowright.position = new Vector2(this._arrowright.width, 0);
    this.add(this._arrowright);
    this._arrowup = new Arrow(1);
    this._arrowup.position = new Vector2(0, -this._arrowright.height);
    this.add(this._arrowup);
    this._arrowleft = ncw Arrow(2);
    this._arrowleft.position = new Vector2(-this._arrowright.width, 0);
    this.add(this._arrowleft);
    this._arrowdown = new Arrow(3);
    this._arrowdown.position = new Vector2(0, this._arrowright.height);
    this.add(this._arrowdown);
    this.selectedAnimal = null;
    this.visible = false;
}
```

Figure 22-2. When the player clicks a penguin, four arrows are shown so the player can choose the direction in which the penguin should move

In the handleInput method, you first check whether the selector is visible. If not, it doesn't need to handle input:

```
if (!this.visible)
    return;
```

You then check whether one of the arrows was pressed. If so, you calculate the desired animal velocity:

```
var animalVelocity = Vector2.zero;
if (this._arrowdown.pressed)
    animalVelocity.y = 1;
else if (this._arrowup.pressed)
    animalVelocity.y = -1;
else if (this._arrowleft.pressed)
    animalVelocity.x = -1;
else if (this._arrowright.pressed)
    animalVelocity.x = 1;
animalVelocity.multiplyWith(300);
```

If the player clicked the left mouse button or touched the screen (it doesn't matter where), you set the state of the animal selector to invisible again:

```
if (Mouse.left.pressed || Touch.containsTouchPress(Game.screenRect))
    this.visible = false;
```

Finally, if the velocity you calculated isn't zero, and there is a target penguin, you update its velocity:

```
if (this.selectedAnimal !== null && animalVelocity.isZero)
    this.selectedAnimal.velocity = animalVelocity;
```

In the handleInput method in the Animal class, you have to handle clicking an animal. However, there are some situations in which you don't have to handle this:

- The animal is in a hole in the ice.

- The animal isn't visible.

- The animal is already moving.

In all these cases, you don't do anything, and you return from the method:

```
if (!this.visible || this.boxed || !this.velocity.isZero)
    return;
```

If the player didn't touch or click the animal, you can also return from the method. Therefore, you add the following if instruction that verifies this:

```
if (Touch.isTouchDevice) {
    if (!Touch.containsTouchPress(this.boundingBox))
        return;
} else {
    if (!Mouse.left.pressed || !this.boundingBox.contains(Mouse.position))
        return;
}
```

The final case you need to cover is if the player touched or clicked the animal but the animal selector was already visible. In that case, you don't have to do anything, and you can return from the method:

```
var animalSelector = this.root.find(ID.animalSelector);
if (animalSelector.visible)
    return;
```

Now that you've handled all the cases, you can make the selector visible, set its position, and assign the animal as the selector's target animal. These are covered in the following instructions:

```
animalSelector.position = this.position;
animalSelector.visible = true;
animalSelector.selectedAnimal = this;
```

As you can see, properly handling user input can be complicated sometimes. You need to take care of all possible actions that a player can take and handle the input appropriately. If you don't do this right, you risk introducing bugs in the game that can lead to a crash (which is bad) or to a possibility for the player to cheat (which is even worse, especially in online multiplayer games).

The instructions you just wrote allow the player to select animals at will and tell them to move in a particular direction. Now you need to handle the interaction between the animal, the playing field, and other game objects.

Handling Input in Reverse Order

The order in which you draw objects on the screen is important. For example, if you draw the penguins before you draw the background image, the player will never see the penguins. However, the order in which objects handle input shouldn't be the same as the order in which they're drawn! In the Penguin Pairs game, this would lead to unexpected behavior.

Suppose two penguins are next to each other on the playing field, and you click one of them. Then four arrows appear. Because the two penguins are next to each other, one of the arrows is drawn over the other penguin (see Figure 22-3). If you click that arrow, what happens? Does the selected penguin move to the left, or do you select the other penguin?

Figure 22-3. What happens when you click the left arrow?

The outcome of this question depends on the order in which input is handled for each game object. If the penguin handles the input before the penguin selector, then the penguin selector will move to the other penguin. If the selector's handleInput method is called first, then the selected penguin will move to the left. Generally, when you develop programs, you want to be in control of the program's behavior. This means you have to choose in which order you want to handle the input and make sure it always happens that way. In this case, the desired behavior is that the selected penguin moves to the left. And as a general rule, you would like *objects that are drawn on top to handle input first*. In other words, you need to call the handleInput method on the objects in the list in *reverse* order of the order in which they're drawn. This can easily be done with the following for instruction, which you put in the GameObjectList.handleInput method body:

```
GameObjectList.prototype.handleInput = function (delta) {
    for (var i = this._gameObjects.length - 1; i >=0; i--)
        this._gameObjects[i].handleInput(delta);
};
```

As a result, objects that are drawn on top now handle input first. Again, this illustrates how important it is to get details like this right when specifying the player interface. An interface that isn't intuitive to the player will very quickly lead to frustration—and the player may no longer want to play your game because of issues with the interface.

Updating Animals

Interaction between animals and other game objects is done in the update method of the Animal class. The main reason for doing this in the Animal class is that then each animal handles its own interaction. If you add multiple animals to the game (as you're doing here), you don't have to change anything in the code that handles the interaction. As a first step, you don't have to update the animal if it isn't visible or if its velocity is zero. Therefore, the first instructions in the update method are

```
SpriteGameObject.prototype.update.call(this, delta);
if (!this.visible || this.velocity.isZero)
    return;
```

As you can see, you first call the update method of the base class. Because the SpriteGameObject class doesn't override the update method, this calls the update method as it's defined in the GameObject class, which updates the position of the object by adding the velocity multiplied by the elapsed game time. Now you have to check whether the animal collides with another game object. Because of the check you do at the start of the update method, you only do this for animals that are both visible and moving.

If the animal is moving, you need to know what tile it's currently moving into. Then you can check what kind of tile it is and whether other game objects are located at that tile. For this, you add a property called currentBlock to the Animal class. How can you calculate the tile the animal is moving into? When a penguin is moving to the left, you can calculate the x index of the tile as follows:

```
var tileField = this.root.find(ID.tiles);
var xIndex = Math.floor(this.position.x / tileField.cellWidth);
```

Because Math.floor results in the closest integer number that is smaller than the value it gets as a parameter, you end up at the tile that the sprite's left position is in. However, this only finds the correct x index when the animal is moving *left*. When the animal is moving to the *right*, you want to calculate the tile that the *rightmost pixel* of the penguin sprite moves into. In order to solve this, you add 1 to the calculated x index if the x velocity is positive. You do something similar to calculate the y index. Here are the complete header and body of the currentBlock property:

```
Object.defineProperty(Animal.prototype, "currentBlock",
    {
        get: function () {
            var tileField = this.root.find(ID.tiles);
            var p = new Vector2(Math.floor(this.position.x /
                tileField.cellWidth),Math.floor(this.position.y /
                tileField.cellHeight));
            if (this.velocity.x > 0)
                p.x++;
            if (this.velocity.y > 0)
                p.y++;
            return p;
        }
    });
```

The next step is finding out what kind of tile the animal is moving into. To do that, you have to add a few methods to the tile field. To do this properly, you add a class called `TileField` that inherits from `GameObjectGrid`, and you add a few methods to that class. One method checks whether given *x* and *y* indices are outside of the tile field. This method is called `isOutsideField`, and it's straightforward:

```
TileField.prototype.isOutsideField = function (pos) {
    return (pos.x < 0 || pos.x >=this.columns || pos.y < 0 || pos.y >=
        this.rows);
};
```

This method is used in another method, `getTileType`, which retrieves the type of the tile for a given tile position. The first thing you check in this method is whether the point is outside of the tile field. If that is the case, you return a background (transparent) tile type:

```
if (this.isOutsideField(pos))
    return TileType.background;
```

In all other cases, you can retrieve the tile type by getting the `Tile` object from the tile field and returning its type:

```
return this.at(pos.x, pos.y).type;
```

Now you can go back to the `Animal.update` method and check whether the animal has fallen off the tile field. If so, you set the animal's visibility to `false` and its velocity to zero, to ensure that the animal doesn't keep moving indefinitely while it's invisible:

```
var target = this.currentBlock;
var tileField = this.root.find(ID.tiles);
if (tileField.getTileType(target) === TileType.background) {
    this.visible = false;
    this.velocity = Vector2.zero;
}
```

Another possibility is that the animal ran into a wall tile. If that is the case, it has to stop moving:

```
else if (tileField.getTileType(target) === TileType.wall)
    this.stopMoving();
```

Stopping moving isn't as easy as it sounds. You could simply set the animal's velocity to zero, but then the animal would be partly in another tile. You need to place the animal at the tile *it just moved out of*. The method `stopMoving` accomplishes exactly that. In this method, you first have to calculate the position of the old tile. You can do that by starting from the *x* and *y* indices of the tile the animal is currently moving into. These are passed along as a parameter. For example, if the animal's velocity is the vector *(300, 0)* (moving to the right), you need to subtract 1 from the *x* index to get the *x* index of the tile the animal is moving out of. If the animal's velocity is *(0, -300)* (moving up), then you need to *add* 1 to the *y* index to get the *y* index of the tile the animal is moving out of. You can achieve this by *normalizing the velocity vector* and subtracting it from the *x* and *y* indices. This works because normalizing a vector results in a vector of length 1 (unit length). Because an animal is only allowed to move in either the *x* or *y* direction and not diagonally, you end up with a vector *(1, 0)* in the first example and *(0, -1)* in the second example. So you set the position of the animal to the position of the tile it just moved out of, as follows:

```
var tileField = this.root.find(ID.tiles);
this.velocity.normalize();
var currBlock = this.currentBlock;
this.position = new Vector2(Math.floor(currBlock.x - this.velocity.x) *
    tileField.cellWidth, Math.floor(currBlock.y - this.velocity.y) *
    tileField.cellHeight);
```

Note that you multiply the position by the width and height of a cell in the tile field. This is because tile indices aren't the same as actual pixel positions on the screen. The tile indices only indicate the location of tiles in the grid, whereas the animal position needs to be expressed as a position on the screen in pixels.

Finally, you set the animal's velocity to zero so it stays in its new position:

```
this.velocity = Vector2.zero;
```

Meeting Other Game Objects

You still need to check whether the animal collides with another game object, such as another penguin or a shark. There are a few special types of animals:

- Multicolored penguins
- Empty boxes
- Seals

You can add a few methods to the `Animal` class to determine whether you're dealing with these special cases. For example, you're dealing with a seal if the sheet index equals 7 and isn't boxed:

```
Animal.prototype.isSeal = function () {
    return this.sheetIndex === 7 && !this.boxed;
};
```

You're dealing with an empty box if the sheet index is 7 and is boxed:

```
Animal.prototype.isEmptyBox = function () {
    return this.sheetIndex === 7 && this.boxed;
};
```

Finally, you're dealing with a multicolored penguin if the sheet index is 6 and isn't boxed:

```
Animal.prototype.isMulticolor = function () {
    return this.sheetIndex === 6 && !this.boxed;
};
```

First you check whether there is a shark at the tile the animal is moving into. To do that, you retrieve the level and use the findSharkAtPosition method from the Level class to find out whether there is a shark:

```
var s = this.root.findSharkAtPosition(target);
if (s !== null && s.visible) {
    // handle the shark interaction
}
```

The findSharkAtPosition method is straightforward; have a look at the method in the example code belonging to this chapter. If a penguin encounters a shark, the penguin is eaten and the shark leaves the playing field with a full belly. In the game, this means the penguin stops moving (forever) and both the shark and the penguin become invisible. The following lines of code achieve this:

```
s.visible = false;
this.visible = false;
this.stopMoving();
```

The next thing to check is whether there is another penguin or a seal. To do that, you use the findAnimalAtPosition method from the Level class. You retrieve the animal as follows:

```
var a = this.root.findAnimalAtPosition(target);
```

If the method returns null or the animal isn't visible, you don't have to do anything, and you can return from the method:

```
if (a === null || !a.visible)
    return;
```

The first case you solve is if the penguin is colliding with a seal. In that case, the penguin doesn't have to do anything—it simply stops moving:

```
if (a.isSeal())
    this.stopMoving();
```

The next case is if the animal collides with an empty box. If that is the case, you move the animal inside the box by setting the sheet index of the box to the sheet index of the animal, and you make the animal invisible:

```
else if (a.isEmptyBox()) {
    this.visible = false;
    a.sheetIndex = this.sheetIndex;
}
```

If the sheet index of animal a is the same as the sheet index of the penguin, or either one of the penguins is multicolored, you have a valid pair of penguins and make both penguins invisible:

```
else if (a.sheetIndex === this.sheetIndex || this.isMulticolor() || a.isMulticolor()) {
    a.visible = false;
    this.visible = false;
}
```

You also have to display an extra pair at top left on the screen, but you deal with that in the next section. Finally, in all other cases, the penguin stops moving:

```
else
    this.stopMoving();
```

Maintaining the Number of Pairs

In order to maintain the number of pairs and draw it nicely on the screen, you add another class called PairList to the game. The PairList class inherits from the SpriteGameObject class. It consists of a frame, on top of which is drawn a number of sprites indicating the number of required pairs. Because you want to indicate the color of the pair that was made, you store these pairs in an array as integer values. This array is a member variable of the PairList class:

```
this._pairs = [];
```

You put integer values in this array because you can define per pair which color it is and how many pairs you need in total. In the member variable pairSprite, you store the sprite representing a pair and set the pair list as the parent of that sprite:

```
this._pairSprite = new SpriteGameObject(sprites.penguin_pairs);
this._pairSprite.parent = this;
```

The image for that sprite is a sprite strip, and the colored pairs are ordered in the same way as the penguins (see Figure 22-4). The rightmost image in the strip (sheet index 7) is the image you display if a pair still needs to be made. So if the _pairs array contains the values {0, 0, 2, 7, 7}, that means the player has already made two pairs of blue penguins and one pair of green penguins, and the player needs to make two more pairs to finish the level.

Figure 22-4. Sprite containing all the possible pair images

You pass along a parameter, nrPairs, to the constructor of the PairList class so you know how large the array should be. You then fill the array so that each element is set to the empty slot (sheet index 7):

```
for (var i = 0; i < nrPairs; i++)
    this._pairs.push(7);
```

You also add a method addPair to the class, which finds the first occurrence of the value 7 in the array and replaces it with the index that was passed along as a parameter:

```
PairList.prototype.addPair = function (index) {
    var i = 0;
    while (i < this._pairs.length && this._pairs[i] !== 7)
        i++;
    if (i < this._pairs.length)
        this._pairs[i] = index;
};
```

This example uses a while instruction to increment the i variable until you find an empty spot.

Now you add a useful property to check whether the player has completed the level. The level is completed if the list of pairs no longer contains any value of 7 (meaning all empty spots have been replaced by a pair):

```
Object.defineProperty(PairList.prototype, "completed",
    {
        get: function () {
            for (var i = 0, l = this._pairs.length; i < l; i++)
                if (this._pairs[i] === 7)
                    return false;
            return true;
        }
    });
```

Finally, you need to draw the pairs on the screen in the draw method. Here you use a for instruction to traverse all the indices in the pair list. For each index, you draw the correct sprite at the appropriate position. Note that you use the same sprite and simply draw it multiple times with different sheet indices:

```
PairList.prototype.draw = function () {
    SpriteGameObject.prototype.draw.call(this);
    if (!this.visible)
        return;
    for (var i = 0, l = this._pairs.length; i < l; i++) {
        this._pairSprite.position = new Vector2(110 + i * this.height, 8);
        this._pairSprite.sheetIndex = this._pairs[i];
        this._pairSprite.draw();
    }
};
```

The call to the base draw method ensures that the background frame is drawn first.

Now that you have the PairList class, you can create an instance of it in the Level class, add it to the game world, a.n it near the top left of the screen:

```
var pairList = new PairList(levelData.nrPairs, ID.layer_overlays, ID.pairList);
pairList.position = new Vector2(20, 15);
this.add(pairList);
```

And in the Animal class, you add a pair to the list if an animal encounters another penguin of the same color or one of the two animals is a multicolored penguin:

```
else if (a.sheetIndex === this.sheetIndex || this.isMulticolor() ||
    a.isMulticolor()) {
    a.visible = false;
    this.visible = false;
    this.root.find(ID.pairList).addPair(this.sheetIndex);
}
```

For the complete example, see the PenguinPairs5 program belonging to this chapter. In the next chapter, you add the final touches to the Penguin Pairs game, and you see a better way to separate game generic code, such as the SpriteGameObject class or the GameStateManager class, from game-specific code, such as the PairList class.

What You Have Learned

In this chapter, you have learned:

- How to program a game object selector
- How to model interactions between different kinds of game objects
- How to maintain and draw the number of pairs made by the player

Chapter 23

Finishing the Penguin Pairs Game

In this chapter, you finalize the Penguin Pairs game. The first step is to reorganize your code a bit so parts of it can be used more easily by other programs. Then you finish the game by extending the user interface and adding sound effects.

Separating Code into Different Modules

Especially when developing more complex applications, it makes sense to group related classes together. For example, if you're developing a complex game, there will be classes related to simulating physics, classes for doing AI such as path planning, classes that provide network playability, user interface classes, and so on. Although the examples used in this book aren't that complex, you can still see a clear distinction between classes that are useful only for a specific game versus classes that are used across different games. For example, all three games have some concept of a basic game object, and both the Jewel Jam game and the Penguin Pairs game use a grid as a basis for their playing field. Also, the concept of a hierarchy of game objects drawn on several layers is something that is used in different games. All in all, this book keeps going back to using similar classes among different games. In fact, you copied classes from the Jewel Jam game and used them as is in the Penguin Pairs game.

As discussed a couple of times earlier in this book, copying code into different projects is a bad thing. Making copies of code means bugs can be copied as well; and if you make any changes or improvements, you'll have to do it everywhere you copied that code. How can you avoid copying code between *different games*? The best way to achieve this is to separate game-specific code from game-generic code. By placing the generic classes together in a separate folder, you can more easily reuse this code in other game projects. By choosing a smart folder structure among different game projects, you can easily ensure that the generic code doesn't have to be copied for each of those projects. In this section, you set up this structure, and you see a neat way to make the distinction between generic classes and game-specific classes in JavaScript by using a concept called *namespaces*.

Variables as Namespaces

Namespaces are commonly used in programming languages to provide some structure for where classes belong. Many programming languages have namespace support baked in the language specification. JavaScript isn't one of those languages, but it's very easy to use the existing functionality in the language to set up something similar.

You've seen in the example code that variables are groups of objects. These objects can be object literals, strings, numbers, or even functions. Because a class is defined by a function in JavaScript, you can group classes together in a variable, making that variable serve as a namespace. For example, suppose you want to create a JavaScript game engine that contains all the generic classes and objects you've built in this book. Let's call this game engine powerupjs. You can start defining your classes as follows:

```
var powerupjs = {
    GameObject : function(layer, id) {
        ...
    },
    GameObjectList : function(layer, id) {
        ...
    }
};
```

Now, whenever you want to use the class GameObject, you type powerupjs.GameObject. In the JavaScript code, this will make it clear to the user that GameObject belongs to the powerupjs namespace. This is great, but it means you have to put all your classes in a single JavaScript file, and this doesn't really improve the readability of your programs. Let's investigate how you can do this in a smarter way.

A Design Pattern for Namespaces

To make using namespaces easier in JavaScript, you use a *design pattern*. Chapter XX briefly talked about design patterns in the discussion of singletons (classes that allow only a single instance). This singleton design pattern was used as follows:

```
function MySingletonClass_Singleton () {
    ...
}

// add methods and properties here
MySingletonClass_Singleton.prototype.myMethod() = function () {
    ...
};
...
var MySingletonClass = new MySingletonClass_Singleton();

// now we can use the variable as a single instance
MySingletonClass.myMethod();
```

The design pattern for putting classes in namespaces uses a JavaScript mechanism that lets you define and call a function at the same time. Perhaps you recall using this before, when defining the function to request the next game-loop iteration:

```
var requestAnimationFrame = (function () {
        return window.requestAnimationFrame ||
            window.webkitRequestAnimationFrame ||
            window.mozRequestAnimationFrame ||
            window.oRequestAnimationFrame ||
            window.msRequestAnimationFrame ||
            function (callback) {
                window.setTimeout(callback, 1000 / 60);
            };
    })();
```

Here the variable requestAnimationFrame contains the result of a function that is defined and immediately called. In a very similar way, you can put the definition of a class in such a function. Have a look at the following example:

```
var powerupjs = (function (module) {

    function Vector2(x, y) {
        this.x = typeof x !== 'undefined' ? x : 0;
        this.y = typeof y !== 'undefined' ? y : 0;
    }

    Object.defineProperty(Vector2, "zero",
        {
            get: function () {
                return new powerupjs.Vector2();
            }
        });

    Vector2.prototype.equals = function (obj) {
        return this.x === obj.x && this.y === obj.y;
    };

    // add more methods and properties
    ...

    module.Vector2 = Vector2;
    return module;

})({});
```

This example creates a function that expects an object literal module as a parameter. In the function, you create the Vector2 class and define its properties and methods. You assign that class to a variable in the module variable, which you then return. The function is executed by passing an empty object literal to the function. The result of the function is stored in the variable powerupjs, which now contains a variable called Vector2 that refers to the class Vector2. For the next class you define, you'll pass the variable powerupjs instead of an empty object literal, so that the powerupjs variable is filled with all the classes that are supposed to be in the powerupjs namespace. You can make this even nicer by using smart JavaScript syntax. Consider the following class definition:

```
var powerupjs = (function (powerupjs) {

    function Vector2(x, y) {
        this.x = typeof x !== 'undefined' ? x : 0;
        this.y = typeof y !== 'undefined' ? y : 0;
    }
    // etc.

    powerupjs.Vector2 = Vector2;
    return powerupjs;

})(powerupjs || {});
```

Here you rename the `module` parameter to powerupjs for clarity; and instead of passing an empty object literal, you pass the expression powerupjs || {}. This expression results in powerupjs if that variable is defined, or an empty object literal otherwise. You add this namespace design pattern to all the generic game classes. Regardless of the order in which these classes are added to the namespace, the first time this is done you start with an empty object literal, and after that, the powerupjs variable is defined and supplemented with the rest of the classes. The example code belonging to this chapter includes a folder called powerupjs; in this folder are all the generic game classes, all of which are in the powerupjs namespace. The remaining examples in this book reuse the powerupjs module (or library) as a basis for the example games.

The namespace pattern is a very useful pattern for grouping related classes together. Whenever you're building a complex application, it's a good idea to use namespaces. That way, you clearly show the users of your code how the classes are related to each other. You can be even more extreme and group namespaces in other, bigger namespaces, using exactly the same design pattern.

Namespaces also provide a bit of extra security. For example, have a look at the following class definition in a namespace:

```
var powerupjs = (function (powerupjs) {

    function GameStateManager_Singleton() {
        this._gameStates = [];
        this._currentGameState = null;
    }

    // add methods/properties here
    ...

    powerupjs.GameStateManager = new GameStateManager_Singleton();
    return powerupjs;

})(powerupjs || {});
```

This example shows the definition of the GameStateManager class, which is a singleton. The fact that this is a singleton can be seen by the fact that you assign an *instance* of the class to powerupjs.GameStateManager instead of the class definition itself. What is really nice is that the class definition is now encapsulated by the namespace—it's no longer possible to access GameStateManager_Singleton in other JavaScript files, thus ensuring that only this single instance of the class can be used, which is exactly the point of the singleton design pattern!

The encapsulation is a result of the function enclosing the class definition. You can use this in other ways to control what functions or classes are available where. For example, perhaps some methods of a class are supposed to be internal (or *private*). You could do this as follows:

```
var powerupjs = (function (powerupjs) {

    ...

    function privateMethod(obj) {
        // do something with the object
        obj._currentGameState = ...;
    }

    GameStateManager_Singleton.prototype.publicMethod() {
        privateMethod(this);
        ...
    }

    powerupjs.GameStateManager = new GameStateManager_Singleton();
    return powerupjs;

})(powerupjs || {});
```

In this example, the method privateMethod can perform operations on the GameStateManager instance, and it can be called from within other methods in the object, but the method isn't accessible from other JavaScript classes.

Organizing classes in modules and folders helps provide a better feeling for the structure of a group of related classes. Figure 23-1 shows how the powerupjs module is organized into different folders. When you create a module, it's a good idea to provide a diagram such as the one in Figure 23-1 for the module's users. Also, because a module can consist of many different classes, you may also want to provide some documentation that describes the module's overall philosophy. In the case of powerupjs, it's important for users to know that the module heavily relies on a running game loop with game objects that update and draw themselves. Furthermore, it's a good idea to provide detailed descriptions of what each method does, what kind of parameters it expects, what calling the method does, and any special cases. The last part of this book discusses documentation in more detail, and you also learn a few ways to make documentation easier to read and more accessible to the users of your classes.

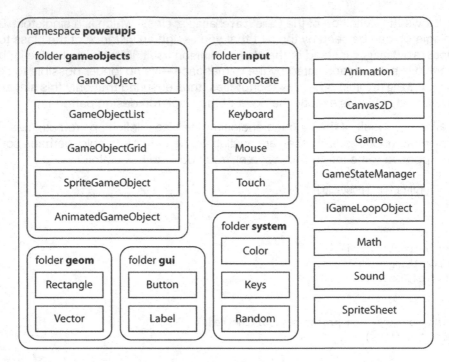

Figure 23-1. An overview of the module and folder structure of the powerupjs *module*

Finishing the User Interface

In this section, you finish the user interface. First you see how to add a hint mechanism to the game. Then you see how to reset and move on to the next level. You complete the game by adding sound effects.

Showing Hints

Now that you've reorganized your code, there are a couple more features to add to the Penguin Pairs game. As a first step, you want to be able to show a hint when the user clicks a button. The hint consists of an orange arrow that is visible for a second. When you load the level, you read the hint position and direction from the levelData variable and create a SpriteGameObject instance to load the arrow, select the correct sheet index, and position it appropriately before you add it to the game world:

```
var hint = new powerupjs.SpriteGameObject(sprites.arrow_hint, ID.layer_objects_2);
hint.sheetIndex = levelData.hint_arrow_direction;
hint.position = new powerupjs.Vector2(levelData.hint_arrow_x * 73,
    levelData.hint_arrow_y * 72);
playingField.add(hint);
```

In order to temporarily display the arrow, you reuse the `VisibilityTimer` class from the Jewel Jam game. You create an instance of this class and add it to the game world as well:

```
this.hintVisible = new VisibilityTimer(hint);
playingField.add(this.hintVisible);
```

You also add a button that the player can click to display the hint on the screen:

```
this.hintButton = new powerupjs.Button(sprites.button_hint, ID.layer_overlays);
this.hintButton.position = new powerupjs.Vector2(916, 20);
this.add(this.hintButton);
```

Finally, you extend the `handleInput` method of `Level` to deal with the Hint button being pressed:

```
if (this.hintButton.pressed)
    this.hintVisible.startVisible();
```

The Hint button can only be pressed if it's visible, which in some cases it shouldn't be:

- After the player makes the first move, the Hint button should disappear, and the Retry button should appear.

- If the player chose to switch off hints in the Options menu, the Hint button should never be visible.

For the first case, you need to keep track of when the player makes their first move. You add an extra member variable `firstMoveMade` to the `Level` class. When you give an animal a velocity, this is done in the `AnimalSelector` class. Once the player has clicked an arrow and the animal is moving, you set the `firstMoveMade` variable to true:

```
this.selectedAnimal.velocity = animalVelocity;
this.root.firstMoveMade = true;
```

Second, you have to handle the Hints setting from the game Options menu. You do this in the `update` method of the `Level` class. You simply check what the value of the Hints setting is in the `GameSettings` variable, and update the Hint and Retry button visibility state accordingly:

```
this.hintButton.visible = GameSettings.hints && !this.firstMoveMade;
this.retryButton.visible = !this.hintButton.visible;
```

As you can see from these two lines of code, the Hint button is visible only if `GameSettings.hints` is true and the player has not yet made a first move. The Retry button's visibility status is always the opposite of the hint button's visibility status. So if the Hint button is visible, the Retry button isn't, and vice versa.

Resetting the Level

After a player moves a couple of animals around, it can happen that the level can't be solved anymore. Instead of having to quit and restart the game, let's give the player a means to reset a level to its initial state.

Thanks to the proper implementation of the reset method everywhere throughout the game object classes, resetting a level to its initial state is now really easy. You have to call the reset method on all the game objects, and then you deal with resetting things in the Level class itself. The only thing you need to do there is set the firstMoveMade variable to false so the player can view a hint again:

```
Level.prototype.reset = function () {
    powerupjs.GameObjectList.prototype.reset.call(this);
    this.firstMoveMade = false;
};
```

> **Note**   There are many ways in which the Penguin Pairs game can be extended. For example, can you write code that determines whether a level is still solvable? You could extend the game by displaying a message to the user if that happens. You might have your own ideas about how the game could be improved. Feel free to try them by modifying and adding to the examples.

Moving to the Next Level

When the player finishes a level (hurray!), you would like to display an encouraging overlay (see Figure 23-2 for a screenshot). When the player clicks or taps the screen, the next level is shown. Because you created the GameStateManager class, let's profit from it by adding another state: LevelFinishedState. The only thing this state does is display the overlay and react to a player clicking. Because the overlay is displayed on top of the level, you still need to do something with the playing state. Therefore, you store it in a member variable. In addition, you load an overlay, position it in the center of the screen, and add it to the game world. Here is the complete constructor method:

```
function LevelFinishedState() {
    powerupjs.GameObjectList.call(this);
    this.playingState = powerupjs.GameStateManager.get(ID.game_state_playing);
    this.overlay = new powerupjs.SpriteGameObject(sprites.level_finished, ID.layer_overlays);
    this.overlay.position = this.overlay.screenCenter;
    this.add(this.overlay);
}
```

Figure 23-2. A screenshot of the overlay shown to the player after they finish a level

You want to display the overlay on top of the playing state, but you don't want the playing state to be able to process input anymore (otherwise the player could still move penguins around). Therefore, you only call the update and draw methods, and not the handleInput method, on the playingState object.

In the handleInput method of LevelFinishedState, you check whether the player has pressed the mouse button or tapped the screen. If so, you set the current state to be the playing state, and you call the nextLevel method on it:

```
LevelFinishedState.prototype.handleInput = function (delta) {
    if (powerupjs.Touch.isTouchDevice) {
        if (!powerupjs.Touch.containsTouchPress(this.overlay.boundingBox))
            return;
    }
    else if (!powerupjs.Mouse.left.pressed)
        return;
    powerupjs.GameStateManager.switchTo(ID.game_state_playing);
    this.playingState.nextLevel();
};
```

How does the nextLevel method work? It has to deal with two possibilities. The first possibility is that the player finished the last level. In that case, you go back to the level menu state. In all other cases, you increment the current level index, and you unlock the next level for the player. Finally, because you changed the level status, you write it to the local storage so that the next time the player starts the game, the game remembers which levels the player has solved. The complete nextLevel method looks like this:

```
PlayingState.prototype.nextLevel = function () {
    if (this.currentLevelIndex >=window.LEVELS.length - 1)
        powerupjs.GameStateManager.switchTo(ID.game_state_levelselect);
    else {
        this.goToLevel(this.currentLevelIndex + 1);
        window.LEVELS[this.currentLevelIndex].locked = false;
    }
    this.writeLevelsStatus();
};
```

The only thing you still need to do is make sure the game goes to the level-finished state when the player has won. You can do this in the update method of the playing state by using the completed property from the Level class:

```
if (this.currentLevel.completed) {
    window.LEVELS[this.currentLevelIndex].solved = true;
    powerupjs.GameStateManager.switchTo(ID.game_state_levelfinished);
}
```

If the player has finished the level, you set the solved status of the level to true, and you change the current game state to the level-finished state.

TUTORIALS

As you've probably noticed, the first few levels of the Penguin Pairs game also serve as a tutorial that explains how the game should be played. When you create a game, players have to learn how to play it. If you don't tell players what the challenges and goals are and how to control the game, they will probably get frustrated and stop playing.

Some games provide extensive help files with long text explaining the story and the controls. Players no longer want to read such documents or screens. They want to jump right into the game. You have to educate players while they're playing.

You can create a few specific tutorial levels in which the player can practice the controls without drastically affecting the progress of the game itself. This approach is popular with casual gamers as an introduction to your game. Seasoned gamers prefer to immediately dive into the action. Be careful not to explain everything in the tutorial levels. Only explain the basic controls. Explain more advanced controls during the game as they're required: for example, using simple pop-up messages, or in a visible spot in a HUD.

Tutorials work best when they naturally integrate into the game story. For example, the game character might start running around in their safe home town, learning the basic movement controls. Next the character practices fighting together with a few friends. And after, that the player goes into the woods to try to shoot some birds with a bow. This will provide all the practice needed for the fights later in the game.

You should make sure your tutorial levels work and that players remember the controls even if they put the game away for a couple of days. Otherwise, they may never come back to the game.

Adding Sound Effects

To finish the game, you should add sounds and music at the right spots. As you may remember, one of the choices in the Options menu is to change the background volume. You do that using the following line of code:

```
sounds.music.volume = this.musicSlider.value;
```

In the PenguinPairs class, you start playing the music:

```
sounds.music.play();
```

Similarly, you play sound effects at appropriate moments, just as you did in the Jewel Jam game. For example, whenever a pair of penguins is made, you play a sound effect (see the update method in the Animal class):

```
sounds.pair.play();
```

If you look at the PenguinPairsFinal example belonging to this chapter, you can see how the complete game works and where sound effects are played back, and of course you can play the game yourself.

WORKING IN TEAMS

The first generation of games was created by programmers. They did all the work. They designed the game mechanics, they created the art (which consisted of just a few pixels), and they programmed the game in an Assembler language. All the work focused on the programming. The game mechanics were often adapted to what could be programmed efficiently.

But when more memory became available, this slowly changed. Creating fancy-looking objects with a limited number of pixels and colors became an art form, and such pixel artists started to play an important role in developing games. In the early days there were no drawing programs (no computer was powerful enough for that). Pixelated characters were designed on graph paper and then turned into hexadecimal numbers to be put into the game code.

With the increase of computer power and storage media like the CD, art became increasingly important, and the artists developed with it. 3D graphics and animations became common, leading to new specialists who could use the new tools and technologies developed to support such work. Nowadays artists make up the majority of game production teams.

At some point, designing the game became a separate job. Game mechanics were tuned to the interests of user groups and were more and more based on principles from psychology and educational sciences. This required separate expertise. Stories assumed a crucial role, leading to the inclusion of writers. And the teams were extended to include producers, sound engineers, composers, and many other types of people. Today, teams for top games can consist of hundreds of people. But without the programmers, nothing would work.

A Few Final Notes

In this part of the book, you've created a game that is quite a bit more complicated than the previous example game, Jewel Jam. You've probably noticed that the number of classes has become quite large, and you're relying more and more on a certain design for the game software. For example, you're organizing game objects in a tree structure and using a class to handle game states. On a more basic level, you assume that game objects are responsible for handling their input, updating themselves, and drawing themselves on the screen. You may not agree with some (or all) of these design choices. Perhaps, after reading the book to this point, you've formed your own ideas about how game software should be designed. That is a good thing. The design I propose in this book isn't the only way to do things. Designs can always be evaluated and improved, or even thrown away and replaced by something entirely different. So, don't hesitate to look critically at the design I propose and try other designs. By trying different approaches to solve a problem, you can better understand the problem and become a better software developer as a result.

What You Have Learned

In this chapter, you have learned:

- How to group classes into a namespace
- How to reset a level to its initial state and handle going to the next level

Part V

Tick Tick

The previous chapters have shown you how to build several different types of games. In this part, you build a platform game with animated characters, physics, and different levels. The name of the game is *Tick Tick* (see Figure V-1), and the story revolves around a slightly stressed-out bomb that will explode within 30 seconds. This means each level in the game should be finished within 30 seconds. A level is finished if the player collects all the refreshing water drops and reaches the finish panel in time.

© Springer-Verlag Berlin Heidelberg 2013

Figure V-1. The Tick Tick game

This platform game includes a number of basic elements that are found in many other games as well:

- It should be possible to play different levels.
- These levels should be loaded from a separate file so they can be changed without having to know how the game code works.
- The game should support animated characters for both the player and the enemies.
- The player should control the actions of a player character that can run or jump.
- There should be some basic physics in the game to manage falling, colliding with objects, jumping on platforms, and so on.

That is quite a list! Fortunately, you can reuse many of the classes you've already developed. The following chapters look at all the items on the list. If you want to play the complete version of the Tick Tick game, get the sample code for Chapter 29 and open the TickTick.html file in the TickTickFinal folder.

Chapter 24

The Main Game Structure

In this chapter, you lay out the framework for the Tick Tick game. Because of all the work you've done for the previous games, you can rely on a lot of preexisting classes. In fact, you build the game on the classes you grouped in the powerupjs namespace/library in the previous chapter. This means you already have a basic design for handling game states and settings, a hierarchy of game objects, and more. You extend the powerupjs library later by adding classes related to animated game objects. You can see these classes in the library; they're discussed in the next chapter.

Overview of the Game Structure

This game follows a structure very similar to that of the Penguin Pairs game. There is a title screen that allows the player to go to either the level-selection menu or a help page (see Figure 24-1). To keep things simple, you won't implement an options page, although adding it would be straightforward because you could use the same approach as in Penguin Pairs. Because the menu structure is so similar, it isn't discussed here. You can see the code in the TickTick1 folder that contains the example code belonging to this chapter.

Figure 24-1. The title screen of the Tick Tick game

The PlayingState class maintains the current level and deals with loading and saving level status (solved/locked), just as in the Penguin Pairs game. The playing state creates Level objects, each of which contains a tile-based game world, again very similar to the way Penguin Pairs is structured.

The Structure of a Level

Let's first look at what kind of things can be in a level in Tick Tick. First, there is a background image. For now, you display a simple background sprite; there is no need to store any information about that in the level data variable. There are also different kinds of blocks the player can jump on, along with water drops, enemies, the player's starting position, and the end position the player has to reach. As in the Penguin Pairs game, you store level information in a global variable. This variable is stored in the local storage so that when the player finishes a level, the browser remembers this the next time the player is playing the game. Or course, this assumes the player doesn't clear the local storage in the meantime.

You define a level using tiles, where each tile has a certain type (wall, background, and so on). You then represent each tile type with a character in the level data variable. Just as in the Penguin Pairs game, you lay out the level as text in a two-dimensional space corresponding to the playing field.

Next to the actual tiles, you also store a hint together with the level definition. Here you can see the instruction that stores the first level in the LEVELS global variable:

```
window.LEVELS.push({
    hint   :    "Pick up all the water drops and reach the exit in time.",
    locked :    false,
    solved :    false,
    tiles  :    ["....................",
                "................X..",
                "..........#########",
                "....................",
                "....................",
                "WWW....WWWW.........",
                "---....####.........",
                "....................",
                "WWW.................",
                "###........WWWWW...",
                "............#####...",
                "....WWW.............",
                "....###.............",
                "....................",
                ".1........W.W.W.W.W.",
                "###################"]
});
```

This level definition defines a number of different tiles and objects. For example, a wall tile is defined by the # sign, a water drop by a W character, and the start position of the player by the 1 character. If there is no tile at the specific position, you use the . character. For the platform game, you need different types of tiles: a wall tile the player can stand on or collide with, and a background/ transparent tile that indicates there is no block in that position. You also want to define a *platform tile*. This tile has the property that the player can stand on it like a wall tile, but if they're standing under it, they can jump through it from below. This kind of tile is used in many classic platform games, and it would be a pity not to include it here! In the level data variable, platform tiles are represented by a - character. Table 24-1 gives a complete list of the different tiles in the Tick Tick game.

Table 24-1. Overview of the Different Kinds of Tiles in the Tick Tick Game

Character	Tile Description
.	Background tile
#	Wall tile
^	Wall tile (hot)
*	Wall tile (ice)
-	Platform tile
+	Platform tile (hot)
@	Platform tile (ice)
X	End tile
W	Water drop
1	Start tile (initial player position)
R	Rocket enemy (moving to the left)
r	Rocket enemy (moving to the right)
S	Sparky enemy
T	Turtle enemy
A	Flame enemy (random speed and direction change)
B	Flame enemy (player following)
C	Flame enemy (patrolling)

Water Drops

The goal of each level is to collect all the water drops. Each water drop is represented by an instance of the WaterDrop class. This class is a SpriteGameObject subclass, but you want to add a little behavior to it: the water drop should bounce up and down. You can do this in the update method. First you compute a *bounce offset* that you can add to the current position of the water drop. This bounce offset is stored in the member variable _bounce, which is initially set to 0 in the constructor:

```
this._bounce = 0;
```

To calculate the bounce offset in each game-loop iteration, you use a *sine* function. And depending on the *x*-position of the water drop, you change the phase of the sine so that not all drops move up or down at the same time:

```
var t = powerupjs.Game.totalTime * 3 + this.position.x;
this._bounce = Math.sin(t) * 5;
```

You add the bounce value to the *y*-position of the water drop:

```
this.position.y += this._bounce;
```

The += operator adds the bounce value to the *y*-position (see Chapter 10 for more about these types of operators). However, simply adding the bounce value to the *y*-position isn't correct, because this is a bounce *offset*—in other words, an offset with regard to the *original y*-position. To get the original *y*-position, you *subtract* the bounce offset from the *y*-position in the first instruction of the update method:

```
this.position.y -= this._bounce;
```

This works because at this point, the _bounce variable still contains the bounce offset from the previous game-loop iteration. So, subtracting from the *y*-position gives you the original *y*-position.

In the next chapter, you add more game objects, such as the player and a variety of enemies. But let's first look at how to define the tiles in a platform game such as Tick Tick.

The Tile Class

The Tile class is very similar to the one used in Penguin Pairs, but it has a few differences. First, you define the different tile types in a variable:

```
var TileType = {
    background: 0,
    normal: 1,
    platform: 2
};
```

In the Tile class, you then declare a member variable type to store the type of tile that an instance represents. In addition to these basic tile types, you also have ice tiles and hot tiles, which are special versions of normal or platform tiles. In the level data variable, an ice tile is represented by the * character (or the @ character if it's a platform tile), and a hot tile is represented by the ^ character (or the + character for the platform version). You add two boolean member variables to the Tile class with their associated properties to represent these different kinds of tiles. Here is the complete Tile constructor:

```
function Tile(sprite, tileTp, layer, id) {
    sprite = typeof sprite !== 'undefined' ? sprite : sprites.wall;
    powerupjs.SpriteGameObject.call(this, sprite, layer, id);

    this.hot = false;
    this.ice = false;
    this.type = typeof tileTp !== 'undefined' ? tileTp : TileType.background;
}
```

As you can see, you check whether the sprite and tileTp variables are defined. If they aren't, you assign them a default value. This allows you to create Tile instances without having to pass along the parameters all the time. For example, the following instruction creates a simple background (transparent) tile:

```
var myTile = new Tile();
```

Now, let's look at the Level class and how the Tile instances are created.

The Level Class

This section shows how the Level class is designed in Tick Tick. It's done in a way very similar to Penguin Pairs. In the constructor of the Level class, you do a couple of things:

- Create the background sprite game object.
- Add a Quit button.
- Create the tile-based game world from the level data.

The first two are straightforward. Have a look at the Level class in the example code to see how they work. Creating the tile-based game world is done in a separate method called loadTiles. Depending on the level index, a different game world is created. The first step is creating a GameObjectGrid instance with the desired height and width, taken from the levelData variable:

```
var tiles = new powerupjs.GameObjectGrid(levelData.tiles.length,
    levelData.tiles[0].length, 1, ID.tiles);
this.add(tiles);
```

You set the width and height of each cell in the grid so the game-object grid knows where to draw the tiles on the screen:

```
tiles.cellWidth = 72;
tiles.cellHeight = 55;
```

Then you create the Tile objects and add them to the GameObjectGrid object:

```
for (var y = 0, ly = tiles.rows; y < ly; ++y)
    for (var x = 0, lx = tiles.columns; x < lx; ++x) {
        var t = this.loadTile(levelData.tiles[y][x], x, y);
        tiles.add(t, x, y);
    }
```

The nested for loop examines all the characters you read from the level data variable. You use a method called loadTile, which creates a Tile object for you, given a character and the x- and y-positions of the tile in the grid.

In the loadTile method, you want to load a different tile according to the character passed as a parameter. For each type of tile, you add a method to the Level class that creates that particular kind of tile. For example, LoadWaterTile loads a background tile with a water drop on top of it:

```
Level.prototype.loadWaterTile = function (x, y) {
    var tiles = this.find(ID.tiles);
    var w = new WaterDrop(ID.layer_objects);
    w.origin = w.center.copy();
    w.position = new powerupjs.Vector2((x + 0.5) * tiles.cellWidth,
        (y + 0.5) * tiles.cellHeight - 10);
    this._waterdrops.add(w);
    return new Tile();
};
```

This particular example creates a WaterDrop instance and positions it in the center of the tile. You place each water drop 10 pixels higher than the center so it doesn't bounce over the tile below it. Look at the Level class to see how to create the various tiles and objects in each level. Figure 24-2 shows a screenshot of the objects in the first level (other than the player character, which you deal with in the following chapters).

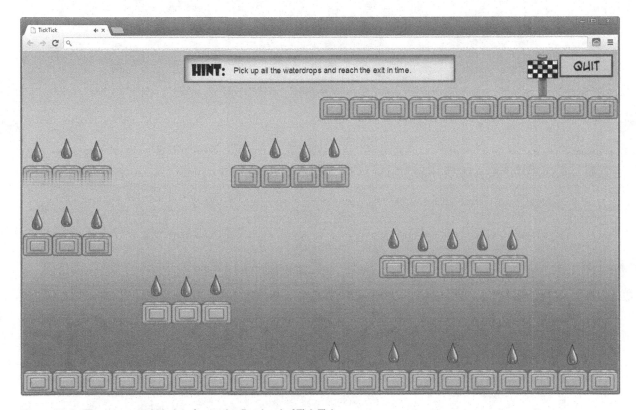

Figure 24-2. The game world belonging to the first level of Tick Tick

What You Have Learned

In this chapter, you have learned:

- How to set up the general structure of the Tick Tick game
- How to create a bouncing water drop

Chapter **25**

Animation

In this chapter, you see how to add *animations* to your game. In the games you've developed until now, game objects could move around on the screen, but adding something like a running character to a game is slightly more challenging. In this chapter, you write a program that contains a character walking from left to the right on the screen. The character is controlled by the player pressing the left and right arrow keys. You don't add touch-interface control in this particular example, but later you see how to control a moving character on touch devices as well.

Another thing that isn't explicitly covered in this book is using the accelerometer that is built into most modern devices. You have access to this data in JavaScript by dealing with events such as ondeviceorientation (or onmozorientation in Firefox) and ondevicemotion, which provides data relating to the device's current acceleration. If you feel you're up to it, you can try to extend the example in this chapter such that it reacts to these events in a meaningful way.

What Is Animation?

Before you look into how to program a character walking around on the screen, you first have to think about what animation is. To grasp this, you have to go back to the 1930s, when several animation studios (among them Walt Disney) produced the first cartoons in black and white.

A cartoon is actually a very fast sequence of still images, also called *frames*. A television draws these frames at a very high rate, about 25 times per second. When the image varies each time, your brain interprets this as motion. This special feature (also called the *phi phenomenon*) of the human brain is very useful, especially when you want to program games that need to contain moving or animated objects.

You've used this feature in the previous games you developed in this book. Every time the draw method is called, you draw a new "frame" on the screen. By drawing sprites at different positions every time, you give the impression that the sprites move. However, this isn't really what is happening: you're simply drawing the sprite at different positions many times per second, which makes the player think the sprite is moving.

In a similar fashion, you can draw a walking or running character. In addition to moving the sprite, you draw a slightly different sprite every time. By drawing a sequence of sprites, each of which represents part of a walking motion, you can create the illusion that a character is walking on the screen. An example of such a sequence of sprites is given in Figure 25-1.

Figure 25-1. *A sequence of images representing a walking motion*

ANIMATIONS IN GAMES

There are different reasons for putting animations in games. When you create 3D games, animation is normally necessary to enhance realism, but for 2D games this isn't always the case. Still, animations can considerably enrich a game.

Animation brings objects to life. But it doesn't have to be complicated to animate them. The simple animation of a character closing and opening its eyes results in a strong feeling that the character is alive. Animated characters are also easier to relate to. If you look at a game like *Cut the Rope*, the main character (named Om Nom) is simply sitting in a corner. But from time to time the character makes some funny moves to show you it's there and wants you to bring it food. This creates a very effective motivation for the player to continue playing the game.

Animations also help to draw the player's attention to a certain object, task, or event. For example, having a small animation on a button makes it clearer for the player that they have to press the button. And a bouncing water drop or a rotating star indicates that this object should be collected or avoided. Animations can also be used to provide feedback. When a button moves downward when you click it with the mouse, it's immediately obvious that the button click was successful.

However, creating animations is a lot of work. So think carefully beforehand about where animations are needed and where they can be avoided, to save time and money.

The Animation Class

For animated characters, you usually design one sprite for each type of movement. The example in Figure 25-1 is the sprite for animating a running character. During the development of the Penguin Pairs game, you designed the SpriteSheet class that represents a strip or a sheet of images. You can use that class in combination with a new class, Animation. In addition to a sprite sheet, an animation requires extra information. For example, you want to indicate how long each frame should be shown on the screen. You also want to be able to *loop* your animation, meaning that once you reach the last frame, the first frame should be shown again. Looping an animation is very useful: in the case of a walking character, for instance, you only have to draw one walk cycle and then loop the animation to get a continuous walking motion. Not all animations should be looped, though. For example, a dying animation shouldn't be looped (that would be very cruel to the character). Here is the complete constructor of the Animation class:

```
function Animation(sprite, looping, frameTime) {
    this.sprite = sprite;
    this.frameTime = typeof frameTime !== 'undefined' ? frameTime : 0.1;
    this.looping = looping;
}
```

An Animated Game Object

The Animation class provides the groundwork for representing an animation. This section introduces a new kind of game object: the *animated* game object, which uses this class. The AnimatedGameObject class is a subclass of SpriteGameObject.

An animated game object may contain a number of different animations, so you can have a character that can perform different (animated) actions such as walking, running, jumping, and more. Each action is represented by an animation. Depending on the player input, you change the animation that is currently active. Then, based on the time that has passed and the properties of the currently active animation (such as whether it loops), you determine the sheet index of the sprite that should be shown on the screen.

To store the different animations, you use a composite object. For each animation, you add a variable to that object. You also need a variable to keep track of the currently active animation. Finally, there is one additional member variable: _time. This variable keeps track of how long you still need to show the current frame, as explained later. Here is the complete constructor of AnimatedGameObject:

```
function AnimatedGameObject(layer, id) {
    powerupjs.SpriteGameObject.call(this, null, layer, id);

    this._animations = {};
    this._current = null;
    this._time = 0;
}
```

You also add two methods to the class: loadAnimation and playAnimation. The first method creates an Animation object and adds it to the _animations variable:

```
AnimatedGameObject.prototype.loadAnimation = function (animname, id, looping,
    frametime) {
    this._animations[id] = new powerupjs.Animation(animname, looping,
        frametime);
};
```

As mentioned, the `AnimatedGameObject` class is a subclass of `SpriteGameObject`. That means when this object is drawn on the screen, it tries to draw the sprite sheet that the member variable `sprite` points to. However, note that you pass `null` as a parameter when you call the base constructor in the `AnimatedGameObject` constructor:

```
function AnimatedGameObject(layer, id) {
    powerupjs.SpriteGameObject.call(this, null, layer, id);
    ...
}
```

You need to assign the sprite belonging to the currently running animation to the `sprite` member variable so this animation is then drawn on the screen. You can easily do this, because each `Animation` instance contains a reference to the sprite that it should animate. Assigning this sprite to the `sprite` member variable is done in the `playAnimation` method.

In that method, you first check whether the animation you want to play is already playing. If it is, you don't have to do anything else and you can return from the method:

```
if (this._current === this._animations[id])
    return;
```

Next, you set the current sheet index and the `_time` variable to 0, and you assign the currently active animation according to the ID that was passed along as a parameter:

```
this._sheetIndex = 0;
this._time = 0;
this._current = this._animations[id];
```

Finally, you set the `sprite` member variable to the sprite that should be drawn:

```
this.sprite = this._current.sprite;
```

Playing an Animation

You've defined a few useful classes and methods for loading and selecting animations. You still need to be able to *play* an animation. What does *playing* mean, exactly? It means you have to determine which frame should be shown, depending on the time that has passed, and draw that frame on the screen. Calculating which frame should be drawn is something you do in the `update` method of the `AnimatedGameObject` class. Because each frame in the animation corresponds to a certain sheet index, you simply have to calculate which sheet index corresponds to the current frame. The `draw` method inherited from `SpriteGameObject` doesn't have to be modified.

In the `update` method, you have to calculate which frame should be drawn. But that means you need to know how much time has passed since the last frame was drawn. If you were to increment the frame index in every call to the `update` method, the animation would be played much too fast. So, you save the time that has passed since the last frame was drawn in the member variable `_time`. You update this variable in the beginning of the `update` method:

```
this._time += delta;
```

Now you can calculate the index of the frame that should be shown. For this, you use a while instruction:

```
while (this._time > this._current.frameTime) {
    this._time -= this._current.frameTime;
    this._sheetIndex++;
    if (this._sheetIndex >=this.sprite.nrSheetElements)
        if (this._current.looping)
            this._sheetIndex = 0;
        else
            this._sheetIndex = this.sprite.nrSheetElements - 1;
}
```

What happens here? The while instruction continues as long as the _time variable contains a value larger than frameTime. In the while instruction, you subtract the frame time from the _time variable. Suppose the time that each frame is displayed is set to 1 second. You enter the update method and add the elapsed time to the _time member variable. Suppose this variable now contains the value 1.02, meaning the frame you're currently showing has been shown for 1.02 seconds. This means you should show the next frame instead. You do this by incrementing the index of the frame you're currently showing, which is the second instruction in the while loop. You then update the _time variable and subtract the frame time (1 second), so the new value of _time becomes 0.02. You put this code in a while instruction instead of an if instruction so you're sure you always show the right frame, even if the time passed since the last update was multiple times the frame time. For example, if the new value of _time was 3.4, you would need to move three frames ahead and subtract the frame time three times from the _time variable. The while instruction takes care of that.

After incrementing the current frame index, you have to take care of what happens once you're past the last frame. To do that, you check whether the sheet index is greater than or equal to this.sprite.nrSheetElements. Depending on whether you want the animation to loop, you either reset the sheet index to 0 or set it to the last element in the sheet.

The Player Class

To use the AnimatedGameObject class introduced in the previous section, you inherit from it. Because the player will control the animated character, let's define a Player class that is a subclass of AnimatedGameObject. In this class, you load the animations belonging to the player and handle the input from the player. In the Player constructor, you load the animations that are needed for this character. In this example, you want the character to walk or stand still. So, you load two animations by calling the loadAnimation method twice. You want both of these animations to loop, so you set the looping parameter to true:

```
this.loadAnimation(sprites.idle, "idle", true);
this.loadAnimation(sprites.run, "run", true, 0.05);
```

Because the idle animation only contains a single sheet element, you don't need to specify the frame time. For the running animation, you specify that each frame should be shown for five hundredths of a second. When the application starts, the character's idle animation should play:

```
this.playAnimation("idle");
```

You also change the player's origin. If you want to draw animated characters moving on a floor, it's useful to use a point on the *bottom* of the character sprite as its origin. Also, as you see later, this is useful for collision checking. For these reasons, you define the origin of the player as the point in the center of the bottom of the sprite element:

```
this.origin = new powerupjs.Vector2(this.width / 2, this.height);
```

Now you need to handle the player's input in this class. When the player presses the left or right arrow key, the velocity of the character should change. You do this in the handleInput method, using an if instruction:

```
var walkingSpeed = 400;
if (powerupjs.Keyboard.down(powerupjs.Keys.left))
    this.velocity.x = -walkingSpeed;
else if (powerupjs.Keyboard.down(powerupjs.Keys.right))
    this.velocity.x = walkingSpeed;
else
    this.velocity.x = 0;
```

> **Note** I chose a value of 400 for the walkingSpeed parameter. Play around with this value and see how it changes the character's behavior. Choosing the right value for parameters such as this one has a big influence on gameplay. It's important to choose values that are "just right." Testing gameplay with a variety of players can help you determine what these values should be so that the gameplay feels natural.

Using the sprite shown in Figure 25-1 allows you to animate a character walking to the right. To animate a character walking to the left, you could use another sprite. However, there is an easier way to accomplish this: by *mirroring* the sprite when you draw it. Mirroring sprites can be useful for any kind of sprite game object, so in the SpriteGameObject class, you add a member variable mirror, which indicates whether the sprite should be mirrored. In the draw method of SpriteSheet, you pass along the value of the mirror variable to Canvas2D.drawImage, as follows:

```
powerupjs.Canvas2D.drawImage(this._image, position, 0, 1, origin, imagePart,
    mirror);
```

You have to extend Canvas2D so it supports drawing a mirrored sprite. You do this by scaling the sprite *negatively*, using the following instruction:

```
if (mirror) {
    this._canvasContext.scale(scale * canvasScale.x * -1, scale *
        canvasScale.y);
    ...
}
```

Next you have to translate and rotate the canvas context while taking the sprite's mirrored state into account. That isn't covered in detail here, but you can have a look at the `Canvas2D` class to see how it's done. To conclude the input handling, you set the `mirror` status according to the velocity if the player is moving:

```
if (this.velocity.x != 0)
    this.mirror = this.velocity.x < 0;
```

In the update method, you select which animation to play based on the velocity. If the velocity is zero, you play the idle animation; otherwise you play the run animation:

```
if (this.velocity.x === 0)
    this.playAnimation("idle");
else
    this.playAnimation("run");
```

Finally, you call the update method in the base class to make sure the animation game-object version of the update method is called as well.

To test your animation class, you create a single `AnimationState` instance, which you add to the game-state manager:

```
ID.game_state_animation = powerupjs.GameStateManager.add(new AnimationState());
powerupjs.GameStateManager.switchTo(ID.game_state_animation);
```

In the `AnimationState` class, you create a `Player` instance, set it at the desired position, and add it to the game world:

```
function AnimationState(layer) {
    powerupjs.GameObjectList.call(this, layer);
    var player = new Player();
    player.position = new powerupjs.Vector2(50, 300);
    this.add(player);
}
```

If you run the program, you see an animated character that you can control with the left and right arrow keys (see Figure 25-2). If the character walks off the visible screen, it doesn't just "stop" off-screen—it keeps going. So, if you hold down the right arrow key for 5 seconds, you need to hold the left arrow key for 5 seconds as well to get the character back.

Figure 25-2. An animated character moving from right to left on the bottom of the canvas

One way around this behavior of being able to walk off the edge of the screen is to implement wrapping: if the character walks off the right side of the screen, it reappears on the left, and vice versa. You can implement wrapping quite easily by adding an `if` instruction to the code that checks the current position of the character and, depending on that position, chooses to move the character to the other end of the screen. Can you change the example yourself to add wrapping?

What You Have Learned

In this chapter, you have learned:

- How to create and control an animation
- How to build an animated game object consisting of multiple animations

Chapter 26

Game Physics

In the previous chapter, you saw how to create an animated character. You also saw how you can load levels and level status from the local storage and how to build a tile-based game world. One of the most important aspects is still missing: defining *how the character interacts with the game world*. You can make a character move from left to right, but if you simply place the character in the level, it can only walk on the bottom of the screen. This isn't enough. You want the character to be able to jump on top of wall tiles and fall down if it moves off a wall tile, and you don't want the character to fall off the edge of the screen. For these things, you need to implement a basic *physics* system. Because it's the character interacting with the world, you implement this physics in the Player class. There are two aspects to dealing with physics: giving the character the ability to jump or fall, and handling collisions between the character and other game objects and responding to these collisions.

Locking the Character in the Game World

The first thing you do is lock the character in the game world. In the examples in Chapter 25, the character could walk out of the screen without any problem. You can solve this by placing a virtual pile of wall-type tiles to the left and right of the screen. You then assume that your collision-detection mechanism (which you haven't written yet) will ensure that the character can't walk through these walls. You only want to prevent the character from walking out of the left or right side of the screen. The character should be able to jump out of sight at the top of the screen. The character should also be able to fall off the game world through a hole in the ground (and die, obviously).

In order to build this virtual pile of wall tiles on the left and right sides of the screen, you have to add some behavior to the grid of tiles. You don't want to modify the GameObjectGrid class. This behavior has nothing to do with the grid of game objects, but it's particular to your platform game. Therefore, you define a new class called TileField that *inherits from* the GameObjectGrid class. You add a single method to that class called getTileType, which returns the type of the tile given its *x* and *y* position on the grid. The nice thing about this method is that you allow these indices to fall *outside* of the valid indices in the grid. For example, it would be fine to ask for the tile type of the tile at position (-2,500). By using an `if` instruction in this method, you check whether the *x* index is out of range. If so, you return a normal (wall) tile type:

```
if (x < 0 || x >= this.columns)
    return TileType.normal;
```

If the *y* index is out of range, you return a background tile type so the character can jump through the top of the screen or fall down a hole:

```
if (y < 0 || y >= this.rows)
    return TileType.background;
```

If both of the `if` instructions' conditions are `false`, this means the type of an actual tile in the grid is requested, so you retrieve that tile and return its tile type:

```
return this.at(x, y).type;
```

The complete class can be found in the example program `TickTick2` belonging to this chapter. If you want to extend the `GameObjectGrid` class in a way more in line with the JavaScript philosophy, you can add the `getTileType` method directly to the `GameObjectGrid` class in a separate JavaScript file. You can call that file `GameObjectGrid_ext.js`, and it will contain a single method addition to `GameObjectGrid` That method will be:

```
GameObjectGrid.prototype.getTileType = function (x, y) {
    if (x < 0 || x >= this.columns)
        return TileType.normal;
    if (y < 0 || y >= this.rows)
        return TileType.background;
    return this.at(x, y).type;
};
```

This way, you don't create a new class, but you simply infuse `GameObjectGrid` with the behavior that you need.

Setting the Character at the Right Position

When you load the level tiles from the level data variable, you use the character 1 to indicate the tile on which the player's character is starting. Based on the location of that tile, you have to create the `Player` object and set it at the right position. For this, you add a method `loadStartTile` to the `Level` class. In this method, you first retrieve the tile field and then calculate the character's starting position. Because the character's origin is the *bottom-center* point of the sprite, you can calculate this position as follows:

```
var startPosition = new powerupjs.Vector2((x + 0.5) * tiles.cellWidth,
    (y + 1) * tiles.cellHeight);
```

Note that you use the width and height of the tiles and multiply them by the *x* and *y* indices of the spot where the character should be located. The cell width is multiplied by x + 0.5 so the character is placed in the middle of the tile position, and the cell height is multiplied by y + 1 to place the character on the bottom of the tile. You can then create the Player object and add it to the game world:

```
this.add(new Player(startPosition, ID.layer_objects, ID.player));
```

Finally, you still need to make an actual tile here that can be stored in the grid, because each character should represent a tile. In this case, you can create a background tile that is placed where the character is standing:

```
return new Tile();
```

Jumping ...

You've seen how a character can walk to the left or right. How can you deal with jumping and falling? If the game is playing on a device that has a keyboard, the character jumps when the player presses the space bar.

Using the space bar to jump is largely a matter of tradition. Other keystrokes are commonly used in games, such as strafing with Q and E; moving directionally with W, A, D, and X; stopping or braking with S; and so on. Using these more or less accepted standards in your game will provide a better experience to your users, because they will already know the interface.

When the player presses the space bar to jump, it basically means the character gets a *negative y*-velocity. This can be done easily in the handleInput method of the Player class:

```
if (powerupjs.Keyboard.pressed(powerupjs.Keys.space))
    this.jump();
```

The jump method is as follows:

```
Player.prototype.jump = function (speed) {
    speed = typeof speed !== 'undefined' ? speed : 1100;
    this.velocity.y = -speed;
};
```

So, the effect of calling the jump method without providing any parameter value is that the *y*-velocity is set to a value of 1100. I chose this number somewhat randomly. Using a bigger number means the character can jump higher. A lower number means the character has to go to the gym more often, or quit smoking. I chose this value so the character can jump high enough to reach the tiles but not high enough that the game becomes too easy (then the character could just jump to the end of the level).

There is a minor problem with this approach: you always allow the player's character to jump, no matter what the character's current situation is. So, if the character is currently jumping or falling down a cliff, you allow the player to make the character jump back to safety. This isn't really what you want. You want the character to jump only when standing on the ground. This is something that you can detect by looking at collisions between the character and wall or platform tiles (which are the only tiles that the character can stand on). Let's assume for now that your yet-to-be-written collision-detection algorithm will take care of this and keep track of whether the character is on the ground by using a member variable:

```
this.onTheGround = true;
```

Sometimes it's necessary to sketch out a class in English (as opposed to JavaScript) before it's written to allow you to write other parts of a game. This is also true in the case of collision detection. You can't test a collision-detection algorithm until you build it in, but you don't want to build it in until you've created the algorithm and tested it. One has to happen first, so you must mentally know what's going on with the other and plan it or keep notes. The CollisionTest example is a program I wrote to test the collision-detection algorithm independent of the game. You may find it useful in some cases to write separate testing programs that help you understand how part of the code should be working.

If this member variable is true, you know the character is standing on the ground. You can now change the initial if instruction so it only allows a character to jump from the ground and not from the air:

```
if (powerupjs.Keyboard.pressed(powerupjs.Keys.space) && this.onTheGround)
    this.jump();
```

If you're playing the game on a device without a keyboard (such as a tablet or a smartphone), you have to handle player input differently. One way of doing this is to add a few buttons to the screen that control the player character only if touch input is available. This is done when the Level object is created:

```
if (powerupjs.Touch.isTouchDevice) {
    var walkLeftButton = new powerupjs.Button(sprites.buttons_player,
        ID.layer_overlays, ID.button_walkleft);
    walkLeftButton.position = new powerupjs.Vector2(10, 500);
    this.add(walkLeftButton);
    var walkRightButton = new powerupjs.Button(sprites.buttons_player,
        ID.layer_overlays, ID.button_walkright);
    walkRightButton.position = new powerupjs.Vector2(walkRightButton.width + 20, 500);
    walkRightButton.sheetIndex = 1;
    this.add(walkRightButton);
    var jumpButton = new powerupjs.Button(sprites.buttons_player,
        ID.layer_overlays, ID.button_jump);
    jumpButton.position = new powerupjs.Vector2(powerupjs.Game.size.x -
        jumpButton.width - 10, 500);
    jumpButton.sheetIndex = 2;
    this.add(jumpButton);
}
```

Controlling the character is done in a way very similar to how you deal with keyboard input:

```
if (powerupjs.Touch.isTouchDevice) {
    var jumpButton = this.root.find(ID.button_jump);
    if (jumpButton.pressed && this.onTheGround)
        this.jump();
}
```

This is a very nice example of how you can automatically adapt the interface of your game to different devices. The buttons are added only when a touch display is available. Another option would be to use built-in sensors in the device, such as an accelerometer. *Doodle Jump* is a good example of a game that uses such sensors to control the character.

... And Falling

The only place where you're currently changing the *y*-velocity is in the `handleInput` method, when the player wants to jump. Because the *y*-velocity indefinitely keeps the value of 1100, the character moves up in the air, outside of the screen, out of the planet's atmosphere, and into outer space. Because you're not making a game about bombs in space, you have to do something about this. What you forgot to add to the game world is *gravity*.

You can follow a simple approach to simulate the effect of gravity on the character's velocity. You add a small value to the velocity in the *y* direction in each update step:

```
this.velocity.y += 55;
```

If the character has a negative velocity, this velocity slowly becomes smaller until it reaches zero and then starts to increase again. The effect is that the character jumps to a certain height and then starts falling down again, just like in the real world. However, the collision-detection mechanism now becomes even more important. If there is no collision detection, the character will start falling down at the start of the game!

Collision Detection

Detecting collisions between game objects is a very important part of simulating interacting game worlds. Collision detection is used for many different things in games: detecting whether the character walks over a power-up, detecting whether the character collides with a projectile, detecting collisions between the character and walls or floors, and so on. Given this very common occurrence, it's almost strange that you didn't need collision detection in the previous games. Or didn't you? Look at this code from the `update` method in the `PaintCan` class from the Painter game:

```
var ball_center = Game.gameWorld.ball.center;
var ball_position = Game.gameWorld.ball.position;
var distance = ball_position.add(ball_center).subtractFrom(this.position)
    .subtractFrom(this.center);
if (Math.abs(distance.x) < this.center.x && Math.abs(distance.y) < this.center.y) {
    this.color = Game.gameWorld.ball.color;
    Game.gameWorld.ball.reset();
}
```

What you're doing here is detecting a collision between the ball and the paint can (although in a very rudimentary fashion). You take the position of the center of each object and see if the distance between those two positions is smaller than a certain value. If so, you say they collide, and you change the color of the can. If you look at this case more closely, you can see that you're representing game objects with basic shapes such as *circles*, and you check whether they collide with each other by verifying that the distance between the centers is smaller than the sum of the radii of the circles.

So this is a first, simple example of doing collision checking in games. Of course, this isn't a very precise way of checking collisions. The ball may be approximated by the shape of a circle, but the paint can doesn't look like a circle at all. As a result, in some cases a collision is detected when there is none, and sometimes a collision isn't detected when the sprites are actually colliding. Still, many games use *simplified shapes* such as circles and rectangles to represent objects when they do collision detection. Because these shapes bind the object within, they're also called *bounding circles* and *bounding boxes*. The Tick Tick game uses *axis-aligned* bounding boxes, meaning you don't consider boxes whose sides aren't parallel to the x- and y-axes.

Unfortunately, doing collision detection using bounding boxes isn't always precise enough. When game objects are close to each other, their bounding shapes may intersect (and thus trigger a collision), but the actual objects don't. And when a game object is animated, its shape may change over time. You could make the bounding shape bigger so the object fits in it under all circumstances, but that would lead to even more false collision triggers.

A solution for this is to check for collisions on a per-pixel basis. Basically, you can write an algorithm that walks over the non-transparent pixels in the sprite (using a nested for instruction) and checks whether one or more of these pixels collides with one of the pixels in another sprite (again, by walking through them using a nested for instruction). Generally, such highly detailed collision detection is too costly for browser games (even though browsers are becoming faster and faster). On the other hand, you don't have to perform this rather expensive task very often. It only has to be done when two bounding shapes intersect. And then you only have to do it for the parts of the shapes that actually intersect. Furthermore, if you're smart about it, you can decide which kinds of objects should use per-pixel collision detection so that you only do it for the objects where bounding boxes don't work well.

When you use circles and rectangles to detect collisions, you need to handle three cases (see also Figure 26-1):

- A circle intersects another circle.

- A circle intersects a rectangle.

- A rectangle intersects another rectangle.

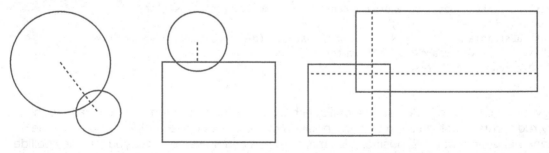

Figure 26-1. Different types of collisions: circle-circle, circle-rectangle, and rectangle-rectangle

The first case is the simplest one. The only thing you need to do is check whether the distance between the two centers is smaller than the sum of the radii. You've already seen an example of how to do that.

For the case where a circle intersects a rectangle, you can use the following approach:

1. Locate the point on the rectangle that lies closest to the circle's center.

2. Calculate the distance between this point and the center of the circle.

3. If this distance is smaller than the radius of the circle, there is a collision.

Let's assume you want to find out if an object of type `Rectangle` intersects a circle, represented by an object of type \expr{Vector2} and a radius. You can find the point closest to the circle's center by clamping values in a smart way. *Clamping* a value between a maximum value and a minimum value is done by the following method:

```
Math.clamp = function (value, min, max) {
    if (value < min)
        return min;
    else if (value > max)
        return max;
    else
        return value;
};
```

Now take a look at the following code:

```
Vector2 closestPoint = Vector2.zero;
closestPoint.x = Math.clamp(circleCenter.x, rectangle.left, rectangle.right);
closestPoint.y = Math.clamp(circleCenter.y, rectangle.top, rectangle.bottom);
```

You find the closest point by clamping the *x* and *y* values of the center between the rectangle edges. If the circle's center is in the rectangle, this method also works, because the clamping has no effect in that case, and the closest point is the same as the circle's center. The next step is calculating the distance between the closest point and the circle's center:

```
Vector2 distance = closestPoint.subtract(circleCenter);
```

If this distance is smaller than the radius, you have a collision:

```
if (distance.length < circleRadius)
    // collision!
```

The final case is checking whether two rectangles collide. You need to know the following about both rectangles in order to calculate this:

- Smallest *x*-value of the rectangle (`rectangle.left`)
- Smallest *y*-value of the rectangle (`rectangle.top`)
- Greatest *x*-value of the rectangle (`rectangle.right`)
- Greatest *y*-value of the rectangle (`rectangle.bottom`)

Let's say you want to know whether rectangle A collides with rectangle B. In that case, you have to check for the following conditions:

- A.left (A's smallest *x*-value) <= B.right (B's greatest *x*-value)
- A.right (A's greatest *x*-value) >= B.left (B's smallest *x*-value)
- A.top (A's smallest *y*-value) <= B.bottom (B's greatest *y*-value)
- A.bottom (A's greatest *y*-value) >= B.top (B's smallest *y*-value)

If all these conditions are met, then rectangles A and B have collided. Why these particular conditions? Let's look at the first condition to see what happens if it isn't true. Suppose A.left > B.right instead. In that case, rectangle A lies completely to the right of rectangle B, so they can't collide. If the second condition isn't true (in other words, A.right < B.left), then rectangle A lies completely to the left of B, which means they don't collide either. Check the other two conditions for yourself as well. In summary, these conditions say that if rectangle A lies neither completely to the left, right, top, or bottom of B, then the two rectangles collide.

In JavaScript, writing the code for checking collisions between rectangles is easy. If you look at the Rectangle class, you can see a method intersects that does this work for you:

```
Rectangle.prototype.intersects = function (rect) {
    return (this.left <= rect.right && this.right >= rect.left &&
        this.top <= rect.bottom && this.bottom >= rect.top);
};
```

Retrieving Bounding Boxes

To handle collisions efficiently in your game, the SpriteGameObject class has a property boundingBox that returns the bounding box of the sprite:

```
Object.defineProperty(SpriteGameObject.prototype, "boundingBox",
    {
        get: function () {
            var leftTop = this.worldPosition.subtractFrom((this.origin));
            return new powerupjs.Rectangle(leftTop.x, leftTop.y, this.width, this.height);
        }
    });
```

As you can see, it takes into account the sprite's origin in order to calculate the correct position of the box. Also note that the bounding box's position is expressed using *world positions*. When doing collision detection, you want to know where the objects are in the world—you don't care about their local positions in a hierarchy of game objects.

Per-Pixel Collision Detection

In addition to the boundingBox property, you add a method collidesWith in the SpriteGameObject class that deals with collision detection. However, only checking whether bounding boxes overlap is often not enough. Figure 26-2 shows an example of two sprites whose bounding boxes overlap, but the images aren't actually colliding. This can happen because parts of the sprites that you draw can be transparent. As a result, if you want to do precise collision detection, you need to look at the pixel level if there is a collision. A collision at the pixel level happens only if at a given position in the rectangle where sprites overlap, both sprites have a non-transparent pixel.

Figure 26-2. Example of two sprites that don't collide but whose bounding boxes overlap

Accessing Pixel Color Data in Images

To do per-pixel collision detection, you need access to an image's pixel color data. This isn't hard to do in HTML/JavaScript, but before you see how, you need to know that per-pixel collision detection is an expensive operation (you see why later). If you do it between each sprite in the game world, you run the risk of your game no longer being playable on older mobile devices or tablets. So, do per-pixel collision detection only when it's really necessary.

Because per-pixel collision detection is expensive, it makes sense to design the code in such a way that it's easy to switch it off for certain sprites. To do this, you maintain a Boolean variable in the SpriteSheet class that indicates whether per-pixel collision detection should be done for that sprite. Because retrieving pixel color data is expensive, you retrieve all that data when the sprite is loaded and store it in an array called a *collision mask*. Why is retrieving pixel color data expensive? Because in order to retrieve that data, you need to first *draw* the sprite and then retrieve to color data from the canvas. You don't want to draw these sprites on the main canvas that the player can see, so you define another canvas just for this purpose in the Canvas2D class:

```
this._pixeldrawingCanvas = document.createElement('canvas');
```

You add a method called createPixelCollisionMask to the SpriteSheet class in which you draw the sprite on the pixel drawing canvas and then extract the pixel color data from that canvas. You initialize the array that will contain the collision mask, and you make sure the pixel drawing canvas is the right size:

```
this._collisionMask = [];
var w = this._image.width;
var h = this._image.height;
powerupjs.Canvas2D._pixeldrawingCanvas.width = w;
powerupjs.Canvas2D._pixeldrawingCanvas.height = h;
```

Then you use the canvas context to draw the sprite:

```
var ctx = powerupjs.Canvas2D._pixeldrawingCanvas.getContext('2d');
ctx.clearRect(0, 0, w, h);
ctx.save();
ctx.drawImage(this._image, 0, 0, w, h, 0, 0, w, h);
ctx.restore();
```

The canvas context has a method getImageData that retrieves the color data for each pixel and stores it in an array. So, let's retrieve all the pixels currently displayed on the canvas:

```
var imageData = ctx.getImageData(0, 0, w, h);
```

The imageData variable now refers to a very large array of numbers. For each pixel, there are four numbers in the array, each between 0 and 255. The first three numbers are the R (red), G (green), and B (blue) values that determine the color of the pixel. The fourth number is the A (alpha) value that determines the transparency of the pixel. An alpha value of 0 means the pixel is fully transparent, and a value of 255 means the pixel is opaque. In the collision mask, you only need to store the alpha values, because the color of objects that collide isn't important: only which pixels represent those objects. So, you use a for instruction to iterate through the array and store each fourth value in the collision-mask array, as follows:

```
for (var x = 3, l = w * h * 4; x < l; x += 4) {
    this._collisionMask.push(imageData.data[x]);
}
```

When creating a SpriteSheet instance, the collision mask is calculated only when the user has set the parameter createCollisionMask to true when calling the constructor. For example, you indicate that you want precise collision detection for the player when the player sprites are loaded:

```
sprites.player_idle = loadSprite("player/spr_idle.png", true);
sprites.player_run = loadSprite("player/spr_run@13.png", true);
sprites.player_jump = loadSprite("player/spr_jump@14.png", true);
```

On the other hand, you don't need such precise information for the tiles, because those are more or less rectangular anyway, so using a rectangular bounding box suffices:

```
sprites.wall = loadSprite("tiles/spr_wall.png");
sprites.wall_hot = loadSprite("tiles/spr_wall_hot.png");
sprites.wall_ice = loadSprite("tiles/spr_wall_ice.png");
sprites.platform = loadSprite("tiles/spr_platform.png");
sprites.platform_hot = loadSprite("tiles/spr_platform_hot.png");
sprites.platform_ice = loadSprite("tiles/spr_platform_ice.png");
```

In order to make it easier to access the collision mast, you add a getAlpha method to the SpriteSheet class to access the collision mask while taking into account the currently selected element in the sheet and whether the sprite is drawn mirrored. Here is the header of that method:

```
SpriteSheet.prototype.getAlpha = function (x, y, sheetIndex, mirror)
```

As parameters, the method expects the *x* and *y* pixel coordinates, the sheet index, and whether the sprite is mirrored. The first thing to do is check whether there is a collision mask associated with this sprite sheet, because not all sprites have such a mask. If there is no collision mask, you simply return the value 255 (fully opaque):

```
if (this._collisionMask === null)
    return 255;
```

Then you calculate the column and row indices corresponding to the current sheet index, in the same way you did in the draw method:

```
var columnIndex = sheetIndex % this._sheetColumns;
var rowIndex = Math.floor(sheetIndex / this._sheetColumns) % this._sheetRows;
```

You can then calculate the actual pixel coordinates in the image (or *texture*), taking into account the sprite element given by the sheet index. You calculate the *x* coordinate by multiplying the width of one sheet element by the column index and adding the local *x* value:

```
var textureX = columnIndex * this.width + x;
```

However, if the sprite is mirrored, you use a slightly different calculation:

```
if (mirror)
    textureX = (columnIndex + 1) * this.width - x - 1;
```

What happens here is that you start from the right side of the sprite element and then subtract *x* to get the local *x* coordinate. For the *y* coordinate, mirroring doesn't have to be checked because you only allow horizontal mirroring in the game engine:

```
var textureY = rowIndex * this.height + y;
```

Based on the *x* and *y* coordinates in the image, you now calculate the corresponding index in the collision mask, as follows:

```
var arrayIndex = Math.floor(textureY * this._image.width + textureX);
```

Just to be sure, you check whether the index you calculated falls in the range of the array. If not, you return 0 (fully transparent):

```
if (arrayIndex < 0 || arrayIndex >= this._collisionMask.length)
    return 0;
```

This way, the getAlpha method also returns a logical result if you try to access nonexistent pixels. Finally, you return the alpha value stored in the collision mask:

```
return this._collisionMask[arrayIndex];
```

For convenience, you also add a getAlpha method to SpriteGameObject that calls the getAlpha method from SpriteSheet with the right parameters:

```
SpriteGameObject.prototype.getAlpha = function (x, y) {
    return this.sprite.getAlpha(x, y, this._sheetIndex, this.mirror);
};
```

> **Note** Not all browsers always allow you to access pixel color data. For example, Chrome and Firefox don't allow this access if you open the HTML page as a local file on your computer. Internet Explorer does allow this, so to test per-pixel collision detection you can use that browser or put the files on a server in order to use either of the browsers. In the *TickTick2* example, I commented out the collisionMask parameter in TickTick.js so the game runs on all browsers, but of course the game doesn't perform per-pixel collision detection in this case.

Calculating the Overlap Rectangle

The collidesWith method in SpriteGameObject handles the two steps of collision detection: first checking whether the bounding boxes intersect and then performing per-pixel collision detection in the overlap rectangle. The first step in this method is to determine whether you need to do any collision detection at all. If either of the two objects is invisible, or if their bounding boxes don't intersect, you return from the method:

```
if (!this.visible || !obj.visible ||
    !this.boundingBox.intersects(obj.boundingBox))
    return false;
```

The next step is calculating the overlapping part of the two bounding boxes. Because this is a useful thing to calculate when dealing with collision detection in general, you add a method called intersection to the Rectangle class that returns a rectangle representing the overlap between the rectangle (bounding box) passed as a parameter and the rectangle object you call the method on (this).

To calculate this overlap rectangle, you need to know the minimum and maximum *x* and *y* coordinates for the rectangle (see Figure 26-3). Using a few useful properties from the Rectangle class in combination with the min and max methods of the Math object, you can calculate these values quite easily:

```
var xmin = Math.max(this.left, rect.left);
var xmax = Math.min(this.right, rect.right);
var ymin = Math.max(this.top, rect.top);
var ymax = Math.min(this.bottom, rect.bottom);
```

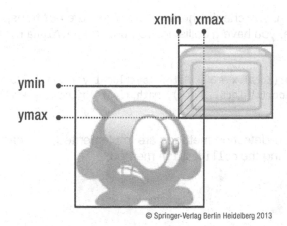

Figure 26-3. Calculating the overlap rectangle using the minimum and maximum x- and y-coordinates

Now you can calculate the position and size of the overlap rectangle and return it from the method:

```
return new powerupjs.Rectangle(xmin, ymin, xmax - xmin, ymax - ymin);
```

In the collidesWith method in SpriteGameObject, you store the overlap rectangle by calling the intersection method from the Rectangle class:

```
var intersect = this.boundingBox.intersection(obj.boundingBox);
```

Checking the Pixels in the Overlap Rectangle

The overlap rectangle's coordinates are expressed in world coordinates because both bounding boxes are expressed in world coordinates. You first need to find out where the overlap rectangle is locally in the two overlapping sprites. Therefore, you need to subtract the world position of each sprite as well as its origin to find the local overlapping rectangle in each sprite:

```
var local = intersect.position.subtractFrom(this.worldPosition .subtractFrom(this.origin));
var objLocal = intersect.position.subtractFrom(obj.worldPosition .subtractFrom(obj.origin));
```

To check whether there is a collision within the overlap rectangle, you use a nested for instruction to walk over all the pixels in the rectangle:

```
for (var x = 0; x < intersect.width; x++)
    for (var y = 0; y < intersect.height; y++) {
        // check transparency of pixel (x, y)...
}
```

In this nested for instruction, you check whether both pixels are *not* transparent at these local positions. If that is the case, you have a collision. You use the getAlpha method to check this for both pixels:

```
if (this.getAlpha(Math.floor(local.x + x), Math.floor(local.y + y)) !== 0
    && obj.getAlpha(Math.floor(objLocal.x + x), Math.floor(objLocal.y + y)) !== 0)
    return true;
```

Now that your basic collision-detection methods are implemented, you can check whether two game objects collide by calling the collidesWith method:

```
if (this.collidesWith(enemy))
    // ouch...
```

Handling Character-Tile Collisions

In the Tick Tick game, you need to detect collisions between the character and the tiles. You do this in a method called handleCollisions, which you call from the update method in the Player class. The idea is that you do all the calculations for jumping, falling, and running first (you did this at the beginning of this chapter). If there is a collision between the character and a tile, you correct the position of the character so that it no longer collides. In the handleCollisions method, you walk through the grid of tiles and check whether there is a collision between the character and the tile you're currently examining.

You don't need to check all the tiles in the grid, only those close to the character's current location. You can calculate the closest tile to the character's position as follows:

```
var tiles = this.root.find(ID.tiles);
var x_floor = Math.floor(this.position.x / tiles.cellWidth);
var y_floor = Math.floor(this.position.y / tiles.cellHeight);
```

Now you can use a nested for instruction to look at the tiles surrounding the character. In order to account for fast jumping and falling, you take more tiles into account in the *y* direction. In the nested for instruction, you then check whether the character is colliding with the tile. However, you only need to do that if the tile is *not* a background tile. The code to do all that is as follows:

```
for (var y = y_floor - 2; y <= y_floor + 1; ++y)
    for (var x = x_floor - 1; x <= x_floor + 1; ++x) {
        var tileType = tiles.getTileType(x, y);
        if (tileType === TileType.background)
            continue;
        var tileBounds = new powerupjs.Rectangle(x * tiles.cellWidth, y *
            tiles.cellHeight, tiles.cellWidth, tiles.cellHeight);
        if (!tileBounds.intersects(this.boundingBox))
            continue;
    }
```

As you can see, you don't directly access the Tile objects. The reason is that sometimes, the *x* or *y* index can be negative because the character is near the edge of the screen. Here you see the advantage of using the getTileType method you added to the TileField class. You don't care if you're really dealing with a tile: as long as you know its type and bounding box, you can do your job.

In the nested for instruction, you also see a new keyword: continue. This keyword can be used in for or while instructions to stop executing the current iteration of the loop and continue to the next one. In this case, if the tile is of type background, the rest of the instructions are no longer executed, and you continue to increment x and start a new iteration to check the next tile. The result is that only tiles that aren't of type background are considered. The continue keyword is related to break, which stops the loop entirely. Unlike break, continue only stops the current iteration.

This code doesn't always work correctly, though. Particularly when the character is standing on a tile, rounding errors when calculating the bounding box can lead to the algorithm thinking the character isn't standing on the ground. The character's velocity is then increased, and the character may fall through the tile as a result. To compensate for any rounding errors, you increase the height of the bounding box by 1:

```
var boundingBox = this.boundingBox;
boundingBox.height += 1;
if (!tileBounds.intersects(boundingBox))
    continue;
// handle the collision
```

Dealing with the Collision

Now that you can detect collisions between the character and the tiles in the game world, you have to determine what to do when a collision happens. There are a couple of possibilities. You could let the game crash (not good if you want to sell your game to many people), you could warn users that they shouldn't collide with objects in the game (results in a lot of pop-up messages), or you could automatically correct the position of the character if it collides with an object.

In order to correct the character's position, you need to know how bad the collision was. For example, if the character walked into a wall on the right, you have to know how far you have to move the character to the left to undo the collision. This is also called the *intersection depth*. Let's extend the Rectangle class with a method called calculateIntersectionDepth that calculates the intersection depth in both *x* and *y* directions for two Rectangle objects. In this example, these rectangles are the bounding box of the character and the bounding box of the tile it's colliding with.

The intersection depth can be calculated by first determining the minimum allowed distance between the centers of the rectangles such that there is no collision between the two rectangles:

```
var minDistance = this.size.addTo(rect.size).divideBy(2);
```

Then you calculate the *real* distance between the two rectangle centers:

```
var distance = this.center.subtractFrom(rect.center);
```

Now you can calculate the difference between the minimum allowed distance and the actual distance, to get the intersection depth. If you look at the actual distance between the two centers, there are two possibilities for both dimensions (*x* and *y*): the distance is either negative or positive. For example, if the *x* distance is negative, this means rectangle `rect` is placed to the right of rectangle `this` (because `rect.center.x` > `this.center.x`). If rectangle `this` represents the character, this means you have to move the character to the *left* to correct this intersection. Therefore, you return the *x* intersection depth as a *negative* value, which can be calculated as `-minDistance.x - distance.x`. Why? Because there is a collision, the distance between the two rectangles is smaller than `minDistance`. And because `distance` is negative, the expression `-minDistance.x - distance.x` gives the difference between the two as a *negative* value. If `distance` is positive, the expression `minDistance.x - distance.x` gives the *positive* difference between the two. The same reasoning holds for the *y* distance. You can then calculate the depth as follows:

```
var depth = powerupjs.Vector2.zero;
if (distance.x > 0)
    depth.x = minDistance.x - distance.x;
else
    depth.x = -minDistance.x - distance.x;
if (distance.y > 0)
    depth.y = minDistance.y - distance.y;
else
    depth.y = -minDistance.y - distance.y;
```

Finally, you return the depth vector as the result of this method:

```
return depth;
```

When you know that the character collides with the tile, you calculate the intersection depth using the method you just added to the `Rectangle` class:

```
var depth = boundingBox.calculateIntersectionDepth(tileBounds);
```

Now that you've calculated the intersection depth, there are two ways to solve this collision: move the character in the *x* direction, or move the character in the *y* direction. Generally, you want to move the character the least possible distance to avoid unnatural motions or displacements. So, if the *x* depth is smaller than the *y* depth, you move the character in the *x* direction; otherwise you move it in the *y* direction. You can check this with an `if` instruction. When comparing the two depth dimensions, you have to take into account that they may be negative. You solve this by comparing the absolute values:

```
if (Math.abs(depth.x) < Math.abs(depth.y)) {
    // move character in the x direction
}
```

Do you always want to move the character if there is a collision with a tile? Well, that depends on the tile type. Remember that `TileType` is used to represent three possible tile types: `TileType.background`, `TileType.normal`, and `TileType.platform`. If the tile the character is colliding with is a background tile, you definitely don't want to move the character. Also, in the case of moving in the *x* direction, you want the character to be able to *pass through* platform tiles. Therefore, the only case where you want to move the character to correct a collision is when it's colliding with a *wall* tile (TileType.normal). In that case, you move the character by adding the *x* depth value to the character position:

```
if (tileType === TileType.normal)
    this.position.x += depth.x;
```

If you want to correct the character position in the *y* direction, things become slightly more complicated. Because you're dealing with movement in the *y* direction, this is also a good place to determine whether the character is on the ground. In the beginning of the handleCollisions method, you set the isOnTheGround member variable to false. So, the starting point is to assume that the character is *not* on the ground. In *some* cases, it's on the ground, and you have to set the variable to true. How can you check if the character is on the ground? If it isn't on the ground, it must be falling. If it's falling, then the *previous y* position is smaller than the current position. In order to have access to the previous *y* position, you store it in a member variable at the end of each call to the handleCollisions method:

```
this._previousYPosition = this.position.y;
```

Now it's very easy to determine if the character is on the ground. If the previous *y* position was smaller than the top of the tile the character is colliding with, and the tile is *not* a background tile, then the character was falling and has reached a tile. If so, you set the isOnTheGround variable to true and the *y* velocity to 0:

```
if (this._previousYPosition <= tileBounds.top && tileType !== TileType.background) {
    this.onTheGround = true;
    this.velocity.y = 0;
}
```

You still have to correct the character position in some cases. If you're colliding with a wall tile, you always want to correct the character position. If the character is colliding with a platform tile, you only want to correct the character position if it's standing on top of the tile. The latter is only true if the isOnTheGround variable is set to true. Therefore, you can write all this in the following if instruction:

```
if (tileType === TileType.normal || this.onTheGround)
    this.position.y += depth.y + 1;
```

Note that to correct the position, you need to add one extra pixel to compensate for the extra pixel you added to the bounding box's height.

What You Have Learned

In this chapter, you have learned:

- How to constrain a character within the environment
- How to simulate jumping and falling
- How to deal with collisions in games

Chapter 27

Intelligent Enemies

As the next step in developing the Tick Tick game, let's introduce some peril to the player by adding dangerous enemies. If the player touches an enemy, the player dies. The enemies generally aren't controlled by the player (that would make it too easy). Therefore, you need to define some kind of smart (or stupid) behavior. You don't want these enemies to be too smart: the player should be able to complete the level. After all, that is the goal of playing a game: winning it. What is nice is that you can build different types of enemies that exhibit different types of behavior. As a result, the player has different gameplay options and must develop different strategies to complete the level.

Defining the behavior of an enemy can lead to some very complex code, with many different states, reasoning, path planning, and much more. You see a few different types of enemies in this chapter: a rocket, a sneezing turtle (seriously), Sparky, and a couple of different patrolling enemies. This chapter doesn't deal with how the player should *interact* with enemies—you only define their basic behavior.

The Rocket

One of the most basic enemies is a rocket. A rocket flies from one side of the screen to the other and then reappears after some time has passed. If the player comes in contact with the rocket, the player dies. In the level description, you indicate with the *r* and *R* characters that a rocket enemy should be placed in a level. For example, consider this level description:

```
window.LEVELS.push({
    hint :      "Many, many, many, many, many rockets...",
    locked :    true,
    solved :    false,
    tiles :     ["................",
                "r..W...........X....",
                "...--..W.......--...",
                "....W.--.......W..R",
                "...--.........--...",
                "r..W......W....W....",
                "...--.....--...",
                "....W.........W...",
```

```
            "...--.........W.--...",
            "r..W.........--.W....",
            "...--.............--...",
            "....W...........W..R",
            "...--.............--...",
            ".1...................",
            "#####..####..#####"]
});
```

A lowercase *r* means the rocket should fly from left to right, and an uppercase *R* means it should fly from right to left (see also Table 24-1).

Creating and Resetting the Rocket

Let's create a Rocket class that represents this particular kind of enemy. You inherit from the AnimatedGameObject class, because the rocket is animated. In the constructor, you initialize the Rocket object. You need to load the rocket animation and play it, and then you need to check whether the animation should be mirrored. Because the animation has the rocket moving to the right, you need to mirror it if the rocket moves to the left. You also store the starting position of the rocket so you can place it back at that position when it moves out of the screen. Finally, you need a variable spawnTime to keep track of when the rocket should appear. This is the complete constructor:

```
function Rocket(moveToLeft, startPosition, layer, id) {
    powerupjs.AnimatedGameObject.call(this, layer, id);
    this.spawnTime = 0;
    this.startPosition = startPosition;
    this.mirror = moveToLeft;

    this.loadAnimation(sprites.rocket, "default", true, 0.5);
    this.playAnimation("default");
    this.origin = new powerupjs.Vector2(this.width / 2, this.height);
    this.reset();
}
```

The last instruction in the constructor is a call to the reset method. In this method, you set the current position of the rocket to the starting position, you set the visibility to false (so the rocket is initially invisible), and you set its velocity to zero. You also use the random number generator to calculate a random time (in seconds) after which the rocket should appear and start moving. You store this time in the member variable spawnTime. You put these instructions in a separate reset method because you call this method later as well, after the rocket has flown out of the screen.

Programming the Rocket Behavior

The behavior of the rocket is (as usual) encoded in the update method. Basically, a rocket exhibits two main types of behavior: either it's visible and moving from one end of the screen to the other, or it's invisible and waiting to appear. You can determine which of the two states the rocket is in by looking at the value of the spawnTime variable. If this variable contains a value larger than zero, the rocket is waiting to be spawned. If the value is less than or equal to zero, the rocket is visible and moving from one end of the screen to the other.

Let's look at the first case. If the rocket is waiting to be spawned, you simply subtract the time that has elapsed since the last update call from the spawn time:

```
if (this.spawnTime > 0) {
    this.spawnTime -= delta;
    return;
}
```

The second case is slightly more complicated. The rocket is moving from one end of the screen to the other. So, you set the visibility status to true, you calculate the rocket velocity depending on the direction it's moving, and you update its position:

```
this.visible = true;
this.velocity.x = 600;
if (this.mirror)
    this.velocity.x *= -1;
```

Finally, you have to check whether the rocket has flown outside of the screen. If that is the case, the rocket should be reset. You check whether the rocket is outside of the screen using bounding boxes. If the bounding box enclosing the screen doesn't intersect the rocket's bounding box, you know the rocket is outside of the screen, and you reset it:

```
var screenBox = new powerupjs.Rectangle(0, 0, powerupjs.Game.size.x, powerupjs.Game.size.y);
if (!screenBox.intersects(this.boundingBox))
    this.reset();
```

This completes the Rocket class, except for interaction with the player, which is something you look at in more detail in the following chapter. For the complete class, see the TickTick3 example code belonging to this chapter. Figure 27-1 shows a screenshot of the level defined in the first section of this chapter.

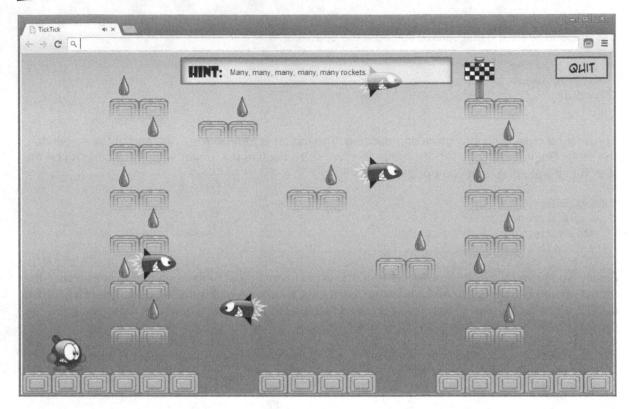

Figure 27-1. A level with many rockets flying around

A Patrolling Enemy

The rocket is a type of enemy that basically has no intelligent behavior. It flies from left to right or vice versa until it flies out of the screen, and then it resets itself. You can also add enemies that are slightly smarter, such as a *patrolling* enemy. Let's set up a few different types of patrolling enemies that you can add to the game.

The Basic PatrollingEnemy Class

The PatrollingEnemy class is similar to the Rocket class. You want the patrolling enemy to be animated, so it inherits from the AnimatedGameObject class. You also need to define the *behavior* of the enemy in the overridden update method. The basic behavior of the patrolling enemy is that it walks from left to right and back again. If the enemy character reaches a gap or a wall tile, the enemy stops walking, waits for some time, and turns around. You can place enemies at arbitrary positions in the level. For the player, you define some rudimentary physics like falling and jumping. You don't do that for the PatrollingEnemy class, because the enemies you define for this game only walk from left to right and back.

In the constructor of the PatrollingEnemy class, you load the main animation for the patrolling enemy character (an angry-looking flame, as shown in Figure 27-2). Initially, you set a positive velocity so the enemy starts walking to the right. You also initialize another member variable called _waitTime that keeps track of how long the enemy has been waiting on one of the edges of the platform it's walking on:

```
this._waitTime = 0;
this.velocity.x = 120;
this.loadAnimation(sprites.flame, "default", true);
this.playAnimation("default");
```

Figure 27-2. A few patrolling enemies

In the update method, you have to distinguish between two cases: the enemy is walking or waiting. You can distinguish between these states by looking at the _waitTime variable. If this variable contains a positive value, the enemy is waiting. If the variable contains a value of zero or less, the enemy is walking. When the enemy is waiting, you don't have to do much. Just as you did in the Rocket class, you subtract the elapsed game time from the _waitTime variable. If the wait time has reached zero, you need to turn the character around. Here is the code to do that:

```
if (this._waitTime > 0) {
    this._waitTime -= delta;
    if (this._waitTime <= 0)
        this.turnAround();
}
```

The turnAround method simply inverts the velocity and mirrors the animation:

```
PatrollingEnemy.prototype.turnAround = function () {
    this.mirror = !this.mirror;
    this.velocity.x = 120;
    if (this.mirror)
        this.velocity.x = -this.velocity.x;
};
```

If the enemy currently is walking, not waiting, you need to find out whether it has reached the edge of the platform it's walking on. It has reached an edge in two cases: either there is a gap, so the enemy can't move any further, or a wall tile is blocking the way. You use the enemy's bounding box to find this information. If the enemy is walking to the left, you check whether the leftmost x value has reached a wall tile or the border of the platform. If the enemy is walking to the right, you check the rightmost x value. You can calculate this x value as follows:

```
var tiles = this.root.find(ID.tiles);
var posX = this.boundingBox.left;
if (!this.mirror)
    posX = this.boundingBox.right;
```

Now you calculate the tile into which this x value falls. You can do that by dividing the x value by the width of a tile. To make sure you always get the correct (lower-bound) tile index, you use the Math.floor method:

```
var tileX = Math.floor(posX / tiles.cellWidth);
```

In a similar way, you can calculate the y index of the tile the enemy is currently standing on:.

```
var tileY = Math.floor(this.position.y / tiles.cellHeight);
```

Note that because you use the *bottom* of the sprite to represent the position of the enemy, the y index you get is the one of the tile *below* the enemy.

Next you have to check whether the enemy has reached a wall tile or the border of the platform. If the tile at the calculated indices is a background tile, the enemy has reached the border of the platform and must stop walking. If the tile at indices (tileX, tileY - 1) (in other words, the tile right next to the enemy) is a wall tile, the enemy also has to stop walking. In order to stop walking, you assign a positive value to the wait time and set the x velocity to zero:

```
if (tiles.getTileType(tileX, tileY - 1) === TileType.normal ||
    tiles.getTileType(tileX, tileY) === TileType.background) {
    this._waitTime = 0.5;
    this.velocity.x = 0;
}
```

Different Types of Enemies

You can make the patrolling enemy slightly more interesting by introducing a few varieties. Here you can use the power of inheritance to write a few subclasses of the PatrollingEnemy class to define different enemy behaviors.

For example, you can create an enemy that is a bit more unpredictable by letting it change direction once in a while. At that point, you can also change the enemy's walking speed to a random value. You do this by defining a class `UnpredictableEnemy` that inherits from the `PatrollingEnemy` class. So, by default, it exhibits the same behavior as a regular enemy. You override the update method and add a few lines of code that randomly change the direction in which the enemy is walking as well as its velocity. Because you reuse most of the `PatrollingEnemy` class code, the `UnpredictableEnemy` class is rather short. Here is the complete class definition:

```
"use strict";

function UnpredictableEnemy(layer, id) {
    PatrollingEnemy.call(this, layer, id);
}

UnpredictableEnemy.prototype = Object.create(PatrollingEnemy.prototype);

UnpredictableEnemy.prototype.update = function (delta) {
    PatrollingEnemy.prototype.update.call(this, delta);
    if (this._waitTime <= 0 && Math.random() < 0.01) {
        this.turnAround();
        this.velocity.x = Math.sign(this.velocity.x) * Math.random() * 300;
    }
};
```

As you can see, you use an `if` instruction to check whether a randomly generated number falls below a certain value. As a result, in a few cases the condition will yield `true`. In the body of the `if` instruction, you first turn the enemy around, and then you calculate a new x velocity. Note that you multiply the randomly generated velocity by the sign of the old velocity value. This is to ensure that the new velocity is set in the right direction. You also first call the update method of the base class so the right animation is selected, collisions with the player are dealt with, and so on.

Another variety I can think of is an enemy that follows the player instead of simply walking from left to the right and back again. Again, you inherit from the `PatrollingEnemy` class. Here is a class called `PlayerFollowingEnemy`:

```
"use strict";

function PlayerFollowingEnemy(layer, id) {
    PatrollingEnemy.call(this, layer, id);
}

PlayerFollowingEnemy.prototype = Object.create(PatrollingEnemy.prototype);

PlayerFollowingEnemy.prototype.update = function (delta) {
    PatrollingEnemy.prototype.update.call(this, delta);

    var player = this.root.find(ID.player);
    var direction = player.position.x - this.position.x;
    if (Math.sign(direction) !== Math.sign(this.velocity.x) &&
        player.velocity.x !== 0 && this.velocity.x !== 0)
        this.turnAround();
};
```

This class defines an enemy that follows the player if the player is moving. This is done by checking whether the enemy is currently walking in the direction where the player is standing (only taking the *x* direction into account). If not, the enemy turns around. You place a limitation on the enemy's intelligence by doing that only if the player isn't moving in the *x* direction (in other words, the player's *x* velocity is zero).

You should never make enemies too smart. In addition, don't make them too fast—it would be a short game if enemies walked appreciably faster than the player while following them. Enemies are there to be beaten by the player so the player can win the game. Playing a game where the enemies are too smart or unbeatable isn't a lot of fun, unless you like dying over and over again!

Other Types of Enemies

Yet another enemy you can add to the game is a sneezing turtle (see Figure 27-3). Why a turtle, you ask? And why a sneezing one? Well, I don't really have an answer to that question. But the idea behind this enemy is that it has both a negative and a positive side. On the negative side, the turtle grows spikes when it sneezes, so you shouldn't touch it. But if the turtle isn't sneezing, you can use it to jump higher. Because you aren't dealing with interaction just yet, you only add the animated turtle for now. The turtle can be used to jump for 5 seconds, then it sneezes and grows spikes for 5 seconds, after which it returns to the previous state for 5 seconds, and so on.

Figure 27-3. Don't jump on the spiky turtle!

The enemy is represented by the Turtle class, which is set up in a fashion similar to the previous enemies. A turtle has two states: it's idle, or it has sneezed and therefore has dangerous spikes. In this case, you maintain two member variables to keep track of which state the turtle is in and how much time has passed in that state: the waitTime variable tracks how much time is left in the current state, and the sneezing variable tracks whether the turtle is sneezing. Again, in the update method, you handle the transition between the two phases, much as you did for the rocket and the patrolling enemies. I don't go into further detail here because the code is very similar to the other enemy classes. If you want to have a look at the complete code, check out the TickTick3 program in the solution belonging to this chapter.

Sparky is the final enemy type that you add to the game. Just like the other enemies, Sparky has two states (see Figure 27-4). Sparky is a very dangerous, electricity-loving enemy. He hangs quietly in the air until he receives a bolt of energy. When that happens, he falls down. While Sparky is hanging in the air, he isn't dangerous; but as soon as he falls, don't touch him! Have a look at the Sparky class to see the code.

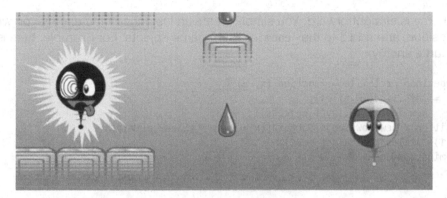

Figure 27-4. Sparky is dangerous when he is electrified

ENEMY SOFTWARE ARCHITECTURE

All these different types of enemies look different and behave differently, but they generally have a common class design. You could probably design a better way to define these enemies by using a couple of generic classes that let you define states and transitions between them. There could be conditions attached to each transition, such as that a certain amount of time must have passed or that an animation should be finished playing. Such a structure is called a *finite state machine*. It's a very common technique using in artificial intelligence systems. If you're up to the challenge, try to write a finite state machine library and redefine the existing enemies to use it!

Loading the Different Types of Enemies

Now that you've defined different varieties of enemies, the only thing left to do is load them when you read the level data variable. The sprites for the different enemies are identified using characters. You store these enemy characters in a GameObjectList object, which you create in the Level class constructor:

```
this._enemies = new powerupjs.GameObjectList(ID.layer_objects);
```

Depending on the character you read when loading the level, you call a different method to load the enemy, by adding a few cases to the switch instruction in the Level class:

```
case 'R':
    return this.loadRocketTile(x, y, true);
case 'r':
    return this.loadRocketTile(x, y, false);
case 'S':
    return this.loadSparkyTile(x, y);
```

```
case 'T':
    return this.loadTurtleTile(x, y);
case 'A':
case 'B':
case 'C':
    return this.loadFlameTile(x, y, tileType);
```

Loading an enemy is straightforward. You simply create an instance of the enemy you would like to add, set its position, and add it to the _enemies list of game objects. For example, here is the method for loading a turtle enemy:

```
Level.prototype.loadTurtleTile = function (x, y) {
    var tiles = this.find(ID.tiles);
    var enemy = new Turtle(ID.layer_objects);
    enemy.position = new powerupjs.Vector2((x + 0.5) * tiles.cellWidth,
        (y + 1) * tiles.cellHeight + 25);
    this._enemies.add(enemy);
    return new Tile();
};
```

You've now defined a few different kinds of enemies with varying intelligence and capabilities. It's up to you to define enemies that are smarter, more devious, or even more stupid, depending on the needs of your game. You didn't apply any physics to the enemies; however, once you start building smarter enemies that, for example, can jump or fall, you'll need to implement physics just as you did for the player. As an exercise, try to think how you can make these enemies more capable without having to rely on physics. Can you let them move faster when the player is nearby? Can you create an enemy that launches particles toward the player? The possibilities are endless, so try these things for yourself!

What You Have Learned

In this chapter, you have learned:

- How to define different kinds of enemies
- How to use inheritance to create variety in enemy behavior

Chapter **28**

Adding Player Interaction

In this chapter, you add more interaction between the player and the objects in the level. Currently, the player can walk around, and a basic physics system allows the player to jump, collide with wall tiles, or fall out of the screen. First you look at a very simple kind of interaction: collecting water drops. Then you see how to create the behavior that allows the player to slide over ice. Finally, you focus on the part of the program that deals with the various player-enemy interactions in the game.

Collecting Water Drops

The first thing to add is the possibility for the player to collect water drops. A player collects a water drop if the bomb character collides with that drop. In that case, you make the drop invisible.

Making a drop invisible once a player collects it isn't the only way to approach the problem of drawing only the uncollected drops, but it's one of the easiest solutions. Another approach would be to maintain a list of water drops that have been collected and then draw only those drops that the player still has to find, but this technique requires a lot more code.

The place where you check whether the player collides with a water drop is in the WaterDrop class. The reason is clear: as before, each game object is responsible for its own behavior. If you handle these collisions in the WaterDrop class, each water drop checks whether it collides with the player. You write this code in the update method. The first step is retrieving the player:

```
var player = this.root.find(ID.player);
```

If the water drop is currently visible, you check whether it collides with the player using the collidesWith method. If so, you set the visibility status of the drop to false. You also play a sound to let the player know the water drop has been collected:

```
if (this.collidesWith(player)) {
    this.visible = false;
    sounds.water_collected.play();
}
```

Later, you can determine whether the level is completed by checking the visibility of each water drop. If all the water drops are invisible, you know the player has collected all of them.

Ice Blocks

Another type of interaction you can add to the game is special behavior when the player is walking over ice. When the player moves over ice, you want the character to continue sliding at a constant rate and not stop moving when the player releases the arrow key. Even though continuing to slide isn't completely realistic (in real life you would slide and slow down), it does lead to predictable behavior that the player can easily understand, which in many cases is more important than achieving realism. To implement this, you have to do two things:

- Extend the `handleInput` method to deal with moving over ice.

- Calculate whether the player is standing on ice.

You keep track of whether the player is standing on ice in a member variable `walkingOnIce` in the `Player` class. Let's assume for now that this variable is updated somewhere else, and let's look at extending the `handleInput` method. The first thing you want to do is increase the player's walking speed when the character is walking on ice. You can do that as follows:

```
var walkingSpeed = 400;
if (this.walkingOnIce) {
    walkingSpeed *= 1.5;
}
```

The value by which the speed is multiplied is a variable that influences the gameplay. Choosing the right value is important—too fast, and the level becomes unplayable; too slow, and the ice isn't different from a regular walking surface in any meaningful way.

If the player isn't walking on ice but is instead standing on the ground, you need to set the x velocity to zero so the character stops moving when the player is no longer pressing an arrow key or one of the touch buttons. To achieve this, you extend the earlier `if` instruction as follows:

```
var walkingSpeed = 400;
if (this.walkingOnIce) {
    walkingSpeed *= 1.5;
    this.velocity.x = Math.sign(this.velocity.x) * walkingSpeed;
} else if (this.onTheGround)
    this.velocity.x = 0;
```

Then you handle the player input. If the player is pressing the left or right arrow key, you set the appropriate x velocity:

```
if (powerupjs.Keyboard.down(powerupjs.Keys.left))
    this.velocity.x = -walkingSpeed;
else if (powerupjs.Keyboard.down(powerupjs.Keys.right))
    this.velocity.x = walkingSpeed;
```

Similarly, if the game is being played on a touch device, you check whether the player is touching one of the buttons, and you adapt the velocity of the player character accordingly.

The only thing you still need to do is find out whether the player is walking on ice and update the `walkingOnIce` member variable accordingly. You already look at the tiles surrounding the player in the `handleCollisions` method, so to extend that method to also check whether the player is walking on ice, you only need to add a few lines of code. In the beginning of this method, you assume the player isn't walking on ice:

```
this.walkingOnIce = false;
```

The player can only walk on ice if they're on the ground. You check whether they're on the ground in the following `if` instruction:

```
if (this._previousYPosition <= tileBounds.top && tileType !== TileType.background) {
    this.onTheGround = true;
    this.velocity.y = 0;
}
```

To check whether the tile the player is standing on is an ice tile, you have to retrieve the tile from the tile field and check its `ice` property. Doing so is straightforward:

```
var currentTile = tiles.at(x, y);
```

Finally you update the `walkingOnIce` variable. You use a logical *or* operator so that if the player is only partly on an ice tile, the variable is also set to `true`:

```
if (currentTile !== null) {
    this.walkingOnIce = this.walkingOnIce || currentTile.ice;
}
```

You only perform this instruction if the `currentTile` variable doesn't point to `null`. You use the logical *or* to calculate whether the player is walking on ice in order to take all surrounding tiles into account. The effect is that the character keeps moving until it isn't standing on an ice tile anymore (not even partly).

Enemies Colliding With the Player

The final kind of interaction to add is collisions with enemies. In many cases, when the player collides with an enemy, it causes the player's death. In some cases, you have to do something special (such as jumping extra high when jumping on the turtle). On the player side, you have to load an extra animation that shows the player dying. Because you don't want to handle player input after the player has died, you need to update the player's current alive status. You do this using a member variable `alive` that you set to `true` in the constructor of the `Player` class. In the `handleInput` method, you check whether the player is still alive. If not, you return from the method so you don't handle any input:

```
if (!this.alive)
    return;
```

You also add a method called die to let the player die. There are two ways the player can die: by falling in a hole out of the game screen and by colliding with an enemy. Therefore, you pass a Boolean parameter to the die method to indicate whether the player died by falling or by colliding with an enemy.

In the die method, you do a couple of things. First you check whether the player was already dead. If so, you return from the method without doing anything (after all, a player can only die once). You set the alive variable to false. Then you set the velocity in the x direction to zero, to stop the player from moving to the left or right. You don't reset the y velocity, so the player keeps on falling: gravity doesn't cease to exist when you die. Next, you determine which sound to play when the player dies. If the player falls to their death, the sound produced is quite different from dying by an enemy's hand (don't try this for real; take my word for it). If the player dies because of a collision with an enemy, you give the player an upward velocity as well. This upward velocity isn't very realistic, but it does provide for a nice visual effect (see Figure 28-1). Finally, you play the die animation. The complete method is as follows:

```
Player.prototype.die = function (falling) {
    if (!this.alive)
        return;
    this.alive = false;
    this.velocity.x = 0;
    if (falling) {
        sounds.player_fall.play();
    }
    else {
        this.velocity.y = -900;
        sounds.player_die.play();
    }
    this.playAnimation("die");
};
```

Figure 28-1. The player dies after colliding with an enemy

You can check in the update method whether the player is falling to death by calculating if the player's *y*-position falls outside of the screen. If this is the case, you call the die method:

```
var tiles = this.root.find(ID.tiles);
if (this.boundingBox.top >=tiles.rows * tiles.cellHeight)
    this.die(true);
```

At the start of the update method, you call the update method of the superclass to ensure that the animation is updated:

```
powerupjs.AnimatedGameObject.prototype.update.call(this, delta);
```

Next you do the physics and collisions (which still need to be done, even if the player is dead). Then you check whether the player is alive. If not, you're finished, and you return from the method.

Now that the player can die in various gruesome ways, you have to extend the enemy classes to deal with collisions. In the Rocket class, you add a method called checkPlayerCollision that you call in the rocket's update method. In the checkPlayerCollision method, you simply check whether the player collides with the rocket. If that is the case, you call the die method on the Player object. The complete method is as follows:

```
Rocket.prototype.checkPlayerCollision = function () {
    var player = this.root.find(ID.player);
    if (this.collidesWith(player))
        player.die(false);
};
```

In the case of the patrolling enemy, you do exactly the same thing. You add the same method to that class and call it from the update method. The version in the Sparky class is slightly different: the player should die only if Sparky is currently being electrified. Therefore, you change the method as follows:

```
Sparky.prototype.checkPlayerCollision = function () {
    var player = this.root.find(ID.player);
    if (this.idleTime <= 0 && this.collidesWith(player))
        player.die(false);
};
```

Finally, the Turtle enemy adds even more behavior. You begin by checking whether the turtle collides with the player. If that's not the case, you simply return from the checkPlayerCollision method, because you're done:

```
var player = this.root.find(ID.player);
if (!this.collidesWith(player))
    return;
```

If a collision occurs, there are two possibilities. The first is that the turtle is currently sneezing. In that case, the player dies:

```
if (this.sneezing)
    player.die(false);
```

The second case is that the turtle is in waiting mode, and the player is jumping on the turtle. In that case, the player should make an extra-high jump. An easy way to check whether the player is jumping on the turtle is to look at the y velocity. Assume that if that velocity is positive, the player is jumping on the turtle. So, you call the `jump` method to make the player jump extra high:

```
else if (player.velocity.y > 0 && player.alive)
    player.jump(1500);
```

And of course, you only want to do this if the player is still alive.

You now have the main interaction programming. In the next chapter, you finish this game by adding mountains and moving clouds in the background. You also add the code that manages transitions between the levels.

TO DIE OR NOT TO DIE?

I made a choice in this section that the player dies immediately when they touch an enemy. Another choice would be to give the player several lives or to add a health indicator for the player that decreases every time the player touches an enemy.

Adding multiple lives or a health indicator to a game can make the game more fun, but you also have to be sure the levels are still challenging enough. A health bar makes sense only if the game's levels are much larger than in this chapter's example. You also need to add side scrolling so that levels can be larger than a single screen.

Implementing side scrolling isn't that difficult: you draw all the game objects in the game world according to a camera offset that moves along with the player. As a challenge, try to extend the Tick Tick game with side scrolling and add a health bar for the player.

What You Have Learned

In this chapter, you have learned:

- How to program various kinds of player interactions with water drops and enemies
- How to program ice tile behavior
- How to cause the player to die in certain situations

Chapter 29

Finishing the Tick Tick Game

In this chapter, you finish the Tick Tick game. First you add a timer such that the player has a limited amount of time to complete each level. Then you add a few mountains and clouds to the background to make the game visually more interesting. Finally, you progress through the levels by adding two extra game states: the "game over" state, and the "level finished" state.

Adding a Timer

Let's first look at adding a *timer* to the game. You don't want the timer to take up too much screen space, so you use a text version of it. Therefore, the TimerGameObject class inherits from the Label class. You want to be able to pause the timer (for example, when the level is finished), so you add a Boolean variable running that indicates whether the timer is running. You also store the time remaining in a variable called _timeLeft. You override the reset method to initialize the timer object. You want to give the player 30 seconds to finish each level. As a result, here is the complete reset method:

```
TimerGameObject.prototype.reset = function () {
    powerupjs.Label.prototype.reset.call(this);
    this._timeLeft = 30;
    this.running = true;
};
```

For convenience, you also add a property gameOver that indicates whether the timer has reached zero. You use this property later to handle the event that the player doesn't finish the level in time:

```
Object.defineProperty(TimerGameObject.prototype, "gameOver",
    {
        get: function () {
            return this._timeLeft <= 0;
        }
    });
```

Now the only thing you still need to do is implement the update method to program the timer behavior. As a first step, you only update the timer if it's running. So if the timer isn't running, you return from the method:

```
if (!this.running)
    return;
```

Then, as usual you subtract the elapsed game time from the current remaining time:

```
this._timeLeft -= delta;
```

Next you create the text that you want to print on the screen. You could simply print the number of seconds on the screen, but let's make the timer a bit more generic so it's also possible to define a timer that can handle minutes as well as seconds. For example, if you want to define a timer that counts down from two minutes, you initialize it as follows:

```
this._timeLeft = 120;
```

You want to display "2:00" instead of "120" on the screen. To do this, you need to calculate in the update method how many minutes are left. You use the Math.floor method for this:

```
var minutes = Math.floor(this._timeLeft / 60);
```

Using this approach, you make sure the number of minutes is never higher than allowed. For example, Math.floor(119) gives you 1 as a result, which is exactly what you need, because 119 seconds remaining translates to 1 minute and 119 − 60 = 59 seconds remaining.

By calculating the remainder after dividing _timeLeft by 60, you get the number of seconds. In order to only have integer numbers, you need to round the number of seconds as well, but you use the Math.ceil method for this. This method always rounds up: for example, Math.ceil(1.2) has a result of 2. You always want to round up because you need to make sure you display zero seconds only when there really is no time left. Here is how you calculate the number of seconds:

```
var seconds = Math.ceil(this._timeLeft % 60);
```

Because you don't want to display negative times, you add the following if instruction:

```
if (this._timeLeft < 0)
    minutes = seconds = 0;
```

Note that you use *operator chaining* here to set the minutes and seconds. The following if instruction does exactly the same:

```
if (this._timeLeft < 0) {
    minutes 0;
    seconds = 0;
}
```

Now that you've calculated the number of minutes and seconds remaining, you can create a string that you draw on the screen:

```
this.text = minutes + ":" + seconds;
if (seconds < 10)
    this.text = minutes + ":0" + seconds;
```

You set the color of the text to yellow so it better fits the design of the game:

```
this.color = powerupjs.Color.yellow;
```

Finally, you want to warn the player if they don't have a lot of time left to finish the level. You do this by alternating between red and yellow when printing the text on the screen. You can do this with an if instruction and a clever use of the modulus operator:

```
if (this._timeLeft <= 10 && seconds % 2 === 0)
    this.color = powerupjs.Color.red;
```

Even though calculating things with time in this manner is sufficient for the Tick Tick game, you might find yourself wanting to do more complex calculations with time. JavaScript has the Date object, which represents time and allows more advanced handling of time, including time zones, conversion to a string, and so on.

Making the Timer Go Faster or Slower

Depending on the kind of tile the player is walking on, time should go faster or slower. Walking on a hot tile increases the speed at which time passes, whereas walking on an ice tile decreases it. To allow for a timer that runs at different speeds, you introduce a *multiplier* value in the TimerGameObject class. This value is stored as a member variable, and you initially set the multiplier to 1:

```
this.multiplier = 1;
```

Taking this multiplier into account while the timer is running is fairly easy. You simply multiply the passed time by the multiplier in the update method, and you're done:

```
this._timeLeft -= delta * this.multiplier;
```

Now that you can change the speed at which time passes, you can do this depending on the kind of tile the player is walking on. In the Player class, you already maintain a variable walkingOnIce, which indicates whether the player is walking on an ice tile. In order to handle hot tiles as well, you define another variable walkingOnHot, in which you keep track of whether the player is walking on a hot tile. To determine the value of this variable, you follow the same approach you did for the walkingOnIce variable. In the handleCollisions method, you initially set this variable to false:

```
this.walkingOnHot = false;
```

Then you add one line of code to update the value of the variable depending on the current tile the player is standing on:

```
this.walkingOnHot = this.walkingOnHot || currentTile.hot;
```

For the complete code, see the `Player` class belonging to the `TickTickFinal` example.

Using the `walkingOnIce` and `walkingOnHot` variables, you can now update the timer multiplier. You do this in the player's `update` method:

```
var timer = this.root.find(ID.timer);
if (this.walkingOnHot)
    timer.multiplier = 2;
else if (this.walkingOnIce)
    timer.multiplier = 0.5;
else
    timer.multiplier = 1;
```

From a game design perspective, it's probably a good idea to explicitly let the player know that walking on a hot tile shortens the time left for finishing the level. You can do this by briefly showing a warning overlay or changing the timer's display color. You can also play back a warning sound. Another possibility would be to change the background music to something more frantic, to make the player realize something has changed.

ADAPTING TO THE SKILLS OF THE PLAYER

Changing the speed of the timer can make a level much easier or harder. You could extend the game so that in some cases the timer would stop or would move back a few seconds if the player picked up a special item. You could even make the level progression adaptive so that if the player dies too often, the maximum time of 30 seconds per level is increased. However, be careful about doing this. If you help the player in a too-obvious way, the player will realize it and adapt their strategy to it (in other words, the player will play worse in order to make the levels easier). Also, the player may feel they aren't being treated seriously. A better way to deal with adapting the maximum time per level is to allow the player to (partly) transfer time left over from previous levels to the current level. That way, difficult levels can be made easier, but the player has to do something to make that happen. You could also consider adding difficulty levels, where a more difficult level has a faster timer but also better benefits such as more points, extra items to pick up, or extra abilities for the player. Casual game players can then select the "Can I play, Daddy?" difficulty level, whereas skilled players can opt for the extremely challenging "I am Death incarnate" level.

When the Timer Reaches Zero

When the player doesn't finish the level on time, the bomb explodes, and the game is over. A Boolean member variable in the `Player` class indicates whether the player has exploded. You then add a method called `explode` to the class that sets the explosion in motion. This is the complete method:

```
Player.prototype.explode = function () {
    if (!this.alive || this.finished)
        return;
    this.alive = false;
```

```
    this.exploded = true;
    this.velocity = powerupjs.Vector2.zero;
    this.playAnimation("explode");
    sounds.player_explode.play();
};
```

First, the player character can't explode if the character wasn't alive in the first place, or if the player finished the level. In either of those cases, you simply return from the method. Then, you set the alive status to false and the exploded status to true. You set the velocity to zero (explosions don't move). Then, you play the "explode" animation. This animation is stored in a sprite sheet and consists of 25 frames of an explosion. Finally, you play an appropriate sound.

Because gravity also no longer affects an exploded character, you only do the gravity physics if the player isn't exploded:

```
if (!this.exploded)
    this.velocity.y += 55;
```

In the update method of the Level class, you check whether the timer has reached zero, and if so, you call the explode method:

```
if (timer.gameOver)
    player.explode();
```

Drawing Mountains and Clouds

To make the level background a bit more interesting, let's add mountains and clouds to it. You do this in the Level constructor. First, let's have a look at how to add a few mountains. For that, you use a for instruction. In the body of that instruction, you create a sprite game object, give it a position, and add it to the backgrounds list. This is the complete for instruction:

```
for (var i = 0; i < 5; i++) {
    var sprid = "mountain_" + (Math.ceil(Math.random()*2));
    var mountain = new powerupjs.SpriteGameObject(sprites[sprid], ID.layer_background_2);
    mountain.position = new powerupjs.Vector2(Math.random() *
        powerupjs.Game.size.x - mountain.width / 2,
        powerupjs.Game.size.y - mountain.height);
    backgrounds.add(mountain);
}
```

The first step is to create the sprite game object. You want to choose randomly between the different mountain sprites that you have. Because there are two mountain sprites, you create a random number (either 1 or 2) to select between them. You use the number to create the ID that corresponds to that sprite.

Then you calculate the position of the mountain. The x position is chosen randomly, and you use a fixed y position so the mountain is at the appropriate height (you don't want mountains hanging in the sky). Finally, the mountain object is added to the backgrounds list.

For clouds, you do something slightly more complicated. You want the clouds to move from left to right or vice versa, and if a cloud disappears from the screen, you want a new one to appear. To do this, you add a Clouds class to the game. You create an instance of this class in the Level constructor and assign it a higher layer value than the background itself and the mountains. This ensures that the clouds are drawn in front of the mountains:

```
var clouds = new Clouds(ID.layer_background_3);
backgrounds.add(clouds);
```

Because the Clouds class contains a number of moving clouds, it's a subclass of the GameObjectList class. In the constructor, you use a for instruction to create a number of clouds and add them to the list. Each cloud is given a random position and a random x velocity. Take a look at the constructor of the Clouds class in the TickTickFinal example to see how this is done.

The Clouds class also has an update method, in which you check whether a cloud has exited the screen. Because you need to do this for each cloud game object, you use a for instruction to traverse all the cloud objects in the list. If a cloud has exited the screen, you create a new cloud object with a random position and velocity. A cloud can exit the screen either on the left side or on the right side. If a cloud is positioned outside of the screen on the *left*, and its x velocity is *negative*, you know it has exited the screen. This is also true if the cloud is positioned outside of the screen on the *right* side, and its velocity is *positive*. You can capture these two cases for a cloud c in the following if instruction:

```
if ((c.velocity.x < 0 && c.position.x + c.width < 0) ||
    (c.velocity.x > 0 && c.position.x > powerupjs.Game.size.x)) {
    // remove this cloud and add a new one
}
```

Removing the cloud is easy:

```
this.remove(c);
```

Then you create a new cloud game object:

```
var cloud = new powerupjs.SpriteGameObject(sprites["cloud_" + Math.ceil(Math.random()*5)]);
```

You assign an x velocity to this cloud, which can be either positive or negative. The y velocity of the cloud is always zero so the cloud only moves horizontally:

```
cloud.velocity = new powerupjs.Vector2(((Math.random() * 2) - 1) * 20, 0);
```

Note in this instruction that you calculate a random number between -1 and 1 and then multiply that number by 20. This allows you to randomly create clouds with either a positive or a negative x velocity. You calculate a random cloud y position by multiplying the screen height by a random number between zero and one. From that number, you subtract half of the cloud height to make sure you never generate a cloud that is drawn fully below the screen:

```
var cloudHeight = Math.random() * powerupjs.Game.size.y - cloud.height / 2;
```

You position the cloud at either the left border or the right border of the screen, depending on the direction in which the cloud is moving:

```
if (cloud.velocity.x < 0)
    cloud.position = new powerupjs.Vector2(powerupjs.Game.size.x, cloudHeight);
else
    cloud.position = new powerupjs.Vector2(-cloud.width, cloudHeight);
```

Now you add the new cloud to the list:

```
this.add(cloud);
```

Figure 29-1 shows a screenshot of a level that has mountains and moving clouds in its background.

Figure 29-1. A Tick Tick level with mountains and moving clouds in the background

Before you finish this section, let's look at the complete code one more time:

```
for (var i = 0, l = this.length; i < l; ++i) {
    var c = this.at(i);
    if (/* c is outside of the screen */) {
        this.remove(c);
        var cloud = new powerupjs.SpriteGameObject(...);
```

```
        // calculate cloud position and velocity
        // ...
        this.add(cloud);
    }
}
```

Look closely at the loop: you're removing and adding objects to a list while traversing it with a `for` instruction. This can be dangerous, because you modify the length of the list in the body of the `for` instruction, and the value of i depends on the length of the list. If you aren't careful, you could run into a case where you remove an item from the list you're traversing, but i is still incremented until it reaches the old length of the list, resulting in an error when you try to access the list outside of its bounds. In this particular case, you won't run into trouble because whenever you remove a cloud, you add a new one; but you have to be very careful when programming these kinds of operations. One way to be sure the program runs correctly in all cases is to simply break out of the loop using either a `break` or a `return` call. This way, as soon as you modify the list in some way, you stop the loop.

Finalizing the Level Progression

To complete the game, you still need to add the game states for dealing with the event that the player has lost or won a level. You approach this in a fashion similar to how you handled it in the Penguin Pairs game, except that here you have an explicit "game over" game state in addition to the "level finished" game state. These states are coded in a fairly straightforward way, similar to how you did it in previous games. You can find the complete code in the `GameOverState` and `LevelFinished` state classes in the `TickTickFinal` example belonging to this chapter.

To determine whether the player has finished a level, you add a `completed` property to the `Level` class that checks for two things:

- Has the player collected all the water drops?
- Has the player reached the exit sign?

Both of these things are fairly easy to check. To check whether the player has reached the end sign, you can see whether their bounding boxes are intersecting. Checking whether the player has collected all the water drops can be done by verifying that all water drops are invisible. This is the complete property:

```
Object.defineProperty(Level.prototype, "completed",
    {
        get: function () {
            var player = this.find(ID.player);
            var exit = this.find(ID.exit);
            if (!exit.collidesWith(player))
                return false;
            for (var i = 0, l = this._waterdrops.length; i < l; ++i) {
                if (this._waterdrops.at(i).visible)
                    return false;
            }
            return true;
        }
    });
```

In the update method of the Level class, you check whether the level was completed. If so, you call the levelFinished method in the Player class, which plays the "celebration" animation:

```
if (this.completed && timer.running) {
    player.levelFinished();
    timer.running = false;
    window.LEVELS[this._levelIndex].solved = true;
}
```

You also stop the timer, because the player is done. Furthermore, you set the solved status of this level to true so that the next time the player starts the game, the browser will remember. In the PlayingState class, you deal with switching to other states depending on the state of the level. Here are the corresponding lines of code in the update method of that class:

```
PlayingState.prototype.update = function (delta) {
    this.currentLevel.update(delta);

    if (this.currentLevel.gameOver)
        powerupjs.GameStateManager.switchTo(ID.game_state_gameover);
    else if (this.currentLevel.completed)
        powerupjs.GameStateManager.switchTo(ID.game_state_levelfinished);
};
```

The code to deal with transitions between levels is fairly straightforward and is almost a copy of the code used in the Penguin Pairs game. Have a look at the code in the TickTickFinal example to see how this is done.

You've now seen how to build a platform game with commonly occurring elements such as collecting items, avoiding enemies, game physics, going from one level to another, and so on. Does it end here? Well, that depends on you. To make Tick Tick a game that is commercially viable, a lot of work still needs to be done. You probably want to define more of everything: more levels, more enemies, more different items to pick up, more challenges, more sounds. You may also want to introduce a few things that I didn't address: playing with other players over a network, side scrolling, maintaining a high-score list, playing in-game movies between levels, and other things you can think of that would be interesting to add. Use the Tick Tick game as a starting point for your own game.

The final part of this book covers a few more things that are useful to know when you're developing games and applications in general in JavaScript. I discuss documentation in more detail, as well as a few ways to protect your game code and let players download your game more quickly.

What You Have Learned

In this chapter, you have learned:

- How to add a timer to a level
- How to create animated backgrounds consisting of mountains and clouds

VI

Into the Great Wide Open

By now you know how to program a game in JavaScript. But what's next? How do you create a full-fledged game that is ready for the market? What do you need to do in order to publish your game? And how should you market it? The final part of this book covers these topics. This part consists of two chapters. The first one deals with producing games, which includes game design, game development, and the operational aspects of game production. The second chapter deals with game publication, including models to earn money from games, marketing your game, and making your game playable in different languages and cultural contexts.

Because it's very useful to hear hands-on advice from people working in the game industry, I interviewed two important such folks. First I interviewed Mark Overmars: he developed the GameMaker application, which is a great tool for creating games quickly. GameMaker has grown into a mature application and is now maintained by Yoyo games, a company that Mark partly owns. He is also the co-founder and CTO of Tingly games, a company that develops so-called greeting games in JavaScript using an in-house built game engine.

Second, I had an inspiring interview with Peter Vesterbacka of Rovio Entertainment, known for its world-famous *Angry Birds* franchise. Peter had a lot to do with the creation of the company. In 2003, he organized a game-making competition while he was employed at HP, with a goal of creating the best possible mobile multiplayer game. This was way before Android or iOS existed. Nokia had just come out with its first smartphone. Three guys—Niklas, Jarno, and Kim, who studied at Aalto University in Finland—participated with a game called *King of the Cabbage World* and won the competition. Peter suggested to them that they start a company, and they did. Fifty-one games later, in 2009, they created the fifty-second game, called *Angry Birds*. Peter is the so-called Mighty Eagle of the company. He describes his primary role as "making sure that big things happen for the company fast enough." Peter is involved in many different aspects of the company, including marketing and branding, and he is looking to help steer the company in new, innovative directions.

The following two chapters are largely based on my interviews with Mark and Peter. Both of them are really inspiring people. Throughout the text, you'll find their views on game production and publication, and they have shared many helpful tips and tricks.

Chapter 30

Producing Games

This chapter covers several topics related to producing games. I talk first about designing HTML5 games and then about development. I briefly cover game asset production as well. Finally, you see the operational aspects of producing games, such as how to collaborate with multiple people on the same code and how to work on a game-production team. Both Mark Overmars and Peter Vesterbacka share thoughts and tips about these topics throughout the text.

> Peter Vesterbacka: "HTML5 and JavaScript have been called the future for a long time when it comes to game development. They haven't quite lived up to their full potential yet, but I see a lot of promise. At the same time, native development tools, interfaces, and ease of use also have improved a lot. Of course, in an ideal world, it would be great to be able to use JavaScript and HTML5 code all over the place. I think there is room for both native apps and HTML5/JavaScript applications."

Designing Games

This isn't a book about game design. Game design is a large field of study, and many books have been written on the subject. The book *Fundamentals of Game Design* by Ernest Adams (New Riders, 2009) is a very good place to start reading about game design. Another interesting book is *The Art of Game Design: A Book of Lenses*, by Jesse Schell (CRC Press, 2008).

> Mark Overmars: "While designing our games, we always keep in mind that the code needs to be efficient. For example, we won't design a game where it is important that tens of thousands of characters move around on the screen, or where a lot of visual things are happening at the same time, or where a very smooth motion is crucial."

This section doesn't cover the design process itself; rather, it mainly discusses how programming web-based applications in JavaScript affects game design. The preceding quote is an example of this approach: because you want your games to play well on a variety of devices, you need to design games that allow for efficient implementation.

> Mark: "Many devices do not have a keyboard, so your game needs to allow control by touch input. For some games, keyboard control is more natural. A challenge then is to ensure that the game is not much easier to play using a keyboard than using touch input. If you develop a game where people play against each other online, or a game that uses an online high-score list, watch out that you're not giving one group of users a large advantage over the others because they use a specific input method."

> Peter: "One of the secrets of the success of Angry Birds is that it was one of the first games that was designed with touch devices in mind. When you design a game for a touch device, typically it will be different from a game designed for a console with a controller. Always develop the best possible experience for the platform in question. Playing on a PlayStation 4 versus playing on an iPad is a very different experience because the situation and the context are very different. In one case you can sit for hours on your couch playing a game on a console, whereas on a phone a game session may take only a few minutes. Both can be great experiences, but in a very different way, and the design should take this into account."

In many JavaScript games, sprites are scaled up or down depending on the device. You've seen how to do this in the games developed in this book. One thing the book doesn't consider is that aspect ratios are radically different between devices. For instance, the iPad has a relatively square screen, unlike the iPhone 6, which has a much more rectangular screen.

In the current implementation of your games, a different aspect ratio means there is white (or black) space surrounding the game screen. If you display a game designed for the aspect ratio of the iPad on the iPhone 5, almost a third of the screen is empty space! While designing a game, it makes sense to try to adapt the design of the user interface, the playing field, that location of overlays, and so on, to the aspect ratio of the device. Ideally, the game should automatically adapt its overall layout to the size and aspect ratio of each device.

> Mark: "In addition to aspect ratio, there is also the choice between portrait and landscape mode. On phones you generally want to use portrait mode, but on a desktop PC or on a television, landscape mode makes more sense. Your mode choice also depends on the type of game, whether you want to use portrait or landscape mode, or whether you wish to allow both.

> In our games, the positioning of game elements is dependent on the aspect ratio. For example, a user interface is placed at the top of the screen, and below it is the game playing field. The game playing field is moved down if there is space available, so that the layout of the elements on the screen looks better. The location of buttons changes depending on the aspect ratio of the screen. Be careful, however, that you also adapt the interactions (finger positions) accordingly. As a result, you can't always use a device's full screen. Furthermore, if you want to place advertisement banners,

room for them has to be subtracted from the part of the screen that is available for playing. This also means you have to use artwork that can be easily scaled or that can be shown partially without taking anything away from the design."

When you design games that work on a variety of devices, you can't always use all of the device's available features. For example, if your game relies heavily on the player tilting the device, then the game isn't playable on a desktop machine. Desktop machines obviously don't have sensors to detect tilt (although that would be fun!). Furthermore, you often depend on versions of browsers and what has been implemented. Audio is a good example. Different browsers play back audio in different formats (or not at all). As a result, you shouldn't design a game that uses audio as a crucial part of its design. Games such as *Guitar Hero* are difficult to port to JavaScript because they rely on having precise control over the audio and measuring the synchrony between the audio and what the player is doing.

If you produce a game, you need to make a trade-off between creating the game for the lowest common denominator (in other words, the device with the fewest capabilities) and thus not using a lot of the features of more modern devices, versus creating a game that uses those features but isn't playable on older devices. If you want to sell your game to a *game-playing portal* (a web site that hosts many different games), the portal will have a list of devices that your game needs to support. So, in many cases, you simply have no choice if you want to publish your game through a portal.

Mark: "One of the most important aspects of game design is the level design. We spend a lot of time tweaking levels in such a way that the difficulty of each level progresses nicely. All parameters that influence the game play are stored in settings files. A designer can then modify these settings files, push new versions of those files to the server, and immediately play the game using the new settings."

Developing Games

If you want to develop games, you need to know how to program, but you also need to know common solutions or approaches for solving programming problems. On top of that, some of those solutions may be more generic than others, and some of the solutions may be more efficient than others. In this sense, programming often is a trade-off between solving a specific problem fast or taking the time to solve a whole class of problems at once. Especially in the game industry, there often is little time to solve classes of problems because of pressing deadlines. So as a developer in the game industry, you need to think very carefully about the approach you choose for solving a problem. On the other hand, writing nice, reusable code doesn't always take more time than writing quick-and-dirty code. As you gain more programming experience, you'll notice that you start developing a mindset that lets you quickly gauge the kind of solution that is required for a certain programming problem. Let's consider a couple of aspects of deciding on a solution.

Third-Party Libraries

Many games and applications rely on code written by different developers. That is why it's so important that when you write code, you do it in such a way that the code is structured logically and is easy for other developers to understand. Often, developers group related code in libraries. For example, a developer may create classes for dealing with physics in games and release that code in a library, to be used in any game that needs physics. Developers have created many libraries in many different programming languages, including JavaScript. For example, jQuery is a well-known JavaScript library that is used to create interfaces on web sites. Then there are tools that combine libraries with a development environment to create complete games, such as Unity (`http://unity3d.com`) which has a script engine that uses something very similar to JavaScript called UnityScript. Another game engine worth looking at is Cocos2D (`www.cocos2d-x.org`). When you want to develop a commercial game, it's a good idea to consider using such libraries or game engines, because they allow you to export your game to a variety of platforms as native applications.

> Peter: "At Rovio, most of our games are native code for iOS, Android, and so on. We do have a version of Angry Birds for HTML5 that uses WebGL, but we mainly do native mobile app development for the time being. We have our own tools that we have developed in-house over the years, so we can very easily write code once and then deploy it to any platform. For some projects, we use Unity, which also enables us to deploy our code to a variety of operating systems and devices."

> Mark: "In large part, we have developed our own engine and write our own libraries. We do this because it is very important for us that we squeeze every last drop of efficiency out of our code. We find that there are many libraries that are beautifully designed and very generic, and because of that they are slow and difficult to adapt to our framework and way of working. In a few cases, we do use libraries, for example for game physics. And we do regularly use tools that have been developed by third parties, such as a code editor or an obfuscation/minification tool such as Closure [see Chapter 31 for more information about Closure and obfuscation and minification]."

In this book, you've used only a single third-party library—Lab.js—which you used to load multiple JavaScript files more easily. You could have opted to use more libraries instead of writing all the code from scratch. In the case of this book, my goal is to teach you the important programming idioms of JavaScript and how they're applied to game programming. I chose to minimize the number of libraries used, so I could keep the code straightforward and in line with the general approach to programming games that I put forward in the book. As a developer, you often have to choose between using a library written by someone else versus programming everything yourself from scratch. If the library is well written and does something you need, it makes a lot of sense to use it in your games. You won't have to do all the work to program the same classes that somebody else already wrote. Furthermore, if a library has a lot of users, the main bugs in the library code probably have already been solved. All in all, if you use libraries, your game code may be a lot more robust than if you program everything yourself. Finally, because libraries are often developed for general purposes, you may find that the library you incorporate solves a problem that you just discovered in your game, so you can simply use the extra functionality that is already there in the library.

In some cases, libraries cause more trouble than they're worth. For one thing, libraries are generally released under a certain license model. If you want to use an open source library in your commercial game, the license may not allow you to sell the game code that includes the library. Therefore, using a library puts restrictions on what you can do with the code, because not all the code was written by you.

> Mark: "Another problem of libraries is that licenses are not always clearly defined, especially because you are distributing the source code in JavaScript. Also, in the end we like to put all our JavaScript code in a single file that is minified and obfuscated, a process that doesn't always work correctly when using third-party libraries."

If you use a library, you avoid having to write all the code, but you're dependent on the library's *limitations*. If you don't properly investigate beforehand whether the library will really solve your problem, you may put a lot of effort into integrating the library into your code and then find out it doesn't actually do the crucial thing you need it to do. Also, sometimes it's a good idea to write code from scratch instead of using a library, because doing so forces you to understand the problem at a deep level; therefore you may find a solution that is more efficient for your application. And finally, if you write all the code from scratch, it's easier to extend or modify the code, because you wrote it.

All things considered, as a developer you have to develop a sense for which parts of the game you want to program yourself (which takes time but leads to better understanding) and which parts you want to use a library for (which gives results faster but may not be a perfect fit for your needs).

Efficiency of Code

JavaScript programs can run on many different devices, ranging from high-end desktop machines to tablets and smartphones. This sometimes puts limits on the computational power that is available. Therefore, it's crucial that JavaScript programs have efficient code. And this depends on how a programmer solves a particular programming problem. Often, there are many possible solutions. For example, consider the simple problem of creating an array and filling it with the numbers 0, 1, 2, 3, and so on. Here is one way to do this:

```
var myArray = {0, 1, 2, 3, 4, 5, 6, 7, 8, 9, 10, 11, 12, 13, 14, 15, 16, 17, 18, 19};
```

You can also use a for loop:

```
var myArray = {};
for (var i = 0; i < 20; i++)
    myArray.push(i);
```

And here's yet another solution:

```
var myArray = {0};
while (myArray.length < 20)
    myArray.push(myArray.length);
```

Each of these solutions delivers an array of size 20 containing the numbers 0–19. But which solution you choose may depend on the context. The first solution (writing out the array) is very straightforward, and by looking at the code it's immediately clear what the contents of the array will be after the code has been executed. For smaller array definitions, this approach works very well. However, this doesn't work if you need an array of size 300. The second solution, which uses a for loop, is much more suitable in that case, because changing the desired length of the array only requires changing one number in the header of the for instruction. The third solution uses a while loop to solve the problem. It avoids having to declare a counter variable (i). However, this solution is probably less efficient than the second solution, because in each iteration the length of the array has to be retrieved twice (once in the header and once in the body).

When you're writing code, always think beforehand about the various solutions that solve a particular problem, and choose the one that fits best. This doesn't necessarily have to be the most efficient solution all the time. If one solution is slightly less efficient but results in much clearer code, it might be a good idea to go for that solution. There are tools that measure the bottlenecks in code. For Firefox, the Firebug tool has a profiler that can analyze your code to give you an idea of where the most time is spent. Similarly, Chrome's developer tools include a Benchmark Suite that can profile JavaScript performance.

Being able to choose the best solution for a problem requires knowledge about what is happening when code is interpreted and executed. Sometimes inefficiencies may be easy to solve, but you don't know they exist. Consider the following basic for instruction, which increments each element in an array by one:

```
for (var i = 0; i < myArray.length; i++)
    myArray[i] += 1;
```

This for instruction is straightforward, but it isn't very efficient. In each iteration of the loop, the length of the array is retrieved and compared to the counter. Because retrieving the length of the array costs time, the following for instruction is more efficient:

```
for (var i = 0, l = myArray.length; i < l; i++)
    myArray[i] += 1;
```

In this case, you retrieve the length of the array and store it in a variable. The condition of the loop is executed each iteration, but because it now uses the variable instead of directly retrieving the length, the code is more efficient.

You can improve the code even more. Incrementing the counter is done by the following instruction:

```
i++
```

Let's look in a bit more detail at this instruction. It's possible to use it as follows:

```
var i = 10;
var j = i++;
```

Although the second instruction looks a bit strange, it's perfectly valid JavaScript code. This is because i++ is also an *expression*, and so it has a *result* that you can store in a variable. The result of the i++ expression is the value of i *before* it was incremented. As a result, j will contain the value 10 and i will contain the value 11 after the second instruction has been executed. Because of this, i++ needs to create a *temporary variable* to store that value and return it. However, in the earlier for loop, you don't use that temporary value. There is another way to increment the variable, as follows:

```
++i
```

This does exactly the same thing as i++, except that it returns the new value of i:

```
var i = 10;
var j = ++i; // j and i both contain the value 11
```

Because it returns the new value, you don't have to store the old value, removing the need for that temporary variable. You can use this to your advantage in the for loop, to make it more efficient:

```
for (var i = 0, l = myArray.length; i < l; ++i)
    myArray[i] += 1;
```

These efficiency improvements may seem minor, but if the for loop is executed 60 times per second for an array containing thousands of particles, minor improvements in efficiency may make the difference between a smooth-running game and an unplayable game, especially on mobile devices with limited computational power. Some browsers may perform optimizations on interpreting and running JavaScript code, and these kinds of inefficiencies are relatively easy to detect automatically. However, not all browsers or versions may perform the same optimizations. By making sure your code is already efficient by itself, your game will run more smoothly on more platforms.

> Mark: "Generally speaking, graphics are the main bottleneck. For some devices it is more efficient to put everything in a large sprite and draw that. For other devices that approach doesn't help because the bottleneck is in the number of pixels that are drawn. As a result, we don't always know where bottlenecks are, because bottlenecks are different dependent on the device, browser type and version, version of the operating system, and so on. Our view is that we need to do everything as efficiently as possible. Traditionally, we would use a profiler to find the bottlenecks and then try to optimize the code accordingly. In JavaScript this is not feasible because of all the different devices and browsers, let alone the fact that it's not always possible to use a profiler for some combinations of device, browser, and operating system."

The games developed in this book don't focus at all on efficiency. A lot can still be improved, particularly when drawing graphics. At the moment, the games in this book redraw the entire image in each game-loop iteration. In many cases, this isn't necessary. Large parts of the screen don't change, so why redraw them? The HTML5 canvas allows you to redraw only a part of the canvas screen. Games are much more efficient if you rewrite the code such that static parts of the screen aren't redrawn. For example, if in a Sudoku game the player does nothing, there is no need to redraw anything. If you use animated effects such as glitters, redraw only the part of the screen where the effect is shown. Another way to improve efficiency in your games is to make a high-resolution version and a low-resolution version. Depending on the capabilities of the device, you can then automatically select which version of the game should be used.

Code efficiency is important, but it shouldn't be at the cost of code clarity. In many cases, efficiency isn't as important as writing clear code. If a button click is handled one hundredth of a second later due to inefficiencies in the code, the player won't notice it. On the other hand, if you've decided to put all input-handling code in a single method to avoid method-calling overhead, your code will be very difficult for others to understand, including a future you.

> Mark: "In many cases, efficiency is not the problem, but hiccups are. An important reason for hiccups are texture swaps. For devices with limited video memory, sprites will be swapped in and out of memory while the game is running, leading to extra computations. What we do to minimize this is to group sprites that are used in the same place in the game on a single sprite sheet. For example, sprites that are used for the title screen are placed on a different sprite sheet than sprites used for the

level selection screen. Another reason for hiccups is garbage collection (destroying objects that are no longer used, and freeing up memory). Unfortunately, there is no way to control when garbage collection happens. Anything that is an object falls under garbage collection. This becomes a problem when your game uses many small objects such as vectors. In that case, try to minimize the number of new objects you create, or pass along x and y values to methods instead of using vector objects."

Coherency of Code

Another thing that is very important when you write code is to make sure your code is *coherent*. Coherency can be achieved on several levels. First, coherency is important in the *design* of the code. For example, in all the games in this book, I have assumed that the game loop does three things:

- Handles player input

- Updates the game world

- Draws the game world

This is a code design decision I made, but other developers might make a different choice. For example, some game engines don't make a distinction between handling player input and updating the game world. Other game engines see drawing as a highly separate process that isn't a part of the game-object classes. What is important is that such a design decision is applied coherently throughout the game. If handling input and updating the game world are supposed to be two separate processes, this should be evident in all the classes. Another example where coherency can be seen in the code design is the way you deal with objects that need only a single instance, such as the game-state manager or the object responsible for drawing on the canvas (`Canvas2D`). For all these objects, this book's examples religiously use the *Singleton* design pattern. When you start programming your own games, think explicitly about the design choices you make, and apply them coherently while you're programming.

Coherency is also important on the *structural* level of your code. Each game-object class has a separate method for each of the game-loop elements. These methods have exactly the same header in each of the classes, and they therefore expect the same parameters. For example, in all the game-object classes, the `update` method has a single parameter `delta`. If you're coherent in the structure of the classes, users of those classes know what to expect. Another example is separating generic classes such as `GameObjectList` (which can be used in many different games) from game-specific classes such as `WaterDrop` by putting the generic classes in a namespace called `powerupjs`. Again, this helps other developers understand how to use the classes and where they belong.

Finally, code should be coherent on the *lexical* level. Make sure all your methods have a similar naming convention. Some developers like method and property names to always start with an uppercase character. This book follows the convention that variable, method, and property names start with a lowercase character, whereas class names start with an uppercase character.

Furthermore, any variables that shouldn't be directly accessed outside a class are preceded by an underscore character. Having such a convention in your code is a good thing. It makes your code a lot easier to understand. Another convention this book follows is that in names consisting of multiple words, each following word starts with an uppercase character:

```
function GameObjectList() {
    ...
}
GameObjectList.prototype.handleInput = function() {
    ...
};
var thisIsAVeryLongVariableName;
```

This way of naming variables is common in programming. Some people have tried to define standards for naming schemes, such as Hungarian notation. In Hungarian notation, variable names also contain information about their type. Have a look at the following example:

```
var bIsAlive = true;
```

The b character tells you that this variable is a Boolean variable. This can be useful information to encode in a variable name, because JavaScript doesn't require programmers to provide the type of a variable when the variable is declared. You may encounter Hungarian notation in code written by other developers, although it's being used less and less now that compilers and development environments can automatically provide all kinds of information about a variable, such as its scope, the type it represents, and so on.

> Mark: "In JavaScript you can write code in a hundred different ways. So, before you start developing, think about what you are actually going to need in the end. If you start out with a wrong approach, you will encounter many problems because of that choice. Making the right choice is not always easy, though. In many cases, the design of the game is not completed yet when you start developing. Sometimes you realize in the end that you need some kind of visual effect in the game, but there is no place in the code to put it."

Producing Game Content

If you want your game to look good, you need nice game assets. Good game assets that show coherency will make your game more attractive to players. This includes not only the visuals but also sound effects and background music. Generally, sound and music are underestimated, but they're important factors in establishing ambience. Watching a film without sound is a lot less fun than watching it while you hear music that emotionally supports what is happening and sound effects that give body to what characters are doing. Games also need music and sound effects, just like films.

To get started, you can buy premade packs of sprites. Here are a few examples of web sites where you can get sprites for free, buy sprites, or hire artists who can create sprites for you:

- www.supergameasset.com
- www.graphic-buffet.com
- www.hireanillustrator.com
- http://opengameart.org
- www.3dfoin.com
- www.content-pack.com

Just like sprites, you can also buy music and sound effects for your games. Take a look at these web sites:

- www.soundrangers.com
- www.indiegamemusic.com
- www.stereobot.com
- http://audiojungle.net
- www.arteriamusic.com
- https://soundcloud.com

If you've already created a few games using these stock assets, it will be much easier for you to set up connections with other indie developers. The games you develop will form a portfolio that shows your capabilities as a game developer.

Working on a Game Production Team

When you're working together with others on a game, you need people with different skills. Generally, a game production team has a project manager who leads the overall production process, game designers, level designers, artists, sound artists, testers, and of course programmers. Sometimes a person fills multiple roles. For example, the project manager can also be the lead game designer. Testers and programmers are very often the same people.

> Peter: "We have many artists, designers, programmers, experts, and Q&A testers. There is a lot of collaboration. A lot of people are involved in making a game nowadays.
>
> When a game company grows a lot, one challenge is finding talent. Also, it is important to stay true to your startup roots, so that you don't become just a big, slow corporation. Try to keep agility in your company, and keep hierarchies in the company to a minimum. As they say, culture eats strategy for breakfast. Keep the startup culture alive, and make sure that you can get stuff done. This holds for many companies that are growing. The challenge lies in maintaining the mentality to keep things moving and agile."

Mark: "Because we are quite a small team, the project manager is also our game designer. Sometimes this leads to problems. The project manager wants the game to be finished on time, while the designer wants to keep improving or changing the game. In that case, the project manager should tell the designer that the game should be done, which is quite hard to do if both are the same person."

You may have a grasp on the various elements that are needed to produce a game but not think you can do everything yourself. If you're a good programmer, it doesn't mean you're also a good artist. And, unfortunately for you, initially it's often the visuals that determine whether a person will try your game. It's a good idea to form a team with an artist and maybe also with a game designer and an audio expert. Try to get connected to others so that you can work together on creating games. Be active in social networks, start your own blog, post on forums, and so on. You're going to be an indie developer, so check out web sites like `www.indiegames.com` to learn what other indies are doing. Be active in game jams like the Global Game Jam (`www.globalgamejam.org`) to meet other developers. Have a look at HTML5 developer forums, such as HTML5 Game Devs (`www.html5gamedevs.com`) or the Web Developer forum (`www.webdeveloper.com/forum/forum.php`).

If you work with multiple developers on a game, you need to find a way to share code and work together on that code. You can use version-management tools such as Subversion (`http://subversion.apache.org`) to do that. Alternatives to Subversion are Git (`http://git-scm.com`) and Mercurial (`http://mercurial.selenic.com`). There are also online equivalents that provide cloud storage in combination with version-management tools. This allows you to work on code and commit it to a server, after which other developers can retrieve the code and use it. Examples of such online code- and version-management tools are GitHub (`https://github.com`) and Bitbucket (`https://bitbucket.org`).

Another thing you need to think about when working with other developers is documenting your code. If you write documentation in a certain format in your source files, there are tools that can automatically read this documentation and create HTML files that show it in a nice layout. Examples of such tools are YUIDoc (`http://yui.github.io/yuidoc`) and Doxygen (`www.stack.nl/~dimitri/doxygen`). Documentation is very useful, but not all game developers take the time to properly document the code they're writing.

Mark: "We use Confluence (`www.atlassian.com/software/confluence`) to manage a game production project. In that tool we store a lot of information about our framework and how to use it. We have written proper documentation for our in-house game engine but not really for the games themselves. Our games are generally developed by a single person and are then finished. We do write a document per game that globally describes how the game code is structured."

Finally, think about how you organize your team. A lot of people forget this aspect and simply start working together, but that may quickly lead to problems because roles and expectations of people on a team are different. If someone believes they are the lead game designer, whereas another person on the team regards that same person as someone who isn't crucial to the cause, this will have repercussions on how well the team works together. When you work on a project, think about why you're doing it, and make sure the others you're working with share your view. One member of your team may want to make a creative statement, but another member may simply want to earn a lot of money.

Peter: "Flat organizations generally work better than deep hierarchical structures. One thing that is very important is that you create an environment where people know what they are supposed to be doing, so that there is clear direction and leadership. It is important to give people jobs with a purpose, no matter if you're coding away at game, doing the artwork, or working on marketing."

Mark: "If you want to create a game company, be very selective in the people you want to work with. If you select the wrong people at the start, you will lose time by having to change the team along the way. Spend a lot of time in the beginning to get the right people."

Chapter 31

Publishing Games

Peter Vesterbacka: "Pretty much everybody on the planet has a smartphone nowadays, make it the biggest gaming platform ever. And we are only at the beginning; it is still growing massively. Mobile is where the volume is, where the center of gravity is."

This final chapter of the book talks about several topics related to getting your game out in the world. First I cover testing and checking code quality to ensure that your game works well on many different platforms. Then I talk about a few things you need to think about when you want to publish your game, such as localization and code optimization. The chapter concludes with a discussion of selling and marketing your game. As in the previous chapter, Peter Vesterbacka and Mark Overmars have provided a number of tips and thoughts.

Testing and Checking Code Quality

Any software you want to make publicly available should be tested before it's released. Especially in the case of JavaScript/HTML5 games, players will own a variety of different devices that run different operating systems with different browsers and browser versions. You have to make sure your game works properly for as many players as possible.

There are many different ways to test software. You can test code by simply reviewing it, checking the structure of classes and methods without actually running the program. You can also test the program by running it and trying a variety of different scenarios and parameter values to ensure that the code does what it's expected to do. It's also important to make sure the code *doesn't do what it is not expected to do*. If the player provides invalid input or a network connection is lost, the game shouldn't crash.

You can do software testing manually, but you can also do it automatically by writing special testing scripts that try a variety of different parameters. This automatic process is also called *unit testing*, because you separately test parts (units) of code.

When you've more or less finished writing the code, there are two other major stages in testing: *alpha and beta testing*. Alpha testing is done internally by a group of people, often the developers themselves. Alpha testing is important because it makes sure all the components the developers have built work together as they should. After the internal alpha testing, software can also be tested externally. This is called beta testing: the software is used by a panel of external users. Often, beta testing is useful not only to remove bugs, but also to find out whether a program works on a variety of devices. In the case of games, beta testing also helps to verify that the gameplay is as intended, that the tutorial levels are clear, and that levels are progressing nicely. In the game industry, this step is called *playtesting*. You can do playtesting internally and externally. Regardless, don't postpone playtesting until your game is nearly finished. Sometimes the results of playtesting can mean a significant change in the way a game works. The earlier in the process you know this, the better.

> *Mark Overmars: "It is important to separate the various testing stages. The developers try to test their code while they are writing it, but they will not able to do that for all devices and all platforms. Our game designer gets an early version of the game fairly soon and can then start doing level design and gameplay testing. These tests are also done by other people in the company (but not the developers, generally). Once we think the game is finished, we put the game online, but hidden from the public. We then test the game on all possible devices and platforms. We first test whether all the aspects of the game itself are working as they should, which is something we don't have to check on all the devices. Second, we let a lot of different people try out the game on different devices and platforms, where we let them go through a basic checklist to verify that audio is working properly, the screens work, the fonts are visible, and so on. If we discover major issues in the game at that point, we pull it offline, and we go through the whole process from the start again.*
>
> *If everything works out, the game is sent to an external test panel that focuses more on gameplay. We'd like to extend and improve this process more in the future.*
>
> *In the past, we have also hired an external party to do extensive testing on all kinds of different devices and platforms. The main goal in that case was to extensively test our engine. Probably we are going to do this again soon, because a lot of useful things came out of that. On the other hand, it also made us realize that our engine was actually working pretty well, which is a nice thing to know. We do have a bunch of different devices and browsers available at our company, but it is impossible to have everything. And the frustrating thing is that—if you look at Android, for example—your game may work on Android 4.0 and 4.2, but not on Android 4.1. Unfortunately, there is no order to how well everything is working."*

Even more so than with other programming languages, it's important that your code is well-written when you write JavaScript code. Debugging and testing JavaScript code is harder than regular applications because so many variables are involved. Therefore, it's crucial that your code is working well before you let it run on a variety of devices. And because JavaScript allows for loose typing, many code-editing environments have trouble doing automatic code completion very effectively, which is a pity because a code-completion feature in your code editor can save you a lot of time—not so much typing time as time you don't have to spend browsing through online help to find how that method that you want to use is spelled and what parameters it needs.

A tool to help you write better code is JSLint (`www.jslint.com`). JSLint is a so-called code-quality checker. It checks your code for things that are generally considered bad practice in coding. For example, JavaScript lets you use variables before they're declared (although in strict mode this isn't allowed). JSLint checks that your code doesn't contain the usage of any undeclared variables. Another example where code-quality checking is useful is that JSLint reports the following kinds of `if` instructions:

```
if (a = 3) {
    // do something
}
```

The condition of the `if` instruction has an assignment instead of a comparison. This is syntactically valid JavaScript code, but the programmer probably meant this:

```
if (a === 3) {
    // do something
}
```

A code-quality checker is helpful for finding these kinds of programming mistakes. Furthermore, if the programmer actually intended to do the assignment in the condition of the `if`, it's still a good thing that JSLint reports it, because assigning something to a variable in a condition is an extremely bad programming practice!

Deployment

When you want to distribute your game, you need to think about a few things. First you need to make sure players all over the world can understand your game. Although many people can read and write English, it's nice if your game adapts itself to the player's region: for example, by translating all the text used in the game into the player's language. This process is called *localization*. If you want to do this properly, you need to separate text from the actual game code as much as possible. This includes the text shown on buttons and help text shown when the player hovers over a user interface element. Localization can be costly if you want your game to be translated into any language in the world; but you can reduce the cost by making sure the game code doesn't contain any text elements and only uses variables that refer to text defined in a single place.

If you use spoken audio in your game, then localization may become very costly. Unfortunately, automatic text-to-speech systems aren't quite there yet in terms of realism, so you'll need to get voice actors to record the spoken audio in any language in which you would like to publish your game.

You can design your game to minimize localization costs, for example by relying mainly on visuals to communicate with the player. Text that says, "Warning: you only have ten seconds left!" requires translation, but a blinking timer doesn't. Most games try to minimize the text displayed to the user, but tutorial levels often contain text. Of course, if you have a word-search game or any other game in which the gameplay heavily relies on text manipulation, you definitely need to think carefully about localization.

Mark: "We have our own localization tool. Every game has its own dictionary file that stores each text in the game with a unique ID, in all languages. We make a special tool to edit these texts. A lot of texts are not game specific, and they are part of our framework, so we export them together with the game-specific texts. Our tool can also generate this data as a spreadsheet so we can send this to a translator who then simply has to fill in a single column. For localization, it is important that all your code works with Unicode, because you want to be able to work with Asian fonts as well."

Peter: "With Angry Birds we created a game that works everywhere, because it is mostly visual. We localize the little text that we have in the game. Although you could build games created for very local markets, we design our games such that we use very little text, so that there is very little requirement to do any localization."

In addition to localization, you need to make sure your code is as compact as possible when you release your game. All the example code in this book is distributed over several files. When you release your game, ideally you want all the code in a single JavaScript file. You also may not want players to be able to easily understand your code. For example, if you've written an innovative algorithm for dealing with physics in games very efficiently, you may want to avoid others copying that code from your game so you retain a competitive advantage. A very useful tool that helps you do all these things is Google Closure (`https://developers.google.com/closure`). Closure allows you to compile your JavaScript files into a single file that is optimized for size so players can download it quickly. You can choose the level of optimization that the Closure compiler uses to generate the optimized JavaScript file. Closure's highest possible level of optimization is known as the *advanced optimization* level. If you were to open and read such a highly optimized file, you wouldn't be able to make much sense of the code. Therefore, this advanced optimization mode is also called *code obfuscation mode*. Obfuscation is useful because it allows you to protect your code from copying by others.

Mark: "We use the Closure compiler from Google for minification and obfuscation, which can be run in three different modes. The first two modes are basically only minification. The third mode is a kind of recompilation where code is rearranged, unused parts are removed, and so on. Our condition is that any game code we release needs to be able to go through that process and still come out working afterward."

Code obfuscation may introduce problems when you call code from an external library. In that case, the obfuscation process shouldn't change the names of functions or variables that you call from that library, because then the names won't match anymore. You have to either provide directives to the obfuscator so it doesn't do renaming operations in those cases, or avoid using external libraries.

Selling Your Game

If you want to make a living with creating HTML5 games, there are quite a few different possibilities. A very simple way to make money with your games is to put them on your web site and add advertisement banners—for example, using Google AdWords. If you get a lot of visitors, you will make revenue from the advertisements. However, this ad income will be low unless you attract a lot of players. Perhaps a more lucrative approach is to sell your games to portals. Most portals offer their games for free, but they also make money from advertisements. There are also a number of broker sites where you can make your game available for a price, such as Game Brokerage (`https://gamebrokerage.com`).

> Mark: *"Selling games to portals can be done on a revenue-sharing basis, where you share in the revenues from advertisements. Revenue sharing is implemented either as the portal paying the developer or as the developer paying the portal. In the first case, the portal puts advertisements in your game and pays you a part of the revenue; in the second case, the developer puts advertisements in the game and pays the portal a percentage of the income. Finally, you can also sell your game through a fixed-fee model, where you get paid once for delivering a game to a portal. Because the HTML5 gaming market is relatively young, portals are still willing to deal with individuals who create and sell games. But more and more HTML5 game companies are starting, so it will probably not stay that way for very long."*

Another way to try to sell your games is through an app store on Android or iOS. You can't directly publish an HTML5 game to those stores, but need to convert it to a native format first. There are wrapper tools that can do that for you, such as CocoonJS (`https://www.ludei.com/cocoonjs`) and PhoneGap (`http://phonegap.com/`). The nice thing about publishing your game as a native app is that you can introduce things like in-app purchases that provide you with extra revenue, in addition to the money you make selling games in the app store. However, be aware that using wrapper tools such as PhoneGap may cause performance lags that need to be thoroughly tested. The app that a wrapper produces may look like a native app, but it's actually a web app that is running in a viewer.

Once your games are out there, you can start to think about other ways to make money with them. For example, if your game allows players to play against each other, you could introduce a subscription service that gives players access to your game when they pay a monthly fee. The players get storage on your server for their profile and their achievements in the game.

Try to think about other ways to make money with your games. Sometimes it helps to involve another party who already has a big network. Create a game for a charity of your choice, and share the revenues with it. You'll help a charity, and it will do marketing for you at the same time! Another way to try to make money with your games is to rely on crowdfunding. There are web sites dedicated to crowdfunding for games, such as Gambitious (`https://gambitious.com`). If you plan to publish your games on Steam (`http://store.steampowered.com`), look at the mechanisms it provides for game developers to sell their work. For example, it has a mechanism called Early Access that allows people to buy and play games that aren't finished yet. This could be a helpful mechanism for you to build up a network of players, gain momentum, get feedback and bug reports, and provide regular game updates. Finally, have a look at the blog by True Valhalla (`www.truevalhalla.com/blog`), which talks about lots of different ways to make money with HTML5 games.

Marketing

Now that you're programming your own games, you may have started to think about how to get them out in the real world. Maybe you don't want to create a game just for the achievement, but to make some money with it. Fortunately, nowadays getting games published is easy. For mobile devices, there are app stores to which you can submit your games after you've exported them to a specific mobile platform. If you sell your games through a portal, then the portal will (partly) take care of the marketing for you. Of course, you can also make your games available on your own web site.

> Peter: "If you look at the fifty-one games we published before Angry Birds, all of them were actually really good games. The main challenge was that the market was really tough. The App Store didn't exist—you had to have good connections in order to get your game out there. What enabled success for us was the App Store. All of a sudden, digital distribution was available to anybody, so you could create a game like Angry Birds and immediately distribute it to fans.
>
> But now that distribution of games has become so easy, this leads to another challenge. Anybody can publish a game through the App Store. As a result, there is an abundance of games and applications. Of course, you need to make great games. But there are already a lot of great games out there. The thing is that for every Angry Birds, there are many "not-so Angry Birds." Many of those games are actually great games, but nobody knows about them. So how do you make your games stand out? In the case of Angry Birds, it is all about the characters. And on the other hand, it is also a brand that asks an interesting question: why are the birds angry? If you are serious about making games, you have to be serious about marketing and branding. It's not enough to just make great games."

Clearly, the challenge lies in making your game visible. On iOS and Android, more than 300 new games appear every day. Most of them are played by just a few people. And if you create your own web site for the game, how are you going to get any visitors?

First of all, you need to produce a quality game. If the game isn't good, people won't play it. Find other people with other skill sets to help you. Don't be overambitious: you aren't going to create the next *Halo*! Set reasonable goals. Start with small but excellent games. Don't trust your own judgment: talk to others about your game, and let them play prototypes to make sure players actually like it. When your game is nearing completion, make a marketing plan. Post about the game wherever you can, make a press kit, create a video, send information to blogs and other web sites, and so on. People will only play your game when they hear about it. Don't expect that this will happen automatically after you've published your game on an app store; you need to make a plan. Before your game is out, build a network of potential players—people who are interested in what you do. Create a Facebook group for your company and/or the game you're creating. Be sure to communicate with followers on social networks such as Twitter. Encourage others to play your game and write about it.

I mentioned the Early Access mechanism on Steam in the previous section. Such an open development mechanism is also interesting from a marketing point of view. It allows you to attract players to your game and get them involved in the game's development. By involving players in the early stages of game development, you can create a very strong bond between the players and the game, because they feel like they're part of the development process. If you're smart about it, these players will act as salespeople for your game, doing a lot of marketing for you.

> Peter: "For us, it is all about our fans and the brand. The power of the brand Angry Birds allows us to spend less money on traditional marketing means such as advertising. If you look at typical game-development studios, I think people don't realize how much they need to spend on marketing. Typically, the game-development costs are a fraction of what is spent on marketing.
>
> We build the brand with our games and with our actions on the marketing side. We started with very strong characters, and we built the brand around that. To build a brand, there are as many different ways as there are companies. If you look at how brands were built traditionally, you can see that starting to happen in the game industry as well, through for example TV advertising. It's not that different from building a brand in any business when it comes to games."

Final Thoughts

This book has covered many aspects of programming in JavaScript. You now have a solid foundation in JavaScript programming and in particular in game programming. As you've probably realized by reading Mark's and Peter's thoughts, the world changes quickly. Operating systems such as iOS and Android are regularly updated with new features. Mobile devices are getting faster and faster. Devices that were popular a few years ago are now obsolete. And in the middle of all that are HTML5 and JavaScript. A striking example of the growing importance of JavaScript is the desktop/PC game *Planetary Annihilation* (www.uberent.com/pa), for which the entire GUI was created using JavaScript and HTML5! It's impossible to predict the future, but one thing is certain: HTML5 and JavaScript are here to stay. I hope that this book helps you come to grips with the language and that it provides you with a good starting point to explore game programming yourself. I'll conclude this book with two things that Mark and Peter said during their interview:

> Mark: "Think about what you want to achieve. For example, you may simply have a creative idea that you would like to implement. This is a very different goal than wanting to earn a living making games. It's not always by definition important that many people play your game. Making a game can be a reward in itself."
>
> Peter: "Don't copy blindly, but try to do things differently instead of doing what everyone else is doing. Think about how you can stand out from the hundreds of thousands of other games. Surprise and delight. It doesn't cost anything to surprise people. That said, learn as much as you possibly can from others. Then do your own thing."

Index

Get the eBook for only $10!

> Now you can take the weightless companion with you anywhere, anytime. Your purchase of this book entitles you to 3 electronic versions for only $10.

This Apress title will prove so indispensible that you'll want to carry it with you everywhere, which is why we are offering the eBook in 3 formats for only $10 if you have already purchased the print book.

Convenient and fully searchable, the PDF version enables you to easily find and copy code—or perform examples by quickly toggling between instructions and applications. The MOBI format is ideal for your Kindle, while the ePUB can be utilized on a variety of mobile devices.

Go to www.apress.com/promo/tendollars to purchase your companion eBook.